D1614460

60000 0000 56461

Killing the Bismarck

Other books by Iain Ballantyne

Strike from the Sea: The Royal Navy & US Navy at War in the Middle East 1949–2003

Warships of the Royal Navy series
Warspite
HMS *London*
HMS *Victory* (With Jonathan Eastland)
HMS *Rodney*

All titles published by Pen & Sword Books

Killing the Bismarck

Destroying the Pride of Hitler's Fleet

Iain Ballantyne

Pen & Sword
MARITIME

First published in Great Britain in 2
Pen & Sword Maritime
an imprint of
Pen & Sword Books Ltd
47 Church Street
Barnsley
South Yorkshire
S70 2AS

Peterborough City Council	
60000 0000 56461	
Askews & Holts	Mar-2012
940.545	£25.00

ISBN 978-1-84415-983-3

A CIP catalogue record for this book is available from the British Library.

Typeset in 11pt Ehrhardt by
Mac Style, Beverley, E. Yorkshire

Printed and bound in the UK by the MPG Books Group

Pen & Sword Books Ltd incorporates the imprints of Pen & Sword Aviation, Pen & Sword Maritime, Pen & Sword Military, Wharncliffe Local History, Pen and Sword Select, Pen and Sword Military Classics and Leo Cooper.

For a complete list of Pen & Sword titles please contact
PEN & SWORD BOOKS LIMITED
47 Church Street, Barnsley, South Yorkshire, S70 2AS, England
E-mail: enquiries@pen-and-sword.co.uk
Website: www.pen-and-sword.co.uk

Contents

For Robert and James

May they never have to fight such battles.
In the words of the great Paddy McAloon,
let's hope those kinds of conflicts are
'as obsolete as warships in the Baltic'.*

* From the first verse of *Faron Young*, from Prefab Sprout's *Steve McQueen* album (1985).

Foreword

The sinking of the *Bismarck* was one of the defining moments of war at sea in the European Theatre and has generated considerable historical study and comment. One might therefore question the value of another book on the subject. My judgement is that this book adds new material and provides us with additional and different reflections on issues that this action has previously raised.

I am particularly struck by the well-researched accounts from a good cross-section of personnel. They, together with the narrative, bring out so much that is enduring about navies and their operations as well as the specifics of this particular operation. The enduring importance of range, damage control and logistics come through strongly in this book, which also shows us the decisive use of naval air power for both reconnaissance and attack.

No commander plans or executes an operation without an eye on the weather. It can be both an enemy and a friend at the same time and this was the case in May 1941. The same weather that made carrier flying so challenging also frustrated the U-boats.

The sheer professionalism of the ships' companies so evident in this action, as is related on the following pages, was the bedrock of the successes that the Royal Navy ground out in the Atlantic, in the Mediterranean and finally in the Pacific over the next four years. It is, of course, part of the legacy that today's sailors and marines aspire to match.

The eyewitness accounts quoted in this book confirm vividly the ferocious pounding the Home Fleet gave the *Bismarck* to ensure her sinking. Additionally, they give support to the view that there was something very personal as well as operational and strategic about the need to destroy *Bismarck*. The loss of the *Hood*, although technically not surprising – she was never given the required modernization –was a huge shock to the Nation as well as the Royal Navy.

Between wars it is always a challenge to continue to afford modernization. This was certainly the case for the Royal Navy and *Hood* was a prime example of that. In the 1940s the Royal Navy had to rely on too many ships of First

World War vintage, including battlecruisers, which were known to be susceptible to plunging shellfire due to inadequate levels of protection.

In considering the strategic context of the story that unfolds here, we must remember that Britain stood very much alone in May 1941. Major reverses had been suffered on the ground. While the threat of invasion had been removed by the successes of the RAF in the Battle of Britain, the German bombing campaign against the cities was in full swing.

The Royal Navy was stretched across the Atlantic and Mediterranean and paying the price for insufficient investment in the 1920s and the late decision to rearm in the 1930s. Add to this the consequences of Arms Control agreements and the Admiralty and Fleet Commanders were at times looking down the barrel of defeat. To have lost the *Hood* and let *Bismarck* avoid retribution would have had a devastating effect on morale and reputation, the latter being particularly important in the perception of the United States and Soviet Union.

The operational, potentially strategic, leverage the German Navy would have been able to exert with the *Bismarck* joining *Scharnhorst* and *Gneisenau* in the Atlantic ports, while undertaking the U-boat campaign, might well have put the Royal Navy past the tipping point. This well written and absorbing book reminds us how this situation was avoided while clearly illustrating the home truths about war at sea. I commend it to you.

Admiral Sir Jonathon Band GCB
Former First Sea Lord & Chief of Naval Staff

Acknowledgements

The genesis of this book can be traced back almost two decades to a conversation over a pint of beer in a Plymouth pub. I was the Defence Reporter of the city's evening newspaper and had arranged to meet a group of men who had served in the battleship *Prince of Wales* during the Second World War, in order to take notes on their experiences for an article that was part of a series on milestones in that conflict. Working in a naval city, which had recently seen its sailors and marines involved in the effort to eject Iraqi troops from Kuwait, it was fascinating to talk to an older generation who had participated in the titanic struggle against fascism of the 1940s. I had been out to the Gulf, spending time in naval vessels engaged in operations applying pressure on Saddam and also aboard warships off the stricken emirate as its oil wells burned. Having gained some insight into life at sea aboard warships – it was the first time British naval forces had been on a proper war footing since the Falklands campaign of 1982 – I had become acquainted with the character of the Royal Navy and its people. In 1990/1, cheerful sailors and marines carried out a job that required great patience and fortitude in trying conditions, for which they got little thanks from a nation that seemed ignorant of the naval dimension of war. By the early 1990s the citizens of the British Isles appeared unable to comprehend the very things that made Britain a great (secure and prosperous) nation: its navy and the control of the sea. As the veterans of *Prince of Wales*, joined by a few from *Repulse*, another Plymouth ship, chatted with me about their experiences I recognised that the essential spirit of the Royal Navy half a century earlier was much the same in the 1990s. Of course, their experiences were so much more dramatic than those of younger generations of sailors and marines, for the Second World War was a globe-spanning drama the like of which we will, hopefully, never see again.

The remarkable men of the 'greatest generation', as they have been called, endured so much. *Prince of Wales*, as her veterans told me, was straight into action out of the builder's yard, took part in the pursuit of the *Bismarck*, then carried Winston Churchill to the USA. She then battled through a hard-fought

Malta convoy run and was sent to the Far East. One supreme irony revealed to me, as we supped our pints in that pub, was that *Prince of Wales* was so busy her sailors and marines never got to sail into their home port of Plymouth. Back then they had never enjoyed a run ashore down Union Street in each other's company, to visit pubs, sup ale and 'spin dits' [tell stories]. What finally brought them together in Plymouth – those that survived the war and the ravages of time – were annual gatherings, during which they would place a wreath at the magnificent Naval War Memorial on the Hoe and say a prayer for lost shipmates. On that same memorial you will find the names of men from other ships lost in the war that also took part in the epic pursuit and destruction of *Bismarck*.

It is now more than seven decades since the start of the Second World War, and the majority of the men who survived so many battles – chatting with me through the years since 1991 in pubs, hotels, services clubs, their own homes, and passing on their amazing experiences via letters – have nearly all passed away.

I acknowledge a great debt to all those veterans, who have brought to life the narrative of not only this book, but also four others I have written for Pen & Sword Books since 2000. This book therefore represents the end of a ten-year cycle of work for me, a quest to record the remarkable stories of ordinary men in extraordinary times, threading them into the fabric of books about the ships they served in and the great events they helped shape. More particularly, those veterans whose testimony I received first-hand for *Killing the Bismarck* are listed in the Sources at the back of the book, so I won't mention them by name here.

Other war veterans, and those connected with warship associations from whom I have received help along the way, similarly deserve my sincere appreciation: Major JEM Ruffer RM, who saw action in the cruiser HMS *Norfolk*; the late Bert Gollop and his shipmate John Cannon who were there in HMS *Dorsetshire*; Ken Satterthwaite and Peter Harrison, Chairman and Secretary respectively of the HMS *Cossack* Association; Bill Kelly, President of the HMS *King George V* Association; Kenneth Davies, Hon. Secretary of the Telegraphist Air Gunners Association.

Veteran Tommy Byers, who saw the horror of the final battle with *Bismarck* up close from his Action Station in the main gunnery control position of HMS *Rodney*, was able to speak across the years via transcripts of interviews with his son, Kevin, and also in a sound recording and letters. Although he sadly passed away some years ago, Tommy Byers still makes one of the most significant contributions towards revealing the true face of war at sea during that gun-blasted finale of the *Bismarck* pursuit. Kevin originally corresponded with me for my previous book, HMS *Rodney*, which also featured his father, and I am truly grateful to him for having the patience to bear with *Killing the Bismarck* as a suitable vehicle for publishing the more provocative elements of his father's testimony.

One of the most remarkable features of the whole *Bismarck* action, which illustrates just how much of a family business the Royal Navy of the Second World War was, can be found in the presence of fathers and sons, as well as brothers, in different ships involved. Among them was young Midshipman North Dalrymple-Hamilton of HMS *King George V*, son of Frederick Dalrymple-Hamilton, Commanding Officer of HMS *Rodney*. Rob McAuley generously made available to me the transcript of an interview with Captain North Dalrymple-Hamilton, conducted for his remarkable TV documentary series *The Battleships*, broadcast in the UK on Channel 4 nearly a decade ago. Although he is primarily based in Australia, I was fortunate enough to meet Rob, and thank him in person, during his yearly visit to the UK. First shaking hands with him in the shadow of Nelson's Column in Trafalgar Square, I soon discovered Rob is a true gent and thorough professional as well as man who knows his stuff when it comes to naval history. Another maritime expert worthy of my appreciation is David Mearns of Blue Water Recoveries, who provided an excellent analysis of what truly sank *Bismarck* in his own book (*see* Bibliography) and later confirmed for me whether or not his verdict still stood. David also kindly offered two images of *Hood* and *Bismarck* lying in the deep.

The painting featured on the cover of this book, and also reproduced as one of the plates, shows the horrifying majesty of *Bismarck*'s final moments, perfectly illustrating the awesome, yet dreadful, reality of destroying the pride of Hitler's fleet. It is by the distinguished British maritime artist Paul Wright, RSMA, whose previous work has graced covers of novels by Patrick O'Brian among others.

I am supremely honoured to showcase Paul's work, which I admire greatly, having originally come into contact with him while putting together a feature for *WARSHIPS IFR* magazine. His support and empathy have been much appreciated.

A rich seam of personal accounts – expressed in letters, sound recordings and autobiographical essays – provided much of the propulsion for the narrative, as well as numerous other documents, all of which were unearthed in UK museums. I would therefore like to convey my gratitude to: the trustees of the Imperial War Museum for allowing access to its collections; the staffs of the Imperial War Museum's Department of Documents, Sound Archive and Photographic Archive; Matthew Sheldon and the staff of the Royal Naval Museum, including Stephen Courtney in its own photographic archive; Susan Dearing and the staff of the Fleet Air Arm Museum; Dr Jane Harrold of the Britannia Museum, Britannia Royal Naval College, Dartmouth. For HMS *Rodney*, the US Naval War College kindly permitted me to quote from the mass of Admiralty signals contained within their book, *On His Majesty's Service*, by Rear-Admiral Joseph Wellings. The same minute-by-minute record was invaluable in putting together its successor, *Killing the Bismarck*. With reference to material that was sourced in the Department of Documents at the Imperial War Museum (and listed in the Sources) every effort has been made to trace copyright holders of the papers of G Conning, AE Franklin, DA Hibbit, Lt Cdr BW Smith and also for the document described as Miscellaneous 3213. The author and the Imperial War Museum would be grateful for any information that might help to trace any of those listed in the Sources whose identities or addresses are not currently known. I would also like to express my thanks to the other copyright holders for granting permission.

Friends and colleagues have offered encouragement, practical help and objective criticism, prompting me to issue my usual proclamation of heartfelt high regard to: Dennis Andrews, Nigel Andrews (not related), Usman Ansari, Jonathan Eastland, Richard Hargreaves and Martin Robinson. Peter Hore did exactly as requested and provided an honest first opinion on the fruits of my labours, also sharing with me a remarkable discovery. Peter deserves the ultimate accolade one can bestow on a naval officer: he is a *true* human being (and a bit of a guru). Among the other players I am indebted to are Derrick Pearce, former Secretary of the HMS *Rodney* Association, and his son Andrew. I am also hugely appreciative of the efforts expended by the Pen & Sword team, including Henry Wilson and Jon Wilkinson, as well as the book's editor, George Chamier. I must also thank Derek Knoll of HPC Publishing for allowing me a flexible enough schedule to write this book during down time, so to speak, from my 'day job'.

Following a summer 2009 interview for *WARSHIPS IFR*, the magazine of which I am Editor, aboard the new destroyer HMS *Daring* at Portsmouth, I asked Admiral Sir Jonathon Band, at the time First Sea Lord and Chief of Naval Staff, to write a Foreword to this book. He was delighted to comply with my request. I am pleased to say it perfectly places the story you are about to read within its broader strategic context, while touching on the intensely personal nature of the *Bismarck* Action to the Royal Navy. My sincere thanks to Admiral Band for his excellent Foreword.

Finally, it remains for me to express my deep appreciation and love for my wife, Lindsey, who has, as ever, displayed her usual heroic stoicism throughout the sometimes gruelling process of creating this epic tale. Fortunately, I was able to buy her off with tea and toast in bed.

Author's Introduction

O'er the glad waters of the dark blue sea,
Our thoughts as boundless, and our souls as free
Far as the breeze can bear, the billows foam,
Survey our empire and behold our home!

Lord Byron, *The Corsair*

There have been many books written on the short life of the German battleship *Bismarck*, considered by the British a corsair bent on piratical exploits in the vast ocean. *Bismarck*'s breakout into the Atlantic in the Second World War and her subsequent pursuit and destruction at the hands of the Royal Navy is one of the epics of naval history, a yarn that continues to exert fascination. Surely the entire story has been told already? Well, actually no, not quite. That is why I decided to write a book defined by what it leaves out, rather than gauging its success by how much could be put in. I hope to alter perspective on this familiar story by presenting a powerful narrative almost entirely from a single point of view – that of the Royal Navy – but spread across a number of ships. This is, therefore, not the story of *Bismarck*, but rather an attempt to piece together what it was like for the men in various vessels of the Royal Navy to pursue and destroy a single warship that could, by escaping their retribution, in the wake of *Hood*'s destruction, shape the whole course of the war. Therefore, this book does not seek to put readers inside *Bismarck*, other than to provide minimal detail necessary for the propulsion of the narrative or illustrate the horror of war. The idea is for the reader to get a feel for what it felt like to be engaged in the desperate hunt for *Bismarck*. To tell the story from the German point of view as completely as that of the British would remove all the tension from each twist and turn. No less a man than the late great popular historian Christopher Hibbert put it this way: 'You've got to make the reader want to know what's going to happen next, even if you're writing about something, the outcome of which is well known. You have to build up an atmosphere, almost like writing a novel or detective story.'[1]

When I was completing my account of British warships named *Rodney* – HMS *Rodney* – I also had to take a difficult decision on what to leave out of that book. It was simply too long. Taking an axe to the three chapters that told the story of battleship *Rodney*'s part in destroying *Bismarck* seemed the wisest option, as anything culled from them could be used as the basis for another book, while other sections would not so easily find a home elsewhere. Material was not, therefore, cut because it was weak, far from it. It actually provided some of the most powerful elements in HMS *Rodney*, revealing the final battle between the Home Fleet and *Bismarck* in a brutally honest fashion that I had not seen presented in any other book. The compressed account that eventually appeared in HMS *Rodney* still, hopefully, did the job well – preserving the balance in a book telling the story of all *Rodney*s, from 1759 to the Second World War, while playing a key role in restoring the reputation of the Birkenhead-built and Devonport-manned battleship as one of the greatest British warships. During the more than two years that I have been working on this book – expanding the scope far beyond anything even I thought possible – I have been nervous about taking a gamble by sitting on some of the extraordinary material culled from the earlier book that is finally published here. Would somebody else present an account of the *Bismarck* episode that negated my efforts? In short, would they beat me to the punch? That has not happened, not because the material isn't out there, but possibly because other people are not looking for it, due to *Bismarck* exerting a peculiar hold on authors' imaginations and motivations. Other people are perhaps not interested in looking for unpublished British eyewitness accounts. The Royal Navy ships, and the achievements of their men, do not necessarily interest them to the same extent as *Bismarck*. Nor do the full eyewitness accounts of the British aviators from HMS *Ark Royal*'s squadrons, who delivered the fatal blow to *Bismarck*'s steering. Their exploits, like much else in the story, are well known, but it is the fine detail, the human element, that is missing in many cases.

I am proud to say that there is plenty of fresh material here, for the reality of what happened on the British side out there in the Atlantic in 1941, as presented in the following pages, is perhaps somewhat more heroic and horrific than some, though not all, earlier accounts would have us believe. Heroic, in that the Royal Navy's men had to contend with old ships and obsolete aircraft operating in extreme sea conditions with only the benefit of early radar to bolster their extraordinary seamanship, bravery and fortitude. I hope my account is also honest, too, in revealing the necessary brutality of the *Bismarck* episode's finale and the fact that a major motivating factor for the British sailors and marines was revenge for the murder of 1,415 of their shipmates on *Hood*. It is fashionable to place a modern, touchy-feely slant on significant events such as those covered in this book, to rewrite people's motivation and censor their darker feelings. What veterans felt after the war, with the softening of old enmities, is sometimes allowed to replace the way they *really* felt during hostilities. The reality is that avenging *Hood* was probably THE major driver for those involved on the British side. They had known *Hood* as a feature of their lives since boyhood and, once they joined the Navy, either served in her, or had friends who were members of the battlecruiser's ship's company, many of them dying at the hands of *Bismarck*. The pursuit and destruction of *Bismarck* was therefore an extremely personal endeavour for the men of the Royal Navy. Sympathy for the German battleship's survivors came after the guns were silent. Killing the *Bismarck* was a horrific and disgusting business, which might explain why a number of those on the British side decided not to make too much of it. Like any rational and right-thinking human beings, the individuals involved were possibly ashamed of what they were forced to do in order to ensure their nation's survival during its darkest hour – as it fought on alone against the Nazis.[2] They did not wish to revisit those baser instincts, those acts of desperate necessity, in detail at a later date. However, not to reveal the full scale of the brutal business of war at sea is to help foster the illusion that it is a long-range, remote, almost bloodless, affair: a tale of machines rather than men.

The images of *Bismarck* lying on the seabed that have been obtained by expeditions to investigate her wreck in recent years do not convey the sheer horror of her end. The smoke, flames, blood and gore have all long gone, leaving only a punctured, pitted shell. This author once received a letter from a *Bismarck* enthusiast claiming his beloved battleship was still intact on the seabed and had therefore gloriously outlived *Rodney*, which, so he crowed in screaming capitals, had been turned into razor blades after the war. Such bizarre reasoning sees warships merely as metal constructs, rather than living, breathing communities afloat that, once the flesh and blood contained within has been eviscerated, no longer exist. Not to lay bare the brutality of the final battle, as well the raw horror of other moments, such as *Hood*'s loss, undermines the courage in the face of adversity shown by ordinary men plunged into extraordinary circumstances, on both sides. To lay out the story as if it was a gigantic game of chess would especially betray the incredible courage of the Royal Navy's ships and men, for the weather was as serious a foe as the enemy. Just finding and hanging on to *Bismarck*, never mind bringing about her destruction, was a superhuman feat. Whether of high rank or just lower-deckers, the men who pursued *Bismarck* were made of remarkable stuff, but were, of course, products of harsh times.

Many had seen action in the First World War and had then endured the global Depression; while everyday life for the majority of people was still far from easy.

Humanity is to the fore in this story, since digressing into deep scientific analysis of technical aspects of the pursuit and final battle would risk making it inaccessible to many readers and suck the emotional marrow out of it, removing drama and pace. There were brave men on the German side, but I am not presenting their acts of courage here. I am interested in the endeavours of British sailors and marines trying to sink a ship that represented Fascism's bid to starve to death the last remaining bastion of democracy in Europe. *Bismarck* was, at the end of the day, a machine of war created to do the bidding of an evil regime, which initiated a war in which millions died. Besides, the *Kriegsmarine* sailors' side of this story is told well elsewhere with no need for in-depth replication in this account.

So much of the *Bismarck* saga is still open to debate, but one thing is for certain: just as *Bismarck* destroyed *Hood*, so the Royal Navy sought revenge and killed *Bismarck* just a few days later.

That is the story contained in this book.

Iain Ballantyne
Plymouth, 2010

Prologue: The Hoodoo Ship

Within the span of seven days
From view to chase and kill
The pride of Hitler's Navy learned
The might of Britain's will*

May 1941
Steaming hard for the Denmark Strait ...

The battleship HMS *Prince of Wales* was fresh out of the shipyard and already had a reputation as a bad luck ship. She was, in the words of her young sailors and marines, who took their slang from American pulp fiction novels and Hollywood movies, a hoodoo. A bastardization of the word voodoo, it invested the battleship with black magic mystique, which meant she was dangerous to keep company with. A dockyard worker had been killed on the slipway when *Prince of Wales* was launched at Birkenhead on the Mersey, and a bomb nearly hit her during a Luftwaffe air raid on the yard. Despite the unease caused by these incidents – for sailors are a deeply superstitious breed – the feeling was that, while others who got too close might suffer misfortune, *Prince of Wales* was in herself a 'happy' ship. She was, after all, one of the most powerful vessels in the Navy. Now, in late May 1941, *Prince of Wales* was steaming hard, in company with the most beloved of ships in the fleet, HMS *Hood*. The 'Mighty *Hood*', as she was universally known, was a First World War battlecruiser blessed with all the grace and beauty denied *Prince of Wales* by brutal, modern lines. The British capital ships formed in line astern battered their way through heavy seas, broad wakes flattening a heaving ocean enough to enable escorting destroyers to follow on and make decent headway. Many miles ahead, Royal Navy cruisers were shadowing the German battleship

* Anonymous poem written by an unidentified member of the Ship's Company HMS *Rodney* following the pursuit and destruction of the *Bismarck* in May 1941. *Source: IWM Department of Documents.*

Bismarck and her cruiser consort, sending back reports to keep *Hood* and *Prince of Wales* on course for battle. In the turrets of *Prince of Wales*, civilian technicians worked feverishly to correct defects in her 14-inch guns. The hydraulic system was leaking so badly gun crews were wearing oilskins. It was not a good omen, but the young men in *Prince of Wales* were inspired by the sight of the biggest and most beautiful ship in the Navy steaming hard and fast ahead of them. One man who was awake to the likely reality of the contest that loomed was the battleship's gunnery officer, Lieutenant Commander Colin McMullen. He was reminded by the presence of *Hood* that at the Battle of Jutland, a quarter of a century earlier, three British battlecruisers were blown apart, for their armour was too thin. To make sure his ship would be 'flash tight' McMullen did his rounds. Inside each of the three massive 14-inch gun turrets, he spoke to the men who operated the guns, telling them to hold steady during the action to come, those dressed in oilskins perhaps especially needing a morale boost. McMullen next climbed down vertiginous ladders inside turret barbettes to the very bottom of the ship, visiting shell rooms and cordite handling rooms, then the magazines, where many hundreds of shells and a corresponding amount of charges were stored: enough explosive power to destroy an entire town. He looked young sailors and marines in the eye, telling them: 'Make sure all the flash tight arrangements are properly obeyed, clips on watertight doors and so on hammered down.'[1] Only clips tightly hammered home could guarantee flash would not seep around the sides.

In the heat of action, with pressure on to feed ammunition to the guns, temptation to leave clips off, or doors slightly ajar, would be great. Some of the ships lost at Jutland even had cordite charges stacked in passageways. When the German shells hit, flash travelled instantly through each ship, detonating cordite and setting off shells, creating enormous explosions, tearing flesh and steel asunder.

When the moment of truth came the following morning, it was one of *Prince of Wales'* youngest sailors who spotted the enemy ships. At around 5.30 am, they were no more than smudges of smoke, the boy shouting his report down from the crow's-nest, his high-pitched voice quavering with excitement: 'Enemy in sight!'

Next, over the horizon came the masts, then rapidly sharpening silhouettes, confirming they were indeed *Bismarck* and a heavy cruiser of the Hipper Class.

Up in the main gunnery control position, at the top of the battleship's bridge tower, Lieutenant Commander McMullen opened his mouth to pass orders for the 14-inch gun crews to lay their weapons on target, but he was drowned out by a bugle call over the Public Address system. This was the 'Still', a signal for everyone to pause in whatever they were doing. The chaplain, the Reverend Wilfred G Parker, a New Zealander, was about to give his prayer before going into battle. Deep in the bowels of the ship, junior rating Joseph Willetts stopped handling cordite charges as the Sin Bosun's[2] voice burst out of the speaker: 'That, which I will recite, was a prayer before the Battle of Edgehill. "Oh Lord, thou knowest how busy we shall be today. If we forget thee, do not forget us".'[3] Then the speakers fell silent. Willetts and the others were told to resume work, and so he began passing cordite charges forward again. Far above, McMullen waited for the prayer to finish, cursing under his breath. Now, finally, he could give orders for the guns to fix on their target. Barely eight minutes of thunderous action had passed when the inside of *Prince of Wales'* gunnery control position was brightly illuminated, as if by a brilliant sunset. Lieutenant Commander McMullen was too busy using his optics to get the measure of the enemy to tear his eyes away and see what had happened.

Chapter 1

Made with Blood and Iron

Battleship *Bismarck* was launched on St Valentine's Day 1939 at the Blohm & Voss shipyard in Hamburg, and while her beautiful lines may have seduced many present among the cheering crowds, the leader of the Third Reich indicated he would not fall head over heels in love with her. The day after the launch, Captain Thomas Troubridge RN, British Naval Attaché in Berlin, a member of the Naval Intelligence Division and therefore a real-life forebear of the fictional James Bond, wrote his report for the Foreign Office, copied to the Director of Naval Intelligence (DNI) and Commander-in-Chief Home Fleet. Troubridge was the great-grandson of the legendary admiral and member of Nelson's 'Band of Brothers', Admiral Sir Thomas Troubridge. Appointed Naval Attaché to the British Embassy in Berlin in the summer of 1936, Troubridge was an imposing figure. A fluent German speaker, he understood the Teutonic mindset completely. This, combined with his habit of frank speaking and incisive wit, made the Germans both respect and fear him. When at home in the UK, he made his feelings about the German dictator crystal clear, telling some British naval cadets during a pre-war lecture: 'Fear God, honour the King and for God's sake don't be bluffed by Hitler.' In his report on *Bismarck*'s christening and launch, Troubridge revealed the ceremony was presided over by 'the Führer, who was assisted by practically every leading personality of the State and fighting services and a vast concourse of people.'[1] As was the German tradition, the name of the new warship was kept secret until the moment of christening, just before she went down the slipway, when a wooden name board was unveiled on the bows. The new vessel was named after the man who forged a unified German super-state in the late nineteenth century, Otto von Bismarck. Troubridge told his masters that Hitler eulogized the 'founder of the 2nd Reich'. Aside from saluting the powerful boost to German prestige represented by the new warship, Hitler used his speech to send a forceful message to the *Kriegsmarine*'s chiefs, indicating they could not expect to claim more than their fair share of rearmament resources. Furthermore, Hitler seemed to be telling his admirals that Germany, a

Continental state founded via the use of its large army under the guidance of Bismarck, would not some seventy years later devote more resources to its fleet than necessary. 'The new construction of a Navy sufficient to our requirements follows hand in hand with the rebuilding of the Army and the creation of a new Air Force,' Hitler told the crowds assembled in the shadow of battleship *Bismarck*'s great hull. The Führer stressed that *Bismarck*, as a tool of the state and its people, would serve the greater good. Perhaps Hitler sought to resist the German Navy's drive to accelerate its Plan Z regeneration scheme, which he had reluctantly approved in January 1939.[2]

No respecter of treaties, Hitler was quite happy to use the Anglo–German Naval Agreement of June 1935 as a means to slap the admirals down. He told those at the launch ceremony: 'Limitations to the number of big ships, which in the circumstances are acceptable and are allowed for in the Anglo-German naval agreement, necessitate a compromise, when naming the vessels, between the understandable desire of the Navy to maintain their own traditions and the claims which the people and the National Socialist State impose upon the Fighting Services.'[3]

Hitler did not necessarily want war with the British and he knew that building a fleet to rival the Royal Navy would provoke them, just as the Kaiser had foolishly done before the First World War. The result two decades earlier was Germany strangled by the Royal Navy's blockade and forced to sue for peace, even though its armies held the enemy at bay. The *Kriegsmarine* was also the least Nazified of the German forces, so Hitler was also possibly telling the admirals: 'I'm the boss.' In his report to London, Captain Troubridge observed that it was interesting to note Hitler used the word '*tragbar*' (supportable) in reference to the Anglo-German Naval Agreement, when the world was accustomed to hearing the Führer refer to 'treaties or conditions which Germany desires to alter' as '*untragbar*' (insupportable). Troubridge took comfort from the apparent enthusiasm of Hitler for building up land forces rather than a navy to threaten British trade and overseas colonies. The British Naval Attaché reflected that, 'the Führer is, in his policy, a disciple of Bismarck, throughout whose age the navy "was left in a half developed state". It is to be hoped that in the Hitler age it will be left in a 35% state[4], which, incidentally, it has by no means yet attained.'[5]

During *Bismarck*'s commissioning ceremony on 24 August 1940, the new battleship's Commanding Officer, Captain Ernest Lindemann, quoted a passage from a speech made to the Reichstag by Otto von Bismarck: 'Policy is not made with speeches, shooting festivals, or songs, it is made only with blood and iron.' Despite understanding little about naval warfare, and wary lest navy suck resources away from his land and air forces, Hitler still recognized hard power when he saw it, for when he visited the ship in early May 1941, he told *Bismarck*'s ratings they were 'the pride of the Navy'. Had Captain Troubridge been there, he might have told the Foreign Office of the German dictator's interesting emphasis on 'the Navy' rather than 'the pride of Germany', or 'the Reich'. Perhaps Hitler sensed the *Kriegsmarine* held itself slightly apart from his designs and was not to be trusted entirely? Sea power and the mechanics of naval warfare were altogether too mysterious for the former infantry corporal and veteran of trench warfare in the First World War. He toured the ship and received a detailed briefing on how *Bismarck*'s gunnery systems worked, but remained uncharacteristically silent, appearing to be struck dumb by the sheer complexity of it all, which no doubt reinforced his aversion to naval matters. Lieutenant Burkard von Müllenheim-Rechberg, fourth gunnery officer and adjutant to Captain Lindemann, gained a clear impression of the Führer's disconnection from matters of naval warfare. While conceding Hitler 'was very much interested in military technology', the young gunnery specialist recorded that Germany's political boss 'could not find a single word to say about this masterpiece of naval construction and weapon technology. He was not moved to comment.'[6] Admiral Günther Lütjens gave a presentation about his experiences during a recent Atlantic sortie. He had just returned from France after disembarking from the battlecruiser *Gneisenau* following her successful 'operation Berlin' commerce-raiding voyage in partnership with sister ship *Scharnhorst*, at the same time as the fast and heavily armed cruisers *Hipper* and *Scheer* were also at large. The four German warships accounted for nearly fifty enemy merchant vessels, around 270,000 tons of shipping sent to the bottom of the ocean or captured. Lütjens said he thought a similar deployment involving *Bismarck* could be even more successful, especially working with *Scharnhorst* and *Gneisenau* and supported by the new heavy cruiser *Prinz Eugen*. Possibly even *Tirpitz* could break out with her sister ship? Certainly, he told Hitler, no single British battleship could hope to take on *Bismarck* and win. This did nothing to settle the German Chancellor's mind, for he privately believed war against commerce might be better pursued via (much more expendable) U-boats, rather than surface raiders. He reminded Lütjens of the lethal potential of British aircraft carriers and their torpedo-bombers, which, as everybody present would have been well aware, had several months earlier put the Italian battle fleet out of action, with a daring raid on Taranto. The admiral conceded they were a threat. One German historian, trying to read Hitler's mind during that May 1941 visit to *Bismarck* and *Tirpitz*, has asked: 'Was he thinking how much more effectively such towering masses of war materials might have been utilized or how much better the 4,700 men comprising the two crews would be better contributing to the war effort if serving in the other branches of the armed forces?'[7] However, having constructed *Bismarck* and *Tirpitz*, the *Kriegsmarine* was not about to let them stay confined to the Baltic. Like their counterparts in the Royal Navy, indeed in all the other leading fleets, German admirals still put their faith in battleships as the principal arbiters of sea power.

However, not only did potential enemies tremble at the sight of a battleship's menacing silhouette steaming over the horizon, so also did governments faced with finding the money to maintain them or build a new generation. Also, every time a battleship set sail it was a gamble with national morale – to lose such a powerful symbol of nationhood would be a serious blow indeed, never mind the potentially huge loss of life. This was probably very much on Hitler's mind during his visit to *Bismarck*, but he preferred not to talk about it. After eating a one-course vegetarian meal in silence, he launched into a monologue about the need to invade Romania to protect 'German minorities'. He also declared America would not enter the war, something Captain Lindemann disagreed with, much to the dismay of staff officers present. Hitler's four-hour visit to the ship came to an end after another speech by Lütjens in which the admiral reiterated the success that might be achieved by *Bismarck*. Lütjens stated emphatically the objective would be to defeat the British wherever they could be found. Von Müllenheim-Rechberg observed that from the Führer there was, again, no response. During his visit Hitler heard no specific reference to the battleship's forthcoming sortie into the Atlantic. The German naval high command had decided to keep the Führer in the dark about it until after *Bismarck* and *Prinz Eugen*, sailed. They feared not being allowed to proceed.

Chapter 2

Germany's Masterly Deception

Prior to the First World War, the naval construction race between Germany and Britain saw two nations leap-frogging each other as their naval architects sought to create bigger and better battleships. Faced with British industrial might, the Germans, who on the whole produced better ships, found they could not win the numbers game. More than two decades on, Plan Z could not hope to fully match the British, who had a head start due to their large, if mostly elderly, extant battle fleet. Barred by the Anglo-German Naval Agreement from creating a fleet more than thirty-five per cent of the Royal Navy's size, the Germans decided to go for quality rather than quantity. They achieved their aim without protest, because the British refused to believe the biggest of the new warships – *Bismarck* and *Tirpitz* – were intended to contest the open seas upon which the empire's trade flowed. In that way the Germans pulled off a masterly deception, even if they received a lot of help from their future enemy in doing so.

Using the Washington Treaty and the later London naval conference[1] as its guide to fair play, the Anglo-German Naval Agreement limited Britain's next generation of battleships to 35,000 tons and it was expected the Germans would do the same. The head of the *Kriegsmarine*, Admiral Erich Raeder told his naval architects to create a battleship that would in reality displace 45,000 tons (standard)[2], but in July 1936 the official figure handed over to the British was 35,000 tons, with a beam of 118ft and a draft of 26ft. The principal weapon would allegedly be the 14.8-inch gun. In reality, the Germans armed *Bismarck* and *Tirpitz* with eight 15-inch guns as primary armament, with twelve 5.9-inch guns as secondary, plus sixteen 4.1-inch, sixteen 37mm and thirty-six 20mm anti-aircraft guns.[3] The UK's Director of Naval Construction assessed that such a broad beam and shallow draught indicated the main theatre of operations for Germany's 'Battleship F' (the future *Bismarck*) would be the Baltic, in other words against the Russians, something with which some senior naval officers agreed. By early 1937 there were those in the Naval Intelligence Division who argued the Germans were probably lying about the new battleship's dimensions

– that she had more displacement, deeper draught, bigger guns and was generally much larger, probably indicating an ability for deep ocean raiding and the endurance to match. Such views were politically inconvenient in an era of appeasing Hitler.

It was easier to invest blind faith in the Germans keeping their side of the bargain. The British have a habit of playing things straight when others might be cheating because it's the done thing, the honourable course. Scrutinizing the reality of *Bismarck's* design might have led to the conclusion that Britain should also cheat, but that would not do. Better not to look too closely.

It was also easier on the public finances. Hitler, who left the technical details of warship construction to his admirals, saw the Anglo-German Naval Agreement as worthwhile only because, in promising not to rival the Royal Navy's supremacy, Germany could build up a navy that would at least be big enough to counter French maritime power and also, of course, to support territorial ambitions in Eastern Europe.

In this way the British agreed to allow Germany five capital ships, a pair of aircraft carriers, twenty-one cruisers and sixty-four destroyers, plus a sizeable number of U-boats.[4] By being so generous they of course permitted the Germans to build the very warships that would prove to be the Royal Navy's biggest worry in May 1941. *Bismarck* was laid down in July 1936, her sister ship, *Tirpitz*, that October. *Bismarck* was, in reality, almost 814ft long and 118ft wide, with a deep load draught of more than 34ft. Even her standard displacement of nearly 41,700 tons – not including fuel oil, feed water for boilers and ammunition – was, of course, a flagrant breach of the Anglo-German Naval Agreement. *Bismarck's* fully loaded displacement was 50,900 tons, though the British did not know that until after the war.

In late December 1936, in a report intended to be seen by the Foreign Office – also copied to DNI as well as C-in-C of the Home Fleet – Captain Troubridge expressed a suspicion there was some kind of bid to outwit the British. He wrote: 'The Anglo-German naval agreement was one of the masterstrokes of policy, which have characterized Germany's dealings with her ex-enemies since the war. When the time is ripe, as history shows, it will unquestionably go the same way as other agreements; but the time is not yet.'[5] However, the final sentence of this passage was not conveyed back to the Foreign Office, possibly because the Ambassador, Sir Eric Phipps, thought Troubridge should restrict his comments to naval matters, rather than speculating on political intent. Nevertheless, the DNI saw it, as did C.-in-C. Home Fleet. The Royal Navy was of course subject to the direction of the democratically elected government of the day, and neither the government, nor the British people was minded to pick a fight with Germany over its naval intentions. After the Second World War, Troubridge was asked by the wartime DNI himself, Rear-Admiral John Godfrey, why he did not flag up more prominently his concerns over where the

Kriegsmarine's expansion plans might be headed. Troubridge responded that while he had initially remained open-minded, though still wary, he hoped the Germans genuinely intended sticking to the restrictions. That they did not became obvious after *Bismarck*'s launch. Troubridge told Godfrey that a British diplomat based in Hamburg assessed *Bismarck* was 'drawing a good deal more than she should'.[6] The truth is that while the Royal Navy would have been quite open to the idea that the Germans were breaking the rules, the political leadership did not want to rock the boat. When Britain guaranteed Poland's security on 31 March 1939, Hitler responded within weeks by applying '*untragbar*' to the naval agreement and tearing it up, leaving the British with new battleships that abided by limitation treaties but were, on an individual basis, inferior to *Bismarck*.

Faced with two battleships, a pair of battlecruisers under construction, and three pocket battleships – each displacing around 16,000 tons (deep load) and armed with six 11-inch guns – already commissioned into service, between April 1933 and January 1936, the Royal Navy decided that despite Germany having nearly defeated Britain through unrestricted submarine warfare in the First World War, the main threat still lay in surface raiders. Funds were funnelled towards modernizing elderly, First World War-era capital ships and building new cruisers and battleships. Since the First World War the British had built only two new battleships, *Rodney* and *Nelson* (both laid down in 1922). Stunted in appearance, with a trio of massive gun turrets, each of which mounted three 16-inch guns, all placed forward, they were nevertheless effective, despite brutish lines and slow speed. The principal British naval aim was domination of the North Atlantic and Mediterranean, to secure those zones from the depredations of surface raiders and keep open supply routes and connections to far-flung parts of the empire. As the menace of Fascism grew through the 1930s, even the pacifist British public and parsimonious governments of the day found they could not ignore the need for new battleships. Initially, because the King George V Class battleships were designed to abide by naval limitation treaties, they were planned with a displacement of 35,000 tons. But the lapsing of those agreements ultimately gave naval architects an opportunity to be somewhat more ambitious, and so their displacement rose by another 5,000 tons. Unfortunately, because the design had originally played by the rules, the 14-inch gun was retained. Upgrading the main armament would have meant going back to the drawing board and, with the drumbeat to war sounding loudly, that simply was not possible. At 745ft long, with a beam of 103ft, the King George V Class ships were 68ft shorter and 15ft narrower than *Bismarck* and *Tirpitz*. The deep load displacement of 42,076 tons was less than the German battleships, although it was believed until after the Second World War that the *Kriegsmarine*'s new battlewagons were about the same displacement as the Royal Navy's. With belt armour of 15 inches (maximum), the British ships were also, overall, less heavily protected than *Bismarck* and *Tirpitz*. With a top speed of 28 knots, they were one knot slower. Prominent among those urging creation of a new breed of ocean-going monsters in the early 1930s was Winston Churchill, who, as First Lord of the Admiralty a quarter of a century earlier, presided over the RN during the final years of its pre-First World War naval build-up.[7] As war clouds gathered, he experienced many sleepless nights wondering if the British navy would manage to keep its lead over the Kaiser's fleet. Now, despite all the blood and treasure spent in the early part of the century, Britain was once more involved in a naval arms race. The interwar treaties had merely postponed the inevitable settling of scores incubated by the unsatisfactory settlement at Versailles. Throughout his wilderness years (1929–1939), when no British government would listen to his dire warnings of a gathering storm, Churchill kept in touch with the Admiralty, which tolerated his forthright advice and lobbying on ship construction matters. The former First Lord of the Admiralty gave the Navy a voice in Parliament, even if it was rarely heeded, at a time when many in government doubted the whole point of the RN. Its bitter enemies included the upstart Royal Air Force, which had gained control of the naval air arm and suffocated maritime aviation ambitions in case they drew scarce funds away. When the government of the day reluctantly ordered new battleships, Churchill immediately offered strident advice to the Admiralty. Some of it was not entirely welcome, in particular his criticism of the decision to opt for 14-inch guns, which were smaller in calibre to those mounted in the new Japanese and American ships. Even the Queen Elizabeth Class battleships Churchill had been midwife to more than two decades earlier packed the punch of a 15-inch gun. He stated in a letter of August 1936 to Sir Samuel Hoare, First Lord of the Admiralty: 'It is terrible deliberately to build British battleships costing £7,000,000 apiece that are not the strongest in the world.'[8]

Originally the King George V Class were to have a dozen 14-inch guns, which Churchill thought gave a weighty punch that offset the smaller calibre. However, the ships were redesigned to take only ten 14-inch guns. Churchill thought this a disaster, not only because it caused a delay in getting them into service but also because the punch was, in his view, not strong enough.

It was maintained by the Admiralty that, even so, the more numerous 14-inch guns – ten of them rather than eight 15-inch or nine 16-inch – had a faster rate of fire. The superior velocity and range of their shells would give them a longer reach and greater penetrative power. Mr Churchill was not persuaded. The former First Lord later grumbled that Britain gambled the fortunes of the Navy, and control of the sea, on 'a series of vessels, each taking five years to build, which might well have carried heavier gun power.' All ships of the King George V Class were laid down in 1937, but completion was slowed due to Britain's withered shipbuilding capacity, which was suddenly burdened with not only constructing battleships, but also aircraft carriers, destroyers, cruisers and submarines. The first of class, *King George V,* named after the recently deceased monarch, was laid down on News Year's Day 1937 and launched in late February 1939, less than seven months before war broke out.[9]

Prince of Wales, named after the prince who became Edward VIII before abdicating in late 1936, was laid down the same day and went into the water in May 1939. *Duke of York,* named in honour of the prince who became King George VI following Edward's abdication, was laid down in May 1937 and would not be launched until February 1940. Two other ships of the class, *Jellicoe* and *Beatty,* were also ordered. Named after the feuding admirals who commanded the British fleets at the unsatisfactory Battle of Jutland during the First World War, their names were subsequently changed, possibly to avoid reminding a country on the brink of war that the Royal Navy's magnificent battleships could sometimes fail to utterly defeat an enemy. *Jellicoe* became *Anson,* named after Admiral of the Fleet Lord Anson, an eighteenth century swashbuckler, who circumnavigated the world on a raiding expedition and reformed the Navy, introducing standard uniforms for officers and improving its fighting efficiency. *Beatty* became *Howe,* to celebrate another legendary Admiral of the Fleet, who, before Nelson, was the Royal Navy's greatest hero in the interminable wars against the French of the eighteenth century. *Anson* and *Howe* would not be completed until 1942. By late 1940 only *King George V* had been commissioned, with *Prince of Wales* racing towards completion. So, while five British battleships were ordered, by the time *Bismarck* and *Tirpitz* were close to commissioning only two of them were anywhere near readiness, with *Rodney* and *Nelson* the most modern fully operational battlewagons the UK possessed on the outbreak of war. The rest of the Royal Navy's capital ships were a mixture of reconstructed First World War-era or, worse, vessels hardly changed at all since that conflict. The RN's ships were also spread across the globe trying to safeguard the Empire, while Germany could concentrate its smaller, but more modern, surface fleet in home waters, ready to send out on raiding missions. The likelihood of the Royal Navy having its capital ships, and enough of them, in the right place at the right time to intercept German raiders was slim. Therein lay the folly of the Anglo-German Naval Agreement. The *Kriegsmarine* had been allowed thirty-five per cent of the British navy's strength when in war it was no easy matter for the Royal Navy to concentrate even that percentage of its power in home waters to counter Germany. The situation was of course made worse by the fact that *Bismarck* was potentially worth at least two British battleships. Had they instead worked to enforce Versailles and the various treaties restricting naval construction the British might have prevented, or at least delayed further, the advent of *Bismarck* and her sister. They might have, therefore, have bought time to rebuild old ships like *Hood.*

In spring 1941, contemplating how the Royal Navy might contain *Bismarck* and *Tirpitz*, Churchill, who had become Prime Minister in May 1940 after a second stint as First Lord of the Admiralty, continued to view the King George V Class battleships with dismay. They were 'gravely undergunned'.[10] Churchill, who was also Defence Minister, applied himself to considering how the Admiralty's pressing need to construct more warships, including a new class of battleship armed with 16-inch guns, could be prioritized, bearing in mind the competing demands for steel to build tanks for the Army. The first two ships of the Lion Class – *Lion* and *Temeraire* – had been laid down just prior to the war, but in October 1939 construction was halted. It was not likely to resume, nor in the end would the final two ships of the class, *Conqueror* and *Thunderer*, even be laid down.[11] All that could be managed in the short-term was completion of *Duke of York*, *Anson* and *Howe*; but work would begin by the end of 1941 on the one-off *Vanguard*, armed with second-hand 15-inch guns, some of which had previously been mounted in the modernized First World War-era fast battleships *Warspite* and *Queen Elizabeth*. The turrets themselves came from the light battlecruisers *Glorious* and *Courageous*, having been in storage since the early 1920s when these ships were converted to aircraft carriers. With no new battleships realistically possible beyond the KGVs, the fact that Britain at least possessed two 16-inch gun battleships must have been a source of comfort, but also of anxiety. Comfort, in that the Royal Navy at least had something to out-match *Bismarck*'s main fire power, but anxiety because the formidably armoured *Nelson* and *Rodney* were so old and comparatively slow, with a top speed of only around 22 knots. It is a poor state of affairs when your most heavily armed battleships were first commissioned nearly two decades earlier. Due to their age they needed constant dockyard attention to keep running. In early May 1941, *Nelson* was in the South Atlantic, having just undergone maintenance in the dockyard at Durban, South Africa, while *Rodney* was due to leave Scotland for Boston in the USA and a major refit.

The man in command of the main striking force expected to intercept and kill *Bismarck* or *Tirpitz* if, and when, they attempted to break out into the Atlantic was fifty-six-year-old Admiral John Tovey. As Commanding Officer of *Rodney* in the early 1930s he knew full well the power of her 16-inch guns and also the vulnerability of her worn-out boilers. With *King George V* as his flagship, Tovey was also aware of the new battleship's flawed main armament. 'Jack' Tovey was no stranger to combat at sea. Having joined the Royal Navy as an officer cadet at the age of fourteen, by the outbreak of the First World War he had command of his own destroyer, winning the Distinguished Service Order and a mention in dispatches for his tenacious command of HMS *Onslow* during the Battle of Jutland.

Tovey commanded the cruisers and destroyers of the Mediterranean Fleet during clashes with the Italians in the early part of the Second World War.

Promoted to command the Home Fleet in November 1940, he would have a prickly relationship with Churchill, whom he felt was full of 'bright ideas' but was 'most dangerous'[12] when he dabbled in matters of strategy and tactics. For his part, Churchill regarded Tovey as 'stubborn and obstinate'.[13]

On Monday, 19 May 1941, *Bismarck* weighed anchor in the bay at Gotenhafen[14], her sailors imbued with supreme confidence. Despite never having been beyond the Baltic, the new Nazi battlewagon had already earned the sobriquet 'most powerful warship afloat' and was now to attempt a breakout into the Atlantic to prey on British shipping. In addition to *Bismarck*'s usual complement of 2,065, there were eighty-two men belonging to the staff of Admiral Lütjens aboard, plus 218 Luftwaffe aircrew and maintenance personnel for the battleship's four aircraft. When it came to the command team for the imminent Rhine Exercise sortie, there was a stark division between the two principal players: Captain Lindemann, *Bismarck*'s Commanding Officer, and Lütjens. They had clashing personalities, described as 'following orders' (Lütjens) versus 'obeying common sense' (Lindemann).[15] Lütjens was not capable of much empathy for those under his command – something he would later prove more than once – and was also a fatalist, perhaps because he knew he could only manage so many lucky escapes from the Royal Navy. In March 1941, Lütjens saw *Rodney*'s menacing silhouette emerge out of the darkness as *Gneisenau* was sinking a merchant ship in the northern Atlantic. The German battlecruiser showed *Rodney* a clean pair of heels. Was fatalism born of such close shaves really the right attitude for a man entrusted with the most important ship in the German fleet, a symbol of the power of the Nazi armed forces essential to the high morale of the nation? And was it right for him to expect the same mindset from *Bismarck*'s eager, raw crew? Lütjens let them know from the outset they would either succeed or die. With little collective experience of naval warfare, *Bismarck*'s sailors probably did not comprehend how horrific the sacrifice might be, at least not on board their brand new battleship, which seemed invulnerable. The presence of Lütjens at the head of the mission already filled some men in *Bismarck* with pessimism. They recognized he had achieved some notable successes, but 'his reputation on the lower deck was by no means enviable'. Furthermore, 'His command in *Gneisenau* was marked by a chain of misfortunes and the superstitious had come to regard him as a Jonah. This reputation had followed him to *Bismarck*, producing, in consequence, a depressing atmosphere.'[16] When she left Gotenhafen, *Bismarck*'s newly commissioned sister ship, *Tirpitz*, took her place in port, an attempt to fool British reconnaissance flights into thinking the former had not yet sailed. However, *Bismarck* was spotted leaving the Baltic by the Swedish cruiser *Gotland*, and this information swiftly leaked to Captain Henry Denham, the British Naval Attaché in Stockholm.

Had *Gneisenau* suffered at the hands of *Rodney* during Lütjens' previous raiding sortie it might well have persuaded Adolf Hitler to ban any further such adventures by his capital ships. Notwithstanding the brush with *Rodney*, the success of the sortie by *Gneisenau* and *Scharnhorst* contributed to the German fleet's decision to send out *Bismarck* just over two months later. *Gneisenau* and *Scharnhorst* were by May 1941 lurking at Brest, alongside the heavy cruiser *Admiral Hipper*. Exercise Rhine originally involved the two battlecruisers making a foray from Brest at the same time as *Bismarck* and *Prinz Eugen*, the operation due to start at the end of April. However, the refit of *Scharnhorst* would take longer than thought, while *Gneisenau* was torpedoed during a daring RAF raid on the Brest Roads and then damaged during British bombing of the port's dry docks. Further misfortune struck when *Prinz Eugen* suffered mechanical problems. The *Prinz Eugen* was one of three German heavy cruisers that were far superior to any British ship armed with the same guns – 8-inch main armament – with the exception of the recently reconstructed cruiser *London*. Completed at Kiel in August 1940, *Prinz Eugen* was named after the Austro-Hungarian Prince Eugene of Savoy, who defeated the Ottoman Turks at several battles in the eighteenth century. Hitler was another Austrian with hopes of victories in the East. The name was also intended to carry on the spirit of the Austro-Hungarian Navy, which had ceased to exist with the end of the empire that used to rule the Adriatic from landlocked Vienna via control of the Dalmatian coast. The previous ship to carry the name had been a 20,000-ton battleship of the Austrian fleet, which, following defeat of the Central Powers in the First World War, was awarded to France. She was used as a target ship, the combined fire of four French battleships eventually sinking her off Toulon in the summer of 1922. Well-designed, the *Kriegsmarine*'s *Prinz Eugen* gracefully cut her way through heavy seas, keeping her forecastle clean. Possessing similar lines to *Bismarck*, except of course on a smaller scale, her vulnerability was a high-pressure steam propulsion system that was prone to break down. Like *Bismarck*, the *Prinz Eugen*'s design was a cheat – meant to displace 10,000 tons, her actual deep load displacement was 18,700 tons. A lot of this went into her impressive protection, with more than an inch of upper deck armour and an armoured deck inside the ship that was two inches thick. Despite this she had a top speed of more than 32 knots. With a standard complement of 1,600, which was more men than it took to run a British battleship, *Prinz Eugen* in May 1941 was commanded by Captain Helmuth Brinkman. He told his sailors at the commissioning of *Prinz Eugen* the previous summer: 'We are a happy ship and we are a lucky ship – but in the long run luck comes only to those who deserve it.'[17] Luck was an essential element of high-seas raider warfare, for the longer a German warship could avoid the tentacles of the Royal Navy, the better to cause distress and damage to the British war effort. As the exploits of the *Admiral Graf Spee* had shown in 1939, even the mere possibility of a singleton high-seas raider on the loose in the Atlantic and Indian oceans was enough to sow confusion and chaos in shipping lanes across the globe. Sailing times for convoys were disrupted and the Royal Navy found its resources stretched to the limit in both protecting merchant shipping and forming hunting groups. The success of *Graf Spee* and her sister ship *Admiral Scheer* in picking off merchant ships and the success of *Gneisenau* and *Scharnhorst* later, combined with the depredations of U-boats, were real threats to the Atlantic lifeline that sustained Britain. With America and Russia still neutral, Britain fought a lonely, losing battle against the Germans, who were triumphant on land everywhere, if not always at sea or in the air. The *Kriegsmarine* hoped that if it was able successfully to stage a surface raider breakout into the Atlantic, then the British might realize their domination of the seven seas was over. Their national morale would be dealt a fatal blow, the population at large would be under threat of starvation, and those who favoured a negotiated peace with Germany might win the argument. The rest of the world not under Nazi dominion might well write Britain off and accommodate Hitler's desires for economic and territorial domination of Europe.

The war would be over.

Chapter 3

Storm-Tossed Sentinels

These were seas that pushed both vessels and men to the limit. According to one Royal Navy cruiser veteran the Denmark Strait was 'a water spout full of violent seas'[1] in which a ship did not just roll with the blows, but was twisted in the ocean's savage grip.

The ship's companies of British cruisers sent to loiter for weeks at a time in the Denmark Strait, awaiting attempts by German surface raiders to break out into the Atlantic, regarded their duty with dread and resignation. For, as one naval officer turned novelist later termed it 'a ship was scarcely a ship, trapped and hounded in this howling wilderness'.[2] In such circumstances a man became nothing more than an automaton, drawing on the last reserves of stamina and training to keep his warship barely functioning. Humanity was sucked out of men who became deadened, hollow-eyed husks, often vomiting where they stood with no care for a bucket. One veteran of British cruisers even recalled seeing his ship's cat chucking up in a bucket. Usually pristine decks were covered in filth, and nobody made an effort to clean them, for what was the point? There was no holystoning the upper deck, or polishing anything below decks[3] in the stormy Arctic, nor were there working parties to repaint the ship or any polishing of brass. Food and drink were spilled as marines and sailors tried, often in vain, to sip or spoon down some nourishment, but it was not cleaned up. As a ship dug into heavy seas the contents of toilets spewed forth and nobody cared to grab a mop, while rust made its mark throughout. Just getting through each day was more than enough effort, never mind striving for cleanliness and pristine 'Pusser's standards'.[4] If a ship was a wet one – in other words, let in water, a common occurrence, depending on size – then water might slosh around inside cabins and claustrophobic compartments, with books, magazines, newspapers, clothes and other personal possessions, thrown to the deck by the movement of the ship, making a squalid soup. The County Class cruisers were perhaps better at keeping water out than other vessels, such as corvettes and destroyers. In Arctic seas their interiors possessed light and some heat, but were also, according to one sailor, 'cold and humid, like a tomb'.[5]

There were those hardy souls, men with iron stomachs and impervious minds, who could overcome it all, such as cooks struggling with hot pots and sizzling trays as the ship pitched and rolled. Somehow they avoided scalding themselves or anyone else, in order to deliver sustenance to those who could keep the food down. For many days, when cooking was all but impossible, bully beef sandwiches, soup and ship's biscuits were all that could be managed. Deep down in the engine rooms – in the heart of the ship, where the centre of gravity lay – old hands of the engineering department rode the roller-coaster with aplomb, making sure the ship could still steam. On the bridge the captain and his officers of the watch found that at least the sight of some vague horizon provided relief for queasy stomachs, enabling punch-drunk brains to function well enough to command the ship. Most British warships had open bridges, assailed by the full fury of the weather against which frail humans wrapped themselves in several layers. Sheepskin coats were only the outermost layer, with hats clamped on sailors' and marines' heads, and jackets, shirts and long johns underneath. They often survived only due to regular deliveries of steaming hot cocoa and, of course, the daily tot of rum, which was like an injection of fire into numbed, weather-beaten brains and bodies. In the severest weather nobody ventured on to the upper deck, for to do so risked being snatched away to an icy death. The sea used its fingers to find the weak spots in any ship design, punching in inch-thick glass on deadlights and making matchwood of boats on upper decks. The ships creaked and groaned with the strain of it all, the age and design of some British cruisers – among them County Class ships built in the 1920s – not helping. They were created to cruise the tropics, as guard ships of the far-flung empire, not to act as Arctic sentinels. In the vast and comparatively benign Indian Ocean, such fast ships might cover hundreds of miles in twenty-four hours hard cruising, whereas in the Arctic it could take a cruiser all her power to manage six miles in the same time period. Tall ships, with high freeboards, the County Class cruisers rolled violently – naval folklore claimed they would roll on a wet handkerchief – but they were tough. The County Class were made with riveted steel, providing flexibility newer, welded, ships lacked and so broke more easily.[6]

In the Arctic summer the Denmark Strait is 180 miles across at its narrowest point, framed by eastern Greenland and northern Iceland, but during the long months of winter, ice closes this cursed, 300 mile-long passage to around 60 miles wide. During the Second World War, the British narrowed it even further, by sowing mine fields. On its western side, the cold East Greenland current – of low salinity – carries icebergs south into the northern Atlantic, while close to Iceland the Irminger Current, a branch of the North Atlantic Current, takes warm water north. The more saline warm water cools as it moves north and sinks. It was an iceberg travelling south from the Denmark Strait that sank the Titanic. Trawlermen still venture eagerly into its turbulent waters to pluck a rich catch from the depths, for warm water meeting cold flowing south, creates upwelling, bringing food supplies for tuna, cod and other valuable fish. Fog is a constant companion due to warm water meeting cold and also because of ice drifting down from the Arctic. In certain stretches of summer those who sail the Denmark Strait live in a world of constant daylight while during the winter there are periods of round-the-clock darkness, further adding to the mind–numbing, spirit–draining experience of weeks on patrol for men of the British cruisers. There could, however, be moments of bewitching beauty in the Denmark Strait, when the weather cleared. The towering glaciers of Greenland shimmered and sparkled on the horizon, above a flat calm, mirrored sea. A brilliant sun, set in clear blue sky warmed the blood, reviving body and soul. The war could be forgotten just drinking in the splendour of the vista, a gently hissing bow wave sparkling like diamonds, icy slush brushed aside, creating a mesmerizing whisper. Often there was no other human life between a warship and Greenland or the Polar ice cap. Adding to the mystery of this unearthly part of Neptune's realm, seemingly lost between sea and sky, was the aurora borealis – the famed Northern Lights – fluorescent ribbons dancing overhead, the product of high energy atomic particles blown by solar wind into the Earth's magnetosphere. Some found it glorious, while others regarded them as satanic, symbolizing the edge of Hades. One cruiser veteran reflected gloomily on a 'dark and sinister Arctic Ocean', in which might be lurking a bringer of death, in the shape of a prowling U-boat. The hypnotic 'unearthly brilliant rays of the aurora borealis only seemed to stress the finality of it all if disaster had struck.'[7]

In May 1941, the unenviable task of standing sentinel in the Denmark Strait fell to two heavy cruisers of the County Class, HMS *Norfolk* and HMS *Suffolk*, the former launched at Portsmouth Dockyard in December 1928 and the latter at Fairfield, on the Clyde, in February 1926. Both armed with 8-inch guns, they received extensive refits in the late 1930s, but remained a type of ship described with contempt by some as 'tinclads' due to their thin armour – around one inch of protection on their sides and turrets with a maximum of just over four inches around their magazines.[8] This was even somewhat less than British cruisers built during the latter stages of the First World War, which had side armour on average three inches thick. But such ships were slower and less heavily armed than the County Class, and the accommodation for their sailors and marines, while bearable for short periods in the North Sea against the Kaiser's fleet, did not lend itself to weeks at sea in the Mediterranean or East of Suez, never mind in the seemingly endless hell of 'Patrol White' in the Denmark Strait.

On 21 May 1941, *Suffolk*, having been relieved of patrol duties by *Norfolk*, set course for Iceland, her men's spirits soaring at the thought of a brief respite.

Lieutenant Commander BW Smith recorded a sudden leap in morale: 'With light hearts and good prospects we waved goodbye to the edge of the floe ice, at which we had gazed with increasing boredom for some days, and steamed away.'[9] Waiting at the Hvalfjord would be sacks of mail containing news from home and, hopefully, some parcels, too. As the cruiser ploughed towards Iceland on the morning of Thursday 22 May, Ascension Day, her men found time to sit down and write their own news, for they knew there would be a very narrow window to get their mail away. The ship was monitoring Admiralty signals traffic, learning that the previous afternoon *Bismarck* and a heavy cruiser had been found and photographed by an RAF reconnaissance Spitfire in Korsfjord, near Bergen. A daring follow-up flight by a naval spotter aircraft discovered the big German ships gone. With that revelation, the Commanding Officer of *Suffolk*, Captain Robert Ellis, realized his men would not have much respite, if any. Lieutenant Commander CT Collett, *Suffolk*'s Air Defence Officer, recalled of the alert: 'We had just completed oiling and were beginning to settle down to our first evening meal in harbour for some considerable time when we got our order to proceed as quickly as possible to patrol our old friend the Denmark Strait in company with HMS *Norfolk*.'[10]

So hopes of a few days in the Hvalfjord, or even of the ship going back to the UK were dashed, *Suffolk* weighing anchor at 11.30 pm. There would be no meals with the ship peacefully at rest – hot meals were impossible without the risk of everything being thrown to the deck. Captain Ellis anticipated his instructions would be simple: *Suffolk* would patrol the Denmark Strait and, if she made contact with *Bismarck* and her escort, fix their position and shadow, so enabling British capital ships to attack the German raiders.

With reconnaissance flights often not possible because of poor weather, the cruisers' talents were vital, although visibility was often only three miles amid thick fog banks, stinging rain squalls and swirling mist – good for either the hunter or the hunted to hide in. It was essential the enemy be given no clue that British warships lay in wait. They could guess, but an intercepted wireless signal could provide the German ships with sure knowledge there were just two 8-inch cruisers on picket duty. They could push through without fear of a capital ship in the vicinity. To prevent the enemy from gaining any such advantage, the commander of the 1st Cruiser Squadron, Rear-Admiral Frederic Wake-Walker, would provide more specific orders via light signal for the forthcoming patrol to *Suffolk*, as she made her way out around Iceland. A torpedo and mine warfare specialist, Wake-Walker was a keen shot who liked to go wildfowling at Scapa. In May 1940 he had been a float commander for the evacuation of British and French troops from the beaches of northern France. His command ship, the destroyer *Keith*, was sunk by German dive-bombers, after which he commanded operations from a small boat. Now, a year later, pursuing a quarry somewhat more substantial – and dangerous – than geese in Orkney, the shooting admiral decided to position *Suffolk*, the ship blessed with the more powerful radar (or Radio Direction Finding equipment, RDF, as it was then known) nearest to the point where *Bismarck* and her attendant cruiser would likely emerge. *Norfolk* and *Suffolk* made their rendezvous at 10.00 am on Friday, 23 May, on the eastern edge of the Denmark Strait, off foggy Isafjordur, a fishing port in the north-west corner of Iceland, under high cliffs towering either side of them. In that majestic Wagnerian setting, signal lamps flickered between the two British ships as Wake-Walker passed over his instructions.

As *Suffolk* sped along, a very large goose left a flight heading north and for a number of hours flew parallel to the ship, level with the upper deck forward. Some keen shots in the wardroom volunteered to bring the goose down – aiming to drop it on to the forecastle. To justify this addition to the dinner menu they suggested the goose was probably an enemy bird carrying out a reconnaissance. Captain Ellis heard the request with patience and humour. Remembering Samuel Taylor Coleridge's, *The Rime of the Ancient Mariner*, in which a ship and her crew were cursed when one of them killed an albatross, he forbade it. *Suffolk*'s Commanding Officer had clearly learned Coleridge's lesson and wanted God on the side of his ship, not the enemy's:

> He prayeth best, who loveth best
> All things both great and small;
> For the dear God who loveth us,
> He made and loveth all.

By the evening of 23 May, the cruiser was at the northern end of the minefield, patrolling south-west, before coming around again to follow a north-easterly course, running like a clockwork mouse between mines and the pack ice. *Suffolk*'s Executive Officer (XO), Commander Ludovic Porter, made a broadcast to the ship's company, explaining that the German ships might well come their way to break out into the Atlantic. The skies above the ice were clear and there remained good vision for about ten miles, but beyond that, all the way to Iceland, was a 'ragged wall of mist'.[11] Wary of being caught out in the open by *Bismarck*, when *Suffolk* headed south-west she hugged the edge of the mist. Should a sighting be achieved, she could swiftly seek cover, to avoid destruction at the hands of the German battleship's guns. However, by the nature of the ship's construction, Captain Ellis and lookouts on the compass platform found her superstructure – including a large slab-sided hangar for *Suffolk*'s embarked aircraft – partially obscured their view astern. The ship's surface search radar was also not able to 'see' in that direction. *Suffolk* might therefore not spot *Bismarck* immediately.

It was very comforting to have the blanket of mist and fog close at hand.

On the north-easterly part of the circuit, close to the ice on the other side of the clear channel, those problems were absent, for the cruiser had a clear view forward, with both radar and the 'Mark One Human Eyeball'.[12]

Of course, there was the slight problem of having nothing to hide in. *Suffolk* was also, potentially, heading straight for much more powerful enemy ships, as the latter came south-west to break out. She would in such an event seek to stay at the maximum possible distance, while hanging on to their tails, sending out a stream of signals to enable the big ships of the Royal Navy to bring them to battle. *Suffolk* must not even sustain minor damage, for it might impair her ability to shadow the enemy. She must be able to keep up her speed. Her steering must be good enough to evade shells, too, while sailors and marines needed to keep their vigilance taut. Should *Suffolk* need to hide in the fog and mist, radar was vital to ensuring contact was maintained. RDF was a recent addition to British warships. Not all of them had it, nor among those that did was it necessarily the most effective variant. *Suffolk*'s Type 284 radar could be trained to cover arcs unavailable to fixed antennae radar, such as that fitted to HMS *Norfolk*, although *Suffolk*'s did, of course, have that blind spot astern. With fixed antennae radar the ship had to be turned to cover arcs, rather than the ship maintaining a fixed course/position and the antennae turning. *Norfolk*'s Type 286M radar had proved troublesome and according to Wake-Walker 'had to be carefully nursed as all spare valves had been used'.[13] *Suffolk*'s Captain Ellis realized the huge potential in radar, so had deeply acquainted himself with its advantages and limitations. Should his ship find herself marking down *Bismarck* he intended using it to the maximum. That ambition was shared by his boss, stationed fifteen miles south in *Norfolk*. As a very technically minded officer, Wake-Walker was keen on using the latest technology to give British warships the edge. He was eager for RDF to prove its worth and well aware history could be made, for it would be the first time radar had been used to shadow an enemy warship. Maintaining a safe distance while not losing contact was a very tricky objective to achieve, as Wake-Walker acknowledged: 'Should the enemy turn on his pursuers when being shadowed from the quarter by a ship using this set [*Norfolk*'s], the shadower must act at once, but in turning away he loses RDF touch astern and is very liable to get caught or retire too far.'[14] Like all of the Royal Navy's cruisers – backbone of a global force – *Norfolk* was a hard-working ship and, since leaving a refit on the Tyne in mid- November the previous year had clocked up vast distances on each patrol. Telegraphist DA Hibbit, on Wake-Walker's staff, proudly noted that this amounted to 'over 53,000 land miles which is more than twice the earth's circumference.'[15] This was an average of 9,000 miles a month. Hibbit also recorded an incident from 20 May, which perhaps gave force to Wake-Walker's decision to deploy *Suffolk*, with her more capable radar, further north and closer to the ice. 'We crashed into the Ice Barrier which was invisible owing to thick white fog,' revealed the young rating 'and we had to go astern in order to extricate ourselves. Slight damage was sustained – no casualties. Damage consisted [of a] hole in the hull of the fo'cstle.'[16]

Knowing *Suffolk*'s blind spot problem was most acute on the south-westerly part of the circuit, Captain Ellis ordered the posting of more lookouts aft. They redoubled their vigilance as the cruiser turned and began heading south-west, at 7.00 pm. The moment of truth came twenty-two minutes later. One of the lookouts, an anti-aircraft gunner, Able Seaman Newall, tasked with looking for enemy air activity and apparently 'feeling rather bored with an empty sky, idly lowered his binoculars into his lap and cast a vacuous eye on the horizon – there he saw two ships.' The officer who related this also caustically observed that 'his mind being equally vacant' Newall initially reported 'Bearing green 140 two ships' believing they could be British. 'Then his eyes popped out of his head! (for this he will probably get a medal).'[17] Captain Ellis and others dashed from the warmth of the enclosed bridge to the starboard bridge wing, raising their binoculars to scrutinize the shapes emerging from a snow flurry some seven miles away. *Bismarck* and *Prinz Eugen*, managing an average speed of 24 knots and skirting the ice, trying not to hit anything too large, recorded their sighting of *Suffolk* at the same time she saw them. Once again, the niceties of life had to be abandoned, as recorded with some excitement by a *Suffolk* officer: 'We were drinking our pre-dinner sherry, when action stations sounded off. The sherry was rather wasted! It was the enemy!'[18] The German ships were well within killing distance of *Suffolk*. Captain Ellis ordered the wheel hard over to port, *Suffolk* racing for the fog to escape destruction. The sighting had a galvanizing effect on the ship's company, including Lieutenant Commander BW Smith who regarded it as 'a rude interruption hearing the emergency action call.' He described a 'quick dash into warm outer clothing and a hurried sprint forward (dodging those sprinting aft of course) and into the fore control[19] went I, with a heart beating a little more rapidly ...' On reaching his action station, Lieutenant Commander Smith picked up some glasses to take a look at the enemy and thought she looked huge, though 'she was to look even bigger later on'. *Suffolk*'s Commander Porter also inspected the German ships, which were 'in plain view, the shape of the cruiser being overshadowed by the great bulk of the battleship. Every moment one expected them to open fire.'[20] The three minutes it took for *Suffolk* to reach safety were agonizing. Everybody on the bridge and in lookout positions was tensed for shell spouts close by, hurling hot shrapnel into the ship, or, worst of all, something substantial hitting the cruiser and in one fell swoop sending her to the bottom of the icy ocean. But *Bismarck* seemed not to have noticed *Suffolk*. Rear-Admiral Wake-Walker later speculated that, unlike the British, the Germans did not use their gunnery radar for anything other than directing weapons, relying on visual observation for sightings. From his excellent vantage point in the anti-aircraft gunnery director, and via high-powered glasses, Lieutenant Commander Collett watched the enemy ships 'slinking along the edge of the ice in a snowstorm [and for some] reason [they] did not open fire on us – at that short range he [sic] could have blown us out of the water.'

Suffolk immediately sent a report, but her wireless equipment was suffering from damp and so it got no further than *Norfolk*. Her Commanding Officer, Captain Alfred Phillips, was tucking into his dinner savoury of welsh rarebit in his sea cabin when he was rudely interrupted by the ship's Chief Yeoman of Signals stumbling across the threshold, breathlessly exclaiming: '*Suffolk's* got 'em, Sir.'[21] The Chief Yeoman handed over a signals intercept of the sighting report.

Action stations were sounded off, *Norfolk*'s sailors and marines finding themselves, as one junior rating described it, 'closed up at our respective quarters'.[22]

Suffolk's escape took her into a narrow space between two sections of a minefield, the ship carefully turning around, maintaining radar contact with the German ships as they continued on a northerly course, edging closer to the ice before turning south-west. Captain Ellis studied the radar screen over the shoulders of the set's operator. Judging the distance to be enough for *Suffolk* to edge out of the mist, Ellis gave the order, but on emerging saw the Germans were still a little too close for comfort, so took the ship back into cover. Circling back, when *Suffolk* came forward again, the enemy were fifteen miles ahead, very close to the edge of the pack ice and pelting along at around 30 knots, trying to outrun their shadower. In *Norfolk*, Captain Phillips ordered his ship to make for the reported position of the enemy with all speed. An hour later, at 8.30 pm, the cruiser plunged out of a fog bank to find *Bismarck* and her escort only six miles off the port bow, the intervening distance disappearing rapidly as the ships closed. Starkly presented with imminent destruction if he did not make a sudden retreat, *Norfolk*'s captain ordered the wheel hard over to starboard and a smoke screen, to give the cruiser protection as she dashed for the mist. *Bismarck* was quick on the draw this time, unleashing a salvo from her 15-inch guns. The shells fell close to *Norfolk*'s stern, on the port quarter, sending splinters scything into the cruiser's X turret. Rear-Admiral Wake-Walker applied a cool, professional eye to the action, describing 'a broad wall of smoke and water at right angles to our line of fire, and I think that the spread for range and line was very small.' The water close to the ship was 'pocked with fragments and one complete burnished shell made what I think was its second bounce 50 yards our side of the salvo and ricocheted over the bridge.'[23] Wake-Walker estimated up to three more salvoes fell, although he only saw one close together 'fine on the starboard quarter' due to *Norfolk*'s smoke screen. The cruiser passed on her dramatic information to the Admiralty, and it was picked up by ships scattered far and wide across the Atlantic who now wondered if they too might be drawn into the action. And so was set in motion 'the intricate mechanism of pursuit'.[24]

In *Suffolk* there was keen rivalry with the other cruiser, Lieutenant Commander Collett proudly observing: 'We were the first to sight the enemy without any doubt whatever although our sister ship *Norfolk* appears to be trying to get the kudos for it!' At 8.30 pm, observers in *Suffolk* saw the enemy's gun flashes in the mist, but while they expected splashes to surround them, nothing happened and it appeared *Bismarck* had been firing on *Norfolk*. The *Bismarck* sustained a serious blow, as her forward radar was put out of action by shock waves from her own guns, so *Prinz Eugen* came forward to take the lead. This enabled her gunnery radar to be used in determining the bearing and range to any likely targets found ahead. German and British ships kept up a bone-jarring speed, rushing headlong down the clear channel – both the mighty pursued and puny pursuers. *Suffolk*'s Lieutenant Commander Smith had a ringside seat from the fore gunnery control position. 'This was a chase – how long it would last and whither the enemy would lead us were very much the unknown factors ... We tore along at 30 knots and apart from snow slightly chilling the ardour of the personnel in exposed positions, our spirits were high.'

Chapter 4

Raise Steam with All Despatch

An officer of the Kaiser's surrendered fleet in 1918, on seeing the bleak
main British fleet anchorage at Scapa Flow for the first time, allegedly
turned to his captors and asked: 'And you really stayed here all the time
– four years?' On receiving an affirmative answer, he shrugged dismissively
and responded: 'Well, you deserved to win.'[1] But beyond the anchorage is a
verdant land, which contrasts starkly with the images lodged in the minds of
many men forced to sit there at anchor, in not so splendid isolation, far from
their loved ones. On a fine summer's day at Scapa the desolate beauty of
Orkney, a collection of islands clustered off the north-eastern tip of the
Scottish mainland, could inspire a feeling of contentment and peace, clearing
both mind and soul of all the clutter of modern, congested civilization.
However, when rain was driving in almost horizontally and a raw gale blew
with ferocity all the way from the Arctic, it truly was the embodiment of dull,
aching misery. That was the image most men of the Navy took away with them,
because their ships' portholes afforded them a narrow perspective. It was here
tens of thousands of them spent many months of their lives during both world
wars of the twentieth century. Was it any wonder the captive Germans scuttled
their once fine fleet in 1919, rather than spend another week in their floating
prisons?

The Kaiser's warships were not designed for weeks of habitability and only
went to sea for a few days at a time. The British derived great pleasure from the
discomfort of the Germans during their internment at Scapa, forced to live as
they were, at anchor in a ship rather than in spacious, warm and comfortable
barracks as was the custom back at Wilhelmshaven. The Germans were being
paid back for the years they forced the Royal Navy's ships to stay far from home
ports and families in Devonport, Portsmouth and Chatham. Now, in the spring
of 1941, the new battleship *Prince of Wales*, a Devonport Division vessel
manned by men from the naval barracks at HMS Drake and Plymouth's Royal
Marines division, was in exile at Scapa. She had never so much as poked her
nose in to Plymouth Sound.

As many of their families endured the Luftwaffe's blitz on Plymouth, the men of *Prince of Wales* formed part of the second generation of Royal Navy sailors and marines resigned to life at Scapa Flow. Unable to spare anyone else, the Commanding Officer of *Prince of Wales*, Captain John Leach, despatched the ship's Padre to go and call on families affected by bombing in Plymouth and bring back news, good or bad. The men, meanwhile, vented their frustrations on the pitches of Scapa, playing hard matches of rugby and football against other ships, including the formidable teams of HMS *King George V*, fleet flagship.

The 'KGV', as she was also known, was commissioned on the Tyne, at Vickers-Armstrong's Walker Naval Yard, on 1 October 1940, under the command of Captain Wilfred R Patterson. On the same day, Midshipman North Dalrymple-Hamilton joined the ship. The Eton–educated son of Captain Frederick Dalrymple-Hamilton, Commanding Officer of battleship *Rodney*,[2] he had wanted to serve in a cruiser. The Royal Navy's young gentlemen believed they stood more chance of seeing action and gaining early responsibility in one of those work horses of the navy than in the more strictly disciplined, and generally less active, battleships. However, Dalrymple-Hamilton senior thought his son would fare far better in a battleship, where his naval education could continue under the eyes of officers specially assigned to tutor midshipmen, whereas in a cruiser there was far less likely to be that level of academic care. Midshipman Dalrymple-Hamilton had first been to sea in his father's destroyer in the Mediterranean Fleet, so he found plenty of space in a modern, roomy battleship to sling a midshipman's hammock. Food aboard ship was also far better than what was available ashore under rationing. North Dalrymple-Hamilton was in the end enormously pleased to be in *King George V*: 'You felt tremendously thrilled for being in Britain's newest battleship, I mean it was most exciting … everybody from the captain down were completely new, a brand new ship and so we were kept very hard at it.'[3] Throughout this time the Luftwaffe was making a determined effort to destroy ships under construction, mounting daylight low-level bombing raids along the Tyne, with *King George V* and the new carrier *Victorious*, under construction at the same yard, prime targets.[4]

Inevitably, as happened in other British cities and towns playing host to yards or naval bases, the Luftwaffe's bombs often fell wide of their target, in this case causing damage to the city of Newcastle itself. The situation was so bad in the autumn of 1940 that, a fortnight after her commissioning, although not yet completed, *King George V* made the tricky journey to sea in the dead of night under blackout conditions. She was destined for Rosyth in order to complete construction in the comparatively safer environment of the Scottish dockyard. *King George V* went down the Tyne with only two out of her four screws in operation; the other two would be fitted at Rosyth, such was the urgency to get

Britain's sole new battleship away from the daily attention of the Luftwaffe. Midshipman Dalrymple-Hamilton felt the civilian population was not sorry to see his ship depart: 'The citizens of Newcastle were very glad to see the last of us because Newcastle had been bombed quite heavily, and they all said: "Well, we wouldn't be bombed if it wasn't for that wretched battleship, *King George V*." So they were glad to see us go …'[5] *King George V* was meant to rendezvous with a pair of destroyers, but *Fame* and *Ashanti* collided while using paravanes to sweep for mines off the mouth of the Tyne. Both ships subsequently ran aground and so, for six hours, *King George V* made her way north unescorted, until replacement destroyers could be sent south. On 11 December, *King George V* joined the Home Fleet at Scapa Flow, but was not yet flagship, as she had yet to work her weapons up to full fighting proficiency, which was traditionally when a battleship was declared fully operational. Before that could be done, the battleship was asked to take a diplomatic delegation to the USA, in January 1941. Two months later, following her final work-up for operations, *King George V* provided distant cover for a commando raid against the Lofoten Islands. In early April she became Home Fleet flagship after Admiral Tovey transferred his flag to her from *Nelson*.

As part of his education, Midshipman Dalrymple-Hamilton spent time in the 14-inch gun turrets during gunnery trials, finding the experience less than spectacular when the ship's main weapons fired, for all he heard was a thump although he conceded 'there was a hell of a roar when you were on the outside.'[6] However, he felt the clubbing blast of the 14-inch was preferable to the 'very painful crack' of 5.25-inch weapons, an experience that Dalrymple-Hamilton found all too familiar. 'When we were working up the *King George V* you could train these guns around, and in a certain place you had to stop them or they fired into the ship, which wouldn't do at all … we had to establish which were "safety arcs".' To do this, the midshipmen were ordered to stand in various places on the upper deck. Dalrymple-Hamilton recalled that 'the guns came around going "bang" and when you literally could stand it no more you'd say "stop" and they put in the training arc stop. Nobody ever thought of telling us to put anything in our ears, and in fact if you did put anything in your ears you were considered rather wet, and so we never did …'[7] Such excitement was not the norm for the young officers, who had their studies to keep them occupied as their ship sat at anchor in Scapa Flow, which Midshipman Dalrymple-Hamilton found utterly lacking when it came to entertainment, unless you were a keen golfer, of which there were quite a few aboard *King George V*. To occupy themselves the battleship's midshipmen decided to resurrect a golf course that had been created by the men of the Grand Fleet during the First World War. More than two decades on, the young officers mapped out the course, restored its fairways and mowed its greens, but, as Dalrymple-Hamilton admitted 'it was never more than just a joke'.[8]

For angling enthusiasts aboard sister ship *Prince of Wales*, which had succeeded *King George V* as newest battleship in the fleet, Scapa offered some fine fishing. On the evening of 21 May, Captain Leach took his Gunnery Officer, Lieutenant Commander Colin McMullen and the latter's brother Maurice, also serving in *Prince of Wales* as a supply officer, ashore in search of trout. By late May, with the water warming up, feeding trout had begun to move out into the lochs but bank and stream fishing still offered fine specimens. The battleship officers were put ashore by Kirkwall, Orkney's capital, but they had not been fishing for much more than an hour when one of the ship's boats crested into view at high speed. The midshipman in charge shouted to them that *Prince of Wales* had received a signal to 'raise steam with all dispatch'. The officers piled aboard the boat with their angling gear. Once back aboard ship, Captain Leach learned *Bismarck*, having been detected at the fjord near Bergen, was presumed to be moving further north in anticipation of a break-out. Admiral Tovey, pondering his next move aboard *King George V*, at anchor nearby, had decided to send a hunting group composed of *Hood* and *Prince of Wales* towards Iceland, in order potentially to carry out an interception either in the Denmark Strait or the Iceland-Faroes gap. Midshipman Dalrymple-Hamilton was aware great things were afoot, even though he did not know exactly what. He sometimes pulled a spell of duty as midshipman of the watch, on the quarter-deck, and on occasion was only 50ft from Tovey, watching as the admiral paced up and down deep in discussion with one or more of his staff officers. On 21 May, Dalrymple-Hamilton was midshipman of the watch again, saluting as both Captain Leach and Vice-Admiral Lancelot Holland, the commander of the Battle Cruiser Squadron, which was composed of *Prince of Wales* and *Hood*, came aboard for a meeting with Tovey. 'It was some time about 20.00 and they had about an hour with the Commander-in-Chief, and then went back to their ships ...'[9] It was not a lowly midshipman's place to know what was happening in terms of the bigger picture, but obviously something big was afoot.

In company with destroyers, *Hood* and *Prince of Wales* would initially take on fuel at the Hvalfjord in preparation for Tovey's further orders. Two months earlier Tovey, on receiving a similar raider alert, had deployed with the entire Home Fleet to cover a potential break-out point south of Iceland. He realized that he had made a major error, for it meant when fuel ran low there was nothing in reserve. This time Tovey intended to retain enough hitting power at Scapa to respond to events as they unfolded.

Prince of Wales had plenty of troubles, and civilian workmen were still trying to put right many defects. Her path to the front-line fleet had not been a smooth one, for she had experienced her share of mishaps. Lieutenant Commander McMullen joined *Prince of Wales* at Birkenhead in January 1940, as she was being completed at the Cammell Laird Yard.[10] McMullen had previously served in the cruiser *Aurora*, experiencing ineffective German high level bombing in the North Sea during late 1939. He regarded *Prince of Wales* as a top line appointment, for being gunnery officer in a battleship was an important job. However, while *Prince of Wales* might have a new gunnery officer, she was at that point in time toothless. On joining, McMullen discovered the battleship 'had no fourteen inch turrets in her, no 5.25-inch gun turrets in her, no pom-poms [2pdr anti-aircraft guns].' Leading Sick Berth Attendant Sam Wood was another new joiner, who had received basic training in HMS *Caledonia*, a training ship berthed alongside Rosyth Dockyard. The former liner had been awarded to the British as part of post-First World War reparations from Germany. In her previous life she had been named *Bismarck*.[11] Now Wood was in the sickbay of *Prince of Wales*, a miniature hospital, with its own X-ray machine, small laboratory, examination rooms, bathroom and isolation room, besides its cots for the sick and wounded. Surgeon Lieutenant Commander Dick Caldwell headed the battleship's medical staff. In action the sickbay was not used and instead the ten-strong medical team, including Surgeon Lieutenant Commander Caldwell, Leading Sick Berth Attendant Wood and other medical officers, senior ratings and junior ratings, was split between stations, the principal one being amidships within the armoured citadel[12] while the other was forward in the seamen's mess deck. The wounded would be assessed and stabilized in these two stations and, after action had ceased, moved to the sickbay itself, by which time it would be safe to treat them there. The sickbay was large and spanned the width of the ship, being forward of the A and B turrets – so the likelihood of it being hit during action was greater than that of both aid stations being taken out. If one of them was destroyed the remaining aid station would deal with the wounded and dying. Joseph Willetts joined *Prince of Wales* during the 1940 August Bank Holiday, having made the long trek north by rail from the south-west of England. As a Devonport Division rating, he too was assigned to the Plymouth naval barracks, HMS *Drake*, and, as he later recalled, was 'anxious to join the ship of my choice'. That ship was *Prince of Wales*, which he knew was building at Birkenhead. He thought a battleship would be tighter on discipline than smaller ships like destroyers or corvettes and, as a man with an orderly mind, Willetts wanted a neat, new ship like *Prince of Wales*. He had initially been disappointed, being told it was 'impossible, because there was already a waiting list of some five hundred people who would have liked to have joined that ship.'[13] However, within a few hours of being told it was unlikely he would get *Prince of Wales*, Willetts was informed he would, after all, 'be required in Liverpool' and was drafted to the battleship as a supply department rating. Joining as a stores assistant, he handled the ordering, storage and issuing of all the ship's many thousands of essential items, from food and clothing to electrical stores, engineering parts and spares, together with upper deck stores. The ship's company[14] had to be fed continually, so there were large storage areas for food. One of his clerical jobs was to keep track of it all; no mean feat in a country on strict rationing and in a ship populated by not only sailors under strict discipline but also hundreds of civilian contractors. In spite of an eager local black market beyond the ship there was no pilfering, at least not on his watch. And despite the *hoodoo* superstition[15] seeded by the death of a dockyard worker during the ship's launch, Willetts found *Prince of Wales* 'the happiest ship'. His naval career would encompass half a dozen warships, but he felt she was the best, as well as the largest and most efficient, in short 'a very, very, very happy ship'. Willetts felt that a huge effort had been made to ensure *Prince of Wales* got the best sailors and marines. Even so, the majority of people in the ship were Hostilities Only (HO) ratings, meaning they were only in the Naval Service until the end of the war, whenever that might be. Willetts was, of course, one of them, having joined up in early 1940. The HOs soon bedded in and gained experience and skill every day, and they all seemed to get on well with the regulars, which was not always the case.

Lieutenant Commander McMullen was, meanwhile, worried about the switch to 14-inch guns after the RN had accumulated so much experience with 15-inch guns, which he felt were a 'well-tried bit of ordnance, completely reliable.' The latter had proved their reliability and hitting power in several battles. However, he recognized that the naval treaties had imposed restrictions. McMullen observed that in the King George V Class this meant the design being altered, 'with B turret, the second turret from forward, instead of being a four gun turret becoming a two gun turret.' McMullen felt the class would have been 'better off really with eight fifteen-inch [guns] because the fourteen-inch turret was completely untried mechanically. Putting four guns into a turret was obviously a much more complicated thing than putting two guns into a turret. So all those ships and especially the first ship in the class, *King George V*, suffered from vast numbers of mechanical teething troubles in their turrets, due to the fact it was an untried, very complicated mass of machinery ... we had vast numbers of problems with our fourteen-inch mountings.' The 5.25-inch (secondary armament) guns were much simpler and McMullen experienced few problems working them up, since they were similar to those fitted in new cruisers, therefore not an unknown element. McMullen's job during the final period of the ship's completion was to check the watertight integrity of the shell rooms and magazines, also to supervise installation of armament. The ship suffered damage during a Luftwaffe air raid in August 1940, the offending bomb falling between the fitting-out basin wall and *Prince of Wales'* port side. The explosion punched a hole in the ship, so much water gushing in that she developed a 20-degree list. At the time a key part of Y turret had not yet been fitted securely and was resting on four gigantic wooden chocks. With the ship listing dramatically, disaster was only narrowly avoided. If she had been in deeper water, *Prince of Wales* might well have capsized, but the bilge keel of the ship hit the bottom of the fitting-out basin. Fortunately, Y turret's heavy metal did not slide. The ship's company, including skilful shipwrights with their wooden constructs, applied themselves to shoring up Y turret, which weighed some 1,500 tons. Lieutenant Commander McMullen was in Y turret at the time, so knew full well the severity of the incident: 'Of course the trouble was that the ship was not in a watertight condition down below because all the bulkheads had been pierced for new electric leads and so on. But we finally managed to isolate the damaged portion. The ship was pumped out and came upright again. But she was very nearly lost while building.' With enough progress made for her to sail in safety, the battleship left Birkenhead on 28 January 1941, but nearly did not make it out of the yard. As she was towed away from the wall, *Prince of Wales* momentarily grounded on the rims of bomb craters in the middle of the basin. The ship's propulsion also failed as she exited the lock from the basin into the Mersey. The battleship's then Commanding Officer, Captain Louis 'Turtle' Hamilton, immediately gave the order to drop anchor, while the engineering department sorted out the problem. Reaching Rosyth, *Prince of Wales* entered dry dock with the aim of putting right defects in the main armament and also completing the ship, a task which had been rendered impossible at Birkenhead by the numerous German air raids. Captain Hamilton handed over command to forty-six-year-old Captain John Leach in early February 1941.

Leach, a gunnery officer who commanded the heavy cruiser *Cumberland* on the China Station in the late 1930s, was more recently Director of Naval Ordnance, responsible for ensuring British warships were armed properly. Leach was alarmed to find his son also drafted to the *Prince of Wales*. When Germany invaded Poland in September 1939, Henry Leach was a midshipman under training at Britannia Royal Naval College, Dartmouth. During Christmas 1940, on completion of training, Midshipman Leach was unexpectedly reunited at home with his father, who was supposed to be somewhere else on important Admiralty business. Captain Leach announced he was off to sea, but could not say which warship he was to command. His wife's face fell, for it was bad enough having a son in a warship, without a husband at risk, too. Captain Leach arranged for Henry to be appointed to the cruiser *Mauritius* instead of *Prince of Wales*, to avoid any conflict of interest caused by father and son serving in the same vessel.[16]

In early 1941, there was a sense of urgency about everything *Prince of Wales* did to get herself ready for commissioning into the front-line fleet – the need for another modern battleship was pressing. She took aboard her full outfit of ammunition and stores plus fresh drafts of sailors and marines to complete her complement before sailing north to Scapa Flow. Following her March commissioning, according to Lieutenant Commander McMullen there were still 'vast numbers of problems'. There were extensive gunnery trials, with fire control and the operation of the guns put through the wringer, to ensure *Prince of Wales* could be brought rapidly to action. It was soon discovered that while recoil, elevation and training of the 14-inch guns worked well enough, the loading process was plagued with problems. The Gunnery Officer noted: 'Of course, in any large mass of complicated machinery you require quite a lot of time in which to get the bugs out of it. Of course, due to the speed with which we had to work up, we were denied that time.' Continuous shoots with *Prince of Wales'* 5.25-inch pom-poms and 14-inch guns proved gruelling for the ship's company but particularly wearing on the gunnery staff. McMullen felt the fire control became very efficient but, even after such intensive work-up, the mechanical workings of the 14-inch guns were simply 'not up to scratch'. When Captain Leach declared the ship operational to the Commander-in-Chief on 19 May, he did so with the proviso that there were still mechanical problems with the 14-inch guns.

Surgeon Lieutenant Commander Caldwell came up with the idea of having a medic available on the battleship's upper decks, ready to move wherever he was needed most during any action. Leading Sick Berth Attendant Wood was that man, tasked with finding a suitable position to await the call to action. After some investigation, Wood decided the armoured conning tower forward of the bridge was a good location. It had wide observation slits that would enable him to see the upper deck on both the port and starboard sides. It also offered a good view over the battleship's A and B turrets, plus the bonus of a telephone link to the ship's forward medical station. The armoured conning tower would be empty in action unless the bridge itself was hit, and only then would the ship be controlled from there, forcing Wood to clear out. He found that usually the only other occupant was a leading seaman who seemed to have nothing much to do except scan the surrounding sea and sky through a pair of binoculars. On getting up there, the first thing Wood did was ring the forward medical station to confirm he was 'closed up and ready'. The leading seaman and Wood took to playing cribbage until an officer of the watch gave them a bollocking, advising them they were not on a pleasure cruise. He confiscated their cards while threatening worse punishment if he caught them at it again.

Wood was armed with the following equipment for saving lives: ten ampoules of morphine, two tourniquets, a forearm splint, bandages of various types, plus cotton wool and lint. He also had an indelible pencil and some labels, although he wondered what use 'such inadequate supplies' would be 'if a major action took place' and there were multiple casualties. His superiors told him to do his best and said that he would hopefully never find out what it was like to treat the dead and the dying under enemy fire. Wood thought it likely that he would be among the first casualties in any action. He would be beyond helping anyone.

Chapter 5

Heavyweight with a Glass Jaw

W hen conceived, HMS *Hood* was the epitome of British naval power, which ruled the oceans, girdling an empire that was the greatest the world had seen. The coffers of Britain, bulging with the gilded fruit of imperium, funded the most magnificent battle fleet ever built. Its battlecruisers were the brainchild of the remarkable Admiral Sir John Fisher, First Sea Lord between October 1904 and January 1910. He reshaped the Edwardian Royal Navy to meet the rising threat of Germany, discarding hundreds of useless warships that were nothing more than Victorian-era showboats, and pushing through a technological revolution that in one stroke – construction of the all-big-gun battleship *Dreadnought* – made every capital ship in every navy, including Britain's, utterly obsolete. Fisher's vision included a new breed of big, fast, heavily-gunned warships that could range the globe, watching over the sea lanes conveying wealth to Britain and holding enemies at arm's length, while inflicting devastation on the impudent scoundrels for daring to assail British trade. The battlecruisers tried to achieve an impossible balance between protection and speed. Starting in 1908, with HMS *Invincible*, the British built a series of ships with battleship hitting power, but only two thirds the protection of a full-blooded capital ship. The problem was that they looked like battleships and so, when war with the German Empire came in 1914, the temptation to let them fight the enemy's biggest and best ships was irresistible. Their lesser armour was combined with an almost cavalier attitude to safety procedures within some British ships – flash screens dismantled, hatches left open, cordite charges stacked in passageways – all of which spelled disaster at the Battle of Jutland, where three Royal Navy battlecruisers were destroyed, with the loss of 3,304 lives. This shattering blow came when *Hood* was already under construction. Conceived in the aftermath of the RN's battlecruiser triumph at the Falklands in late 1914, *Hood* was meant to be a speedier version of the highly successful Queen Elizabeth Class fast battleships that a retired Fisher helped First Lord of the Admiralty Winston Churchill create just prior to the outbreak of war. The Queen Elizabeths were what the battlecruisers should have been all along – big, fast, well armed and heavily armoured enough to fight, and beat, any enemy battleship. *Hood* was originally laid down on the Clyde on 31 May 1916 – the day the RN lost those three battlecruisers at Jutland. The keel laying was repeated on 1 September that year to give her thicker belt armour, but only the fore part of the ship received the greater protection. Work on three sisters vessels – *Howe*, *Rodney* and *Anson* – was suspended indefinitely in March 1917 and they were formally cancelled in November 1918. *Hood* was the last battlecruiser ever built for the Royal Navy, faith in the concept having been broken. However, with the British Empire drained economically by war, and the Grand Fleet destined mostly for the scrap yard, *Hood* and two other relatively new battlecruisers, *Renown* and *Repulse*, were retained in service. Completed in 1920, *Hood* toured the world flying the flag for the British Empire. An imperial icon, she also summed up the material state of the Royal Navy between 1921 and 1937 – externally impressive, seemingly invulnerable and still the biggest, but actually a thin shell, an illusory gloss hiding vulnerabilities that would be starkly exposed during the Second World War. *Hood* was a heavyweight boxer with a glass jaw. Lacking essential full modernization, but benefiting from an exaggerated reputation as the world's most beautiful and powerful warship, in 1941 the so-called 'Mighty *Hood*' was ill prepared to fight the latest capital ships. Between 1920 and 1939, *Hood*, for all her faults, still appeared to present a combination of speed and hitting power unrivalled by any other capital ship. Some might have bigger guns, such as the 16-inch weapons of American and Japanese battleships, and the Royal Navy's own *Nelson* and *Rodney*, but they could not hope to catch *Hood*. On a good day she was capable of destroyer speeds – shifting her nearly 50,000 tons and eight 15-inch guns through the water at 30 plus knots. As a new naval arms race gathered pace in the 1930s, *Hood* remained busy flying the flag – maintaining the impression of the Royal Navy as ruler of the seven seas – but newer, even more heavily-armed and faster ships were taking shape. They had the sort of protection needed to survive a slugging match that *Hood* so sorely lacked. In early 1939 it was suggested *Hood* should go into a deep refit that would rectify her vulnerabilities in overhead protection and also replace obsolete secondary armament.

This major work would have changed her graceful silhouette, making her more a beast of modern war. Not only would she have received modern 5.25-inch anti-surface/anti-aircraft secondary turrets, as fitted to the King George V Class ships, her torpedo tubes (mounted in an exposed position on the upper deck) would have been deleted. She would also have received better torpedo defences. *Hood*'s distinctive 650 tons conning tower was to be removed, saving weight that could be spent elsewhere. The battlecruiser would have received a new aircraft hangar, plus better engines. Most crucial of all was the need to upgrade her armour, protecting *Hood* better against both flat-trajectory and plunging fire. In the end, all she received was twin 4-inch guns, the extra weight putting *Hood*'s quarterdeck well under water in anything but the calmest of seas. In northern waters even the boat deck, high up in the waist of the ship, was swept with waves, such was the alarming increase in displacement. She had originally been 45,200 tons deep load, but now was in excess of 48,360 tons. Assigned to Force H at Gibraltar as flagship, *Hood*'s guns were blooded during the unfortunate bombardment of French warships at Oran, in early July 1940, an operation designed to stop France's capital ships falling into German hands. In mid-January 1941, *Hood* was sent to Rosyth for more work – engine repairs (the main item) plus Type 284 radar. She also received two new motor launches.

On 15 February, a new commanding officer arrived, in the shape of Captain Ralph Kerr. His style was less forceful than that of his predecessor, Captain Irvine Glennie, who had just been promoted to Rear-Admiral. Kerr had a scar on his face and was held by one young sailor to be 'quieter, less prepossessing, and did not want everyone to get out of his way just because he was captain of *Hood*.' Glennie was 'a typical dour Scot and a four-ringed captain who wanted everyone to know it.'[1] Ralph Kerr was aged forty-nine, having joined the Royal Navy in 1904, subsequently seeing action at Jutland in the battleship *Benbow*, but specializing in destroyers for much of his career right up until the time he assumed command of *Hood*. Among *Hood*'s ship's company was seventeen-year-old Ted Briggs, a Yorkshireman who first saw the battlecruiser from the beach at Redcar in 1935, when he was twelve years old. Briggs instantly fell in love, never forgetting *Hood*'s grey-painted hull bleached white by summer sun, nor the graceful bows and long, powerful 15-inch guns with their glittering tampions. Then there was the pleasing symmetry of her superstructure, appearing to taper aft, where two more 15-inch gun turrets lurked under a dazzling, cream awning. An entranced Briggs watched small boats bustle around this ship of legend, the star of cigarette cards and newsreels, lead player in photo essay magazines and books for boys, all extolling the awesome power of the British navy and enduring supremacy of the Empire.

It was a dream come true when junior rating Ted Briggs was drafted to *Hood*. On 1 March 1941, while the ship was still at Rosyth, eighteen-year-old Briggs was promoted to Ordinary Signalman, so passing from boy sailor to man, although he would have to be twenty-one years old before he could draw a tot of rum aboard ship. He was, however, allowed to drink as much as he liked ashore.

Another of *Hood*'s junior ratings was twenty-year-old Robert Tilburn, the son of a policeman, from Leeds. At the age of ten Tilburn fell in love with the idea of a life in the Royal Navy, following a holiday with relatives in Portsmouth during which he attended Navy Week, touring several warships. His father took a lot of persuading, but finally at the age of 16 Tilburn was allowed to join as a boy seaman. He was sent out to join *Hood* at Gibraltar during the Munich Crisis of September 1938, and was with the ship through the latter stages of the Spanish Civil War and later the action at Oran.

Midshipman William Dundas, from Perthshire, joined *Hood* in early January 1941 at the age of seventeen. Keen on a naval career, he had entered Britannia Royal Naval College in May 1937, passing out in December 1940. Dundas finished eighteenth out of thirty-four in the college's Second Division, a cadet captain – equivalent of a school prefect – for, while not highly academic, he had demonstrated a talent for leadership. Dundas passed out from BRNC at the same time as young Henry Leach, son of *Prince of Wales*' captain.[2]

By mid–March, *Hood* had emerged from the dockyard and was moored in the Firth, just upstream from the Forth Bridge. Not yet worked up to full fighting efficiency, as she headed north to Scapa on 18 March *Hood* got the call to action. Admiral Tovey, in *Nelson*, was leading a hunt for *Gneisenau* and *Scharnhorst* south of Iceland, the two raiders, under the command of Admiral Lütjens, having caused chaos in shipping lanes. *Gneisenau* was nearly caught by *Rodney*, on 16 March, the British battleship appearing 'silhouetted like a mountain against the light in the west.'[3] The German raiders were later spotted by aircraft from the *Ark Royal* around 600 miles west-north-west of Cape Finisterre. The Germans had headed south for France, rather than attempting to reach home by going north around Iceland. Tovey set off in pursuit, but the enemy evaded the British group, reaching Brest by 22 March. In a single day during 'Operation Berlin' the raiders managed to sink five merchant ships, a total of 25,784 tons, and altogether notched up twenty-two vessels, representing some 116,000 tons of enemy shipping and all the cargo that entailed.[4]

On 23 March, her sailors and marines disappointed at another failure to bring the enemy to action, *Hood* arrived at Scapa Flow. She was by then flagship of the Battle Cruiser Squadron, carrying Admiral William Whitworth (Holland's predecessor) and for much of the next month, would be at sea, only returning to Orkney to take on oil. *Hood*'s main task was to keep watch on the enemy fleet, much as wooden-wall British battleships did during the Napoleonic Wars. Some 137 years later the Royal Navy's warships were positioned 350 miles to the west of Brest, their duty as wearing as that of their forebears, tedium and rough weather draining morale. *Hood* went to action stations at dawn and dusk every day, but if the routine was hard on the men in the big ships, the destroyers in escort had it a lot harder.

Chapter 6

The Navy's Here

Among ships riding shotgun on *Hood* at this time was the legendary HMS *Cossack*, command vessel for the 4th Destroyer Flotilla, under the dynamic Captain Philip Vian. At 1,870 tons, *Cossack* and her Tribal Class sister ships were minnows compared to the likes of *Hood* and *Prince of Wales*. Of their kind they were modern and very fast – capable of speeds in excess of 36 knots. Well armed for ships of their size, with four turrets, each mounting a pair of 4.7-inch guns, they also had four 21-inch torpedo tubes and one pom-pom anti-aircraft mounting. The Tribals were worked extremely hard, frequently at the forefront of the action, winning 'a magnificent fighting record'[1] and paying the price as a result. During the Second World War, of the sixteen commissioned into the Royal Navy, all but four had been lost by the end of 1942, eleven of them sunk in battle. *Cossack* was launched at the Walker Naval Yard on the Tyne the same day in June 1937 as sister vessel *Afridi*, a local newspaper paying tribute to 'two trim vessels, alike as two peas' which 'took the water beautifully'. The Tribals were believed to cost 'about £480,000, a big increase on previous destroyers'.[2]

Both ships saw combat off Norway in 1940, and while *Cossack* came through intense action, *Afridi* fell victim to German air attack. *Cossack*, however, first sprang to renown during the famous *Altmark* Incident of February 1940. With Vian on her bridge, she steamed into Norway's Jossing Fjord and rescued thirteen merchant ship captains together with 286 merchant navy officers and men. They came from vessels intercepted and sunk by the German high seas raider *Graf Spee* before the latter was cornered and ultimately driven to destruction by the cruisers *Exeter*, *Ajax* and *Achilles* in December 1939. The supply vessel *Altmark* was used as a floating prison for the captured mariners and sought to carry the prisoners home to Germany as trophies to offset the loss of *Graf Spee*. The *Cossack*'s thirty-three armed men boarded *Altmark*, despite her being in neutral waters, killing four Germans and wounding five others, with only one of the merchant mariners injured.[3] The daring escapade achieved world renown, particularly for the legendary shout, as *Cossack*'s men stormed in, 'The Navy's here!' Vian's imprint was stamped all over the *Altmark* Incident. He was prepared to take chances in the face of extreme risk. Described as 'ruthless, extremely hard-driving'[4] Vian was as harsh with himself as he was with others. Vian was admired, even if he did not inspire the same love as some other commanders in the Service's history, such as Nelson, to counter-balance his hard edges. Joining the Royal Navy in June 1907, Sub-Lieutenant Vian witnessed Jutland from the destroyer *Morning Star*, then in the early 1920s served on attachment to the Royal Australian Navy as a gunnery officer in the battlecruiser *Australia* and cruiser *Adelaide*. Back with the RN, he was promoted to Captain in 1934, specializing in destroyer command and protecting British merchant vessels from attack as they sailed off the Iberian coast during the Spanish Civil War. Appointed to command *Cossack* and the 4th Destroyer Flotilla in early 1940, Vian's ruthless ambition would later have an impact on efforts to track down and destroy *Bismarck*, but the gamble he would take, while portrayed by some as Nelsonian, was seen by others as reckless.

Cossack was hit by eight enemy shells during the close-quarter fighting in the fjords of Norway during the Second Battle of Narvik in April 1940, but Vian was by then commanding the flotilla from *Afridi*, while *Cossack* was under the command of Captain Robert Sherbrooke, another man not afraid to go in harm's way.[5] When Sherbrooke left *Cossack* in May 1940, Vian, having survived the loss of *Afridi*, returned to the ship. Christmas Eve saw *Cossack* sailing from Scapa with four other destroyers, providing escort for *Hood* as she took up station east of Iceland, standing guard in case German raiders attempted to break out into the Atlantic. By early January, *Cossack* was at Southampton for a refit, including a modification to her Type 286 radar that enabled it to use a rotating aerial. Concluding her refit in early March 1941, on her way back to Scapa Flow *Cossack* set off an acoustic mine in the Irish Sea, but fortunately sustained only minor damage. In early April, the destroyer joined up with the Battle Cruiser Squadron, having spent a few weeks on numerous escort duties, including for battleships *Rodney* and *King George V*.

By mid-April, *Hood* was at Scapa, taking on fuel for another spell off Brest and was headed back to that station when diverted north, where cruisers were waiting to track *Bismarck*. Briefing *Hood*'s ship's company over the PA, Admiral Whitworth explained that, should it come to a battle, the battlecruiser would close fast, presenting a narrow bows-on profile. This, according to Ted Briggs, was the first time it dawned on some of the ship's officers that *Hood* was extremely vulnerable to plunging fire, though they still held faith with the 12-inch belt armour to soak up punishment. Nobody sought to explain 'this type of Achilles heel'[6] to sailors of the lower deck as they contemplated fighting the so-called most deadly warship in the world. Having left Kiel, on this occasion the German battleship did not head out into the Atlantic, but rather sailed to Gotenhafen, from where she would complete work up in the comparatively safe environment of the Baltic. *Hood* called in at the Hvalfjord on 21 April with the rest of the hunting force. They were kept at two hours notice to sail. One of *Cossack*'s young sailors, Boy Seaman KFW Rail, gazing in awe at the 'Mighty *Hood*', decided to see if he could wangle an invitation for a visit.

He succeeded, going across to see one of the ship's engineering department sailors, a friend of his father's. 'It was good to meet him [and] we planned for a get together when [the war was] all over.'[7] *Hood* stayed in Iceland for just twenty-eight hours, cruisers *Suffolk* and *Norfolk* arriving while she was there. With them *Hood* sailed to cover two convoys and spent three days at sea on a mission of 'bone-chilling vigilance in [an] arid area of frost-smoke and water-laden skies'[8], returning to the Hvalfjord without seeing action. During stormy patrols in the North Atlantic, *Hood* could easily lose track of escorts like *Cossack*. Some waves were 60ft high, capable of shifting a 15-inch gun turret of 1,000 tons – more than half *Cossack*'s entire displacement. It is easy to see how such sea conditions could make life in destroyers hell. Vian remarked: 'The battlecruisers liked to travel fast as a security measure against U-boat attack, and, in the prevailing heavy seas, speed was ever a problem for the destroyer escort.'[9] Should U-boats attempt to attack a battlecruiser or battleship, it would be destroyers like *Cossack*, with depth charges and sonar, that would be expected to prevent it, strike back or even sacrifice themselves to save the capital ships. But even without an actual attack, lives were still very much at risk in destroyers on escort duties.

Vian revealed: 'although there was a strong disinclination to slow the battle-cruisers down, on the other hand there was urgent need to minimize damage to the deck fittings of the destroyers, and above all to prevent officers and men being washed overboard as watches were relieved.'[10] On one stormy day in the north Atlantic between Iceland and the Faroes, three sailors working on *Cossack*'s upper deck were washed overboard, two of them 'never to be seen again'.[11] The third, Able Seaman S Remnant,[12] was washed back aboard. In bad weather, officers coming forward from their accommodation aft, for watch-keeping on the bridge, tried to stay inside the ship, taking a circuitous route through the gearing compartment and engine room. Even so, they still had to face thirty yards exposed on the upper deck. Vian conveyed the misery of destroyer life in such weather: 'It was a lucky officer who did not start his watch soaked to the skin in icy sea water.'[13] Vian suffered a harsh loss. Captains of warships are awarded their own steward, a kind of seagoing butler, who looks after their every domestic need, from laundry to making sure they receive their meals on time and in a style they deserve. The relationship between steward and captain is a close one, even if still marked by the protocol of rank. So, when his Maltese steward, Joseph Aquilina,[14] was washed overboard during a patrol off Iceland, it was an 'unnecessary loss' that Vian confessed he 'felt keenly'.[15] Aquilina regularly delivered meals to Vian in his sea cabin located below

Cossack's bridge, and was ordered to use the engine room route. However, to ensure the captain's meals were still hot, Aquilina habitually took the risk of using another route, which entailed more time on the upper deck. Inevitably, the sea claimed him. Vian lamented: 'We searched vainly in the turmoil of the gale, but nothing more was seen of him.'[16] Aboard the much bigger *Hood*, relatively safe from being snatched away, junior rating Robert Tilburn much preferred being on the upper deck, even on the fiercest of days. Initially his action station was deep inside the ship, in the A turret shell room, but on promotion to seaman gunner he served in the crew of a 4-inch anti-aircraft gun. He recalled: ' I loved watching the water, seeing the waves, seeing the power of the water.' Tilburn marvelled at seabirds keeping up with the ship despite howling gales. A favourite pursuit of his was to hurl some bread into the air 'and down they'd swoop and grab it.'[17]

Once it was certain *Bismarck* was in Polish waters, *Hood* headed back to Scapa, arriving there on 5 May. Admiral Whitworth departed for a desk job in London and was replaced by Vice-Admiral Holland, not only as commanding officer of the Battle Cruiser Squadron but also deputy commander of the Home Fleet. *Hood* held intensive gunnery practice for her 4-inch and 15-inch gun crews, scoring some good hits and straddles on practice targets. The ship's company was almost cocksure, Ted Briggs summarizing their attitude as: 'We were confident that our aim would be steady if our path crossed that of *Bismarck*.' One of Briggs' jobs was to fetch and carry messages to the Flag Lieutenant – or Flags – who filtered Admiral Holland's signals. At 8 pm on 21 May, he was tasked with taking a message to Flags – Lieutenant Commander Wyldbore-Smith – in the form of a signal containing instructions from Tovey. This message told Holland to prepare the Battle Cruiser Squadron for deployment at one minute past midnight on 22 May. The destroyers *Icarus*, *Electra*, *Achates*, *Anthony*, *Antelope* and *Echo*, would escort Holland's big ships.

The *Cossack* was absent from *Hood's* side because at the end of April she had been sent south, to operate temporarily out of Plymouth, hunting down German destroyers and E-boats causing trouble in the English Channel.[18] By 21 May, *Cossack* and the rest of Vian's flotilla were at Greenock, preparing to escort a convoy from the Clyde as far as Gibraltar. It looked like she would miss out on any forthcoming action with *Bismarck*.

Among those ships escorting *Hood* and *Prince of Wales* was a vessel that would distinguish herself as a supporting player in more than one drama to come. In May 1941 HMS *Electra* was seven years old, another Tyne-built warship, a destroyer of the E Class, a comparatively old design dating back to 1929, a new batch of which was ordered in haste as the nation finally awoke to the need for a regenerated navy. When her thirty-two-year-old gunnery officer, Lieutenant Timothy Cain, first set eyes on her, one misty morning in early 1939 at Greenock, on Scotland's west coast, *Electra* 'with her thrusting bows and lean funnels [appeared] eager, aggressive, and extraordinarily graceful.'[19] She was lightly armed compared to her Japanese and German equivalents, for *Electra* had only four 4.7-inch guns, mounted singly in four turrets, compared to the half dozen 4.7- and five 5-inch guns, respectively, of equivalents in the navies of Germany and Japan. The E Class were what the British navy called good sea-boats and *Electra* could stay at sea for considerably longer than her German or Japanese equivalents. A sailor with eighteen years under his belt, who had joined as a boy seaman and risen through the ranks, Cain now held the appointment Gunner (T), the letter in brackets signifying his sub-specialisation in torpedoes. *Electra* was confronted with the reality of war early, having steamed at high speed to the scene of the first casualty at sea, the liner *Athenia*, which was attacked by a German U-boat within hours of war being declared by Britain on 3 September 1939. Arriving as the liner slowly sank, *Electra* took aboard survivors, mostly civilians in their nightclothes, including children. Some of *Electra*'s men were ordered aboard the dying liner to search for anyone still trapped below but only came back with a single living soul. In June 1940, escorting *Ark Royal* on a strike against Trondheim, *Electra* suffered severe damage during a collision with the destroyer *Antelope*, but somehow limped home. Going into refit, she was back in action by the end of 1940. In May 1941 *Electra*'s captain was Commander Cecil Wakeford May, the ship and her sailors by then weather-beaten and fully seasoned, but still eager to prove their worth in battle. Cain – known as 'Guns' – squeezed poetry out of the destroyer's heroic endurance in turbulent seas: 'Time after time, streaming green-white pennants of foam from her stem, had she swept upwards from the valleys of the wind-driven ocean before reeling corkscrew-wise into the seething turmoil of the trough ...' At other times *Electra* 'skimmed with her wake like a snowy plume behind her, across the black surface of a sinisterly silent sea.'[20] As the war in the Mediterranean – where the real action seemed to be – intensified, the men of *Electra* found their eagerness for combat slightly dulled, for, as Cain later reflected, there was not a mess-deck nor wardroom in any ship in the Home Fleet that had not lost somebody in that theatre of war.

Aboard *Prince of Wales* at Scapa Flow when the call to prepare for deployment came on 21 May, supper had just finished and the men of the lower deck were settling down to an evening of swapping stories, playing bingo, writing letters home, or reading pulp fiction. 'Special sea duty men, close up at the double!' came the call over the speakers, causing some to abandon whatever they were doing and race to duties on the upper deck. As *Prince of Wales* made her stately progress out of Scapa, the call 'Action Stations!' blared over the loudspeakers. Leading Sick Berth Attendant Wood gathered his gear together and made the long dash to the armoured conning tower. Reporting in via the telephone, he saw *Hood* passing through the anti-submarine boom just ahead of his ship.

The battlecruiser's unmistakeable silhouette was just visible: 'Tiny dark figures could be seen scurrying about the upper deck as her crew set about their duties of securing for sea.' The destroyers had previously exited via the Switha Gate after raising anchor and slipping their buoys in Gutter Sound, and on the bridge of *Electra* Lieutenant Cain scanned a starless sky. The preparations for combat had been well underway aboard *Electra* as she swept through the Gate, with ammunition for the guns brought up from below decks to be placed close at hand in ready-use lockers. Elsewhere, torpedoes were armed and depth charges primed, while checks were made on the 4.7-inch guns themselves, to make sure they would deliver destruction to the enemy when required. The destroyers loitered patiently in the Pentland Firth, like a pack of hounds awaiting the huntsmen. Cain relished the drama of the moment: 'The hunt was on, and we were ahead of the pack.'[21]

The capital ships exited the anchorage via the southern, Hoxa Gate, a small vessel hauling aside the massive underwater net designed to ensure U-boats could not sneak in. *Prince of Wales* followed closely in *Hood*'s wake, a cold north wind biting into those on her exposed upper deck. To be going forth on their first war mission in company with *Hood* infused the sailors and marines of *Prince of Wales* with great confidence. As Lieutenant Commander McMullen later reflected, the majority of them mistook her size and reputation for battle worthiness: 'We were the new boy but we felt perfectly confident that there was the mighty *Hood*.'[22]

Chapter 7

Rushing to their Destiny

In *Prince of Wales* a voice blared out from the public address system: 'The Captain will speak to the ship's company.' After a pause, Captain Leach told the battleship's sailors and marines: 'Two German warships, namely *Bismarck* and *Prinz Eugen*, are at sea and, according to intelligence sources, are going to enter the north Atlantic convoy shipping lanes via the Arctic Circle.'[1] Their exact location was not known, so *Prince of Wales* and *Hood* were still heading for waters around Iceland, where they would join forces with cruisers. Leach said he expected *Hood* and *Prince of Wales* to give a good account of themselves if forced into battle.

In *Electra*, following on behind, the ship's company thought there was a fair chance of action, even if the Germans evaded their squadron in the dreadful weather. Surely the rest of the Home Fleet still had to be reckoned with? However, as Cain acknowledged, it was like looking for a needle in a haystack and 'even the greatest of ships is reduced to needle-sized proportions when you come to look for it in the immensity of the sea.' Yet confidence in *Hood*'s power flowed through *Electra*. One of her ship's company, staring admiringly at the huge silhouette looming on the destroyer's quarter, remarked: 'Jerry's going to have a bit of a shock when he sees her ahead of him. When it's *Hood* v. Hitler I back British all the way ...' Cain himself thought *Hood* had never looked more impressive 'as she drove towards Iceland and her destiny, as she narrowed by half a mile a minute the distance between her and the fateful German guns.'[2]

As he ate breakfast in HMS *Hood*, Briggs listened to the ship's executive officer, Commander William Cross, provide a briefing over the public address system stating that *Bismarck* and a Hipper Class cruiser had been spotted at Bergen and expected to make an attempted break-out. *Hood* and her squadron were being sent to Iceland, to be better positioned to intercept any such endeavour. The verdict of the lower deck was that it would all come to nothing, as was usually the case. Should it turn into an actual interception, *Hood*'s 15-inch guns would be able to handle a 'jumped-up pocket battleship'[3]. At 10.30 pm on 22 May, a signal was received from Admiral Tovey, in which the

Home Fleet commander instructed Admiral Holland: '*Bismarck* and consort sailed. Proceed to cover area south-west of Iceland.'[4] Tovey, who wanted to remain linked to the telephone land line as long as possible, to be in full, instant and above all secure communication with the Admiralty in London, had only departed Scapa Flow around thirty minutes earlier. He fired the signal off before imposing radio silence, for fear of giving away the position of the Home Fleet's main striking force to the enemy. *King George V* was in company with carrier *Victorious*, battlecruiser *Repulse*, cruisers *Aurora*, *Hermione*, *Galatea* and *Kenya* plus assorted escorting destroyers. An officer in *King George V* would note an encounter on 23 May that illustrated why the fleet was trying so desperately to intercept *Bismarck* and *Prinz Eugen*: 'On Friday forenoon we passed a large homeward-bound convoy. It was just such a convoy as this that the enemy wished to find; had he been able to do so, the loss of valuable ships and cargoes and the even more valuable lives of the seamen would have been immediate.'[5]

King George V was heading to cover the north-west of Iceland. However, *Bismarck* and *Prinz Eugen* were already slipping around the north of Iceland into the Denmark Strait. *Hood* and her group were ordered by the Admiralty to alter course.

Commander Cross came on the PA again to advise the ship's company of the latest developments, raising tension and anticipation throughout the vessel. Ted Briggs began to sense this would not be just another frustrated foray after all: 'Looking around me, I could see my mates yawning nervously and trying to appear unconcerned. We all knew it was an act, yet we did not discuss the possibilities of action seriously.' However, Briggs wondered again if it was going to be 'another false alarm'. That evening he was playing a game of cards in his mess-deck when suddenly the PA blared out: 'Flag Lieutenant's messenger report to the SDO [Signals Distribution Office] at the double!' That meant Briggs, so he rushed up to the SDO, where a message was thrust into his hand. Briggs made haste to Lieutenant Commander Wyldbore-Smith's cabin. The officer already knew the contents of the signal in Briggs' hand but he had to see it in writing, too. It was short, sharp and to the point, conclusively revealing that this was no wild goose chase and that battle surely lay ahead: 'From *Suffolk* – enemy in sight.'[6] The shadowing cruisers were sending out updates on the enemy's course and speed at regular intervals. As soon as the sighting report came in, Admiral Holland gathered his staff officers and the ship's senior officers around a chart table, to study where the enemy was and the best course of action to bring about an interception. *Bismarck*'s location was plotted as three hundred miles away and due north, prompting Holland to ask Captain Kerr to increase the ship's speed to 27 knots and for the navigator to alter heading by 295 degrees – interception course. Holland, who had been using the Admiral's bridge, now went to the enclosed compass platform to be alongside Captain Kerr. Young Briggs went, too, as he still had messages to run. While *Hood* was not yet at full action stations, and with an estimated ten hours to interception, Briggs did sense a metaphorical girding of the loins throughout the battlecruiser: 'The back of my neck began to prickle with excitement, and I found myself stuttering slightly, a nervous habit which until then I had managed to conquer since the age of ten.'

In the aftermath of her close shave with *Bismarck*'s 15-inch guns, *Norfolk* reported at 8.32 pm: 'One battleship, one cruiser in sight.' Holland, Tovey and everyone else reading signals to the Admiralty, now knew the Germans were definitely in the Denmark Strait. As the Battlecruiser Squadron shaped course for interception, the weather deteriorated, with high seas and snow flurries.

Never mind the Germans, the chief foe as the ships sped north was the dreadful weather, which Sam Wood in *Prince of Wales* experienced in the raw, the wind howling 'like a million screeching devils trying to dodge the rain.' The seas were mountainous: 'Looking for'ard, sometimes the bows would disappear under a swell of green frothy sea and a great surge of water would engulf the main for'ard A and B turrets. Slowly the bows would rise from the sea in defiance and tons of water would run from the decks back into the sea.' There was something gothic about the night, like some horror story scene in the eerie half light of the Arctic – crashing, hissing, booming waves, spray leaping high into the air, drenching anyone in an open position. The rumbling, roaring ocean buffeting the ship battered the eardrums, the wind keening through aerial wires, screaming like a tortured soul, a banshee. The destroyers had it really rough, waves submerging them before they leapt free again. In *Electra*, Commander May, who was also commander of the destroyer flotilla, became fearful of the damage his small ships would sustain, if they continued to batter themselves at full speed into the rough seas. He signalled Holland: 'Do not consider destroyers can maintain present speed without danger.' Holland ordered a signal flashed by light at 8.55 pm: 'If you are unable to maintain this speed I will have to go on without you. You should follow at your best speed.'[7] The destroyers continued to try and hang on until around 9.30 pm, when they gave up the unequal fight and slowed down, disappearing fast astern of the two capital ships.

In *Prince of Wales* everybody, including Wood, stayed where they were, no matter how exposed to the elements. The sheer scale of the storm – simultaneously awe-inspiring and frightening – made the efforts of men seem puny. Wood was terrified by the sight of 'two great ships being tossed about like corks … About a mile expanse of sea in front of the ship's bow would lift high above the ship itself, the bow would rise with this swell and the rest of the ship would follow. When we were riding high on this mountain of water a glance to port would show the *Hood* lying about half a mile away below our view like some small toy ship. The next moment we would be sliding down the swell at a rapid rate of knots and the ship would vibrate as if a million hammers were beating a tattoo on her shell, whilst the *Hood* would appear towering above us with our roles reversed and us the small toy ship. Hour after hour this foul weather persisted and the ship's company seemed to settle into a routine of going about their duties like staggering robots.' Wood was sustained in his lonely vigil by deliveries of corned beef sandwiches and hot, strong tea, but alcohol was the real salvation, for, as Wood noted, the 'daily tot of rum came up with unfailing regularity. What a life saver!' Action stations for Supply Assistant Joseph Willetts – he was not needed to do paperwork while the ship was at such an alert state – was down in a cordite charge handling compartment for the Royal Marines' 14-inch (Y) turret, which was aft. He described his action station as 'about seven decks below the upper deck'. He got to it by 'climbing hand-over-hand down vertical ladders from one deck to the next – not always the same ladders because the ladders were placed in various parts, so that if one became unusable there would be another that we could use. I was in there for a little more than two days in company with six others.'

At Chequers, the official weekend retreat of British Prime Ministers in the Buckinghamshire countryside, Winston Churchill was entertaining a very special guest. Averell Harriman, President Roosevelt's special envoy to Britain, who had been sent to the UK in order to assess the situation after nearly two years of war, was being taken fully into the Prime Minister's confidence about the *Bismarck* threat. Harriman, who would ultimately spend several weekends with Churchill at Chequers, described it as being drawn into the Prime Minister's 'agitation'.[8] It suited British aims for the Americans to be in the loop, and Harriman kept Roosevelt up-to-date on the hunt for *Bismarck*, as much as did Churchill, who had a direct line of communications with the American leader. Churchill need not have worried about Harriman being on-side, for the dashing American diplomat had already judged the USA would eventually have to fight Germany, observing: 'We are going to have to come into the war some time … The sooner we come in, the shorter the job will be.'[9] On 22 May – the day before he and Harriman left for Chequers – Churchill sent President Roosevelt a telegram in which he revealed: 'We have reason to believe that a formidable Atlantic raid is intended.' Churchill added: 'Should we fail to catch them going out your Navy should surely be able to mark them down for us …'[10] He finished the message: 'Give us the news and we will finish the job.'[11] Churchill's fear of *Bismarck* had been at its height in November 1939, with, as he put it, Britain 'straining every nerve to finish *King George V* and *Prince of Wales*' before the end of 1940, for it was anticipated *Bismarck* would be ready for action not long after that point. Churchill believed 'the arrival of the *Bismarck* on the oceans before these two ships were completed would be disastrous in the highest degree, as it can neither be caught nor killed, and would therefore range freely throughout the oceans, rupturing all communications.'[12] Churchill had, of course, been aboard *Hood*, most recently in March 1940, when he briefly visited her at Scapa Flow while still First Lord of the Admiralty. Nine months later – December 1940 – he sent President Roosevelt a realistic, but still upbeat, letter on the British position, including an assessment of comparative battleship strength. He said the Royal Navy's position would be eroded over the next six or seven months by the commissioning of *Bismarck* and *Tirpitz*, which Churchill felt would be ready by January 1941. He remarked that *Rodney* had recently been diverted to transatlantic convoy duty, something that made him very uneasy with effective Home Fleet battleship numbers so low. The only vessels capable at all of fighting *Bismarck* and her sister were of course *King George V* and *Prince of Wales*, with *Rodney* and *Nelson* older and slower, but heavily armed and protected. The battlecruisers were not really in the equation as far as any serious assessment of strength was considered, while the unmodernized Revenge Class battleships were in Churchill's view fit only for convoy escort work and could at best hope to handle combat with a heavy cruiser, but nothing bigger. The Mediterranean Fleet did have the rebuilt Queen Elizabeth Class battleships but they were needed in their operational theatre and could not be committed to any fight against *Bismarck* in the Atlantic. Churchill told Roosevelt that 'at any time when numbers are so small a mine or torpedo may alter decisively the strength of the line of battle.'[13] He explained the British situation would get better in June 1941, when *Duke of York* was expected to be ready for service and by the end of the year when *Anson* was ready, expressing the fervent wish that something might postpone the moment of truth. He told Roosevelt: 'Even a few months' delay in *Bismarck* will affect the whole balance of sea-power to a serious degree.' Churchill cultivated high hopes the RAF's Bomber Command might be able to disable *Bismarck* and *Tirpitz*, but these were not realized. In the end, of course, it came down to a contest at sea, the moment Churchill feared arriving during that late May weekend with Harriman at Chequers. Well aware how the chase was developing, thanks to constant updates from the Admiralty[14] in central London, on the night of 23 May Churchill found he could not sleep, and his American guest would also suffer a restless night.

In the north Atlantic the storm gradually died away, with Captain Leach in *Prince of Wales* explaining over the PA that evening how *Suffolk* and *Norfolk* were continuing to shadow the German ships. With the likelihood of action at dawn the next day, after the speaker went silent Sam Wood contemplated what might lie ahead within a few hours, asking of himself: 'How will I react under gunfire?' With a new sense of purpose, their fate sealed, the ship's company again settled down at their action stations, the rhythm of the engines and vibrations of her lunging momentum surging through *Prince of Wales* as she barrelled north in *Hood*'s wake. Even up in the armoured bridge, Wood could sense 'a new form of energy was pulsating through the ship as it [sic] forged ahead through the half light, half dark of the Arctic night.'

Busy with preparing the guns for action Lieutenant Commander McMullen made his rounds of *Prince of Wales'* turrets, magazines and shell handling rooms. Assessing the spirit of the ship, he found 'everyone had a little bit of butterflies in their tummies' but despite that morale was 'very high really'. He felt they were all 'splendid chaps'.

McMullen had drilled endlessly for this moment throughout his naval career, so perhaps a few more hours would not make much difference. For the *Prince of Wales'* gunnery officer, more than anyone else in the ship, it would be a personal battle and he reflected: 'One found it hard to realize that this was it. This was going to be me versus the *Bismarck*'s gunnery officer on the other side.' From his lofty action station in the gunnery control position, McMullen gazed at *Hood* still charging hard ahead and, again, it was a comfort. In the meantime, he ordered the guns' circuits tested by firing 'a tube' in each one.[15]

At 9.55 pm the Admiralty sent out an 'all hands' signal: 'One BB [battleship] and one cruiser reported by *NORFOLK*'. This was definitive confirmation for the entire Royal Navy, picked up by vessels spread across the globe, that a confrontation with the so-called most powerful warship in the world was coming within hours. Five minutes after that signal was sent out, *Bismarck* reversed course and came at *Suffolk*, beginning her turn in a rainstorm that disguised her intentions, until the curtain was momentarily torn aside and the cruiser's men saw the German battleship apparently coming straight for them. This was what Captain Ellis feared most, so he ordered the helm hard over and *Suffolk* put in some distance, expecting *Bismarck* to come charging out of the rain. This did not happen, so the cruiser turned back, steaming hard to make up the four or five miles she had lost and re-establish contact. *Bismarck* had merely been toying with *Suffolk*.

In *Hood* Commander Cross made an electrifying broadcast to the ship's company, telling them: 'We are expected to intercept at 0200 tomorrow morning. We will go to action stations at midnight. In the meantime prepare yourselves and above all change into clean underwear.'[16] This latter measure was to prevent infection in case of a wound.[17] The last time *Hood*'s men heard it was prior to their attack on the French fleet at Oran. Briggs, who had been down to his mess-deck for a cup of cocoa, was besieged by conflicting emotions. Not exactly afraid, he wanted the battle to be over and done with as soon as possible but was also happy for it not to happen at all. He hoped he would wake up in his hammock the following morning and discover it had all been 'a mistake'. As midnight approached, Briggs pulled on clean underwear and socks, then his number three sailor suit, lifebelt and a waterproof coat, together with flash hood and gauntlets.

A gas mask hung in front of his chest and, to top it all off, a steel helmet sat snug on his head. The youngster waddled off encumbered like some armoured knight of old. He hoped several layers would protect him against not only infection in case of wounding, but also the cold and wet, and flash burns, giving him a chance of survival and therefore being picked up if he landed in the water. What unnerved him most was not the idea of 'instant oblivion' but of 'being fearfully wounded or mutilated and screaming out in painful insanity'. Briggs feared he would be exposed as a coward but took comfort from the quiet confidence that seemed to suffuse the ship. Stopping by the SDO to collect some signals for the flag lieutenant, Briggs met one of his good mates, a sailor named Tuxworth. They paused for a brief exchange of banter, bolstering each other's shield of bravado.

Tuxworth asked: 'Do you remember, Briggo, that when the *Exeter* went into action with the *Graf Spee* there was only one signalman saved?'

Briggs laughed and fired back: 'If that happens to us, it'll be me who's saved Tux.'[18] Back in late 1939 *Exeter* had been damaged and limped to the Falklands for battle damage repair before making a triumphant return to Devonport.

Such was the heroic fate *Hood*'s men might have imagined for themselves – bloodied but unbowed, heroes all. The young sailors' exchange was interrupted by a bugle call over the PA declaring 'Action Stations'.

On the compass platform, Briggs felt like he was on the stage – footlights replaced by the hooded, soft lights around the chart table and glow of the binnacle. There were ten players in all, including Briggs, with Vice-Admiral Holland sitting centre stage in the captain's chair, Captain Kerr at his right hand and, a few paces further to starboard, Commander 'Tiny' Gregson, the Battle Cruiser Squadron gunnery officer, the man who would order the signal for *Prince of Wales* to open fire. The flag lieutenant was also there to do the admiral's bidding while Briggs was ready to run messages for Flags, collect signals and acknowledge voice pipes. There was another youngster there, too, Bill Dundas who, as midshipman of the watch, acted as a messenger and lookout. With the exception of Admiral Holland, they were all clad similarly to Briggs, except he was the only one wearing shoes while they all had stout sea boots on. Holland was sitting bolt upright in the captain's chair, wearing a navy issue short greatcoat rather than a long duffel coat. The admiral's fingers tapped nervously on binoculars hung around his neck. A gunnery specialist, Holland was aged fifty-four, with white hair that made him look older than he actually was. To sailors in *Hood* he seemed 'shy and withdrawn'[19] but a year earlier Holland had seen combat at Spartivento in the Mediterranean, commanding a squadron of cruisers in action against the Italians. It was originally his intention that *Suffolk* and *Norfolk* should take on *Prinz Eugen*, an equal match, while the two capital ships handled *Bismarck*, but for some reason this was not conveyed to them.

By midnight it was believed the Germans were only 100 miles away[20] and fifteen minutes later Holland ordered *Hood* to fly her battle ensign. This massive flag, which was 24ft long and 12ft wide, streamed out behind the ship from her mainmast, making a blood-stirring sight,[21] but then came news of the cruisers losing contact with the Germans ships.

At around 11.30 pm *Bismarck* and *Prinz Eugen* had disappeared into a snowstorm and once *Suffolk* also entered it visibility closed down to not much more than a mile. Radar tracking was rendered ineffective. This development was conveyed to *Hood*'s men, who now went to a relaxed state of action stations.

On the compass platform there was a conference around the charts. To try and strike a likely interception course, and also give the cruisers time to reacquire the Germans, *Hood*'s speed was slowed to 25 knots and for a time the ship headed north. The cruisers would not reconnect with *Bismarck* and her consort for another three hours and the gap came at the worst possible moment. Holland was now concerned that if he headed out wide to the north-west, the Germans would slide by to his south and break into the Atlantic. Without sighting reports he had to take a judgement call and contemplated the possibility of a turn to the south-west. In doing so, he would risk not crossing the Germans' 'T', which would allow him to present his broadsides to *Bismarck* and *Prinz Eugen*'s bows, while only their forward firing main guns (and therefore half their armament) would be able to bear on the British ships. Meanwhile, in *King George V*, realising the moment of truth was fast approaching and thinking of the two British capital ships' relative strengths and weaknesses, Admiral Tovey considered breaking radio silence to send a signal. According to one naval officer, who saw action in the looming battle, Tovey was 'so worried about the *Hood*'s deck armour that he drafted out a signal to Admiral Holland suggesting that *Prince of Wales* went in towards the enemy end on and drew the fire while *Hood* lay off at a distance. He considered this. He wrote the signal out then he thought he mustn't interfere tactically with the admiral on the spot. He tore the signal up.'[22]

In *Hood*, grappling with the same dilemma, Holland still hoped to close quickly and hit hard while presenting a narrow profile. This necessity had guided his whole approach strategy. He knew *Bismarck* could not head due west, owing to the Greenland ice pack hemming her in, and there were minefields on the Germans' port side. Therefore, it was a reasonable to guess that the German admiral in command, whoever he was, might, in attempting to achieve break-out, head south-east. If Holland had not found *Bismarck* and her cruiser by 2.10 am he was going to order his warships to head south.[23]

The uncertainty of whether or not there would be an interception at all was kept from *Hood*'s ratings during the night. They tried to settle their spirits and minds for the battle they thought would come within hours, although Briggs, in his privileged position on the compass platform, got an inkling of what was really going on. He quizzed Lieutenant Commander Wyldbore-Smith, to be informed that the cruisers losing contact had plunged Admiral Holland into anxious uncertainty. Holland's nervous energy expressed itself by his constant swivelling of his chair, face clouded with doubt. Spray spattered the glass screen around the compass platform as Hood headed for 'no definite destination'.[24] Not long after dawn Holland ordered a turn to the south and then adjusted it to south-east. Calculating the enemy would still be north of his position, he persisted in attempting to stay on the German ships' bows. To give himself early warning – because he did not know if the cruisers would re-establish contact in time – Holland sent the destroyers, which had caught up as the weather improved, out far ahead as a scouting screen. As she headed off towards the north, *Electra* managed an impressive 31 knots, throwing up walls of water either side of her sharp bows, spray falling on her like a heavy rainstorm. The rest of the escorts were buried beneath the waves as they fought their own private battles to maintain momentum. Rapidly falling away behind them, 'the battlewagons rose and fell with the sound of thunder…jettisoning great streams of water from around their cable chains, and steaming around their "nostrils" – the gaping hawse-holes that flanked their bows – like a pair of angry dragons.'[25] The destroyer men looked forward to action, with *Electra*'s captain, as senior officer in the escort force, intending to wield them as a rapier, in lightning thrusts, while the broadsword of the big ships clanged down on *Bismarck*. However, Admiral Holland would not recall the destroyers when he adjusted heading to south, presumably because he wanted them to cover the possibility of *Bismarck* and her consort heading back to Germany via the northern route.

The *Hood*'s compass platform became a 'somnolent citadel', with the 'cold fingers of the Arctic draughts … whistling through.'[26] To wake the ratings up Briggs was sent to fetch a container full of hot cocoa from the galley while Dundas got something warming for the officers from the wardroom galley.

At 2.47 am, there was huge relief when a signal was received from *Suffolk*, revealing she had found *Bismarck* and her consort again. The four big ships were heading on a similar course – the British on 200 degrees, the Germans on 220 degrees, in other words slightly diverging. This was not the best position, but Holland would have hoped the Germans were still not aware enemy capital ships were in hot pursuit and about to catch up with them. *Hood* and *Prince of Wales* adjusted course again to ensure they did not actually end up passing directly ahead of the Germans. Sailors off-watch in their hammocks and bunks were given a prod to wake up by a broadcast over the PA system, though probably not many of them were actually asleep. The engine room department in *Hood* was urged to squeeze as much as possible out of her tired boilers, the ship somehow managing just over 28 knots, 'blackish, purple smoke' pouring from her funnels.[27]

Ted Briggs gazed at the vista laid out before him, as *Hood* 'screamed into battle', finding he had little to do but watch. This rendered him vulnerable to his fears, leaving the youngster 'a somewhat frightened observer'.

Dawn on 24 May was daubed across the eastern horizon in golden orange splashes on the pale blue canvas of the Arctic. It lightened with every minute, melting away to yield a morning that left an indelible impression on Leading Sick Berth Attendant Wood in *Prince of Wales*: 'the light of dawn swept away every shadow in its path. It was one of the most beautiful sights I have ever seen and its grandeur remains imprinted in my memory to this day, I shall never forget it.' From his vantage point in *Hood*, Ted Briggs saw only menacing grey clouds, waves rolling down from the north-east hammering the battlecruiser's hull, the drumbeat of imminent battle, a haze of spray hissing against the forward turrets of the great ship. Now *Hood*'s own radar picked up *Bismarck* some twenty miles to the north-east. Fate was sealed. Within the hour there would be a battle. Briggs swapped a few words with his pal Ron Bell, down below on the flag deck, manning the other end of the same voice pipe. Briggs was amazed by the lack of fear in his shipmate's voice. 'Near him would be Tuxworth, helping to handle the halyards and still joking, no doubt. Alongside in charge of the flags I guessed that Yeoman Bill Nevett would be as outwardly calm as ever, despite the pallor of his face.' Then there was Petty Officer Stan Boardman in charge of a pom-pom anti-aircraft gun nicknamed Sally on *Hood*'s starboard side, a loving family man with a newborn baby at home. Having served in the sickbay during his early days in *Hood*, Briggs also thought of his shipmates down there, too, including Sick-Bay Petty Officer Stannard, whom he imagined would be 'sterilizing operating instruments, laying out blankets, making sure bandages were handy …' His thoughts returned to himself: 'God, don't let me be wounded. I guessed a lot of blood would be flowing there today, and it made my own feel colder.' Briggs pondered whether or not God was on his side. While not an unbeliever, he was not a churchgoer either, but the ship's chapel was a place of peace he found calming. As a keen student of naval history, it always made him think of Nelson before the battle of Trafalgar and the legendary admiral's famous prayer. Now, some 136 years later, the young sailor offered up his own plea to God, which was 'a pitiful silent prayer'. While Nelson's prayer might have been a symptom of the admiral's feeling that his hour of destiny was upon him and the fate of a nation on his shoulders, the teenage Ted Briggs simply asked God for courage and stamina to get through the forthcoming ordeal. His resolve was sorely rattled when, at 5.00 am, the call went through the ship: 'Prepare for instant action.'[28]

There was a smudge of smoke on the horizon and in *Prince of Wales* Lieutenant Commander McMullen heard the seventeen-year-old boy sailor in the crow's nest shout: 'Enemy in sight, bearing green 40.' The German ships were on the starboard bow. In his first aid station, Sam Wood scanned the vista with keen eyes, to see what the lookout had spotted, finding 'two upright blurs, which gradually showed themselves to be the top masts of fighting ships coming into view over the curvature of the earth.' Over the PA came the call to tighten up action stations, and now *Prince of Wales'* own massive battle ensign unfurled at the ship's masthead. Wood was transfixed by the view though one of the slits in the armoured bridge tower: 'As I gazed out into the distance the oncoming masts grew larger and the fighting tops of two capital ships became clear to the naked eye. Soon the complete silhouettes of two capital warships stood out on the horizon, dark and looking powerfully fearsome.' The turrets of *Hood* and *Prince of Wales* trained to meet the enemy, guns raised to achieve the correct trajectory and adjusted as both range and bearing changed. The British and German ships were converging at a high rate of knots, rushing to their destiny, their men living in the moment, with no thought for the future or past anymore, but only what might unfold in the next few minutes.

Chapter 8

Death of a Battlecruiser

At his action station, Sam Wood checked his medical supplies again, settling down to absorb a moment in history. Peering out through the observation slit, he took in a vista of astonishing beauty: 'The reflection of the dawn light danced upon the surface of the sea and stretched from our bows out towards the German warships. The ruffled surface of the sea seemed to constantly change from brilliant white diamond sparkles to dazzling ice blue, to flashing green and then to deep awesome red. It seemed as though our ships were forging ahead through a garden of sparkling jewels ...' Overhead was a vaulted sky of pale orange light. There was a very light wind, which the young medic thought whispered: 'You who are about to die today, don't be afraid, for this is what heaven is like.' However, the men in *Prince of Wales* knew the Grim Reaper was about to make his harvest, as Wood later admitted: 'Make no mistake, we all knew someone would undoubtedly die but it would be someone else ...'

The morning held its calm, developing fine and clear, offering maximum visibility across the dark sea, but it soon clouded over. The shadowing cruisers were thoroughly relieved to see their own capital ships coming over the horizon, as it meant they had succeeded in fixing the enemy for destruction. The likelihood of *Bismarck* and *Prinz Eugen* turning on them now diminished, for the Germans had bigger problems. In *Suffolk*, Ludovic Porter used binoculars to survey the scene: 'Against the light horizon were silhouetted the German ships, while away to port, and barely distinguishable against the low cloud forming their background, were *Hood* and *Prince of Wales*. As they tore along with their guns cocked up in the air they were a gallant sight, and we watched with the feelings of a producer who has set his stage and now awaits only the rising of the curtain.'

Some sixty miles to the north, as the hours slipped by the men in the destroyers had experienced a gnawing anxiety they were wasting their efforts, pursuing a red herring, and that the matter was being decided far to the south. Perhaps the Germans had even slipped away and evaded the Royal Navy again?

The electrifying signal they now intercepted confirmed their intuition had been correct: 'FROM HOOD. ENEMY IN SIGHT. AM ENGAGING.'[1]

This dramatic news spread swiftly throughout *Electra* and everybody expected she would soon be turning around and leading the rest of the flotilla south to battle.

In *Prince of Wales*, charging hard behind on *Hood*'s starboard quarter, McMullen was at the heart of the drama. He found his vessel's design was making life extremely difficult, for the King George V Class were very wet ships. The lack of flare on their bows meant that at speed, or during heavy weather, rather than shrugging the sea aside, leaving a clean forecastle, they dug in. As *Prince of Wales* lunged towards the enemy at 28 knots, into both wind and the run of sea, tons of water cascaded over the forecastle. Impenetrable spray flew up and blanketed A and B turrets, preventing their range-takers from calculating opening fire ranges. This was a bitter irony, as the whole reason *Prince of Wales* and her sisters lacked flared bows, was to enable their two forward turrets to fire directly ahead. McMullen decided a range-taker in the 14-inch gunnery control position should take over the job of calculating the range. The gunnery officer would also apply some of his own instinct about the likely firing solution.

Meanwhile, just under 400 miles to the south-east, *King George V* was steaming hard, at 27 knots, having very early on 24 May picked up that *Prince of Wales* and *Hood* would soon be in action. While glad the enemy was successfully intercepted, the men of *King George V* were concerned their vessel would not now get a chance to engage her opposite number in the German fleet: 'At this moment our feeling of satisfaction that our heavy ships had made contact was spoilt by the probability that the *Bismarck* might be destroyed or turned back without the *King George V* having a hand in the matter. Ever since the Prime Minister had spoken to us at Rosyth, we had all looked on the *Bismarck* as our own particular target.'[2] Confronted with the cold reality of facing the enemy, there was no such bravado on *Hood*'s compass platform. As soon as the enemy ships had been sighted a signal was sent to both the Admiralty and Tovey, notifying them of the composition of the enemy force, their heading and distance from *Hood*, as well as the position, heading and speed of the Battlecruiser Squadron. Radio silence simply had to be broken in such circumstances to announce battle was imminent. The decisive moment was therefore upon them, Vice-Admiral Holland giving an instruction for *Hood* and *Prince of Wales* to make a turn of 40 degrees to starboard. Unfortunately it ensured only the forward turrets of the British capital ships would be able to fire on the enemy, but he was desperate to present as narrow a profile as possible until his vulnerable flagship was within the so-called immune zone. Once inside the immune zone, the enemy's fire would not be plunging, with a chance of penetrating *Hood*'s weak uppers, but on a flatter trajectory and more likely to hit the armour belt.

The only sound on the compass platform was the officer of the watch calmly giving his steering instructions and the voice of the senior rating below repeating the orders back for confirmation via voice pipe.

Holland, in a steady voice, declared: 'Open fire.' On the nod from the Fleet Gunnery Officer, Chief Yeoman Carne bellowed for the Yeoman to raise signal Flag 5, which instructed *Prince of Wales* to open fire as soon as she was ready. With the range closing to around 13 miles, more flag signals flew from *Hood*'s halyards, to be read and noted by the Yeoman on *Prince of Wales*' bridge. 'Engage the left hand ship.'

The logic of both British ships concentrating their fire on a single German vessel was to avoid wasting time trying to tell whose shots were falling around what target, so enabling swifter adjustment. If both *Prince of Wales* and *Hood* aimed at *Bismarck* they would have more or less the same corrections to make and, most importantly, could concentrate on eliminating the more serious threat first. However, McMullen suspected this was NOT *Bismarck* he was being ordered to shoot at. He felt it was an easy mistake to make: 'Over the horizon came these two ships, one leading the other, exactly the same silhouette, four turrets, one funnel.' Inspecting the enemy through his 'very powerful modern binoculars', McMullen thought the first ship in line, the one on the left, 'looked definitely smaller than the ship astern of her...We immediately realized that the *Hood* had made a mistake.' McMullen ordered that a light signal should be flashed to *Hood*: 'Make IMI.' This was a request for *Hood* to repeat her signal, a hint that perhaps the more senior ship had a made a mistake. Feeling his irritation rising, and believing that a huge error was being made, McMullen urged the signalman: 'Make IMI, IMI, IMI.'[3]

McMullen later expressed sympathy for *Hood*'s mistake in the heat of the action, for the older ship had a lower bridge, which meant the silhouette of the left hand German vessel looked bigger than it did to those in *Prince of Wales*. McMullen reflected it was 'very cunning on the Germans' part to have these silhouettes so exactly alike. Of course the *Prinz Eugen*, although she was a cruiser, was a very big ship.' Adding to McMullen's frustration was the fact that, as the most modern battleship in the Royal Navy, *Prince of Wales* had very good gunnery radar, but she was not within effective range, which was 'graduated out to 24,000 yards'.[4] McMullen estimated the opening fire range was around 25,500 yards – some fourteen and a half miles – so if *Hood* waited just a little later then perhaps *Prince of Wales*' radar could achieve decisive hits very quickly?

The gunnery officer of *Hood* gave the order: 'Shoot!'

The ting-ting of the fire gong sounded over the speaker system and, exposed almost to the full force of the guns, Briggs both saw and felt *Hood*'s opening salvo, as it 'belched out in an ear-pulsating roar, leaving behind a cloud of brown cordite smoke, which swept by the compass platform. Seconds later a duller boom came from our starboard quarter as the *Prince of Wales* unleashed her first fourteen-inch salvo.' With no correction as yet to the original signal, *Prince of Wales* had to follow suit and fire on the lead German ship. It was just as McMullen was about to finally issue the 'open fire' order that the Padre made his intervention, the prayer for protection in battle blocking out the communications circuit and infuriating the gunnery officer, McMullen noting his astonishment at the poor timing: 'You never dream of such a thing happening.'[5]

While the Padre may have aggravated McMullen, many sailors deep inside the battleship, unable to see any of the action, and relying on whatever was broadcast via the public address system for information, appreciated the benediction. Among them was Joseph Willetts, in the Y turret cordite handling room, who thought it had a most unexpected effect. The bugle call for 'Still' ordered everyone to stop what they were doing and all Willetts could hear was 'the wash of the sea on the ship and the various noises of the engines, which weren't much [and] to suddenly hear the chaplain's voice with a prayer of that description – it was a very, very touching thing to experience.'

The gun flashes were brighter than the dawn streaking the Arctic sky, enormous clouds of smoke obscuring the capital ships' silhouettes – death was on its way.

For many men on both sides brave thoughts and fatalism gave way in a split second to a desperate plea – muttered or heard in the mind – at least to survive the next few moments. Watching from *Suffolk*, Ludovic Porter saw 'a flare of orange light on the horizon, which showed that the British ships had opened fire …' In *Hood*, fear bled away as Briggs was caught up in the excitement and fascination of the moment, counting off the seconds of his ship's shells in flight, waiting for the moment of impact. He saw 'tiny spouts of water, two extremely close to the pinpoints on the horizon.'

The Germans had rehearsed this moment many times in combat exercises, with *Hood* their most feared opponent, but even though the British had opened fire, Lütjens hesitated to give assent for his ships to hit back. His orders were to avoid engaging capital ships if he could. While he had envisaged tackling perhaps one British battleship at a time, here were two. Standing beside the admiral on the bridge, Lindemann angrily watched seconds of hesitation turn into minutes. 'I will not let my ship be shot out from under my ass,' he muttered, before using the internal telephone system to advise his gunnery officer: 'Permission to fire.'[6]

From *Hood*, Ted Briggs was intrigued to see 'four star-like golden flashes, with red centres, spangle along the side of *Bismarck*.' Four 15-inch shells from the German battleship's main armament were coming straight at *Hood* and Briggs felt 'deep, clammy numbing fear' flood back. A familiar sound, like an express train, which *Hood*'s sailors had last heard when being fired at by the big guns of the French fleet at Oran, filled the air as shells passed overhead. They fell somewhere on the port side. With the German ships getting closer, the enemy's aim was sure to improve. But then came the crushing revelation that an error had been made, with a call from someone in *Hood*'s spotting top saying *Bismarck* was in fact the second ship in line, the one on the right, not the left. The most powerful German ship had been left free to fire at whomever she chose. Admiral Holland displayed no emotion on his face and merely said, with no trace of anger or disappointment: 'Shift target to the right.'[7] *Hood* sent a signal to *Prince of Wales* admitting her mistake and instructing the switch.

Bismarck and *Prinz Eugen*'s guns flashed again, their gunnery officers' bracketing *Hood*, shells falling on the British battlecruiser's starboard side, dirty brown plumes erupting and hissing as they collapsed back into the sea. Watching through the slit in the *Prince of Wales*' armoured bridge, Sam Wood felt the cold grip of fear, but then the roar and shock wave of his own ship's A and B turrets firing cudgelled his senses. The young sailor was momentarily overcome by blinding, choking, nausea-inducing cordite smoke but his initial fear was subsiding. Wood soon felt bloodlust rising: 'Everything seemed to be falling into a pattern, our guns would elevate or deflect slightly as they received new range directions, then would follow the blinding flash and the smoke as they fired their cargoes of death and destruction. The noise was deafening. In my foolish youth I was brainwashed and excited by the battle. It never crossed my mind that the two opposing sides were hurling tons of screaming, exploding, hot steel at each other in an attempt to tear apart the human beings at each receiving end.' However, the horrifying reality of war would not long be denied young Sam Wood.

The lack of any likely threat from enemy aircraft left *Suffolk*'s air defence Officer, Lieutenant Commander CT Collett, free to watch the spectacle of battle unfold from his ship's air defence position. 'We were mere spectators of this part of the battle and it was thrilling – watching those big ships fire at one another at terrific range with such accuracy. I could see the splashes made by our shells falling all 'round the Germans and I saw two vivid spurts of flame onboard the *Bismarck* indicating that she had been hit. But it only lasted a few minutes.'

Hood sent off a salvo every twenty seconds from her forward turrets – six times in two minutes.[8] While shell splashes erupted around the German ship, the battlecruiser's observer saw no visible hits, except what appeared to be a small fire on the *Bismarck*'s upper decks. Amid the thunder, an attempt was being made to give the British ships a decisive edge, by putting the *Prince of Wales*' amphibious aircraft overhead to spot fall of shot. It had been impossible to use the aircraft earlier to scout ahead of the force, the weather being too rough to recover the Walrus, which needed to land on flat water next to the ship before being craned back aboard. Having put the aircraft on the launch catapult and fuelled it, when the enemy was spotted the Walrus was defuelled, to avoid posing an additional fire risk. Now the weather was calmer, a decision was taken to use the aircraft after all, so it was refuelled. With time pressing, the Walrus was to be launched with its tank two thirds full. The aircrew already aboard, making their final checks, the engine at full throttle, the catapult officer was holding his flag aloft.[9] When the flag dropped the Walrus would shoot off the rail but before that could happen, a shell struck the after funnel. Hot metal splinters peppered the aircraft, rending it unsafe to fly, and the disappointed aviators climbed out. Instead of pulling the lever to send the Walrus off to observe the battle from on high, it was instead jettisoned over the side.

Now came the first strike on *Hood*, which threw everyone on the compass platform to the deck. An officer went to look back down the ship, trying to spot the point of impact, reporting back calmly to the admiral and Captain Kerr that *Hood* had been hit at the base of the mainmast and was on fire. The 4-inch ammunition in the ready-use lockers on the starboard side was blazing and flames were reaching the UP rockets.[10] On *Hood*'s compass platform, they heard calls of 'Fire' through voice pipes and via the ship's telephone system. An inferno was consuming the boat deck amidships and explosions could be heard. In addition to shells detonating, the rockets also started exploding. Ted Briggs' courage began to crumble: 'Fear gripped my intestines again as agonized screams of the wounded and dying emitted from the voice pipes. The screeching turned my blood almost to ice. Yet strangely I also began to feel anger at the enemy for the first time.' Captain Kerr issued an order for the gun crews to seek shelter wherever they could until the explosions had exhausted themselves, but the exposed upper deck positions had already been turned into 'a charnel house ... screams of the maimed kept up a strident chorus through the voice pipes and from the flag deck.'[11] Briggs was certain he heard his friend Ron Bell shouting for help.

Robert Tilburn, who enjoyed being on the upper deck in the fresh air so much, was crewing one of the port 4-inch guns in the midst of the rapidly unfolding horror. Tilburn thought three shells had hit *Hood* and heard the gun crews ordered to take cover inside the ship's superstructure, but[12] with two other sailors, was held back and ordered by a gunner's mate to douse the exploding ammunition. It was going off in 'small explosions, rather like a big Chinese cracker',[13] creating a 'very fierce blaze', which was 'pinkish in colour, with not much smoke'[14] Tilburn and the others declared they would tackle the fire: 'When it stops exploding.'[15] The gunner's mate went to phone the gunnery officer, but at that moment a German shell hit the recreation space where the gunners were taking cover, according to Tilburn killing everyone inside, some 200 men. The three survivors threw themselves to the deck, all hell breaking loose around them, *Hood*'s own anti-aircraft shells whizzing off all over the place and exploding. But this storm was not visible to the command team, with Admiral Holland and Captain Kerr keeping their binoculars firmly focussed on the enemy. Seeing such detached calm, Briggs felt his nerve return. *Hood* had been under fire for a mere two minutes, but to the young sailor it had seemed like as many hours.

The flagship's signal to *Prince of Wales*, instructing her to switch targets, was too late – for *Bismarck* had been left free to concentrate her fire on *Hood*, unmolested by incoming British shells. Admiral Holland decided to risk turning his ships, so they could bring all their guns to bear. Having at 5.49 am conducted a turn of 20 degrees to starboard, at 6.00 am, *Hood* and *Prince of Wales* altered course by 20 degrees to port, opening arcs of fire for aft turrets, the speed of both German and British vessels still 28 knots. The range between the opposing ships was now less than nine miles, the turn having increased the range only a little. Immediately *Hood*'s X turret roared, the frustrated and impatient gunners finally able to play their part. While *Prinz Eugen* had already delivered a sixth salvo against *Hood* before switching fire to *Prince of Wales*, the *Bismarck*'s fifth salvo came at 6.01 am and delivered a killer blow, which utterly changed Ted Briggs' world. There was a blinding flash, which enveloped the outside of the compass platform and he was picked up and 'dumped head first on the deck'. However, unlike the earlier occasion, when he was knocked off his feet, this time there was a far more sinister aspect. 'Everything was cold and unreal. The ship which had been a haven for me for the last two years was suddenly hostile.'[16]

From *Prince of Wales'* compass platform, Captain Leach had been keeping an eye on *Hood*'s amidships fire, glancing over every now and then to see if it had gone out or was developing into something more serious. To him it appeared 'reddish yellow and there was a certain amount of smoke, but no more than I should expect to see from a fire of that size.' Then Leach saw the killer salvo from *Bismarck*: 'There were, I think, two shots short and one over, but it may have been the other way round. But I formed the impression at the time that something had arrived on board *Hood* in a position just before the mainmast and slightly to starboard. It was not a very definite impression that I had, but it was sufficiently definite to make me look at *Hood* for a further period. I, in fact, wondered what the result was going to be, and between one and two seconds after I formed that impression an explosion took place in the *Hood* which appeared to me to come from very much the same position in the ship. There was a very fierce upward rush of flame the shape of a funnel, rather a thin funnel, and almost instantaneously the ship was enveloped in smoke from one end to the other.'[17]

Taking shelter on *Hood*'s boat deck, Tilburn felt the impact, which seemed further aft. It shook the entire ship, blast and shrapnel buffeting the midships position, but the explosion did not seem any worse than the effect of *Hood* firing a salvo.[18] Taking cover by the UP launcher splinter shield, Tilburn avoided immediate death or injury, but the other two gunners were not so fortunate, one of them being 'blown away'.[19] The other was disembowelled by a shell splinter which to Tilburn was a vision of horror: 'It opened him up like a butcher and all his innards were coming out.'[20] In the seconds after the explosion there was 'dead silence'[21] but debris, bodies, and parts of bodies, started falling from the sky. Tilburn looked up: 'Some of the bodies I saw falling were those of officers [and *Hood*] shuddered and seemed to stop altogether.'[22]

On the compass platform, Midshipman Dundas got the impression *Bismarck* had sent shells through *Hood*'s spotting top that did not explode, but still caused carnage, hence the human remains thumping down on to the upper deck. Dundas was asked by Captain Kerr to check who exactly had fallen close by, but the midshipman had to report back that he could not tell, since the corpse had no face. Nor did it have any hands. All he could say was that it was a lieutenant. The enemy shells were coming in thick and fast, and Dundas judged: 'It was the fifth salvo that really did for us. Wreckage began raining down again, and I saw a mass of brown smoke drifting to leeward on the port side.'[23]

The whole of the ship was gripped by savage juddering, and then slowly listed to starboard. Once *Hood* had a ten-degree list on, the helmsman shouted up the voice pipe to the officer of the watch: 'Steering's gone, sir.'

Almost as if on a peacetime exercise, the officer responded: 'Very good.'

Captain Kerr interceded, ordering a switch to emergency steering.[24] Ted Briggs was once again reassured by the reactions of the older, more senior men, who still maintained an icy calm. Admiral Holland, in the captain's chair, glanced back at *Prince of Wales* and then, once again, fixed his binoculars on *Bismarck* and *Prinz Eugen*. The *Hood* righted herself for a second, provoking relief. However, she then rolled violently to port. On reaching 45 degrees it was clear she was not going to right herself again and was doomed. Briggs was surprised at how cold and detached he was in the face of utter disaster and what was probably his own death. In fact, he was amazed at how calm everybody was as they made their way in single file out of the starboard door, a task which became increasingly difficult as the deck grew ever steeper. Some decided to try and exit the compass platform via the port door, surely a fatal error, while others, perhaps feeling the Grim Reaper's breath on their necks, tried to smash windows at the front. Even so, to Briggs, it was all done with eerie calm, 'as if in drill' for there was 'no order to abandon ship; nor was a word uttered. It just was not required. The *Hood* was finished, and no one needed to be told that.'[25]

The Battle Cruiser Squadron navigating officer, Commander John Warrand, even stood aside, gesturing for Briggs to go first through the starboard door. The young sailor looked over his left shoulder and saw Admiral Holland slumped in his chair 'in total dejection'. Following the tradition that the captain is the last to leave his ship, Kerr stood beside Holland, struggling to keep upright as the angle of the deck became ever steeper. Midshipman Dundas doubted he could make it up the steeply sloping deck, so, as he later remarked, opted for 'kicking a window on the starboard side until I made a big enough hole to squeeze through.'[26] Briggs began climbing down a ladder on to the Admiral's bridge but as he descended the ship tilted so dramatically that a few seconds later he was 'walking on the side of the bridge, instead of the ladder.' He discarded anything that would weigh him down, divesting himself of helmet and gas mask, pulling off his anti-flash hood and gauntlets. The lifebelt was under his coat and Briggs found he could not inflate it. Looking around, he could not see anyone else, although he felt some of the officers must be close at hand.

In *Prince of Wales*, Lieutenant Commander McMullen did not see the cataclysm, at least not directly: 'Suddenly the whole of the inside of our spotting top [lit up] as if there was a sudden sunset.' Others in the battleship were stunned to see *Hood* torn apart, her bows rising vertically in the air, the twin 15-inch guns of A turret firing one last, defiant, salvo. Sailors and marines in *Suffolk*, witnessing the horrifying turn of events from a distance, found it almost beyond the capacity of their minds to process. Commander Porter saw that 'a salvo appeared to hit *Hood* aft.' And then: 'A tremendous column of flame shot hundreds of feet into the air, following [sic] by dense clouds of black rolling smoke, rising to form a funeral pall for what had a second before been the largest fighting ship in the world. It must have been instantaneous for seventeen hundred [sic] officers and men of her gallant company. So swift was the disaster that for a moment the mind was stunned.' The cruiser's CT Collett was uncertain which of the two British capital ships had exploded: 'I saw a terrific sheet of scarlet flame suddenly reach up high into the Heavens in the direction of our ships and then die down to be followed by billowing clouds of thick black smoke. I knew at once that a magazine in one of our two ships had gone up and that this must be an end to her.' Unlike the men in the distant cruisers, for medic Sam Wood, staring through a slit in the armoured bridge of *Prince of Wales*, the destruction of *Hood* was terrifyingly close: 'there was a terrible explosion and blinding flash of light followed by a pall of acrid black smoke...We watched the scene with horror, minds numbed as the bow section drifted forward out of the smoke.'

Wood lifted up the phone, telling Sick Berth Petty Officer Percy Silk down below in one of the aid stations: 'The *Hood*'s gone.' There was no response, so, still stunned, Wood replaced the handset.

Even as *Hood* was ripped apart her final salvo of shells curved over the German ships, observers in *Prinz Eugen*, already staring in wonder at the smoke column where the British battlecruiser had been, noting with astonishment some 15-inch shell spouts astern and to starboard of their own ship. Voices on the heavy cruiser's bridge called out: 'They were firing as they blew up! They fired to the end!'[27]

In *Bismarck*, Lieutenant von Müllenheim-Rechberg, who, as the officer in charge of the battleship's aft gunnery control had been tasked with keeping a close eye on *Suffolk* and *Norfolk*, had temporarily handed over surveillance to a petty officer to use other optics in order to watch the duel with *Hood*. As he swung the optics towards the British battlecruiser's position he heard someone shout: 'She's blowing up!'

What he saw next was incredible, for instead of the legendary enemy warship he found 'a colossal pillar of black smoke reaching into the sky'.

He made out the bows of the battlecruiser pointing upwards, which he realized was 'a sure sign she had broken in two'. Then he saw something he would not have believed possible had he not seen it with his own eyes: 'A flash of orange from her forward guns! Although her fighting days had ended, the *Hood* was firing a last salvo. I felt great respect for those men over there.'[28]

Being hit by human remains probably saved Tilburn's life as he took cover on *Hood*'s boat deck: 'Bits of bodies were falling over the deck and one hit me on the legs. I thought, "I'm going to be sick", so I got up and went to the ship's side to throw up.'[29] Tilburn looked up and around, seeing that *Hood* seemed to be going down by the stern and tilting at an alarming angle to port. Out of the corner of his eye he saw something that looked a little like an ammunition locker hurtling down on him from out of the sky, prompting him to make a rapid exit.[30]

Pulling himself to his feet, he leapt onto the forecastle, which was already half covered in water. Like Briggs, he decided to discard anything that might weigh him down including his duffel coat, helmet and gas mask, until the water swept him over the side. Having survived the butcher's shop of the boat deck, Tilburn now swam for his life. Not far away, Ted Briggs calculated he must kick out quickly, away from the deckhead of the compass platform above. This he successfully did, but was gripped by boiling water and suction as a large section of *Hood*'s hull began its death plunge, taking him with it. As pressure built up in his ears he began to panic, realizing these could be his last seconds of life. Briggs thrashed about, trying to gain some upward momentum. Lungs burning, he thought he was not going to reach the surface and might as well give up. Taking in a mouthful of water, tongue thrust to the back of his throat, his strength seeped away. Panic was replaced by calm. Deciding to stop swimming, he let himself drift toward death: 'The water was a peaceful cradle. I was being rocked off to sleep. There was nothing I could do about it – goodnight, mum. Now I lay me down … I was ready to meet God.'

Tilburn's belt was restricting his breathing, so, using the knife he customarily carried, he cut it off, but, as he did so, saw the midships section of *Hood* rolling over on top of him, a huge mast swinging down. Caught across the back of his legs, a radio aerial wire ensnared him, wrapping itself tightly around his feet. As the wreckage sped into the darkness Tilburn was tugged down, taking a deep breath as he vanished under the surface of the sea. Pulling at the aerial wire and bowing his body, Tilburn used the knife to cut the laces of his sea boots. As they were ripped off his feet and taken down into the deep, he found himself shooting back to the surface, his ascent assisted by air bubbles. Tilburn broke through, gasping for air, water streaming from his head and shoulders, gaining his last sight of the warship that had been his home: 'Just the bows were stuck out of the water, practically vertical, and then she slid under.'[31]

In making his escape, Midshipman Dundas found that, as he eased himself out of the compass platform window, he was also sucked down, everything becoming a dark blur. 'The next thing I knew was that I shot to the top, and I was swimming to the surface.'[32] Briggs, having accepted death, was also saved by huge air bubbles, which grabbed him and lifted him to the surface of the sea 'like a decanted cork in a champagne bottle'. His head bursting into the air, he frantically trod water.[33] 'I panted in great gulps of air. I was alive. I was alive.' The sea was bubbling and hissing like 'hundreds of serpents', Briggs spinning in the water to find *Hood*'s bows not more than 150ft away, sticking up vertically. There was no sign of the B turret, which had been blown off along with the armoured control tower just behind it when a magazine detonated. Some eyewitnesses in other ships reported seeing what could have been the 1,100-ton turret, or even the 650-ton conning tower, spinning through the air.[34] The gun barrels of A turret were slumped drunkenly to port. The bows were 'flame-seared', the paintwork 'bubbling, as if under the heat of a giant blow-lamp' and Briggs saw this part of the ship sucked down 'savagely and speedily'.

It would haunt his soul: 'It was the most frightening aspect of my ordeal and a vision which was to recur terrifyingly in nightmares for the next forty years.' Briggs thought that he might be sucked down again, so swam away as fast as he could, struggling through a four-inch thick coating of oil in which dozens of small rafts were bobbing slowly to the surface. He hauled himself onto one of them and, looking around, saw a patch of burning oil marking where *Hood* had been. There was no sign of any other survivors. The two massive magazine explosions that broke the ship apart both fore and aft extinguished life in many terrible ways, ensuring there would not even be corpses to show where the Royal Navy's biggest warship had been destroyed. Explosions and firestorms dismembered and eviscerated hundreds of men or incinerated them.

Others were killed by concussion, drowned as the sea gushed in, or squashed by heavy machinery and fittings ripped off mountings by gravity during the ship's death plunge. The remains of the ship sped to the seabed, compartments containing air soon crushed by pressure, along with anyone left alive in them, the sea muffling the screams and desperate, fleeting prayers of the doomed.

Thundering on behind, *Prince of Wales* was forced to take evasive action to avoid colliding with the battlecruiser's stern, which had remained afloat for a moment. Passing not much more than 20ft away from Briggs, *Prince of Wales'* stern swept through the oil and debris, 14-inch guns roaring and German shell splashes sprouting around her. Briggs expected to see *Prince of Wales* shudder to heavy blows and go the same way as *Hood*. The British battlecruiser had opened fire at 5.53 am. She was destroyed eight minutes later.[35] In *Prince of Wales*, Sam Wood reflected the shock of those who had witnessed the brutal manner of *Hood*'s passing: 'All that remained was a huge pall of smoke where just a few moments earlier had sailed the pride of the Royal Navy. We could not believe it ...'

Chapter 9

The Entrails of Hell

T here was a chance *Hood* could strike one last lethal blow, even after she had blown up, for her torpedoes, launched just moments before her demise, still sped towards the German ships. Travelling at 30 knots, and with a range of 16,000 yards, could *Hood*'s torpedoes reap some measure of revenge?

In *Prinz Eugen*, highly-trained hydrophone operators heard three tinfish in the water. The cruiser's commanding officer, Captain Helmuth Brinkmann, displaying steely cool under fire, turned his ship sharply to starboard three times, evading torpedoes at 6.03 am, 6.06 am and 6.14 am.[1] During her second turn away, *Prinz Eugen*'s aft 8-inch gun turrets kept firing, while her A and B turrets trained on their maximum aft bearing to port, seeking to reacquire the enemy at the earliest opportunity. *Bismarck*, acting on the torpedo warning, also momentarily altered course to starboard before turning back to resume her assault on *Prince of Wales*. Brinkmann, who spotted two of the torpedo tracks himself, was hailed as having saved his ship through his 'powers of quick decision [from] serious damage, even from annihilation.'[2]

While *Hood*'s torpedoes failed to find their mark, the same could not be said of German shells, which surrounded *Prince of Wales* with a forest of towering splashes. For Sam Wood, a primeval instinct for preservation kicked in, and he felt compelled to find a less confined space. He thought, 'if the same thing was to happen to us and we were to go the *Hood*'s way I would be better off on the open deck of the bridge above me.' Unfortunately, he chose to follow his roaming commission at the very moment calamity struck *Prince of Wales*. 'I was climbing the ladder and had reached the top two steps, two thirds of my upper body were through the hatch whilst my legs were still firmly on the ladder. Suddenly there was a blinding flash in front of my eyes and I felt enveloped in a pocket of searing heat. I heard no explosion and everything appeared in slow motion. I was sucked up the ladder and seemed to float across the bridge area. After floating for what seemed an age I finally came to rest on the deck amidst a shambles of torn steel fixtures, collapsed searchlights and human bodies. As I regained my senses the sweet smell of burnt flesh mingled with the acrid stench of high explosives in my nostrils. Gradually my brain cleared and the red fog lifted from my eyes. Everything was enveloped in dark grey smoke.' At 6.03 am, one of *Bismarck*'s 15-inch shells had ploughed through the bridge, not exploding until it exited, killing or disabling everyone except Captain Leach, the navigating officer, Lieutenant Commander CG Rowell and the Chief Yeoman. Rowell was seriously wounded, though, with a jagged splinter of wood through his mouth and sticking out his cheek.

Somehow Rowell was still on his feet. Of two midshipman standing together directly in the path of the shell nothing remained, except a gore-spattered cap. In a compartment below the bridge a lieutenant plotting the course of the battle heard a rumble above. He used a voice pipe to ask what had happened but the only response he got was a trickle of blood, which dripped on to his white plotting paper.[3]

In a surreal moment of comedy, as Wood struggled to regain his senses, he felt one of the bodies on top of him stir and heard its owner say: 'Hang on Doc, I think we've been hit.' Once whoever the voice belonged to had removed himself, Wood was able to move again, giggling at the sheer stupidity of the remark. Getting unsteadily to his feet, still a little dazed, Wood looked around to see who he could help and spotted a sailor he recognized as Leading Seaman Tucker still alive, but buried under debris.

As he came over, Tucker told him: 'See to the others, I don't feel too bad.'

Ignoring the man's instruction, Wood cleared wreckage away, finding Tucker's left leg 'hanging on by a narrow strip of flesh and his femoral artery spurting like a fountain.' Wood's reaction was instinctive: 'I quickly [applied a] tourniquet [to] his leg, injected morphia and organized his removal to the main medical station below. Other casualties were dealt with as I came across them, losing count of how many.' Among those he treated was Lieutenant Esmond Knight, a movie star in peacetime, who had serious head injuries, with blood pouring from wounds around his eyes, rendering him blind.[4] Wood wondered if the actor would ever return to the silver screen. Alleviating the suffering of others kept his mind in neutral, but the young medic still saw things he would never be able to forget. 'I remember Boy Signalman Johnstone, recognizable only by the crossed flags on his arm and later by his paybook; the navigator with a hole in his cheek, and so on it went, for how long I can't recall. The bridge and compass platform were a complete shambles, the dead were collected by hastily organized working parties.' In all, during the battle, *Prince of Wales* suffered thirteen killed (two officers and eleven ratings) along with nine wounded (an officer and eight ratings). Lieutenant Commander McMullen, having been far too busy trying to hit *Bismarck*, now tuned into the exchanges of conversation on the ship's internal communications network, hearing someone gasp in shocked disbelief: '*Hood* has gone ...'

The gunnery officer mentally noted that this would not have a positive effect on his ship's fighting morale at a time when she, too, could be sunk. 'So there we were, at one moment full of confidence astern of the mighty *Hood*. Next moment, as a new untried ship, we were facing *Bismarck* and the *Prinz Eugen*, both of which then concentrated on us.' Lieutenant Commander McMullen had also not registered the serious blow to his own ship, finding he was 'quite unaware of the damage to the bridge just below us, except I can remember some white smoke coming up in front of my binoculars: so it was a completely impersonal episode ... almost as if one wasn't there ... one was doing a job one had been trained for.' The Germans were scoring some telling hits. An 8-inch shell from the *Prinz Eugen* hit the boat deck of the British battleship, wrecking boats and setting them on fire, before punching its way into the working chamber below a 5.25-inch gun turret. Without exploding, the shell ran around the chamber, coming to a rest by a terrified sailor's foot, passing so close to the back of one man's head it took off every hair, leaving behind fresh, pink skin.[5] Hearing the commotion below, the petty officer in the turret above opened a hatch and, peering down into the deathly, silent darkness, asked: 'What's going on down there?'

A tremulous voice replied: 'We've got an unexploded German shell.'

The petty officer turned to Boy Seaman Alan McIvor, a gun layer, and asked him to telephone the gunnery control position and ask for advice on what to do. Right then, McIvor, who was only seventeen, wished he had never defied his parents to join the Navy. Now it seemed McIvor's mother's worst fears were about to be realized.[6] When the young sailor phoned him Lieutenant Commander McMullen replied that he was too busy to deal with it at that moment. On hearing this, the exasperated senior rating exclaimed: 'What do they want us to do!? Hatch it out?'

He asked McIvor to give the gunnery officer another ring. This time it was explained they should hang on to the shell, so a munitions expert could look at it later. After an interval, during which he contemplated the apparent stupidity of the instruction, the petty officer told McIvor to ring the gunnery control position yet again and ask if someone was coming down soon. McIvor was to explain that they were not too keen on having an unexploded shell lying around so close to their own ammunition. McIvor picked up the handset, but this time only pretended to speak to someone. Putting the phone down he decided to be bold with his lie: 'They said ditch it.'

'Ditch it?'

'Yes.'

This was great news, so the petty officer and a veteran able seaman grabbed a heaving line – normally used to transfer supplies between ships – and secured it around the nose and base of the shell. Very carefully, the two men edged the shell up through the hatch from the working chamber, then out of the turret onto the upper deck. Equally gingerly, they lowered it over the side of the battleship as she raced along, still trading blows with the Germans. So focused were they on getting rid of their turret's unwelcome visitor, the sailors barely flinched at the extraordinary cacophony of the 14-inch guns firing nor the great fountains of spray and shrapnel kicked up by German shells.

The same near misses were heard only as rumbles, crashes and clangs by sailors deep inside *Prince of Wales*, but Captain Leach occasionally provided a commentary on events, including the loss of *Hood*. Junior rating Joseph Willetts, at his action station in a cordite magazine, just couldn't believe it: 'That sounded impossible and we waited for confirmation. And we were very anxious that we should serve the guns quickly because if the *Hood* had been sunk then we would have a double job.' Working conditions for Willetts and his shipmates in the cordite magazine were difficult: 'the condensation was such that the water on the floor was between four and six inches deep, which was swirling from one side to the other, which rather meant that all of us were wet to the knees.' He felt it was a 'dreadful existence'. The cordite fumes affected his eyes, were in his mouth and in his lungs. It would be several days before Willetts recovered: 'It had a very nauseating effect.'

Despite this and the loss of *Hood*, Willetts thought there was 'no fright whatever. People just went about doing their job including me and everybody else. There was nobody afraid of anything. We were quite confident ...'

The sailors bent to their task, and it was hard work. A complete charge of cordite for a shell was 320lbs and this was in four canvas bags, which were each of 80lbs, about 3ft long, kept in a barrel about 15-16 inches diameter. By putting his shoulder to it the young Willetts was just about able to haul one from its storage barrel. The firing end was marked red. The charges were put in a lift and up they went to the gun.

Despite his close call with death, Captain Leach, who had moved to the Admiral's bridge to control the ship, was still able to function and take command decisions. Acutely aware of the poor mechanical state of the battleship's turrets, he realized, with some telling hits suffered and facing the fury of *Bismarck* and *Prinz Eugen* alone, he could well lose his ship, a double blow Britain could not withstand. He ordered *Prince of Wales* to turn hard aport and make a smoke screen to mask her withdrawal to join the cruisers. This decision was not popular with his gunnery officer, who lamented: 'Although we were well over at the start we quickly straddled and the shoot was going very well, which was borne out later of course by the fact that we did hit her [*Bismarck*] three times.'

Cursed with his own communications problems, having been unable to raise anyone on the phone, McMullen sent someone to find out what was happening. 'Go down and tell the Captain everything's going fine,' he yelled after the boy sailor scurrying down the ladder.

The youngster came back white-faced with shock. He had been unable to find Captain Leach, discovering only the wrecked bridge, with its torn corpses and moaning wounded attended by medics. Although he was angry about action being broken off McMullen soon realized the captain had made the right decision 'because with two ships concentrating on us we would probably have been sunk as well as *Hood'*.

Not only that, the teething problems with the main armament had proved severe, with at times only three out of ten 14-inch guns capable of being fired, despite the best efforts of the Vickers contractors.

As *Prince of Wales* turned away, the forward 14-inch gunnery director could not bear on the targets anyway, but there was a switch in the transmitting station, which transferred control of the main armament to the after 14-inch gunnery control position. Unfortunately the Royal Marine officer in charge of the aft-facing Y turret[7] overrode this and went to what is termed 'local control', firing two salvoes at *Bismarck*, which were not accurate. However, even this turret soon fell silent, because, as the ship turned hard aport at full speed, centrifugal force jammed the shell ring,[8] putting the turret completely out of action for around an hour. During the action Lieutenant Geoffrey Brooke was spotting officer in the after 14-inch gunnery control position. Should the main gunnery position be taken out his job was to record the fall of shot, so the aim of the main armament could be corrected. He had been an eager spectator during the battle, awaiting his turn to take an active part, but hoping it would not be necessary, for it would mean McMullen was probably dead and the ship in deep trouble.

He had heard another officer exclaim over the internal communications network: 'My God! The *Hood*'s gone!'[9] Once the ship had stood down from action stations, Brooke went off to see what damage *Prince of Wales* had sustained. Making his way forward, he passed through a compartment that contained radar-operating equipment. There were shrapnel holes in internal bulkheads and its external skin, allowing in dusty beams of light, which penetrated the gloom. To Brooke it appeared the compartment's door was either open or had been ripped off. As the ship rolled, the light beams played up and down, revealing horrors, including the upper half of a man who had been cut in two by a shell hit. It was a leading seaman he knew. 'His eyes were open but his white face looked utterly peaceful.' It occurred to Brooke that the dead could smile. The light beams revealed something worse: a boot with part of a severed leg sticking out of its top. Feeling a sudden urge to vomit, Brooke made a swift exit to a nearby 'heads'[10], bending over a toilet pan and retching, but somehow he controlled his stomach and the feeling passed. Going out into the fresher air of the boat deck, amid the smoking remains of the battleship's small boats, Brooke found a stretcher party looking for wounded and corpses. He directed them to the radar office. Staring down at the pitted and charred surface of the deck, Brooke noticed German shell fragments and, amid all the debris, small bits of metal that he felt must be from *Hood*. He picked up a rivet that he recognized as being of the kind used to pin the British battlecruiser's plating to her frame. As Brooke put this grisly souvenir into a pocket, a messenger from Captain Leach found him and asked him to go to the Admiral's bridge. Leach asked Brooke to create a sketch of *Hood*'s demise for an action report. After taking notes Brooke went below to start work on a drawing that replicated what the captain had seen.

Taking a break from his ministrations on the upper deck and absorbing the broader picture, Sam Wood realized his ship was wreathed in her own smoke screen, which cast a black and evil shadow over the blood-spattered wreckage of the bridge. The stunning beauty of dawn, as *Prince of Wales* and *Hood* raced to their destiny across a calm sea, was nothing but a distant dream. Wood mourned the transformation of his world: 'I reasoned that if I had seen heaven earlier that day when everything had appeared so beautiful, I was now viewing the entrails of Hell.' With the last casualty gone from the bridge, Wood slumped onto the deck for a rest, trying to make sense of what had just happened. He was overcome by irrational thoughts: 'I was covered in dirt and blood, my head throbbing like mad, one of my shoes was missing, my uniform was in tatters and a strange sensation in my confused mind was telling me I should not have let the *Hood* go down, that I should have reached out and grabbed the bows as they were disappearing into the depths of the ocean.' He conceded it was 'crazy thinking…but everything seemed crazy that morning.'

Chapter 10

After-Shock

At Chequers, Churchill shook Averell Harriman awake around 7 am. On opening his eyes, the American diplomat found Britain's war leader looming over his bed 'in a yellow sweater, covering a short nightshirt, his pink legs exposed'.[1] Churchill told Harriman: 'Hell of a battle going on.'

The evening of 23 May had dragged on, as Churchill, Harriman and other weekend guests waited in vain for concrete news from the Admiralty.

They knew *Prince of Wales*, untried and untested, was in company with *Hood*, and discussed how the latter might be old but was well armed, big and fast.

They also knew there were cruisers trailing *Bismarck* and *Prinz Eugen*, one of them at least holding onto the German ships via use of radar. The duty captain in the Admiralty was on the other end of a telephone and so had the pleasure of dealing with the Prime Minister's frequent enquiries. Despatch riders on motorcycles also brought messages to Chequers from military, Foreign Office and Secret Service sources. As expected, the German ships were trying to make their break-out via the Denmark Strait rather than other routes, but the Admiralty messages could provide no further detail, as the drama was still unfolding. Everything was still uncertain and unknowable. So, finally, everybody went to bed around 3.00 am, with no definitive news of whether or not the German ships had been brought to battle. Four hours later Harriman barely had time to digest the fact that *Bismarck* had been engaged before Churchill gloomily remarked: 'The *Hood* is sunk. Hell of a battle.'

He asked about the fate of *Prince of Wales* and Churchill brightened a little, remarking: 'She's still at her.' Showing the tenacity in the face of adversity for which he was well known, Churchill added: 'The *Hood* has blown up, but we have got the *Bismarck* for certain.' His defiance at such a dark moment made a significant impression on Harriman, who would report back to Roosevelt that the bulldog spirit burned bright. Churchill later confessed that when first told about the battle, and the cruel fate of one of Britain's 'most cherished naval possessions'[2] he was afflicted by 'bitter grief'.

The Prime Minister went back to bed, but at 8.30 am was awoken by his Principal Private Secretary, John Martin. Hoping *Prince of Wales* had avenged *Hood*, Churchill enquired: 'Have we got her?'

'No,' responded Martin, 'and the *Prince of Wales* has broken off the action.' The Prime Minister felt 'a sharp disappointment'.[3] The loss of *Hood* and the failure of *Prince of Wales* to achieve revenge heaped misery upon misery for the mercurial British leader. There were also very heavy naval casualties in the Mediterranean at this time, Admiral Andrew Cunningham's fleet suffering grievously at the hands of the Luftwaffe as it tried to prevent the Germans from seizing Crete. In the space of a few days, many key ships were lost, and, with *Hood*'s destruction added in, 3,500 sailors and marines were killed.[4] In the Atlantic, should *Bismarck* evade her pursuers, the loss of life could be heavier still, with Canadian troops on their way in a UK-bound convoy and thousands more British servicemen and women headed for the Middle East and Indian Ocean in other, equally vulnerable, convoys. However, the Royal Navy remained the most powerful maritime force on the face of the planet, with an unsurpassed record of success. While hard pressed, surely it still had the flexibility and strength in reserve to hunt down and destroy a single German battleship? But, with *Prince of Wales* breaking off the action, which way had *Bismarck* gone? North, and home to a heroes' reception for destroying the biggest warship in the British fleet? Churchill confessed: 'Here was my great fear.'[5] He continued to be nagged by a feeling of anger at the inability of Britain's new battleships to tackle *Bismarck* on equal terms. In late October 1940, Churchill had visited *King George V* at Rosyth. Dressed in his yachting cap and naval reefer jacket, the Prime Minister gave a speech to her ship's company, telling *King George V*'s men how important it was for the ship to get in fighting order as soon as possible to be ready to take on *Bismarck*. Afterwards, in private, Churchill again expressed his dim view of the King George V Class battleships, due to their lack of gun power. Now, seven months later, two of those flawed battleships were perhaps Britain's best chance of stopping *Bismarck*, with one of them, *Prince of Wales*, further handicapped by battle damage.

News of the clash pulsated around the globe, via navy-wide signals, but neither the name nor nationality of the ship destroyed during the fight in the Denmark Strait was revealed at first. In *Rodney*, several hundred miles to the north-west of Ireland, escorting the troop ship *Britannic* to Canada, the battleship herself heading for a refit in Boston, Gunnery Officer Lieutenant Commander William Crawford, initially hoped the unidentified sunk ship was *Bismarck*. Within seconds the awful truth was revealed, via a follow-on signal from Rear-Admiral Wake-Walker in *Norfolk*: '*Hood* has *blown* up.'

Elsewhere in *Rodney*, Lieutenant Peter Wells-Cole found 'the loss of the *Hood* was a great shock to everybody', while spirits in some parts of the lower deck were less than buoyant. He added: 'Morale at that time was already low and on a point of honour we knew we were going to have to sink *Bismarck*.'

The atmosphere in *Rodney*'s wardroom was subdued – there was none of the usual good-natured banter and laughter, and those who chatted did so in hushed tones. The ship's doctor gave the opinion, without lifting his head from a newspaper, that if death should come in a sea fight, then it had better be swift, like *Hood*'s. He added: 'One has no time to think in the heat of battle, but it's better not to talk about it.'[6] In HMS *Cossack*, Captain Vian read the words '*Hood* has *blown* up' and felt real pain. He would recall: 'I believe I felt no stronger emotion at any time in the war than at the moment I read this signal.'[7] Having headed north from Plymouth as recently as 20 May, *Cossack* was now a key component of the escort force for convoy WS8B, which departed the Clyde on 22 May, carrying troops for the Middle East and East Indies. Some of *Cossack*'s older salts would have recalled that they had lost somebody they knew well, for Captain Kerr, the battlecruiser's commanding officer, had at one time served in their destroyer.[8] Also hearing news of the battlecruiser's destruction, Lieutenant Commander William Donald, in command of the Harwich-based corvette *Guillemot*, recalled a prophetic meeting with Kerr, when the latter was in command of all Rosyth-based destroyers. Donald, at the time First Lieutenant of the sloop *Black Swan*, which was in dockyard hands for repairs to mine damage, had called on Kerr to ask about being appointed to another warship. Smiling at the young officer's eagerness for action, Captain Kerr responded that he might actually get a ship command. Kerr added: 'I'm hoping for one myself soon.' Recalling Kerr's jest, Donald reflected: 'His little joke had a tragic sequel.'[9]

The *Electra*'s shock at hearing of *Hood*'s loss was all the greater for having just hours earlier been in company with her. When the fatal moment came, due to being sent north by Admiral Holland, *Electra*'s men found themselves 'out of sight behind the far horizon; frustrated, bewildered, and powerless to help.'[10]

The yeoman, who had been infused with eager excitement just five minutes earlier, when he took the news of *Hood* engaging the enemy to Commander May, now climbed up to the bridge looking utterly crestfallen. Perturbed, Cain asked him: 'Any further news?'

'From *Prince of Wales*, Sir ... *Hood* sunk!'

Cain was stunned for a second and then felt a rush of blood to his head and exploded in anger: 'You can keep your sense of humour to yourself!'

Reeling, the tearful yeoman responded: 'My God, Sir, but it's true, Sir. It's just come through – I have told the Captain.'

Commander May was instantly thinking of the survivors in the water who would need rescuing. *Electra*'s navigator informed him the scene of the disaster was sixty miles to the south. Ordering the ship turned around, May signalled the other destroyers under his command to follow suit. Meanwhile, Lieutenant Cain glanced at his watch and thought it must have stopped, for it was indicating only ten minutes had passed since he had heard news of *Hood* opening fire and here he was, an aeon later, trying to absorb the dreadful revelation of her destruction.

Cain thought: 'Our watches are still ticking ... and the *Hood* is dead.'[11]

Aboard the cruiser *London*, off the coast of Portugal, escorting the liner *Arundel Castle*, carrying evacuees from Gibraltar back to the UK, Surgeon Lieutenant R Ransome Wallis felt a deep sense of personal loss. He had been boyhood friends with the battlecruiser's First Lieutenant and recently treated a young midshipman in *London*'s sickbay who, having narrowly survived the sinking of his ship, heard with pleasure that he was being drafted to *Hood*.

The plucky youngster told Ransome Wallis: 'I shall be all right now sir, I am going to the *Hood*.'[12]

In the sloop *Egret*, escorting a slow moving convoy in the North Atlantic, signals traffic revealing the *Bismarck* break-out had been studied with anxiety by Ordinary Telegraphist Derric Breen. Now he double-checked his decrypt of the fateful signal about *Hood* before sending it up to the bridge. He sent it up: 'the voice pipe whistled – it was the navigator, demanding I check the signal.'

Breen did as he was told and confirmed again that it said *Hood* had been blown up, but still there was a reluctance to accept it was true: 'It took time, however, for the full import of the signal to be digested. Then the engines kicked up and over and, like a sheepdog, we set to work herding and chivvying our convoy, scraping another half-knot out of them while we rode shotgun.' Some convoys turned around, but *Egret*'s was right in the middle of the area through which Breen felt the German raiders might now sail. Breen imagined that his small ship would only have time to lay a smokescreen before being sunk by the enemy's big guns. 'Those like us with our heads in the trap could do no more than whip 'em up and keep running ... We searched the horizon with eyes sharpened with dread.'[13]

In the Home Fleet flagship, now around 360 miles south-east of the Denmark Strait, Admiral Tovey received news of *Hood*'s loss from an emotional Commander Jacob, his fleet wireless officer. Tovey told him to calm down, adding: 'There's no need to shout.'[14] Because it was *so* incredible, different cipher officers in *King George V* were tasked with producing their own transcripts of the signal, just in case there had been an error. Perhaps it actually said *Hood* had been damaged? However, the only conclusion was: '*Hood* has *blown* up.' This was conveyed back to Admiral Tovey, who had already convened a meeting of his key officers to decide what to do next.

Before Captain Patterson could even make a broadcast on the public address system, news of *Hood*'s loss spread swiftly throughout the flagship. Royal Marine Henry Bridewell, one of the crew of a 5.25-inch gun in the starboard secondary armament, felt it plunged the ship's company into deep depression.

'A mood of dismay and disbelief best described the feelings at that point. No one said very much – there wasn't much to say.'[15]

Midshipman Dalrymple-Hamilton had pulled the middle watch, from midnight until 4 am, but was shaken awake in his hammock down in the gun room to be told *Hood* had blown up. He thought it 'unbelievable'. Like many of his fellow midshipmen in *King George V*, he knew a lot of *Hood*'s midshipmen. *King George V*'s young men felt it was 'most appalling and shattering news and we could hardly believe it that she had blown up.' They realized that it now fell to the rest of the Home Fleet to get the German battleship, for, as Dalrymple-Hamilton reflected: 'We knew quite a lot about the *Bismarck* – it had always been accepted that our whole reason for being at Scapa was to get the *Bismarck*, and nobody was under any illusion that she was an extremely tough nut to crack.' As *King George V* knuckled down to the pursuit, her midshipmen speculated about what might happen next: 'After *Hood* had been sunk we were pretty shaken and we knew that we'd really got a job on our hands.'[16]

Three of *Hood*'s ship's company still clung to life. Having watched *Prince of Wales* plunge past, guns blazing, Ted Briggs looked around, finding burning oil on the surface of the sea nearby. He decided to paddle away, in case it spread, flames consuming the raft and him along with it. The exertion got his blood pumping, staving off the onset of hypothermia. Out of breath, having ingested some oil, and with his arms weakening, Briggs paused, glancing back to see if the oil fire had extinguished itself. On the horizon he could see hazy outlines of what he thought were British cruisers. Then, he spotted somebody on a raft, arms waving frantically. Close by was another raft with someone else trying to attract his attention. Sprawled face down on his raft, Briggs paddled over, discovering Tilburn and Dundas. Having escaped going down with *Hood*, Tilburn had spotted a patch of debris, so swam over. He found a raft floating in oil, so decided against trying to reach it. With the warmth seeping out of his body, limbs growing heavier by the second, Tilburn realized he wouldn't last much longer if he stayed in the water, so paddled around looking for an alternative.

He noticed Briggs and Dundas on their rafts and, on finding his own, laid himself across it, chest down, propelling it over to them.[17] Somehow, Dundas had managed to get himself into a sitting position. The other two attempted to do likewise, but every time they tried they slid off into the water. Briggs and Tilburn gave up, and settled for lying face down across their rafts. The trio of survivors hung onto the ratlines of each other's rafts, a bid to ensure they stayed together. Tilburn thought it was all very well the three of them joining up, but they were hundreds of miles from the nearest land, there appeared to be no other survivors and now there was no sign whatsoever of any ships, British or German. Dundas was relentlessly cheerful, realizing that anyone who gave in to the strong desire for sleep would slip into a coma and die of hypothermia. He therefore made them sing 'Roll Out the Barrel'.[18] Despite this, Briggs found the lure of sleep increasingly hard to resist. It would be easy to slip into the blessed relief of unconsciousness after everything that had happened, but he was prised from death's embrace by Tilburn suddenly shouting: 'There's a plane!' The *Hood* survivors splashed the water with their hands, shouting at the tops of their voices: 'Help! Help! Help!'

The RAF Sunderland flying boat flew on, unable to see them in the debris field. Briggs' teeth started chattering uncontrollably. Dundas suggested they stay awake by telling stories of how they each survived *Hood*'s destruction. Agreeing none of them had heard any loud explosion before she sank they felt it was a real puzzle.[19] Dundas and Tilburn compared injuries – the former had sprained an ankle when he kicked the compass platform window out, while the latter managed to cut himself in the act of hacking away at his sea boots. Briggs had escaped without even a scratch. He and Dundas agreed they went into the water on *Hood*'s starboard side. Recalling that he broke the surface on the port side, Briggs realized he must have been sucked right under the ship. All the talk was actually counter-productive, for, together with the cold, it exhausted them so much the ratlines slipped through their fingers, the rafts drifting apart.

Meanwhile, at Chequers, Harriman next saw Churchill at 10.00 am and asked for news of the battle. During the interim the Prime Minister had been studying telegrams and trying to shape events with a series of messages to the Admiralty. Churchill claimed he kept anxiety at bay through action, observing that 'as long as one is doing something the mind is saturated and cannot worry'. He was able to tell Harriman that *Bismarck* was steaming south.[20] One of Churchill's major fears was that, in order to pursue and bring *Bismarck* and *Prinz Eugen* to destruction, convoys were being steadily denuded of their escorts. The German wolves might soon be among the convoy sheep, with no warship shepherds to beat them off. Churchill rang the duty captain at the Admiralty and questioned him about a troop convoy to the south of Ireland, being reassured there was 'a lot of salt water'[21] between those ships and the Nazi raiders. Churchill had high hopes that, so long as British vessels maintained contact with *Bismarck*, they could 'dog her to doom'. However, the Germans could still get away in the vastness of the Atlantic and the British were 'vulnerable almost everywhere'.[22] The Prime Minister was most anxious to deliver some good news to MPs when he next addressed the House of Commons in a few days' time, on Tuesday 27 May. Just a fortnight earlier, Parliament had been forced to evacuate its usual home at the Palace of Westminster by a Luftwaffe bomb. MPs decamped to nearby Church House, which Churchill described as 'a port in a storm'. It had the extreme inconvenience of, as it were, not having any conveniences. Nor did it have the usual smoking, dining or writing rooms, but instead poor substitutes. Heaped on top of that, the Luftwaffe was still making a nuisance of itself, causing further interruptions to Parliamentary business. MPs were likely to be in a foul mood, so they would not react well to news that *Hood*'s loss was unavenged, convoys 'cut up or even massacred', or that *Bismarck* had reached a German or French port.[23] Then there was the situation in the eastern Mediterranean, where Crete was a lost cause and heavy casualties had been suffered. Pondering all this, Churchill managed to mask his true feelings, 'smiling in the face of adversity'.[24] For, as he later admitted, 'it costs nothing to grin.' The British leader, somewhat mistakenly, believed the Royal Navy's senior commanders at sea were not aggressive enough. Without having all the facts, he was contemplating pressing the First Sea Lord, Admiral Sir Dudley Pound, to court-martial Captain Leach of *Prince of Wales* for breaking off the action with *Bismarck*. The Prime Minister believed the Navy was generally too cautious with its ships. On 22 May, before leaving for Chequers, and nearly two days before *Hood*'s great sacrifice, when discussing British warship losses off Crete with his Private Secretary, John Colville, Churchill declared Royal Navy vessels were there to be risked for the greater good. He asked querulously: 'What do you think we build ships for?'[25]

In the north Atlantic, for *Hood*'s survivors the allure of sleep grew strong again, so Dundas returned to bawling 'Roll Out the Barrel'. Due to a distance of several hundred yards between rafts, and 'sleepy mist' in his brain, Briggs heard this only dimly. He tried to tune in to the words, but found it too much effort and grew irritated, thinking: 'Oh why don't you shut up, man, so I can get some sleep.'[26] On his raft, tossing up and down on the considerable swell, Tilburn drifted off into a drowsy fog. He recalled something Jack London wrote in one of his novels, about the effect of extreme cold in Canada: 'You go to sleep and die [so] I thought, if I'm going to die, I might as well die in my sleep.'[27]

However, before he could drift off into death, Tilburn heard Dundas stop his infernal singing and shout: 'What's that?'[28]

The midshipman then yelled: 'There's a destroyer coming along.'[29]

Tilburn snapped out of his doze, looked around and, sure enough, saw a destroyer steaming hard. 'What a beautiful sight,' he thought but she went straight by.[30]

Two of *Electra*'s three boats had been wrecked during the night, leaving one to be sent off and search for survivors, so as their ship steamed south the destroyer's men worked hard on preparing other means of getting people aboard. Thinking back to their *Athenia* experience in late 1939, they anticipated saving hundreds of lives, so scrambling nets, climbing ropes and lifebelts were all made ready on the upper deck. Surgeon Lieutenant Seymour, the 'Doc', decided to turn the destroyer's main mess deck into a makeshift hospital to back up his sickbay, while the officers' bunks would also be needed for the many patients he expected to treat. Crashing south at top speed, just before 8 am smoke was sighted to the south-west. Realizing the moment was upon them, Lieutenant Seymour took Cain to one side, suggesting that some of the younger sailors should be sent below, in order to avoid seeing some of the more gruesome injuries many survivors would no doubt have. Cain responded sharply: 'Bloody nonsense! We'll need everyone we've got to help the poor devils inboard!' But the spike in tension was for naught as the smoke turned out to be a merchant vessel, which soon lay in their wake. Not long after, *Electra* cut through a large patch of oil and a small amount of wreckage, but there was no sign of the hundreds of bobbing heads they anticipated. Cain thought: 'Where were the boats, the rafts, the floats...? And the men, where were the men?' An image of the massive *Hood*, her large ship's company – like a small army – assembled on her quarter-deck for divisions, flashed into his mind and the scale of disaster was hammered home. This was it. All that remained of the 'Mighty *Hood*' and her men. Then someone shouted out that there was someone in the water, to starboard in the distance. Two men appeared to be swimming and one looked like he was sitting on a raft. One of *Electra*'s senior ratings released an anguished cry: 'But there must be more of them – there can't only be three of them! Where the hell are the others?' There were no others and Cain felt that it was 'a moment never to be erased from the memory. It was a revelation of horror.'[31]

Ted Briggs recognized the ship's pennant number as she flashed by and, joining the other two in waving arms frantically, screamed: 'It's the *Electra*... *Electra*! *Electra*! *Electra*!'[32]

The destroyer cut her speed and turned towards the survivors, approaching each of the separated rafts one at a time, with the utmost care. Sailors with climbing ropes at the ready to throw down lined *Electra*'s upper deck and the scrambling nets were put over the side. As his saviour approached, out of sheer delight at being saved from a watery grave, Midshipman Dundas broke into song again: 'Roll out the barrel, let's have a barrel of fun.'

Electra's surviving sea-boat was lowered and was rowed off to see if anyone else could be found, alive or dead. Tilburn found himself hoisted up 'like a sack of spuds'[33] onto the destroyer's upper deck by two sailors who had clambered down to render assistance. He looked around at a circle of sailors staring at him as if he was some kind of circus curiosity. Shaking himself, like an angry dog shrugging off water he snarled: 'And what's up with you – you poverty-stricken crowd? Ain't you got no bloody boats?'[34]

Briggs was thrown a line, which he held on to for dear life, but was too cold and exhausted to haul his raft over to the scrambling net, so *Electra*'s sailors pulled him over and then bundled him up on to the ship. As a Portsmouth rating through and through, Briggs couldn't resist a rather caustic joke: 'Now isn't that just my rotten luck – to be picked up by a Chatham ship!' *Electra*'s sailors forgave his jibe and smiled indulgently. The youngster's eyes filled with tears, which ran hot and bitter down his black, oil covered cheeks. Briggs turned to gaze out across the surrounding sea, lamenting: 'Oh God...my mates!' They gently laid him on the deck, cutting off his wet, oil-sodden clothes, a calloused hand placing a cup against his lips as he was softly urged to drink. Briggs did as he was told, the fire of his first taste of Navy rum blazing a path through oil covering the inside of his throat. He immediately threw up.

To the men of *Electra* the third survivor's behaviour was most peculiar, and Cain thought he'd never seen 'a man more nonchalant, or less put out by his unexpected circumstances.' From his position on the destroyer's bridge Cain could see that this man 'made no attempt to precipitate his rescue by trying to swim ...' Instead, Dundas waited calmly, perched on his liferaft, for someone to come and rescue him. The *Electra*'s sailors threw lines to him, hoping he would make some effort to catch them but not even curses could provoke him to move. Eventually one of the sailors was lucky enough to land the end of a line in the survivor's lap. Grasping it, Dundas was hauled over to the ship and helped up a scrambling net. Welcomed aboard by *Electra*'s First Lieutenant, he apologized for losing his cap, which meant he was unable to offer a salute. Identifying himself as a midshipman and probably the most senior survivor from *Hood*, Dundas tried to stand up but found he could not, due to his ankle injury. Lifted onto a stretcher, he was taken down to the destroyer's sickbay, protesting all the way that he was perfectly well.[35] *Electra*, together with *Anthony* and *Icarus*, stayed a while longer, their sailors scanning the surrounding ocean for any further signs of life, but all they saw was drifting debris and not much of that. Bobbing down *Electra*'s side came a desk drawer. Two of the destroyer's men clambered down a scrambling net to fish it out the water. Inside the drawer were dozens of ratings' personal records

It must have come from a desk in a clerical office well below decks in *Hood* and had been blown into the air, for both drawer and documents were unscathed. Cain and his shipmates thought it a bitter irony 'that the blast had not used its human victims with an equally freakish tenderness.'[36] Giving up the futile search for more survivors, *Electra* and the other destroyers, running low on fuel, headed for Iceland, a blanket of depression smothering them.

Senior rating Bill Lowe, who had been a member of *Hood*'s ship's company in the early 1930s, was on leave in Brighton. Going out for a beer with his dad, as they entered the pub a man coming out told them in shocked voice: 'The *Hood* has been sunk.' Lowe exchanged a disbelieving look with his father, gasping: 'No! No, I don't believe that.'[37] There were hushed conversations about the loss of *Hood* on all sides – nobody could get their heads around the news they had just heard over the pub's radio.

In the wake of this body blow, the following morning the *Sunday Pictorial* thundered on its front page: 'British warships cleaved their way through the North Atlantic last night seeking vengeance for the battle cruiser *Hood* ... which was sunk by a freak shot in battle with the Germans early yesterday. Thoughts of every British sailor, as our ships chased the Germans, were fixed on *Bismarck* ... It was every man's hope to see her sunk.'[38]

Chapter 11

The Hunters and the Hunted

For the cruisers, watching from a distance as titans clashed, the action ended as suddenly as it began. They saw a British ship exploding, another on fire and retreating. Lieutenant Commander Collett, in *Suffolk*, stared anxiously at the pillar of smoke marking the demise of a capital ship and thought of his brother, John, in P*rince of Wales*. Was he among the dead? 'It seemed an eternity waiting for the news as to which ship had been sunk because it was fairly obvious from the size of the explosion that there could not be many survivors …' In impotent fury, *Suffolk* fired three salvoes with her 8-inch guns that fell far short of the enemy. The shattering signal came through and while Collett was relieved to discover his brother's ship was not the victim, he was still devastated. It was 'a terrible shock … I found [it] difficult to believe that our biggest and most beautiful ship had gone so suddenly … and that I had seen it go, but a relief to know that the *PoW* [*Prince of Wales*] was still afloat – but had been hit.' But, what if brother John was among casualties in *Prince of Wales*? When *Suffolk* intercepted a signal listing dead and wounded, Collett was relieved to find his brother was not among them.

After destroying the British battlecruiser, Admiral Lütjens and Captain Lindemann disagreed profoundly on what should happen next. Lindemann said *Bismarck* MUST pursue and destroy the apparently badly damaged British battleship, which they believed to be *King George V*, but Lütjens refused to yield. 'The Admiral stuck to his incomprehensible decision.'[1]

Unaware of this bitter disagreement between their commanders, *Bismarck*'s ordinary sailors celebrated their achievement, believing they would now turn for home. However, as *Bismarck* and *Prinz Eugen* pressed on into the Atlantic, the German battleship was already suffering from a handicap that would, ultimately, doom her. One of three 14-inch shell hits achieved by *Prince of Wales* punctured oil tanks, and a pumping station was out of action in a flooded section of the forecastle, denying the ship access to 1,000 tons of fuel. Another hit – probably the source of the fire British warships claimed to see – destroyed boats on *Bismarck*'s upper deck. *Bismarck* suffered no casualties but flying wreckage on the boat deck damaged the aircraft launch gear. With two holes in her hull, she rapidly took in 2,000 tons of water, losing two knots off her speed and leaving an oil trail. Not only was *Bismarck* down by three degrees on the bow, she also developed a nine degree list to port, although counter-flooding corrected this. She had also, of course, damaged her forward radar when firing at *Norfolk* on 23 May. Considering the damage to his ship, Lindemann counselled returning to Germany, but Lütjens insisted *Bismarck* should head to St Nazaire for repairs, possibly because he had in mind a later venture into the Atlantic with *Scharnhorst* and *Gneisenau*.

Bismarck and *Prinz Eugen* had by now disappeared over the horizon, but lookouts in *Suffolk* spotted a Sunderland flying boat overhead, which swooped down to make a light signal. The RAF aircraft advised the cruiser it could provide directions to the probable location of *Hood*'s survivors. However, with two German raiders making good their escape to rampage among sea lanes bulging with British merchant ships, that was *not* a job for a cruiser. *Suffolk* flashed a signal back, asking the Sunderland to find and report the location of *Bismarck* and *Prinz Eugen*. It flew off in search of the enemy ships, a trail of oil glinting on the surface of the ocean pointing the way. With the necessary information passed back by the flying boat, *Suffolk* steamed hard to resume her shadowing duties. Of *Norfolk* and *Prince of Wales* there was no sign. Re-establishing contact with the enemy and marking them for destruction might be down to *Suffolk* alone, but her men were near the limit of their endurance. Collett realised: 'I had been standing up straining my eyes to catch sight of the German ships for close on 11 hours, without anything to eat or drink, and no dinner [since] the night before! I suppose it was about 6.30 am, but I completely lost all count of time. Some v.g. sandwiches were dealt out at about this period and they put new life into me. After about half an hour we sighted smoke on the horizon and, as we came nearer to it [then] it became obvious that it wasn't only smoke from a funnel, but from what must have been a considerable fire onboard *Bismarck*.[2] We were steaming at full speed and soon masts and bridges of the German battleship and her attendant cruiser were visible and we reduced speed so as not to get too close …'

And so the knife-edge duty of shadowing was resumed, with its mix of long stretches of boredom interrupted by intense moments of extreme danger. According to Commander Porter, *Suffolk*'s ship's company had 'lived, and eaten at odd moments at the guns. An odd doze snatched during lulls served for sleep. Some slept on their feet. But the work and watching of arduous months had been worthwhile…'[3] There were lighter moments. One of the cruiser's older officers, who had seen action at the Battle of Jutland in the battlecruiser *Princess Royal*, calmed his nerves by knitting 'while perched on his uncomfortable seat in the after [gunnery] director.'[4] Some of the cruiser's anti-aircraft crews kept their spirits up by holding sing-songs, while Royal Marine gunners allowed out of their turret for a breather rolled up an old rag for a game of football.

While *Prince of Wales* had retired from the fight, the prospect of further combat could not be discounted. The ship remained taut at action stations, so there was no time for rest and recuperation, although a hot drink and a sandwich fortified medic Sam Wood. 'After a mug of cocoa and a corned beef "doorstep" I reported to the Surgeon Commander for further instructions. I was told to remain at my action station after obtaining further medical supplies.'

The *Prince of Wales* was 'quite seriously damaged',[5] the 8-inch shells of *Prinz Eugen* doing the most visible harm. In total she had been hit seven times – four 15-inch shells from *Bismarck* and three 8-inch from the *Prinz Eugen*. There were hits aft, both above the water-line and below it – with flooding of some spaces, not forgetting the 15-inch shell from *Bismarck* that passed through the bridge and caused such mayhem. The most dangerous was a hit below the water line on the starboard side. An unexploded 15-inch shell lay between the outer armoured skin and the inner hull of the ship, next to a magazine. The Chief Engineer had detected water contamination in oil from tanks in that area, indicating shell penetration. It could explode at any moment, though nobody in the ship was aware of quite how perilous the situation might be. A grim battle-readiness assessment was given to Captain Leach: out of ten 14-inch guns, only three were capable of firing; the Y turret, which had jammed when the ship made her turn away from battle, could not be rotated; around 400 tons of water had been taken in astern; the maximum speed the ship could make was 27 knots. Meanwhile, *Suffolk* found she needed to make only 22 knots to keep up with *Bismarck*, a further indication that the German battleship had slowed due to damage. By now, *Norfolk*, in company with *Prince of Wales*, was not far behind *Suffolk*, all three coming under the command of Rear-Admiral Wake-Walker.

The weather, which had been fair all day, deteriorated and mist banks and rain squalls frequently obscured the German ships. *Suffolk*'s Commander Porter, reflected on the dangers of hanging on to the coat tails of powerful enemy ships in such tricky conditions: 'To maintain contact in the filthy weather which now set in, the shadowers closed up on the enemy. Each time the Germans disappeared into one of the patches of rain and murk one was reminded of the traditional habit of the wounded buffalo to lie up in a thicket to savage his pursuers.' As the clock marked 6.30 pm, the German ships melted into a thicker patch of fog and squalls, *Bismarck* making a sharp turn to the west. This was the second time she had conducted that manoeuvre in order to mask attempted separation from *Prinz Eugen*, which was ordered by Lütjens to head off, first of all to seek fuel from one of the pre-positioned tankers lurking in the Atlantic, then to hunt down and destroy enemy merchant ships. The first time this move was attempted, at 3.40 pm, the British ships were too close and weather not quite bad enough to hide what was going on. Three hours later, as both ships entered a fog bank, *Bismarck* again signalled 'Hood', the agreed codeword to initiate the manoeuvre. The battleship turned sharply away to the west and then north to confront the enemy and distract them, while *Prinz Eugen* steamed south. This coincided with a British show of aggression triggered by a signal from the Admiralty, itself prompted partly by Churchill piling on pressure from Chequers for *Prince of Wales* to avenge *Hood*'s loss. The signal asked Wake-Walker: 'Request your intentions as regards the *Prince of Wales* re-engaging?'

With such a dangerous quarry in poor weather conditions, Wake-Walker could not be blamed for keeping a 'respectable distance'.[6] The poor state of affairs in *Prince of Wales*, plus the inherent vulnerabilities of lightly protected cruisers against two adversaries who had destroyed a battlecruiser in short order, also had to be taken into account. Wake-Walker believed Tovey and the *King George V* group were close enough to effect an interception by the early hours of 25 May – if he could just hang on to *Bismarck* and *Prinz Eugen* long enough to mark them down. Shadowing was surely the wisest course? However, Wake-Walker, prompted by the career-threatening tone of the Admiralty signal, decided to go on the offensive. The Admiralty was implying that more was needed in the aftermath of the Royal Navy's most famous ship being lost along with 1,415 men. Wake-Walker decided, in consultation with Captain Leach via light signal, that his force should creep up on *Bismarck*, with *Prince of Wales* in the lead. They would bring about a short engagement, then withdraw to the east, hoping the Germans would take the bait and follow. This would shorten the distance to Tovey, making it more likely the Royal Navy could destroy the German ships.

However, observers in *Suffolk* saw *Bismarck* turning just as she slid into a patch of mist. Wary of a trap, *Suffolk* proceeded carefully, changing course and withdrawing a little. As one of her officers wrote a few days later, in a letter to his family, the British cruiser 'went where angels normally fear to tread'.[7] *Suffolk*'s radar operators warned that the range to *Bismarck* had decreased from fifteen miles to just ten, indicating she was coming their way. Four minutes later, with lookouts straining their eyes to catch sight of the enemy, not more than two miles away 'the great bulk of *Bismarck*' emerged[8]. *Suffolk*'s Lieutenant Commander Collett, reported: 'Suddenly, she appeared out of the mist, a huge terrifying monster and much too close for our liking! Once again Providence protected us. For some unknown reason she held her fire: it was as though her Captain had decided to give us a sporting chance! – whilst everyone gaped at her, expecting to see the vivid orange flashes from her guns, which would almost certainly have caused us grievous harm if they had gone off at that time.'

Suffolk immediately piled on the knots as her helm was put hard over, turning away to seek safety. *Bismarck*'s turrets trained on the British cruiser, guns flashing. Officers whose action stations were below decks, and who were referred to by those in more exposed positions as 'the idle rich', had come up for a breath of fresh air. Commander Porter reported that, as *Bismarck* 'appeared from her lair in the murk ['the idle rich'] thought she was a [British] battleship of the *Ramillies* Class [sic], until they saw the flash of her guns and stayed not on the order of their going.' At his action station, Commander Porter counted off the seconds to impact. 'For half a very slow minute we waited, and then short of us the huge fountains of water leapt into the air. Again and again she fired, the salvos jumping nearer and nearer.' Three 15-inch shells plunged into *Suffolk*'s wake, spaced no more than two yards apart, throwing up a single gigantic column of water. The British cruiser fired back, to no effect, for *Suffolk*'s snaking manoeuvres threw her aim off. Fifteen seconds later another salvo of 15-inch shells hit the water, in the same spot as the first. *Suffolk* was long gone, twisting and turning as she endeavoured to put as much distance as possible between herself and *Bismarck*. Collett saw the third of *Bismarck's* salvoes fall 'about 300 yards astern and it was obvious that she was getting our range!' Then, came the enemy's fourth: 'I saw the flash of her guns for that fourth salvo and I must admit that the time that elapsed between those flashes and the fall of shot was most unpleasant to me, as I expected us to be hit – I did, in fact, dodge behind our gun director[9], which is a most flimsy affair and couldn't possibly have protected us against anything but the smallest of splinters ... a sort of vain endeavour to obtain shelter! It was a most absurd thing to do but the urge to get behind something was terrific! I should like to add here that I was by no means the only person to act in this manner. People who had something to do and to occupy their minds were lucky because they probably did not realize our imminent danger or if they did they couldn't just drop it and hide! Our captain, however, had a similar idea as to where this salvo might fall and, as her guns fired, the helm went over and we altered course about 45 degrees to port. This almost certainly saved us because the shells fell, as far as I could judge, just exactly where we should have been if we hadn't altered! Her next salvo fell in line with us but about 300 yards short and then we altered course again and started making a smoke screen, which we eventually retired behind and hid ourselves in.' Veiled by the smoke, *Suffolk* still caught sight of *Prinz Eugen* and unleashed some 8-inch shells. These fell so short the German cruiser did not even notice she was being fired at, believing *Suffolk*'s gunfire was part of the general battle in the far distance. The men of *Prinz Eugen* heard rumbles and saw orange and yellow flashes reflected by the clouds. As the weather cleared all the way to the far horizon, they caught their last sight of 'big brother' *Bismarck*. 'Encircled by a halo from the salvoes of her own heavy turrets, militant and proud [*Bismarck*] disappeared, firing beyond the clear horizon. It was a scene which none of the men of the *Prinz* who saw it would ever forget.'[10]

Bismarck fired around seven salvoes and *Suffolk* in return fired a hundred 8-inch shells, but the German battleship lost interest when the cruiser disappeared into the smoke screen. As *Suffolk* retired towards them, *Prince of Wales* and *Norfolk* – the former at the limit of her guns' range and *Norfolk* well beyond that of hers – entered the fray, more as a gesture of protection for the other British ship than with any realistic hope of hitting *Bismarck*. The Germans had pre-empted the British attack plan, which was now a damp squib. In *Norfolk*, Rear-Admiral Wake-Walker watched three 8-inch salvoes fall short, while it appeared, despite the extreme distance, *Prince of Wales* managed to straddle *Bismarck*.[11]

In *Suffolk*, Collett wondered what the hesitant encounter looked like to his brother. 'We heaved a sigh of relief as we joined up with *Prince of Wales* and *Norfolk*. I couldn't remember what John's action station was [in *Prince of Wales*] but I remember wondering whether he was watching our little battle and what his reactions were.'

Chapter 12

Swordfish Strike

By 8 pm on the evening of Saturday 24 May, *King George V* was 450 miles south-west of Reykjavik, with the enemy to the west by some 180 miles.

Admiral Tovey still hoped he could meet *Bismarck* and *Prinz Eugen* in battle on the morning of 25 May. It was possible they could be brought to action via an attack by torpedo-bombers from *Victorious*. The timekeeping in *KGV* was British Mid-summer Time – two hours ahead of GMT. This meant that as the ship was by then 30 degrees west, sunset would not be until 00.31 am on 25 May and dawn would break at 6.00 am – just five-and-a-half hours of what passed for darkness in those latitudes. The British admiral decided to detach *Victorious* from his force. The carrier headed off at high speed, to reach a position where she was within range to launch her aircraft. Tovey hoped this could slow the enemy down by inflicting critical damage. As *Victorious* departed on her mission, with four cruisers in escort,[1] *King George V*'s men settled down to await news of the looming air strike's success or failure. It would, in turn, decide whether or not they took up the fight against *Bismarck* the next day. As he turned in to snatch a few hours' sleep in his sea cabin bunk, the commanding officer of the flagship, Captain WR Patterson, wrote in the Captain's Order Book: 'Course 212 degrees, speed 27 knots. Call me in accordance with standing instructions. Pass enemy reports down the voice pipe as they come in. Call me at once if cruisers lose touch with enemy and at 0530. 14" turrets to close up at 0200.'[2] *King George V*'s guns would be ready for action before dawn.

The young naval aviators of *Victorious* were embarking on a mission that was the true definition of British pluck. If the Royal Navy had been asked to pick any Swordfish unit to undertake Tovey's bidding, it would not, in ideal circumstances, have been 825 Naval Air Squadron. It had suffered heavy casualties and had therefore recently drafted in novice naval aviators. Their squadron leader, assisted by two veteran sub-flight commanders, was Lieutenant Commander Eugene Esmonde. Though born in England, his aristocratic family hailed from Tipperary and was of Norman origin. The 825

NAS boss was a descendant of Colonel Thomas Esmonde, who won a Victoria Cross during the Crimean War for rescuing wounded men under fire, at one point snuffing out a fizzing cannon shell by smothering it with his body.[3]

A scion of both Irish nationalists and British patriots, one forebear of Lieutenant Commander Esmonde's was hanged for treason in the late eighteenth century while another from the same era became captain of the British frigate *Lion*. After proving himself unsuited to life as a Catholic missionary, Eugene Esmonde joined the Royal Air Force in 1928, finding he relished the challenge of flying fighter-bombers from the Royal Navy's aircraft carriers in an era when the Senior Service had to rely on the grace and favour of the RAF to provide a naval air arm. In the mid-1930s Esmonde left the air force for a career as a commercial pilot, flying on postal and freight routes between India and Australia, also taking the controls of luxury flying boats run by Imperial Airlines. In 1939 he received a letter from the Admiralty, which was anxious to recruit anyone with experience of carrier operations for the newly established Fleet Air Arm. After some negotiation over pension entitlement, necessary because Esmonde wanted one day to play his part in financing his family's large ancestral home, the thirty-year-old aviator joined the Royal Navy as a Lieutenant Commander. Esmonde was appointed to a squadron in the carrier *Courageous*, surviving her sinking off Ireland on 17 September 1939, thereafter being sent to command a Swordfish training unit at Lee-on-Solent and serving at other shore bases before receiving orders to take command of 825 NAS.[4]

Victorious and her fledgling aviators were the only solution available to Tovey in late May 1941, all other operational carriers being committed elsewhere. Launched on the Tyne eleven days after war broke out, *Victorious* had only been commissioned into service on 29 March 1941. A product of the desperate race to build warships in the years just prior to the war, she was an armoured-deck fleet carrier of the Illustrious Class, true cutting edge ships for their day.[5] The aircraft that formed the main striking weapon for *Victorious*, were, however, not exactly at the forefront of military technology. The maiden flight of the Swordfish biplane torpedo-bomber was in the spring of 1934, but the first squadrons were not formed until the summer of 1936, around a year before *Victorious* was laid down. A large, ungainly looking aircraft, the Swordfish appeared peculiarly old-fashioned, especially compared to sleeker, faster monoplane naval aircraft, such as the US Navy's Douglas Devastator torpedo-bomber, ordered the same year the Swordfish first flew, which had its own maiden flight in 1935 and was in service by late summer 1937. The Swordfish was also slow, with a top speed of 138 mph, while the Devastator could manage 206 mph. The British torpedo-bomber looked like a flying museum piece, but, for its role, was a superb workhorse, some of its perceived faults actually proving to be advantages. Its low take-off speed meant the Swordfish could get airborne even when a ship was at anchor. At sea, during storms, when it wasn't possible for a carrier to manage the forward momentum needed to launch other, more modern aircraft, it could still get into the air. The Swordfish had a low stall speed, which meant it could land back aboard ship even in gale force winds and was also highly manoeuvrable. During the famous raid on Taranto of November 1940, Swordfish torpedo-bombers showed their dexterity by flying between the cables of barrage balloons meant to deter air attack.[6] As the German Navy would soon discover, the slow speed of Swordfish also made them difficult to shoot down. Constructed principally from wood and metal struts, across which was stretched fabric, the Swordfish might seem too fragile for modern warfare. However, the fact that anti-aircraft shells would pass through without exploding, rather than detonate on hitting a metal-skinned machine, made it surprisingly tough. The true worth of the sturdy Swordfish can be seen in the fact that, while it served in several different guises until the end of the Second World War – with some 2,400 built – only 130 Devastators were ever constructed, the type being withdrawn from combat service in 1942. However, the Americans were putting huge investment into carrier aviation, the Devastator having a short shelf-life because the US Navy was able swiftly to bring into service more formidable strike planes, like the Avenger, which far outclassed the Swordfish and most other British naval aircraft. The less well-funded Fleet Air Arm stuck with the Swordfish and made the most of it, particularly as so-called successors, such as the Albacore, were little better.

As it emerged that *Bismarck* was intent on a breakout, the nine Swordfish of 825 NAS were ordered to join *Victorious*, just in case. They made a short flight from the naval air station at Campbeltown, on the Kintyre peninsula in the west of Scotland, landing to refuel in Orkney and then flying on to *Victorious*. For many of the young aviators it was their first landing on a ship. Indeed, there were no more than seven people with relevant flying experience in the squadron. The squadron should have been blessed with eight weeks of work-up training on joining a carrier, but not even that number of days was available, much less hours. As the carrier returned from a flying training session in waters beyond Scapa, some of the aircrews and ship's company watched *Prince of Wales* and *Hood* sailing north-west at top speed, on their ill-fated pursuit of *Bismarck* and *Prinz Eugen*. To the men of *Victorious*, the rate at which those departing ships were steaming signified something big was afoot. Instead of sailing for the Clyde to meet the elderly battlecruiser *Repulse*, to help escort a convoy to Malta – carrying forty-eight crated Hurricane fighters for the defence of the fortress island – *Victorious* was soon accompanying the fleet flagship in pursuit of the most dangerous quarry in the world. A few days later, the young men of 825 NAS assembled in their ready rooms, in a state of barely suppressed tension, coiled for action and awaiting the order to man their aircraft. With the shock of *Hood*'s destruction, just that morning, at the forefront of their minds, the

Swordfish crews regarded themselves as have-a-go pugilists, with *Bismarck* a dreaded heavyweight challenging the Royal Navy to last ten rounds. Sub Lieutenant Pat Jackson, one of the 825 NAS pilots recalled: 'The prelude to our Air Strike was horrible, sitting and waiting your turn to get into the ring. You feel, "God, I'd get out of this if I could ..."'[7]

Since being detached, *Victorious* had steamed north-west at her top speed of 30 knots, into an increasingly severe gale. The ship rode a 32ft swell, lunging ahead and crashing down, the angry, frothing sea cascading across her bows, washing around the superstructure, her flight-deck whipped and pummelled by driving rain and howling wind. The plan was for the Swordfish, under the protection of Fulmar fighters that would take off from *Victorious* shortly after the torpedo-bombers launched, to attack *Bismarck* first. Then, with the Fulmars maintaining contact, the Swordfish would recover to *Victorious*, rearm and then assault the Hipper Class cruiser.

The aircraft were tightly packed at the rear of the flight-deck, wings folded back. With butterflies fluttering in their stomachs, the young aviators emerged from below, walking across the drenched flight-deck, spray and rain stinging their faces, bodies leaning into the wind. Each of them wore a well-insulated Sidcot flying suit and heavy, lined boots, with a Mae West life vest over the top. This assembly was crowned with a leather flying helmet and goggles, the latter kept raised until pulled down just prior to take off. There were no oxygen masks with microphones in Swordfish, for they did not fly high enough.[8] Instead the observer, pilot and telegraphist air gunner (TAG) communicated by shouting down a flexible voice tube.

The men climbed up the high sides of their aircraft, assisted by the helping hands of squadron handlers. Each Swordfish was armed with a single 18-inch torpedo fitted with a contact fuse, set to run at 31ft, as it was estimated *Bismarck* had a draught of around that depth. Their aircrews exposed to the savage weather in open cockpits, one by one the Swordfish were brought forward, their wings unfolded and locked into place. On the signal they rumbled down the flight-deck and staggered into the sky. At least one Swordfish, hurling itself into the stormy night, dropped alarmingly, wheels skimming the heaving waves before clawing its way into the murk. With sunset not expected for a further two hours, the torpedo-bombers set course for the enemy in daylight, but were swiftly swallowed up by a rain squall. Ahead of them was a 120-mile flight into strong wind and lashing rain. Behind the controls of his Swordfish, Pat Jackson felt his nerves settle: 'Once you get into the cockpit and start up and fly in formation, you're doing what you're trained to do.'[9] The torpedo-bombers formed on their leader, Esmonde, climbing to 1,500 feet and flying south-west at 85 knots through patches of stratus cloud. The idea was to fly at the bottom of the cloud layer, so it would mask their attack. To help find and fix *Bismarck* for strike, the Swordfish were making use of Air to Surface Vessel (ASV) radar.

This duly picked up a contact but, sighting a warship through a gap in the clouds, 825 NAS found *Prince of Wales*, which they only realized was not *Bismarck* by virtue of the four guns mounted in her A turret. A signal lantern flickered aboard the British battleship, advising that *Bismarck* was off her starboard bow, fifteen miles distant.[10] *Norfolk* also provided directions to the enemy, gleaned from her own radar. As dusk finally came on, the light faded dramatically and the sea rose, the Swordfish turning over *Suffolk*, from which Lieutenant Commander Collett bade them good hunting, feeling that they 'were a cheering sight and we waved to them and wished them the very best of luck.'[11]

Between the strike group and their target lay the US Coast Guard cutter *Modoc*, searching for survivors from a recently sunk merchant vessel. *Modoc* would find herself risking destruction not once, but twice, merely for looking on as the latest episode in the great drama unfolded. With a displacement of less than 2,000 tons, she was tiny in comparison with the battleship that now crossed her path. The Americans knew of *Bismarck*'s breakout, having picked up news of *Hood*'s demise via radio. *Modoc* later encountered a British corvette that revealed the Germans were still heading south. The possibility of being mistaken for the enemy by either side had occurred, so *Modoc* was flying huge US Coast Guard battle ensigns and making regular radio broadcasts to identify herself as neutral. Now her lookouts' binoculars were filled with a battleship around ten miles away, steaming south, emerging from the gloom and giving no sign of having seen the American cutter, the ship's gun turrets remaining pointed fore and aft. The vessel ignored *Modoc*'s light signal inquiry: 'What ship?' Attempts by radio to ensure the battleship knew *Modoc*'s identity and nationality gained no response and the Americans suddenly realized it was *Bismarck*, news going swiftly through the cutter. Men off watch rushed up ladders and along passageways to gain a vantage point on the upper decks, gawking at *Bismarck* as she exited stage right into the fog. Then there were shouts as *Modoc*'s lookouts spotted biplanes dropping from the low clouds. These aerial intruders seemed to float like leaves on the air current rather than be subjected to powered flight. Having climbed back into cloud to gain cover for the final leg of their attack run, the ASV of Esmonde's Swordfish had picked up a contact, which looked likely to be *Bismarck*, exactly where he had been told she would be, but it was *Modoc* they were preparing to attack. Aboard the cutter, general quarters sounded, men dashing to man her three anti-aircraft guns. As the British aircraft swooped on their target, they realized it was too small to be *Bismarck*, whose location was given away by her own anti-aircraft gunners opening fire. The Swordfish had totally lost the element of surprise.

Suffolk's men were not able to see the Swordfish press home their assault, relegated as they were to watching a 'horizon [which] was lit by flickers of flame and by the pin-point bursts of anti-aircraft fire', although Lieutenant

Commander Collett claimed he saw '*Bismarck*'s AA shells bursting in the gloom'.[12] *Modoc* was, of course, much closer, her crew enjoying a ringside seat as the Swordfish attacked. *Bismarck* twisted and turned, her guns sparkling, upper-works wreathed in smoke; some of the shells headed towards *Modoc*, whose captain, Lieutenant Commander Harold Belford, saw them landing 'dangerously close to our bows'. There was a stark band of light on the horizon in the north and west, but a gathering darkness in the south and east. The attacking British torpedo-bombers were organized into two sub-flights of three and one of two from the north-east, hoping to be hidden in the gathering darkness while they turned in against *Bismarck*, finding her silhouetted against a setting sun. One Swordfish had lost contact with the squadron and did not take part in the attack but the others pressed on. The German battlewagon's 15-inch main armament and her secondary battery contributed to the barrage, creating fountains of spray amid a rainbow-coloured storm of tracer. As the torpedo-bombers skimmed in, *Bismarck* raised her speed to 27 knots. The Swordfish dropped to 100ft and under, initially approaching on *Bismarck*'s port quarter, the German ship making a hard turn to starboard. Their pilots watched for the heavier guns firing, some taking evasive action to ensure they skirted around the shells' point of impact. Pat Jackson's Swordfish was in the second sub-flight of three aircraft, led by Lieutenant Percy Gick and he found it 'chaotic as we went in for the attack. Heavy flak bursts all around and the stench of burning explosives.'[13] Petty Officer Les Sayer was Gick's TAG, finding that whether he lived or died depended on the skill of a pilot who hardly ever spoke to him. Such was the class divide between officers and lower deck ratings, even in the close confines of a Swordfish crew.

Heavy shell spouts some 100ft high erupted between the aircraft, some Swordfish flying through them, faltering and dropping momentarily, before shaking the water off and going on. Sayer's Swordfish had its fabric fuselage punctured.[14] He could see his aircraft's torpedo through a hole between his feet. With all hell breaking loose around the aircraft – the sky filled with lazy arcs of tumbling, glowing shells that looked like 'pretty fireflies'[15] – Sayer stared at the red tail fin of the torpedo, waiting for it to disappear, signifying the fish was on its way. While he had been working around to the *Bismarck*'s starboard side, 'swerving across the enemy bows'[16] the lower aileron of Esmonde's aircraft was damaged by enemy fire, throwing it briefly out of control. Having got his Swordfish back on course, Esmonde decided to come in as he was, dropping his torpedo from an altitude of 100ft and just 1,000 yards off *Bismarck*'s port beam. *Bismarck* turned tightly to port, successfully combing not only Esmonde's torpedo but also those of the other two aircraft in his sub-flight. Gick, whose aircraft had flown under Esmonde's as the former began his attack run around midnight, was not happy with his first approach to target, on *Bismarck*'s starboard side, so turned away. However, the other two Swordfish in Gick's sub-flight carried on, dropping their torpedoes to no avail, as *Bismarck* again skilfully evaded them. The two Swordfish of the third sub-flight unleashed their torpedoes on *Bismarck*'s port side and also missed, the German ship twisting and turning to evade harm, her anti-aircraft guns putting up a storm of steel. The Germans grudgingly admired the suicidal bravery of aircrews who, it seemed, did not expect to return from their mission. Amid the smoke from *Bismarck*'s own weapons, Lieutenant von Müllenheim-Rechberg caught glimpses of the attack via his gunnery director optics. To him the 'antiquated' British aircraft appeared to be moving so slowly they were 'standing still in the air'. They got so close before releasing their torpedoes, it looked like the enemy aircraft intended flying right over *Bismarck*, which struck him as the 'height of impudence'.[17] As each Swordfish turned away its TAG sprayed *Bismarck* with machine-gun bullets. Though this did no damage, it made the enemy duck for cover. Esmonde, having used up his chance to strike a mortal blow, tried to assist by leading other Swordfish that had expended their torpedoes past *Bismarck*, a valiant attempt to draw fire away from those that might still land a blow. Gick flew a wide dog leg, bringing his Swordfish back in on *Bismarck*'s bow around sixty seconds after Esmonde's attack, flying at 'about six feet over the water, right ahead of the enemy'.[18] Les Sayer stood up, looking past his aircraft's observer and pilot, seeing the huge bulk of the battleship getting bigger and bigger. The Germans had still not spotted the lone Swordfish. Sayer thought his aircraft would be ripped to shreds the moment *Bismarck* woke up. It was a single torpedo, a pair of light machine guns and just three British aviators 'against the might of the German Navy ...'[19] They couldn't possibly survive. But no, the Swordfish kept going and nobody in *Bismarck* noticed until after the torpedo was dropped. The aircraft leapt in the air as it parted company with the weapon at around 500 yards out, turning low over the waves to make an escape, zigzagging as it flew away, chased by criss-cross tracer arcs. The *Bismarck*'s anti-aircraft guns could not get the range – they were calibrated for targets flying a minimum speed of 100 knots, but the Swordfish were flying at 90 knots, the required speed for dropping torpedoes.[20] The mixed calibres of the German AA guns did not help either, nor did the violent manoeuvres of the ship herself, making it virtually impossible for the gunnery directors to keep their weapons on target. The Germans tried again with their larger calibre guns, but the British aviators watched for the flashes, trying to calculate the time of flight and fall of shot, throwing their aircraft away from where they fervently hoped the shells would land. One shell passed rather too close to Les Sayer's Swordfish, ripping another hole in the fabric of the biplane's fuselage. As the battered aircraft high-tailed it away from *Bismarck*, Sayer exclaimed over the voice pipe: 'It's bloody draughty back here!'[21]

About thirty seconds after Gick's torpedo was dropped, one of the British aviators saw a 'white cloud which may have been spray' erupting on *Bismarck*'s starboard side 'quickly followed by a large dark cloud, which eventually rose to a height of 500 feet then drifted away.'[22] Two Fulmar fighters watched from a distance, ready to take up shadowing duties in the aftermath of the strike. Fulmar pilot TW Harrington, of 800X NAS, later revealed that, in common with the other fighter, his aircraft was not allowed to tune its wireless set to the exact wavelength in case the Germans got a fix on *Victorious*. This would make it difficult to send a sighting report once they had confirmed contact with *Bismarck*. Harrington banked his aircraft, which was buffeted by the gale, rain running in wavy rivulets down the outside of the cramped cockpit, and somehow saw 'something very black with breaking water on our port bow. We altered course towards this faint object and lo and behold "it" opened fire at us – well done the *Bismarck* for making up our minds.' Despite the poor light and rain squalls, Harrington spotted the German battleship was trailing oil and he estimated she was heading south-east, at a speed of 18 knots. The Fulmar's observer sent out a sighting report, a fragment of which was picked up.

Bismarck continued firing at the Fulmars, until they retired to about ten miles, before turning back for *Victorious*, as their fuel got low. It was anticipated that a pair of relief Fulmars would soon take up shadowing duties. One of the departing Fulmars reported a hit on *Bismarck* to *Victorious*, confirming an earlier signal from Esmonde that only a single torpedo had struck home. The weather had deteriorated so severely that there were fears the Swordfish could not be brought back aboard *Victorious* safely. The 825 NAS pilots had barely got the hang of landing aboard a carrier in daylight, so coming back on a stormy night would test their fledgling skills to the limit. They would have to cope with a heaving flight-deck, driving rain and howling wind. As if this wasn't bad enough, the homing beacon supposed to help guide them back to the ship was out of order. The Swordfish would be able to use their radar to find *Victorious*, but what if they found her, only to run out of fuel before they could land?

It was imperative they get it right first time, especially as the crews would be very tired and probably, in several cases, flying damaged aircraft. However, just as they were homing in on a radar contact, a rain squall masked the ship and they flew by *Victorious*. As the drone of passing aircraft was heard amid the storm, a huge risk was taken, *Victorious* shining searchlights and signal lamps into the clouds. Fortunately, there were no U-boats prowling nearby.

Wary of the possibility there might soon be, Rear-Admiral Alban Curteis, cruiser squadron commander and also senior officer in the task group, ordered the commanding officer of *Victorious*, Captain HC Bovell, to turn the light show off. He acknowledged this instruction by using his brightest signal lamp, hoping the errant Swordfish might spot it. In the end, the intrepid torpedo-bomber crews turned around and were able to find their way home thanks to the cruisers guiding them back by using low intensity signal lamps. The second Swordfish down managed to land just as the carrier's bows plunged into the sea, a huge surge of water washing over the aircraft as it taxied forward to the parking area. Fortunately, the bottom of the cockpit had been shot out, so the water swiftly drained away.[23] All the Swordfish had been recovered safely by 2.00 am, while three of the five Fulmars also returned safely. TW Harrington found landing his fighter a daunting prospect for, in addition to having never before seen the layout of the new ship's flight-deck lights in the dark, the exhaust vents on the aircraft's nose had no baffles. Therefore, as he brought the aircraft in to land, Harrington was blinded by 'lots of red exhaust gas flaming in just the area where you were trying to see the batsman [landing officer]'. Climbing down from his cockpit, Harrington was congratulated by the batsman for making a perfect landing.[24]

However, the other two Fulmars failed to find *Victorious* and were forced to ditch on running out of fuel, with only one aviator being rescued, many hours later, by a merchant ship named *Ravenshill*. Meanwhile, back aboard *Victorious*, the aviators were rewarded for their heroic endeavours with a delicacy that was very rare in wartime: bacon and real eggs. They were also warmed with a special tot of rum. Les Sayer and the other TAGs were not privy to the post-mission debrief, which was for officer aircrew only. However, Sayer was also convinced a hit had been achieved, which he felt certain he had seen.[25]

In reality the damage to the German battleship was negligible. Just one of her sailors was killed – a senior rating passing ammunition forward hurled against 'something hard'.[26] The corpse of this first fatality in *Bismarck*, Warrant Officer Kurt Kirchberg, was sewn into a sailcloth shroud and placed in a boat on the upper deck for burial later. The flooding of the boiler room was exacerbated by collision mats used to stem the flow being shaken loose by the ship's violent manoeuvring. *Bismarck* was forced to reduce speed to 16 knots and institute further temporary repairs after which she attained 20 knots, continuing her race south ahead of shadowing British warships. Shortly after the Swordfish undertook their attack, *Prince of Wales* was involved in her own drama. Lieutenant Commander McMullen found himself resisting orders to destroy *Modoc*, which he sighted on the starboard beam 'in the murk', ordering *Prince of Wales'* 14-inch guns trained on the target as a precaution. In *Norfolk*, Rear-Admiral Wake-Walker ordered '*Flag 5*', which was the signal for *Prince of Wales* to open fire on the unidentified ship. McMullen, and his spotting officer, Lieutenant AG Skipwith, scrutinized the mystery vessel using their powerful binoculars. 'We could see this ship was pitching,' said McMullen. 'She was a small ship. Twice we were given the order to open fire by the admiral. Twice we failed to do so …'[27]

McMullen phoned Captain Leach and told him: 'That's *not* the *Bismarck*, Sir.' Had McMullen obeyed the admiral and let rip with his ship's three operational 14-inch guns or the secondary armament, he would have undone all of Winston Churchill's careful work behind the scenes with dispatches to President Roosevelt and the charm offensive on Harriman at Chequers. McMullen reflected: 'Skipwith and I reckoned that we practically saved the war because if we'd sunk the American coastguard cutter it would not have helped our relations with the Americans.' *Modoc's* captain and upper deck contingent watched in fear as *Prince of Wales'* guns held their aim. Well aware that a single hit from the British capital ship's big guns would shatter his small ship, Lieutenant Commander Belford discussed what might be the best course of action with his executive officer, Lieutenant Robert Furey. Belford asked: 'What are we going to do?' Furey's response was to the point: 'I'd change course and get the hell out of here.'[28] *Modoc* beat a hasty retreat, the elderly cutter pushed to her bone-shaking top speed of 12 knots.

An hour after the torpedo-bomber attack, when it became clear *Bismarck's* reduction in speed was just a temporary measure, Wake-Walker decided to try his hand at slowing her. This time when he instructed *Prince of Wales* to open fire, she did, sending two salvoes directed by RDF in *Bismarck's* direction, at 1.15 am from the considerable range of around 16,000 yards. The German response was a little while in coming, the British admiral recording that it 'consisted of a single gun salvo and then a four-gun salvo a long way short.'[29] It was not completely dark but the marginal visibility made it very difficult for *Bismarck* to see *Prince of Wales*. When darkness finally fell, the weather took a decided turn for the worse. Young medic Sam Wood, probably suffering depression in the aftershock of that day's events, felt it reflected his world, for 'sleet and rain came down in endless torrents, conditions were atrocious, seas mountainous and to step out onto the open deck was like walking through a waterfall. Lookouts and others in exposed positions were soon soaked to the skin despite protective clothing…It was a miserable night, fit only for howling banshees.'[30] The British were forced to rely on *Suffolk's* radar alone to keep track of *Bismarck*, with all three shadowing warships on the German port quarter. This gave Lütjens an opportunity to break contact, for *Bismarck's* hydrophones and radar had confirmed there were no enemy warships following off the starboard quarter. *Bismarck* turned sharply to the west, then headed north-west, east and south-east – a huge circle – before finally heading for St Nazaire. The British, worried about U-boats, were carving out zigzags as they headed south. *Suffolk* made her last contact with *Bismarck* at 3.06am, before turning away. However, on returning, she was unable to re-establish radar contact, as expected, at 3.30 am. After nearly thirty-two hours and 1,000 miles of hanging on to the German battleship's tail, *Suffolk* had lost *Bismarck*. The news of this calamity raced through *Prince of Wales*, Sam Wood recording the bitter blow ('we all felt utterly depressed …'). As the new day dawned, British lookouts strained their eyes, the battleship and cruisers hunting in vain, for all the while the wary *Bismarck* might be trying to pull another surprise attack. Ludovic Porter noted: 'Through the murk the British ships searched, at times able to see only two miles, and once again the simile of the wounded buffalo came to mind.'[31]

However, *Bismarck* really was gone.

Chapter 13

A Day of Fearful Gloom

When news that *Bismarck* had been lost hit Chequers, it plunged the mercurial British Prime Minister into dark depression and again stirred up latent anger at the Navy's performance. In his diary entry for 25 May, Churchill's Private Secretary, John Colville, recorded: 'A day of fearful gloom ensued. The PM cannot understand why the *Prince of Wales* did not press home her attack yesterday and keeps on saying it is the worst thing since Troubridge turned away from the Goeben in 1914.'[1] Churchill's fury and depression had its roots in his experiences during the First World War. Rear-Admiral Ernest Troubridge was in command of a cruiser squadron in the Mediterranean that, as hostilities commenced in August 1914, shadowed the German battlecruiser *Goeben* but failed to bring her to action. *Goeben*'s escape to Turkey, along with the cruiser *Breslau*, was an event that is held to have brought the Ottoman Empire into the war on the side of Germany. Rear-Admiral Troubridge, father of Captain Thomas Troubridge, the Naval Attaché in Berlin who was to be present at *Bismarck*'s launch in 1939, felt the full fury of First Lord Winston Churchill. Troubridge was arraigned before a court martial aboard the pre-dreadnought battleship *Bulwark* at Portland, in November 1914. He was acquitted on the charge of negligence but never received another sea command. In 1941, looking back at the consequences of *Goeben* reaching Turkey, Churchill would have no doubt feared *Bismarck*'s escape could lead to similar national and personal disaster. The Dardanelles campaign of 1915–16 that tried to take Turkey out of the war cost many thousands of lives, led to Churchill losing his job as First Lord of the Admiralty and to his subsequent resignation from government. A quarter of a century later there was a feeling at large, and it also seems to have gnawed at the Prime Minister, of the Home Fleet representing a great investment in national treasure, so needing to prove its worth. The Grand Fleet of the First World War – a magnificent weapon in large part created by Churchill when he was in charge at the Admiralty – had been the shining hope of a quick victory for Britain. As Churchill knew only too well, it had appeared to fumble the ball at

Jutland. Would the Home Fleet now do the same with *Bismarck*? One contemporary observer acknowledged the pressure on the Home Fleet to deliver at a time of high crisis in the Second World War but also pleaded for greater understanding of the mysteries of exercising sea power. The movements of the Home Fleet as it closed in on *Bismarck* had to be kept hidden from the enemy, but this meant its activities were therefore also kept away from a British public hungry for news, especially in the wake of *Hood*'s loss. Pressure was on the Home Fleet to deliver 'spectacular action of the type which, although it could not win the war in a few minutes, might well lose it.' The same Royal Navy officer also observed: 'It is remarkable that in a seafaring nation there should have been in our history so many instances of inability among landsmen and politicians to appreciate the silent and secret work of those commanding the main fleet.'[2]

Churchill naturally understood that exercising sea power could be a mysterious and uncertain process, but that did not help erase the painful memory of *Goeben* and the Dardanelles. He would have recalled sharply how much energy he had expended in 1916, even after leaving the Admiralty, in trying to explain to the public how the magnificent Grand Fleet still held the strategic upper hand despite suffering more losses at Jutland than the Germans. In May 1941 it was one thing to have cruisers shadowing *Bismarck*, with various units converging on her ... but now the German battleship appeared to have pulled a disappearing act. The admirals would not have to face MPs nor would they need to explain to the public how *Bismarck* had escaped retribution, or find excuses for the Navy's dismal performance in letters to President Roosevelt. Churchill had become Prime Minister after the Norway disaster, which had made Chamberlain's continuing as British leader impossible.[3] Could the same now happen to him, all because of the Royal Navy letting him down not only in the Atlantic but also elsewhere? The situation in and around Crete remained dire and Churchill felt Cunningham's Mediterranean Fleet continued to show 'a tendency to shirk its task of preventing a seaborne landing'.[4] He complained that losing half the Mediterranean Fleet would be worth it, to prevent the Germans from taking Crete. What sacrifice would the British leader therefore permit in order to bring about *Bismarck*'s destruction? In the vast Atlantic, ships, even big ones like *Bismarck*, were specks of no significance. The hunt for *Bismarck* could be compared to 'a number of snails searching for a particular snail who is doing his best to avoid them on Lord's Cricket Ground in thick fog.'[5]

Tovey's slim hopes for a morning battle on 25 May had evaporated, and now the Home Fleet commander weighed up three potential courses of action the Germans might take: attempt a rendezvous with supply ships and U-boats to unleash a sustained campaign against merchant shipping; head for a French port; sail back to Germany via the Greenland-Iceland Gap. *King George V* had

Victorious close by, and Tovey could also number four cruisers and nine destroyers in his immediately available striking group. Considering the calamity that had befallen *Hood*, he had already decided to keep battlecruiser *Repulse* out of harm's way, sending her away to refuel. Meanwhile, the Admiralty was considering which of its scattered units should be instructed to converge on the area where the two German ships might now be. In this way it could marshal far-flung assets and hopefully put them at Tovey's disposal. Among them was battleship *Rodney* and escorts, to the south-east of the Home Fleet flagship, while further to the south was the old and slow battleship *Ramillies*. The Gibraltar-based Force H – spearheaded by *Renown*, carrier *Ark Royal* and cruiser *Sheffield*, under the command of the formidable Admiral James Somerville – was steaming hard, heading north-west into the Atlantic. The 4th Destroyer Flotilla, led by the supremely aggressive Captain Vian, was still escorting a convoy but could be pulled away. Cruisers *Edinburgh* and *Dorsetshire* were on convoy duty off the coast of West Africa and heading north. Also among those potentially available was the heavy cruiser *London*, which had been diverted away from convoy escort duty early on the evening of 24 May and asked to head north-west, specifically tasked by an Admiralty signal with proceeding at 'economical speed' to close the enemy and 'prepare take over shadowing duties' on *Bismarck*. However, at 9.19 am on 25 May the Admiralty re-tasked *London* with playing a key role in preventing *Bismarck* from mounting a prolonged raiding sortie should she evade the Home Fleet. The signal instructed *London* to 'search for enemy tanker'.[6] In all these ships, as the Admiralty's instructions flew out, the feeling of shock at *Hood*'s loss gave way to a grim determination to avenge her and the men who had lost their lives. They would hunt *Bismarck* down and kill her. 'The disposition [of ships] made, all that could be done on Sunday was to steam and hope.'[7]

It was too dangerous to send troop reinforcements from west to east across the Mediterranean, so Convoy WS8B[8] was initially headed for Gibraltar and then would skirt the west coast of Africa before heading into the Indian Ocean. This was one of the convoys that Churchill felt was at risk should its escorts be diverted. Riding shotgun on WS8B in *Cossack*, Captain Vian was monitoring signals intercepts and wondering, indeed hoping desperately, that his flotilla - *Cossack*, *Zulu*, *Maori*, *Sikh* – would soon be called to participate in the hunt for *Bismarck*. Other ships in the escort force were the Polish destroyer *Piorun*, anti-aircraft cruiser *Cairo*, carrier *Argus* and destroyers *Eridge*, *Restigouche* and *Ottawa* (the latter two Canadian). The cruiser *Exeter*, legendary veteran of the Battle of the River Plate, was also providing cover at a greater distance, carrying a Royal Navy Commodore. This was the convoy that *Repulse* and *Victorious* had originally been assigned to cover. On 24 May, at around 8.30 am, a German Focke-Wulf Condor long-range maritime strike bomber flew low over the convoy, between its two westernmost columns of ships. This provoked an angry barrage from both merchantmen and escorting warships. Two bombs were dropped, exploding in the sea close to the liner *Abosso*, causing shock damage that stopped her port engine. To enable repairs the convoy was slowed down, for while a damaged cargo vessel might be left to fend for herself, a ship packed with hundreds of troops could not possibly be abandoned to her fate. By the morning of 25 May, WS8B was far to the west of Ireland, sailing south-west. While Tovey had to consider all eventualities, Vian fortunately only had to take precautions to protect the convoy, which would be most at risk if *Bismarck* continued at speed on a south-easterly course, as last reported before contact was lost. It was decided to send *Cairo* thirty miles to the west, so that she could provide early warning should *Bismarck*'s deadly silhouette crest over the horizon. However, while Vian was left as the tactical 'Local Escort' commander, the buck did not stop with him. With so many lives at risk in the convoy the overall boss of WS8B was Vice-Admiral Sir Geoffrey Arbuthnot, Commander-in-Chief East Indies Station designate, who was taking passage in the liner (now troop ship) *Georgic*, to Ceylon. Vian recalled that he communicated with Sir Geoffrey via 'a code of my own devising'.[9]

Vian acknowledged that it was at least wise to keep the convoy ships informed of events as they unfolded 'to avoid giving what might well prove to be needless alarm...'[10] The thrusting destroyer flotilla commander decided it was of the utmost importance panic did not spread through the troop ship *Georgic* due to rumours of *Bismarck* and *Prinz Eugen* bearing down on the convoy. Therefore in the coded messages, sent by flag and light signal, *Bismarck* was referred to as 'Beaver' while *Prinz Eugen*, in reference to the fact that the man the German cruiser was named after fought alongside John Churchill in the Seven Years War, was dubbed 'Marlborough's friend'. Judging that John 'Jack' Tovey in *King George V* would be seeking to join forces with Frederick Dalrymple-Hamilton in *Rodney*, in one signal from *Cossack* to *Georgic*, Vian told Arbuthnot that 'Jack and Freddie' could be 'in the picture'. Hinting at his skepticism at such a command arrangement, the combat-proven destroyer captain would observe rather sarcastically of this pantomime: 'As the senior officer present he had evidently to be informed.'[11]

At around 1.00 am local time in Gibraltar on 24 May, men of the naval provost had been sent out into streets and alleyways nestled at the foot of the Rock, to winkle out those sailors and marines of Force H with special dispensation to sleep ashore. The Admiralty in London had sent a signal ordering Force H to raise steam and prepare to sail in two hours. News of this order interrupted a sing-song in the ward room of *Sheffield*, while men who had been on a run ashore, or hauled from their beds, were soon streaming up gangways, many of them carrying string bags bulging with bananas and oranges. A few hid bottles of Spanish brandy, illicit copies of *Lady Chatterley's Lover* or smutty postcards depicting senoritas in various states of undress. Force

H had departed Gibraltar shortly after 3.00 am and at 7.00 am, as her men consumed a breakfast of chopped kidneys on fried bread, *Sheffield*'s commanding officer, Captain Charles Larcom told them via the public address system about the rapidly evolving situation in the northern Atlantic.[12] For the time being Force H was to ready itself to provide protection for convoy WS8B as it came further south. To many it seemed their ships, being so far south of the scene of the action hundreds of miles to the north, would not be drawn in. Fate was to decide otherwise. The ships of Force H picked up the signals revealing *Hood*'s destruction, and like sailors and marines in British warships around the world, the men of *Sheffield* could barely believe it: 'It came as a terrific shock to all of us to hear about the loss of the *Hood*…'[13] As his ship battered her way north-west, an aviator in *Ark Royal* thought it 'unbelievable news' that 'the greatest, most impressive and handsome warship in the world to most of us since we were boys' was no more.[14]

One Swordfish pilot in *Ark Royal*, Sub Lieutenant Alan Swanton, yielded a pithy reaction to news *Hood* had been sunk: 'Well, bugger me!'[15] For many in *Ark Royal* the battlecruiser was familiar as their ship's partner in the uncomfortable attack on the Vichy fleet at Oran. Swanton felt that throughout *Ark Royal* there was 'a strange mixture of incredulity, anger and loss'. How dare the bloody Germans blow the pride of the Royal Navy out of the water and every single man aboard? Later, as they noted the deciphered instructions directing ships from all over the Atlantic to join the pursuit of *Bismarck*, the aviators in *Ark Royal* reflected with grim satisfaction that vengeance would assuredly be achieved. Swanton declared: 'We soon came to realize that the Admiralty weren't going to let Adolf get away with sinking *Hood*.' The thirst for revenge, the sheer excitement of being involved in one of the great dramas of the war distracted *Ark*'s men from the weather, which at other times would have made their lives miserable. *Sheffield*'s men had confidence *Suffolk* and *Norfolk* would hang onto *Bismarck* to enable *Hood*'s loss to be avenged. Then they picked up more bad news: 'It was not until Sunday morning that we heard that these two ships had lost touch, just before day-light, that we realized for the first time that the *Renown*, *Ark* and ourselves were the only ships between *Bismarck* and Brest.'[16]

Force H steamed north-west at 26 knots, the weather deteriorating by the hour, the six escorting destroyers suffering most. New orders from the Admiralty took the force away from convoy escort duty and instructed Admiral Somerville to place his ships between *Bismarck* and the French Atlantic coast. Somerville was aware that lurking in Brest were *Scharnhorst* and *Gneisenau*, which might come out at any minute to reinforce *Bismarck*, or, for all he knew, might already be at sea. With *Hood* destroyed, *Prince of Wales* damaged, the strike by torpedo-bombers from *Victorious* having failed, what chance did Somerville's ships stand if they had to step into the ring with *Bismarck*?

Completed in September 1916 at the Fairfield yard on the Clyde, Force H flagship *Renown* was a contemporary of *Hood*, but unlike the latter, had received a major rebuild that took place between autumn 1936 and September 1939. *Renown* emerged from this the day before Britain declared war on Germany. With a deep load displacement of just over 36,000 tons, she retained her six 15-inch guns (mounted in pairs, in two turrets fore and one aft) although an improvement to elevation gave them a much greater range, and the anti-aircraft weapons fit had been boosted. The most striking aspect of *Renown*'s reconstruction was a new, heavily armoured bridge tower structure. While the ship's protection elsewhere was also improved, the Royal Navy was under no illusions, especially after *Hood*'s demise, that *Renown*, like other ships of her kind, was not suited to slugging matches with battleships. In April 1940 she had, however, conducted a long-range duel with *Gneisenau* and *Scharnhorst* – the very same ships now lurking in Brest – in dreadful weather off the coast of Norway. In mid-August 1940 *Renown* replaced *Hood* as flagship of Force H. The battlecruiser's designated role, for which she had been modernized, was to act as escort ship for the new fast carriers, and it was just that function she performed for *Ark Royal*. Already by May 1941, the *Ark* had gained an illustrious record, seeing action off Norway and in the Mediterranean. One of a kind, the 22,352-ton *Ark Royal* was the first purpose-built large aircraft carrier constructed for Britain's navy – her predecessors of similar displacement utilized the hulls of decommissioned battlecruisers. While the RN's other large aircraft carriers at the time of her construction – *Furious*, *Glorious* and *Courageous* – were unattractive conversions, *Ark Royal* had the clean, modernistic lines that we today recognize as belonging to aircraft carriers. Ugly and utilitarian looking in the eyes of those who loved battleships, with seafaring grace sidelined by the need for functionality, *Ark* was, after all, a floating airfield. Built on the Mersey by Cammell Laird, launched in spring 1937 and commissioned the following November, the air group envisaged for *Ark* was impressive: up to forty-eight Swordfish and twenty-four Sea Skua fighter-bombers.[17] One of *Ark*'s Sea Skuas made history by shooting down a Dornier seaplane over the North Sea in late September 1939, the first British aerial kill of the war. *Sheffield* was a Southampton Class cruiser, completed in late August 1937, armed with a dozen 6-inch guns and displacing 11,350 tons fully loaded. Blooded off Norway in 1940, Old Shiny, as she was nicknamed, had also seen action in the Mediterranean. These three ships had more battle experience than *Bismarck*, but they were extremely vulnerable to the German ship's big guns and singly no match for the Nazi battlewagon. However, combined – and provided they could keep their distance – they might at least be able to slow her down for the Home Fleet to do the job of killing. *Sheffield* could find and shadow *Bismarck*, while *Ark Royal* stood off at a safe distance, again using a Swordfish strike as the principal weapon. *Renown*, depending on whether or not *Ark*'s aircraft had inflicted a telling wound, might, as a last gasp measure, be able to close with and fight *Bismarck*, but this was not a prospect that filled her men with much enthusiasm.[18]

Force H was usually responsible for Royal Navy operations in the western Mediterranean and also in the Atlantic, from the Bay of Biscay out to the Azores and down the West African coast. It had already gained a formidable reputation, under Somerville, an admiral who, like many of the RN's senior commanders – including Cunningham in command of the hard-pressed Mediterranean Fleet – did not always enjoy a harmonious relationship with the hands-on, and incessantly interfering, Winston Churchill. An episode at the tail end of the previous year perfectly illustrated the underlying tensions between the Royal Navy's admirals and the British war leader. *Ark Royal*, *Renown* and *Sheffield* were all present at the controversial Battle of Spartivento, on 27 November 1940, when Force H faced two Italian battleships – the brand new *Vittorio Veneto*, with nine 15-inch guns, and the modernized *Guilio Cesare*, with ten 12.6-inch – plus seven heavy cruisers and nearly twenty enemy destroyers. Force H was, therefore, heavily outnumbered. Aside from *Ark*, *Renown* and *Sheffield*, Somerville had only another cruiser, the *Berwick*, armed with eight 8-inch guns, nine destroyers and four corvettes to see off the Italians while also protecting three merchant ships carrying sorely needed tanks and other supplies to the British Army in North Africa. After an hour's battle, in which *Berwick* suffered damage and a single Italian destroyer was also hit, and with two air strikes from *Ark Royal* failing to find their mark but scaring the Italian commander, the enemy retreated. Instead of ordering a pursuit, Somerville decided that safeguarding the merchant ships was paramount and successfully delivered them to their destination, bringing much needed relief to efforts on land. However, Churchill was extremely displeased and ordered the Admiralty immediately to send a Board of Enquiry to Gibraltar, to await the return of Force H and demand answers as to why Somerville had failed to chase the Italian fleet to destruction. This was deeply unpopular within the Navy, which felt the commander on the spot was better placed to make crucial life-or-death tactical decisions than somebody sitting in a London bunker hundreds of miles from the scene of battle. While Somerville was regarded by the men of Force H as an inspirational, and above all humane, leader, the Prime Minister did not share this good opinion. Churchill's view of Somerville only improved after the latter conducted a successful – and risky – bombardment of the Italian port of Genoa in early February 1941. A visitor to Chequers around this time had the temerity to ask the Prime Minister why a Board of Enquiry had been established following Cape Spartivento. This provoked a grudging acknowledgement from Churchill that it was a rash gesture: 'My boy, in war mistakes are often made.'

Somerville was a man who led by example and made great efforts to ensure every member of the Force H team felt valued, their problems understood, that everybody was 'all of one company'. This was no mere show of due care and attention – the sailors and marines under his command *knew* Somerville was genuine.[19] When it came to the aviators of *Ark Royal*, Somerville decided he should get in the cockpit with them whenever possible, in order to enhance his appreciation of their particular risks, which he always took care not to underestimate, especially after he experienced some exciting flying exercises in Swordfish, Skuas and Fulmars. His nephew, Mark Somerville, an observer in *Ark*'s Fulmar squadron, was frequently teased about needing to shoot down more enemy aircraft for his uncle. The admiral wrote home to his wife: 'Having seen and talked to the pilots and observers before they took off one waits anxiously for their return and it's a joyous feeling when you've counted them back.'[20] Somerville also confided, when contemplating the hazards of naval aviation during a foray by Force H into a stormy Atlantic: 'It gave me cold shudders to see them trying to land-on with the *Ark* pitching and rolling like mad.'[21] Several months later, with his fighting force making top knots in its bid to place itself across *Bismarck*'s path, Somerville was again contemplating the risks he would be asking his brave young aviators to take. As the Force H ships headed out into the Atlantic, he also nursed bitter grief over the loss of his nephew, killed just over two weeks earlier, when his Fulmar was lost defending Force H from an Italian torpedo-bomber attack. And Somerville took the loss of *Hood* personally, too, for he had known her ship's company well during her time as Force H flagship. Like so many others in the Royal Navy, Somerville vowed to avenge *Hood*. It was not going to be an easy task, for, as 25 May wore on, Force H was driving into the teeth of heavy Atlantic gale – wind force 7.

Chapter 14

Steering to Intercept Enemy

In the immediate aftermath of *Hood*'s sinking Captain Frederick Dalrymple-Hamilton recognized that HMS *Rodney* – old, slow and desperately in need of the refit she was due to start in Boston at the end of May – might well be required to do her bit in the pursuit and destruction of *Bismarck*. The Commanding Officer of the sixteen-year-old battleship decided to put together a war cabinet of sorts, which was dubbed the Operations Committee. It combined the best tactical brains aboard ship, in order to help Dalrymple-Hamilton make what he considered could be decisions of crucial importance to Britain. Among its members were *Rodney*'s navigator, Lieutenant Commander George Gatacre, her executive officer, Commander John Grindle, and the torpedo officer, Lieutenant Commander Roger Lewis. Two of its members did not belong to the ship's company, being among the 512 supernumeraries taking passage to Canada and the USA in the battleship.[1] Captain Cuthbert Coppinger was the newly appointed commanding officer of the superdreadnought *Malaya*, undergoing repairs at New York Navy Yard, while Lieutenant Commander Joseph Wellings was an Assistant Naval Attaché from the US Embassy in London. In July 1940 Wellings had been expecting to join the destroyer USS *Hopkins* in Hawaii but was instead sent to the United Kingdom, where he witnessed the Battle of Britain unfold overhead and bombing raids on London, also clocking up sea time in a number of British naval vessels including the destroyer *Eskimo*, battlecruiser *Hood*, and cruisers *Birmingham* and *Curacoa*. Tasked with conveying secret documents to Washington DC, Wellings was finally going home to be reunited with his wife and young daughter. On New Year's Day, he had joined shipmates in *Hood* for a toast to victory and peace in 1941. Now a good many of them were dead. Wellings would be a key player in *Rodney*'s Operations Committee, working closely with Lieutenant Commander Gatacre, who was actually on attachment from the Royal Australian Navy.

Formidably armed – carrying nine 16-inch guns, the heaviest fitted to any British capital ship of the Second World War era, and with a dozen 6-inch guns as secondary armament – *Rodney* was 40,000 tons fully loaded and very heavily protected. Should *Bismarck* confront *Rodney*, in terms of armament and protection she would find the British ship very hard to beat. However, *Rodney*'s top speed of 23 knots (at a push) was some six knots slower than *Bismarck*'s. It was unlikely she could catch *Bismarck* in a chase. If the German ship chose to stand off at long range, in order to bombard *Rodney* with plunging fire, then the latter would be unable to close the range to get within the so-called immune zone. Such salient facts were very much in the forefront of Captain Dalrymple-Hamilton's mind as he discussed options with his Operations Committee. Many hundreds of miles to the north, in *King George V*, Admiral Tovey, a former captain of *Rodney*, was well aware of her strengths (a tough, hard-hitter) and weaknesses (old and slow). He recognized that while *King George V* was faster, newer, and well protected, her 14-inch guns did not offer the same certainty of devastation as *Rodney*'s. A combination of the two ships would be the most effective means to wipe out *Bismarck*. Turning his attention to how best to make a rendezvous with Dalrymple-Hamilton's ship, whose exact location he did not know thanks to radio silence, Tovey was mindful that, with *Rodney* so far south, the only way a meeting could happen, if at all, would be if *Bismarck* was still heading south-east.

Tovey would have been aware that *Rodney* was due to depart Greenock on 22 May, destined to accompany the troop ship *Britannic* across the Atlantic, with four Tribal Class destroyers – *Eskimo*, *Tartar*, *Somali* and *Mashona* – in escort. They soon hit heavy weather and this took its toll on the destroyers, forcing *Rodney* to reduce speed as signals traffic revealed dramatic events in the Denmark Strait. Always aware that at any moment he might be required to assist, Dalrymple-Hamilton as yet saw no reason to divest himself of the encumbrance of *Britannic*, for the course his group of ships was pursuing would place *Rodney* perfectly if *Bismarck* broke out and headed south. But then again, Dalrymple-Hamilton reasoned that it was all a case of 'what if', for surely other ships further north would take care of business? He must have wondered if his son, Midshipman North Dalrymple-Hamilton, serving in *King George V*, would soon be seeing action. When the signal came through early in the morning of 24 May that a British capital ship had been destroyed, Dalrymple-Hamilton was no doubt gripped with high anxiety for his boy. While relieved it was not *King George V*, the revelation that *Hood* had been annihilated would have filled him with resolve to stop *Bismarck* if the opportunity presented itself. At 10.22 am on 24 May, *Rodney* received a signal from the Admiralty providing the enemy's last reported position and speed, ordering: 'Steer best closing course.'

Four minutes later, the Admiralty signalled *Rodney*: 'If *BRITTANIC* [sic] can't keep up let her proceed alone with one destroyer.'[2] Therefore at noon, around 500 miles north-west of Ireland, *Britannic* was left behind with *Eskimo* as her escort. At 2.28 pm, as she headed west, hopefully placing herself on

Bismarck's anticipated course, *Rodney* signalled the remaining trio of accompanying destroyers: 'Am steering so as to intercept enemy ...'

With *Suffolk* sending regular shadowing reports, it seemed to *Rodney* and her escorts that they were likely to be in battle sooner rather than later. Everyone in the battleship was 'getting excited about possibility of making contact'.[3] and at 7.01 pm the destroyer flotilla commander, Captain Clifford Caslon, sent a visual signal to *Rodney*: 'Please confirm that as soon as enemy is contacted DDs [destroyers] are free to attain position for attack.' *Rodney* flashed back: 'Yes – confirmed.'[4]

Rodney picked up a signal from *Suffolk*, sent at 4.01 am on 25 May, confirming she had lost radar contact with *Bismarck*, and Dalrymple-Hamilton immediately convened a meeting of the Operations Committee. It was decided *Rodney* should attempt to stay where she was, well placed to prevent *Bismarck* reaching Brest.

The battleship's second gunnery officer, Lieutenant Peter Wells-Cole recalled of this phase: 'We just plodded along, hoping we could catch her.' It was of the utmost importance the battleship maintained radio silence, in order not give away her perfect interception position, but on the other hand it was essential Tovey knew where his most powerfully armed unit was. When he read in an intercepted signal that *Repulse* had been sent off to refuel at Newfoundland, Dalrymple-Hamilton correctly deduced Tovey would be even more anxious to link up with *Rodney*, so at 9.00 am he decided to let the Home Fleet boss know where he was. As well as transmitting his ship's position, Dalrymple-Hamilton suggested he could loiter with the intention of intercepting *Bismarck* if, and when, she tried to go south-east in a bid to reach safety. He also informed Tovey he had three destroyers with him and visibility was ten miles. It was Dalrymple-Hamilton's only wireless transmission of the entire pursuit, but it was perfectly timed, confirming for Tovey he had the firepower needed to defeat *Bismarck* decisively – God and fuel willing. It was all a huge gamble, but in the best traditions of the Royal Navy calm professionalism reigned. Polish Sub Lieutenant Eryk Sopocko was taking the mid-morning watch on *Rodney*'s bridge on 25 May, where he saw 'the captain was talking in quiet tones to the navigator. I could hear the measured tick of the electric log, occasionally the patter of bare feet[5] as a messenger ran with an order. Someone near sighed tiredly. At times rain rattled on the bridge screen; at times one heard the whine of the wind as it swept over us in gusts.'[6] Lieutenant Commander Gatacre and Lieutenant Commander Wellings analysed Admiralty signals traffic and composed a summary to assist Captain Dalrymple-Hamilton in making a decision on what *Rodney* should do next. It was likely *Bismarck* was damaged, something given away by her oil trail and reduced speed; the single hit by a torpedo during the *Victorious* strike may have made the German battleship's condition even more precarious; an attempt to return home via the northern route could be tricky, as RN forces would now be lying in wait. Such a course would take *Bismarck* within range of British bombers. Both Brest and St Nazaire could handle major repairs on capital ships, and *Gneisenau* and *Scharnhorst* would soon vacate the dry docks at Brest. The Luftwaffe and German U-boats could combine, once the *Bismarck* was within 400 miles of the French coast, to provide very effective protection.[7] Wellings and Gatacre also said they believed Brest was more likely than St Nazaire, as it was an easier port to get into, by virtue of its wide, well-protected bay. Now it was Dalrymple-Hamilton's turn to carefully weigh up the options. He asked a few questions to clarify his thoughts. He decided *Rodney* should head north, to place herself better for a rendezvous with the Home Fleet while retaining the possibility of blocking *Bismarck*'s run to the French Atlantic ports.

At 10.47 am on 25 May Admiral Tovey ordered all ships to search north of *Bismarck*'s last confirmed position, for a serious error had been made in *King George V*, with the German battleship's position plotted wrongly.

Admiral Lütjens did not believe he had managed to shake the British off, so had made long wireless signals to the German naval headquarters in France, which were picked up by intercept stations in Britain. In the Admiralty they plotted *Bismarck*'s estimated position and it appeared the German battleship was heading south-east. It was suggested *Bismarck*'s plotted location should be transmitted to *King George V*. However, before sailing from Scapa Admiral Tovey had instructed that raw data only should be sent, as he would have destroyers with him equipped with radio direction-finding equipment and they could use it to try and achieve a precise triangulation. However, the destroyers were no longer with *King George V* and when the intercept data was applied to a chart in the British flagship an error was made, seeming to indicate the German battleship was heading north.[8] *Rodney* had plotted the same land station intercepts, but came to the conclusion *Bismarck* was heading towards Brest. *Rodney*'s Operations Committee was astonished to read the general signal instructing British warships to 'search accordingly' to the north, when they reckoned *Bismarck* was actually sixty miles south of where Tovey stated she was. Dalrymple-Hamilton could not imagine the order applied to his ship – if *Bismarck* really was going back to Germany via the northern route, then *Rodney* was too far south and too slow to be of any use. The Operations Committee agreed it was best for *Rodney* to remain where she was, just in case Tovey was wrong. Captain Dalrymple-Hamilton predicted the Admiralty would soon correct Tovey's instructions. At 11.58 am, a signal was sent by the Admiralty, telling *Rodney* it was probable *Bismarck* was heading for Brest or St Nazaire. At that moment she was positioned just 100 miles south of the most likely direct course *Bismarck* would take.

In *King George V*, Admiral Tovey read intercepts of Admiralty signals to *Rodney*, and found they fed a sense of unease. He began to suspect the

Admiralty was taking a different view of *Bismarck*'s course and so sent an irritated signal asking why nobody had thought to share their doubts with him. Tovey wanted to know if Admiralty analysts thought *Bismarck* was heading south, rather than escaping back to Germany on the northern route. However, on balance, once he had calmed down, Tovey decided the signal to *Rodney* was merely a precautionary move by the Admiralty to cover all options. However, in *Rodney*, the Operations Committee was reading a decoded signal sent at midday to shore bases including Plymouth and Portsmouth, which said: 'The Admiralty believes the *Bismarck* is headed for Brest.'[9]

With her propellers pushing their ship through the sea at 21 knots, *Rodney*'s men fully expected to see *Bismarck* cresting over the horizon at any moment. When this looked less likely, the 16-inch gun crews, who had been closed up just in case, were allowed to relax. The Admiralty signalled new instructions to *Rodney*. She was no longer to head for Biscay and should instead steer north-east. *Rodney* had, however, already altered course away from Brest, sailing south towards Cape Finisterre, to place herself across the route to both French and Spanish ports. The majority of the British fleet had been heading in the wrong direction for nearly four hours and now the Admiralty could not make up its mind where *Bismarck* was headed. Having not encountered *Bismarck* by 4.20 pm, Captain Dalrymple-Hamilton went into a huddle with the navigator and executive officer. They decided to now comply with the Admiralty's orders and sail north-east at speed. It was later reckoned *Rodney* missed *Bismarck* by only twenty-five miles. At that range the German vessel would anyway have been below the horizon.

Lt Commander Lewis later reflected: 'If we had sighted her... we would have had a private action between the *Rodney* and *Bismarck*, so we did think about what would happen and we were very dubious of the result.' With *Bismarck*'s speed so much superior to *Rodney*'s, he thought, 'she could out manoeuvre us and complete the whole engagement at maximum range until she'd hit us. I think, in point of fact, we wouldn't have sunk her, we'd possibly have been damaged a bit ourselves and lost the chase.' Instead, for gunners in the 16-inch and 6-inch turrets there was the usual boredom of being closed up with nothing to do, except maybe read a book or play cards. At 6.05 pm the Admiralty sent a signal to *Rodney*: 'Proceed on the assumption that the enemy's destination is a French port.' By 6.10 pm on 25 May, Admiral Tovey had decided, on the balance of all available information, *Bismarck* was probably heading south-east after all and turned *King George V* around, with instructions issued for other ships to do the same. At 7.15 pm Tovey finally received confirmation from the Admiralty that it was felt *Bismarck* had to be heading for the French Atlantic ports. A signal advised: 'BISMARCK is heading for a port on the West Coast of France.' Until that evening the Admiralty had believed *Bismarck* could also possibly be heading north, but its judgement had now 'hardened'[10] in favour of the German battleship heading for France. *Rodney* was, meanwhile, still carrying out her lonely search and Dalrymple-Hamilton, having not sighted *Bismarck* by 9 pm, ordered his ship around to head south-east, directly towards Brest, at a speed of 21 knots. At 11 pm, as dusk finally fell, *Rodney*'s men were again relaxed from action stations. Sub Lieutenant Sopocko had earlier managed to get his head down, in the 16-inch shell room below X turret. He found he slept there, head nestled on a folded coat, better than anywhere else in the ship. The idea of sleeping at action stations surrounded by so much explosive, which had bothered him when he first joined *Rodney* two months earlier, no longer troubled the young Pole.

Now, like hundreds of other *Rodney* sailors and marines, Sopocko was able to return to his proper resting place, in his case a hammock slung on the poop deck. However, everyone was ordered to sleep in their clothes, for the call to action stations would come at dawn. They must close up with speed, just in case *Bismarck* loomed out of the rising sun.

At Chequers, the British war leader remained a twisted knot of anger and anxiety even though he might try to put a brave face on it for his guests. But nobody could fail to notice the obvious signs of Churchill's agitated and depressed condition throughout the weekend. There was his vigil over a huge map of the North Atlantic, on which were marked last known positions of *Bismarck* and her pursuers; his wet cheeks on the morning of *Hood*'s loss; fury at his son-in-law Vic Oliver for playing Beethoven's funereal 'Appassionata' on the piano, which provoked him to thunder: 'Stop it! I want no "Dead March", I tell you.'[11]

Then there was his neglect of paperwork and his hangdog expression. During dinner on 25 May his dismay over events led Churchill to declare melodramatically that he would resign as Prime Minister to take direct command in the Middle East. With a flash of black humour he added that he would even renounce cigars and alcohol if it won him the prize of showing how the war could be better managed in the eastern Mediterranean. No such dinner table hubris was noted when it came to the *Bismarck* situation. While Churchill may have seen combat as a young cavalryman in the Sudan, briefly led a battalion in the trenches on the Western Front during the First World War, was First Lord of the Admiralty twice, he had never commanded a warship in peace or war, never mind a fleet. That was a task which even a man as naval-minded as him surely realized contained mysteries of judgement best left to the professionals of the Senior Service, which is possibly why he reserved his greatest ire for its leaders.

Out there, in the vast ocean, they contended with the vagaries of weather, time, distance, never mind the logistics of applying firepower to a moving target, often at huge distances, and inspiring men to risk their lives in battle. In naval warfare, ultimately the loneliness of command belonged to the ship captains and admirals alone. For Captain Dalrymple-Hamilton, the need to use utmost care in positioning *Rodney*, may have brought to mind another fraught pursuit some one hundred and thirty-six years earlier. In the summer of 1805 the exact position of a Franco-Spanish fleet had been lost for several weeks, until Vice-Admiral Robert Calder, thanks to judicious direction from their Lords of the Admiralty, found his fleet in a similar location to that of *Rodney* in 1941. Calder initiated an action that failed to defeat the enemy ships decisively and saw them escape to the protection of Spanish ports. While Calder did manage to prevent the enemy fleet from joining forces with French warships in the Channel, Nelson, arriving too late to take part in the action, was extremely frustrated to find a truly devastating blow had not been inflicted. It would take the Battle of Trafalgar finally to destroy the Franco-Spanish Combined Fleet, which Nelson had chased to and from the Caribbean prior to Calder's action. Bearing in mind Churchill's love-hate relationship with the Royal Navy's top brass, *Rodney*'s Dalrymple-Hamilton was possibly anxious not to find himself in the same position as Calder, who was later court-martialled for his hesitant brush with the enemy.[12] In 1941, of course, there was a steady stream of signals flying out from the Admiralty to British warships, but initiative was still a key quality. With more firepower in his single steel battleship than in an entire wooden-wall battle fleet of the type commanded by Nelson, Dalrymple-Hamilton's opportunity for action, or a missed chance to safeguard the nation, was just as great as Calder's. Fortunately, as she was a steam-driven battleship, *Rodney* was not at the mercy of the wind and could, at any time she chose, head in any direction, in order to achieve an interception. Through the ability to send signals over hundreds of miles, rather than just line of vision using flags and rockets, Dalrymple-Hamilton had been able to let the latter day equivalent of Nelson – John Tovey – know approximately where he was, hopefully enabling a decisive concentration of firepower denied to the Royal Navy in the summer of 1805. And, due to the use of airpower (something else unavailable to Nelson and Calder) the British at least stood a chance of sighting *Bismarck* beyond ship's visual range, and even halting her progress.

Hundreds of miles away, in leafy Buckinghamshire, there was a post-dinner film show at Chequers, including the Prime Minister's favourite, an instalment of *Time Life*'s *March of Time*, a mix of stills, news footage and re-enactments depicting milestones of world events. As a man who had already made his mark on history, Churchill possibly revelled in seeing events he had helped to shape. His anxiety over the situation in the Atlantic might also have prompted him to worry about how future instalments of 'March of Time' might portray that weekend's events. As a welcome distraction from such thoughts, the Chequers film show also included a recently released cowboy movie, *Western Union*, starring Robert Young and Randolph Scott, directed by Fritz Lang, the German-Austrian director who had quit the Third Reich in the mid-1930s.

The Prime Minister had woken up on 25 May anticipating a battle between the Home Fleet and *Bismarck* that morning, allowing the stain of *Hood*'s loss to be wiped away and giving him good news of some kind to announce to MPs. In the early hours of 26 May he concluded: 'The day which had begun so full of promise ended in disappointment and frustration.'[13] Churchill finally went to bed at 2.15 am, making a parting comment to his guests about the weekend's place in history: 'These three days have been the worst yet.'[14]

However, he was taking to bed some glimmer of hope, for he had been briefed by the Admiralty that *Ark Royal* and Force H, together with *Rodney*, stood a good chance of catching *Bismarck* before she could reach the safety of a French port. That required the German battleship to be found again. Another long day of uncertainty lay ahead for Churchill and the Royal Navy.

Chapter 15

Remorseless Determination

Edward Palmer, who served in *Rodney* as a junior rating during the late 1930s, but was now signals officer of HMS *Deptford* on convoy escort duty, saw the all too familiar silhouette of his old ship looming over the horizon. Having monitored signals traffic, Palmer was aware the *Bismarck* chase was well underway and his ship – at 1,500 tons displacement a midget compared to such a giant – had been exercising proper caution. *Rodney* was not exactly delighted to encounter the Devonport-built Grimsby Class sloop. 'We knew the *Bismarck* was somewhere not too far away and she passed ahead of our convoy in the dark in the early hours of the morning,' recalled Palmer. 'A few hours later I saw the *Rodney* pass ahead. She'd be about three miles ahead in the mist and I did nothing about it. *Rodney* then discovered that there was a convoy close on their starboard side and made me a furious signal demanding to know why I hadn't challenged...I said: "I think discretion is the better part of valour." My ship had two 4.7-inch guns, *Rodney* had nine 16-inch guns and twelve 6-inch guns, the *Bismarck* had eight huge guns and even more 5.9-inch guns, so challenging them would have been suicidal.'[1]

Hundreds of miles to the south of HMS *Deptford*, the cruiser *Dorsetshire* was filled with 'remorseless determination to get revenge'[2] for *Hood*. Bert Gollop, one of her junior ratings described the feeling aboard: 'We had just left Cape Town and the ship was escorting a large convoy with the back-up of an armed merchant ship. Soon after we heard the news of HMS *Hood* and we were all devastated, could not believe it.'

Signals were scrutinized intently as they flashed back and forth between the Admiralty and other vessels actively involved in the pursuit of *Bismarck*. Calculations were made, even though contact with the German battleship had been lost. The cruiser's command team pondered which direction *Bismarck* might be heading – possibly south towards Brest and therefore within reach of *Dorsetshire*? Nobody was keener for the fight than the cruiser's commanding Officer, Captain Benjamin 'Pincher' Martin who had risen from the lower deck, having joined the Royal Navy as a teenage boy seaman in 1907.

In Nelson's time lower-deckers were encouraged to become officers if they had the talent, but in the Victorian era the Royal Navy became less meritocratic. However, from 1912, ordinary sailors were again able to gain commissions, Martin becoming only the second lower-decker to reach the rank of Captain since then. On his way up the ladder, he had served as a Warrant Officer in the super dreadnought *Malaya* at Jutland, receiving his commission in the immediate aftermath of the battle.[3] Martin was regarded by sailors who served under him in *Dorsetshire* as 'this sod of a captain' but one whom they 'rated so highly'.[4] Tough task master though he might be, Martin was a consummate seaman, a true fighting captain, always careful to do what was right by his ship's company – never risking their lives unnecessarily – and also what was best for the Navy and the nation. Martin approached each task ready for action, going at things with vigour, ready to hit the enemy hard. On 6 May, *Dorsetshire* had rescued thirty-five survivors from a merchant ship named *Oakdene*, adrift aboard two lifeboats in the south Atlantic. The cruiser approached them at speed, her guns, torpedoes and depth charges ready to fire, having spotted what she thought was a U-boat nearby. It did not come to a fight, however, as no enemy submarine was found. The *Dorsetshire* offloaded the *Oakdene* survivors at Freetown in Sierra Leone before departing on 11 May as escort to UK-bound convoy SL74, alongside the Armed Merchant Cruiser *Bulolo*. Convoys sailed at the speed of the slowest ship, which in this case was around seven knots, painfully turgid going for *Dorsetshire*. The current tasking was particularly aggravating, especially in light of the heavy traffic between the cruiser's wireless room, where general signals were intercepted, and the cipher office where they were decoded. The ambitious Captain Martin devoured the transcripts, looking for his chance to get involved in finding and killing *Bismarck*.

Meanwhile, Vian, another supremely aggressive captain, was instructed in the early hours of 26 May to leave his convoy and take his four destroyers, plus *Piorun*, to join *King George V* as escort, for Tovey's own had withdrawn to refuel. Convoy WS8B was left in the care of the cruisers *Exeter* and *Cairo* supported by Canadian destroyers *Restigouche* and *Ottawa*. Unknown to *Exeter*, or anyone else at the time, shortly after Vian's ships departed, she cut across *Bismarck's* intended course, the German battleship being about 100 miles to the northwest at the time. William E Johns, one of *Exeter's* senior ratings, later observed of this moment that it was 'no great distance at sea', adding, 'our convoy would have been in danger had the German warship altered course to starboard.'[5] At 10.35 am, a Catalina flying boat of the RAF signalled the position of a mystery battleship, 700 miles west-northwest of Brest and heading south-east. *Rodney* assessed it was *Bismarck*, some 110 miles to her south-west. Contact had been re-established after a gap of thirty-one hours, and *King George V* was 135 miles to the north of the German battleship. *Exeter* read the signals, her men gripped by a sense of growing anticipation, but due to her vital task of escorting WS8B, she was not called into the fight. William E Johns noted with a tinge of disappointment: 'Now every ship within a thousand miles seemed routed to the kill – everyone, that is, except *Exeter*, who steamed along with her convoy of troops, ironically, as charts later showed the nearest warship to *Bismarck* ...'

.   In *Cossack*, also monitoring signals traffic, Vian noted *Bismarck*'s speed, course and position, and decided she was heading for a port in the Bay of Biscay. *Rodney* was already heading south-east towards Brest, so continued on the same course. Tovey was, meanwhile, concerned the Catalina had spotted *Rodney* rather than *Bismarck*, so signalled the Admiralty at 10.51 am: 'Request a check that contact was not *RODNEY*.' Confirmation duly came and so it seemed the chase was entering its final phase, the German ship appearing to be headed for Cape Finisterre – still well-placed for both French and Spanish ports. *Bismarck* was now fixed firmly in the sights of converging British warships.

At 11.00 am, *Dorsetshire* intercepted the sighting report, the cruiser and her convoy being around 600 miles to the west of Cape Finisterre. *Bismarck* was just 300 miles due north, Captain Martin calculating he had a good chance of finding her if she was headed for Brest. He judged the best thing he could do was follow Nelson's instruction to his sailors before the Battle of Trafalgar: 'In case Signals can neither be seen or perfectly understood, no captain can do very wrong if he places his Ship alongside that of an enemy.' For the lower deck sailors of *Dorsetshire*, not privy to their captain's decision, the increase in speed suggested an urgent mission but, bearing in mind their relaxed alert state, also that action was not imminent. *Dorsetshire* gratefully departed the slow work of convoy escort, leaving the merchant ships in the care of *Bulolo*. Heavy weather was soon encountered: 'Giant waves rolled over the bows of the ship, driven on by a howling wind. The cruiser plunged one minute into a deep trough and the next being swept up a sheer wall of water to reach the crest of yet another wave. Like a dog shaking off water she rid herself of the glistening spray before ploughing her way down and onwards.'[6] Ordinary life was made impossible by the ship's constantly rolling and pitching. Some of the junior ratings grumbled that Martin's ambition for promotion was getting them involved in business far away that perhaps they were better staying out of. For the galley crew feeding the sailors and marines, preparing meals was a gymnastic effort, a battle against the violent movement of the ship they did not always win. Injury was a distinct possibility: 'Below decks it was like riding a roller-coaster, but without the screams of delight...At meal times the 'cooks' of the mess had great difficulty getting from the galley to the mess-deck.[7] It was not easy to hold a hot tin dish with two hands and find another limb to grasp a fixture when the ship rolled.'[8]

One sailor sent from his mess to fetch an evening dinner tray piled high with tripe and onions came to grief after trying in vain to steady himself at the top of a 'steep sloping ladder'. Disaster struck: 'Putting his leg over the hatch coaming he waited for the opportune moment to start his descent. Suddenly the ship lurched, and contrary to the sailor's estimates, he slithered down the steel steps, upending the tray of white concoction over himself and the mess space.' Sickbay was his final destination, with an injured back. Captain Martin came on the public address system and explained the reason for such haste, which was not much consolation for the injured man. 'No words of patriotic zeal could console him, fighting the *Bismarck* did not feature on his list of priorities. He put the blame for his misfortune squarely on the shoulders of the captain for speeding in such foul weather.'[9] Many of the listening sailors may have been eager to avenge the *Hood*, but they also feared the outcome of a contest with *Bismarck*. They admired Captain Martin's aggression, but it was also their main cause of anxiety. 'They knew that if the occasion arose "Pincher" Martin would point his ship at the enemy battleship ... and engage no matter what the consequences might be.'[10] Vibrations under foot became stronger, the whole ship shaking and rattling from stem to stern as she plunged ahead at 29 knots. The usual preparations for action took place. Her boats were swung in. Ornaments, pictures, anything fragile and precious that might be shattered and smashed – due to the firing of her own guns, impact of enemy shells or violent manoeuvring – were removed and stowed away. Then, the call for Action stations blared throughout *Dorsetshire*. Far below decks the men went to their positions in the cordite magazines and shell handling rooms. The guns were manned and checked to make sure they were in full fighting order. The ship battered on through the storm, spray leaping up either side of bows 'into a wind howling and roaring ...'[11] The turrets trained, water cascading off the guns, aiming at a smudgy silhouette just visible rising and falling on mountainous seas. It turned out to be a small Portuguese merchant ship that very quickly gave her identity, semaphore light winking from her bridge, lest she be blown out of the water by the British warship that lunged out of the murk. *Dorsetshire* stormed by, not slackening her speed for a second, while the ship's chaplain, the Rev. EBD Laborde, found his service well attended and the ship's sailors never more fervent in prayer.

During the mistaken chase north, *Prince of Wales* had turned around to search for *Bismarck* and by the time the error had been discovered was too far away to be of any use, particularly in her battered condition. Also short of fuel, she was instructed to head for Iceland, land casualties for treatment, effect temporary repairs and then proceed to Rosyth Dockyard. On the way to Iceland, *Prince of Wales* buried her dead in rough seas, the ceremony taking place off the aptly named Cape Farewell, southern Greenland, 'in a howling, freezing gale'.[12] Thirteen corpses were wrapped in canvas and laid out in a single row on the quarterdeck, the chaplain delivering a service no one could hear because the wind whipped his words away. The dead slid one by one over the side into heaving seas. There were no tears on the faces of the living; they were not only numb from the bitter cold weather, but also from the shock of a baptism of fire in which the 'Mighty *Hood*' had exploded, snuffing out the lives of more than 1,000 fellow sailors. After taking on fuel at Iceland, *Electra* was sent out to escort *Prince of Wales* into harbour, the destroyer's men thinking the battleship looked rather sorry for herself, with damage plainly visible. There were no cheerful greetings between ships during what Lieutenant Cain described as 'a miserable meeting'.[13] Nobody at that point fully appreciated how decisive *Prince of Wales'* hits had really been.

That day on the south coast of England, in the pleasant cathedral city of Chichester, heartbreak was delivered to Mrs Sarah Henshaw of 6 Shop Wyke Road, in the form of a telegram from the Commodore of the Naval Barracks at Portsmouth.

REGRET TO REPORT THAT YOUR SON OWEN W HENSHAW STOKER FIRST CLASS P/KX 96061 IS MISSING PRESUMED KILLED ON WAR SERVICE.[14]

Henshaw was in *Hood*, and of course the telegram bearing the news of his demise was just one of 1,415 being sent out. It was soon joined by a letter from Buckingham Palace conveying the King and Queen's condolences, assuring Mrs Henshaw of their 'heartfelt sympathy in your great sorrow'.[15]

Yorkshire schoolchildren who had been pen pals of men serving in *Hood* no doubt prayed that by some miracle their sailor or marine had somehow survived the great calamity broadcast on the radio and splashed across the newspapers.

The only three survivors of that disaster were by then at sea in a transport ship named the *Royal Ulsterman*, travelling incognito back to the UK under special orders not to reveal they were *Hood* sailors. It was important an early debriefing of the only men left from her ship's company preceded the inquiry into the loss of the battlecruiser.*

In the Home Counties, the Prime Minister's motorcade departed Chequers shortly after noon, headed for the seat of power in London, where a Cabinet meeting was held, described by one participant as 'very gloomy and unpleasant'.[16] News that *Bismarck* had been found by an RAF Catalina flying boat took the edge off the all-pervading dark anxiety. Anthony Eden, who was Foreign Secretary and one of Churchill's closest advisers, tried to buck him up with a cheery note, which said that while 26 May had been a bad one, he was sure *Bismarck* would be sunk the following day.[17] However, the question of fuel was elbowing itself to the forefront of Churchill's hopes that *Hood* might yet be avenged, for the Royal Navy's ships had now been steaming hard for four days and he realized they might soon have to give up due to lack of oil. The faster they went after the Nazi battleship, the swifter their oil reserves dwindled. However, if they slowed down, *Bismarck* would get away.

The fuel issue would soon vex Captain Dalrymple-Hamilton more than anything else. He fully expected *Rodney* to join *King George V* within hours, sending *Mashona* off to search for her in the west, with orders to pass on *Rodney*'s position, again using visual signals to avoid giving the Germans any inkling, via their own wireless intercepts, of how close the British actually were. *Rodney*'s gunners climbed through hatches in the tops of their respective turrets and down on to the forecastle, where they enjoyed some fresh air and a cigarette. X turret's Sub Lieutenant Sopocko found the weather was trying to cheer up: 'The wind had gone down a little and the sun came in occasional glimpses through the clouds. The waves are still high.' A rumbling stomach reminded him it was some time since he had eaten, but fortunately when he returned to the turret he found someone had been down to the galley and fetched kettles of steaming hot soup and chunky corned beef sandwiches. At 2.40 pm, the cruiser *Edinburgh*, which had left her convoy far behind to join the hunt for *Bismarck*, sent a visual signal to *Rodney* asking if she had sighted *King George V*. *Rodney* responded that she had not and asked another of her escorting destroyers, *Tartar*, by signal lamp if she had. The response was negative. The destroyers were now dangerously low on fuel and Dalrymple-Hamilton, as senior officer on the scene, thought he might order them to detach at 5.00 pm and head for Plymouth. However, this depended on the Polish destroyer *Piorun*, with Vian's squadron, arriving to take over screening duties. Vian's other destroyers – *Cossack*, *Sikh*, *Maori* and *Zulu* – were supposed to provide protection for the fleet flagship. There was concern U-boats might be gathering to protect *Bismarck,* and British battleships would be too vulnerable without such protection. With *Piorun* still not present, *Rodney* could not really dispense with her existing destroyer protection, for the battleship's fuel state was critical – especially as she needed enough in reserve to fight *Bismarck* – and ruled out evasive action to counter U-boats. The escort commander was informed by Aldis lamp that *Rodney* 'cannot afford to zigzag'[18]. It was a standard tactic to make life more difficult for enemy submarines attempting to target a surface warship. That afternoon a Luftwaffe Focke-Wulf Condor scouting aircraft managed to spot *Rodney* and her three destroyers, provoking a storm of fire from British ships, but the Germans got away unharmed. According to *Rodney*'s Midshipman GR Shaw, this was partly because 'shooting was pretty bad'.[19]

It was realized *Bismarck* would be advised of Royal Navy units hot on her heels. A signal was duly sent by German naval headquarters that afternoon, with the morale-boosting claim that the British battleship and her escorts were 200 miles behind. Although they feared her 16-inch guns, the German battleship's command team knew *Rodney*'s slow top speed meant *Bismarck* would be able to make France, provided their luck held. Shortly after 3.00 pm, *Rodney* was sighted by lookouts in *King George V*, ahead on the port bow. They were slow off the mark, for some twenty-four minutes earlier *Rodney*'s sailors had spotted Tovey's flagship, fifteen miles distant, in the west. Tovey was keen for his old ship to join him for the kill, but was also aware she was seven knots slower than *King George V.* He sent a visual signal to *Rodney* at 3.19 pm: 'Good luck, you may be there in time yet.' *Rodney* flashed back: 'Very much thanks. We are doing our best and much want to be with you.'[20] However, as the British ships tried desperately to bring their quarry to heel, the long, painful pursuit descended into farce, with an episode of mistaken identity that so nearly heaped yet more blood-soaked humiliation on the British navy.

Chapter 16

Sorry for the Kipper

As soon as the Catalina sighting report came in, action stations were sounded off in the Force H ships, which altered course to 'intercept and shadow the enemy'.[1] Even prior to contact being renewed with *Bismarck*, preparations to fly Swordfish off on reconnaissance missions to find, fix and hold the German ship's position had been initiated. The decision was made to hold back Vernon Graves, the senior observer of 818 NAS, so that, once *Bismarck* was located by the *Ark*'s aircraft, his high level of skill with the radio could be brought into play. Graves would be in a follow-on Swordfish that was launched to take over the shadowing job. Graves' special assignment meant a vacancy in a Swordfish flown by the commanding officer of 818 NAS, Lieutenant Commander Tim Coode, who selected Lieutenant Edmund 'Splash' Carver as his replacement observer. Carver's part in the drama was in many ways accidental. He was an old hand in *Ark Royal*, having been an aviator in her Sea Skua fighter squadron until April 1941, when it was disbanded and replaced by Fulmars. Carver was sent back to *Ark Royal*, to crew a Fulmar and lead flights of Hurricane fighters flown off for Malta. After that mission was interrupted and Force H sent to intercept *Bismarck*, Carver found he was a bit of a 'spare number'. Of course he felt perfectly at home, as he knew everybody in the *Ark*'s wardroom, having served with them so recently. Carver was particularly friendly with Coode, frequently playing Liar Dice[2] with him, and so it was the duo took a reconnaissance Swordfish aloft at 8.30 am on 26 May. The wind was blowing hard from the north-west, getting stronger and, as Coode's aircraft approached the end of an outward sweep, its TAG heard a report by another Swordfish, which had sighted *Bismarck*. Coode turned his aircraft around and wound it up to top speed, in the words of Carver 'hurrying back to arm with torpedoes.'[3]

Meanwhile, aboard *Ark Royal* an extra fuel tank was being fitted to another Swordfish in place of its TAG, giving the aircraft a flight endurance of six hours. Crewed by a pilot and Vernon Graves, it took off and headed into the murk to send back radio reports on a regular basis, fixing the *Bismarck*'s position for the final showdown.

Coode and Carver's Swordfish landed at around quarter past noon. Once it had come to a halt and its engine was off, the aircraft's wings were immediately folded back and it was taken down on the lift to be refuelled in the hangar.

It would be held in reserve with other Swordfish while the first strike on *Bismarck* was launched. Fifteen Swordfish were arranged on the flight-deck, fourteen to be launched on the strike and one in reserve. *Ark Royal* was forced to reduce speed to just eight knots, but even then there was still 40 knots of wind, the ship rising and falling 55ft on huge waves. Twenty aircraft handlers were assigned to each Swordfish, their job being to push it into position and await take-off, hanging on to ensure it did not slither into its neighbour.

As they pushed a Swordfish towards the back of the flight-deck it might, literally, be an uphill task, but then, as the ship plunged down again, the aircraft would suddenly roll forward, forcing them to put their shoulders into restraining it. The handlers might also find themselves hanging on for grim death and 'breaking into a canter as the ship topped a swell and the aircraft rolled happily forward.'[4]

Finally, the aircraft were ready and, as with the *Victorious* strike group two days earlier, the attempt to halt *Bismarck* would be led by an aircraft equipped with ASV, in this case a Swordfish in the leading sub-flight. The 810 Naval Air Squadron boss, Lieutenant Commander James Stewart-Moore, a senior observer, would lead the attack, which would be split down into six sub-flights. There were only observers in each of the sub-flight leaders' aircraft, the other crews being reduced to a pilot and a TAG, to save weight and therefore extend fuel range. The Swordfish equipped with ASV was the exception as it carried a sub lieutenant to operate the radar equipment.

At 2.00 pm on 26 May *Sheffield* was ordered by Somerville to steam ahead at top speed to establish contact, one of the cruiser's sailors recording the excitement of the chase. 'You can have no idea of the thrill we got as the ship forged ahead at full speed and left the squadron astern. What we had all been training for ever since we joined the Navy, was at last about to be put to the test of "Action Stations" ...'[5] A £2 reward was promised, to be paid on the spot, to whoever sighted the enemy ship first. The cruiser's speed soon topped 31 knots, despite heavy seas, the heat off *Sheffield*'s funnels so intense their paint blistered. The cruiser's gun crews remained closed up, and with the Luftwaffe expected to appear in force to shepherd *Bismarck* to the safety of a French port, nobody kept a keener eye open for trouble than Midshipman JDL Repard, who was in a gunnery control position on the cruiser's upper deck, helping to co-ordinate air defence weapons. Through very large binoculars, mounted on a robust stand, his attention was drawn to the sight of Swordfish tumbling 'like falling leaves out of the low clouds'.[6] On red alert, *Sheffield*'s air defences were taut and ready but Repard advised them to check their fire for these were obviously friendly aircraft.

An hour after take-off, Stewart-Moore had glanced across from his aircraft to the Swordfish closest in the sub-flight – the one fitted with ASV – and saw Sub Lieutenant Norman Manley-Cooper, charged with operating the equipment, waving to attract his attention. The youngster used semaphore flags[7] to indicate a radar contact around twenty miles to starboard and so the attack group turned in that direction. Having been told during the pre-flight briefing there were no British ships in the attack sector, the aviators were confident they were about to assault the enemy. There was reason to believe the cruiser with *Bismarck* might still be lurking out there, too. Whatever size grey ship appeared out of the murk was fair game, as they believed it had to be the enemy.

Through gaps in the clouds, Stewart-Moore gained glimpses of what was clearly a cruiser and assumed it had to be the Hipper Class ship, most likely, as suspected, still keeping company with *Bismarck*.[8]

The Swordfish dropped out of the clouds, diving to sea level for their attack runs, but Stewart-Moore's pilot, Lieutenant H de G Hunter, yelled down the voice pipe: 'It's the *Sheffield*!'[9] Pulling out of the dive and turning away, Hunter waggled the wings of his Swordfish to indicate to the other pilots something was wrong. Only two got the idea and pulled away from the attack, the rest pressing on to drop their torpedoes.

Aboard *Sheffield*, Midshipman Repard was struck dumb with incredulity. Sailors down in *Sheffield*'s RDF compartment heard somebody exclaim via a voice pipe: 'My God, they're attacking *us*!'[10]

On the bridge Captain Larcom shouted for 'full speed ahead' and ordered that no guns should open fire on the errant aircraft, the cruiser pointing her bows straight at the tinfish in the water. One was successfully evaded, but then three others were spotted splashing into the water on the starboard bow.

A shout from an excited sub lieutenant behind him on the bridge about this did not distract the grim-faced Larcom as he conned the ship to comb the torpedoes.[11] A Swordfish had no sooner dropped a torpedo off the cruiser's starboard bow when, struggling 'slowly at bridge height' across *Sheffield*'s bows, it signalled by Aldis lamp: 'Sorry for the kipper.'[12] This did not soothe Captain Larcom who was 'purple with rage'[13], his anger having been stoked by another Swordfish actually having the cheek to spray the cruiser with machine-gun fire as it flew past. Disparaging comments flew around *Sheffield*'s anti-aircraft gun crews, touching on the theme of 'fly boys who wouldn't recognize their own mothers.'[14] Actually, fortune smiled on the British that day thanks to faulty technology, for a new design of magnetic detonator was fitted to the warheads, which proved rather temperamental, with six out the eleven torpedoes dropped exploding on hitting the sea, *Sheffield* successfully combing all the others.

The Swordfish formed up on Stewart-Moore's aircraft for the flight back to *Ark*, his attention attracted once again to the aircraft with the ASV, in which Midshipman Manley-Cooper was indicating with the semaphore flags that he had picked up another contact, around ten miles away. Three destroyers came into view below, which the aviators at first suspected might be German ships coming out to help escort *Bismarck*, but they flashed a British identification signal. It was Vian's 4th Destroyer Flotilla, battling rough weather in poor visibility as it struggled south. Junior rating Ken Robinson, a loader on *Cossack*'s 2pdr pom-pom anti-aircraft weapon recalled of this encounter that one of the biplanes flew 'practically alongside us as the pilot waved to us before they flew away.'[15] Having checked the destroyers out, the Swordfish turned back towards *Ark Royal*. Stewart-Moore was tapped on the shoulder by his TAG, Petty Officer RH McColl, who handed him a piece of paper, which was headed 'Most Immediate'. The signal advised: 'Look out for *Sheffield*, which is in your vicinity.'

This was bitterly ironic, and Stewart-Moore contemplated sending a rude signal back but dismissed the idea, having considered the following biblical fragment: 'Behold, the half was not told me.'[16] As they approached *Ark*, the Swordfish were instructed to ditch any torpedoes they retained. This obviously applied only to the three aircraft that had not attacked *Sheffield*, so now they dropped their tinfish, ensuring they were well away from any British ships, the torpedoes running until they reached the end of their range and exploded. The young aviators returned to *Ark Royal* shame-faced and there was what one of them described, with true British understatement, as an 'animated' debrief. Resolutions were made about learning lessons from the first, abortive attack. A spectator of the first attack, Alan Swanton, who had counted the Swordfish back from their ill fated mission, observed: 'They say that bad luck runs in three. If HOOD had been one, losing BISMARCK for a day had been two, then this strike was definitely number three.'[17] When he went below decks after landing, Stewart-Moore was greeted with 'profuse apologies' over the failure of the admiral's staff in *Renown* to advise *Ark Royal* that *Sheffield* had been sent ahead into the danger zone. When he went into the debriefing room nobody seemed interested in the tendency of torpedoes fitted with magnetic warheads to explode on hitting the sea. Every effort was being put into planning a follow-on strike that night. Stewart-Moore persisted and, finding the ship's torpedo officer, after a discussion they agreed the mechanism was faulty. Permission was sought to use contact warheads. The advantage in the ship's own magnetic field detonating torpedoes was that they could be set to run under a vessel, with the blast ripping a huge hole in the vulnerable underbelly. The explosive force of contact warheads was diminished, as the charge was set off by the nose of the torpedo hitting the side of the ship, much of it being dissipated in the sea or the air. Stewart-Moore and *Ark*'s torpedo officer reckoned the torpedoes used in the *Sheffield* attack detonated because they had been trying to keep their depth in a very heavy swell. As Stewart-Moore put it, each torpedo had found itself 'steering alternately upwards and downwards, changing its attitude to the earth's magnetic field rapidly and suddenly',[18] a process that fooled the weapon's galvanometer into detonating the warhead.[19] Such sea conditions were not likely to change, so it was best to revert to contact warheads, in spite of their lesser effect. Stewart-Moore's request was presented to *Ark Royal*'s commanding officer, Captain Maund, who decided to contact Admiral Somerville in *Renown*. As a former torpedo specialist, Somerville instantly understood the predicament and gave his assent to using contact warheads.[20]

By 3.51 pm, the main British hunting group was 500 miles to the west of Land's End and another Condor was spotted and fired on by *King George V*'s 5.25-inch guns, without result due to the extreme range. A single aerial intruder was not much for a battleship to worry about, but every mile they steamed towards the south-east brought *King George V* and *Rodney* closer to being within range of land-based enemy bomber squadrons, which were a different prospect altogether. However, it seemed the net was closing on *Bismarck* and, with some luck, her destruction could be achieved before the Luftwaffe had a chance to intervene. All that was needed was for something to slow *Bismarck* up, or 'the chance of bringing him to action would be small'.[21] *King George V* had been managing a constant 25 knots, but at 5.24 pm signalled *Rodney* she had slowed to 22 knots 'to economize'. Eleven minutes later, having considered her own situation, *Rodney* sent back: 'Engine room conditions are quite severe but I do not wish to slow since you may go on and I get left behind.' *Somali*, *Mashona* and *Tartar* hung on, too. There was still no sign of Vian's destroyers.

Sheffield's officer of the watch, Sub Lieutenant Paul McLaughlan, a Canadian, was scanning the horizon with his binoculars when, at 5.40 pm, he detected something with a warlike silhouette on the horizon. McLaughlan declared: 'I think I can see something on the port bow.'[22] And sure enough, there was 'a dim grey shape indistinctly seen through the haze'.[23] Lookouts and officers covering that sector twiddled the knobs of their glasses, trying desperately to bring the shape into sharper relief. Could this really be the fabled *Bismarck*? The *Sheffield* was making quite a few knots and, with the intervening distance disappearing rapidly, any doubts soon disappeared as the German battlewagon's distinctive shape loomed larger. Midshipman Repard ran his glasses along *Bismarck*, which he saw was 'constantly doused in heavy spray' a mere twelve miles ahead. The captain ordered the wheel put hard over to starboard, *Sheffield* turning away, to stay out of range of the enemy's guns and began the process of edging around behind *Bismarck*. One of the cruiser's sailors gazed at the Nazi behemoth, expecting to see her guns blaze at any second: 'She seemed horribly close to us and we all felt that she must have seen us and any moment expected a salvo of 15-inch shells about our ears. However, all was well, and nothing happened as we made our way round the stern of her, keeping about ten to twelve miles away.'[24] Like *Suffolk* and *Norfolk* before her, *Sheffield* began to send out a stream of regular reports on *Bismarck* to the rest of the fleet and the Admiralty. Like those other two cruisers she had to maintain a fine balance between being close enough to maintain contact while not straying too near.

Should *Sheffield* get too close, thought one of her sailors, 'we should undoubtedly lay ourselves open to being sunk or badly damaged.' The nearest friendly ship that might be called on for support was more than fifty miles away and so the cruiser's men found it 'tense work, nobody dared to relax a moment.'[25]

As the Admiralty broadcast that *Sheffield* was shadowing *Bismarck*, sending a surge of anticipation throughout ships scattered across the globe, in the cruiser's A turret one of the gunners, Colin Ross, remarked: 'Every ship in the Navy must be plotting us on their charts now. If we lose him we'll never be able to lift our heads again.'[26]

At 5.58 pm *King George V* sent another visual signal to *Rodney*: 'Very probably will have to return for fuel at midnight. In case torpedo bombers get in another attack it is most important you should be able to continue steaming at not less than 20 knots.'[27] *King George V* having used up sixty-eight per cent of her fuel Dalrymple-Hamilton now informed Tovey that *Rodney* would have to depart the scene at 8 am the following morning, to ensure she could get home with enough in reserve to take evasive action if attacked by German aircraft. Tovey decided that, should *Bismarck* not be caught by midnight, he would turn *King George V* around and head home, although he would still ask *Rodney* to stay a little longer in hope of a decisive engagement. In preparation for a wireless signal to Admiral Somerville, at 6.20 pm *King George V* asked *Rodney* for information on her best speed, the latter replying by visual signal: '22 knots'. Tovey subsequently warned Somerville that *King George V* would be forced to turn for home if the German ship was not slowed down by air attack in the next six hours, but, he added: 'RODNEY will be able to continue chase but without destroyer escort. Recommend you stay with aircraft carrier.' Tovey clearly felt *Rodney* should at least have the advantage of Swordfish strikes from *Ark Royal* to aid her in whatever battle transpired. But it seems even *Rodney* was doubtful, particularly as it was feared the enemy was marshalling wolf packs of submarines as well as hundreds of Luftwaffe bombers; speed would be essential to escape their depredations. There was also much agonizing on leaving battleships to carry on the chase without destroyers, but they did not have the endurance, especially when the battlewagons could not supply fuel – as they might normally do via flexible pipes during replenishment on the move – due to their own dire need for it. The risk seemed acceptable given the circumstances, especially bearing in mind no battleship had yet been sunk at sea by air power, and it was felt likely even *Rodney*'s top speed would provide protection against submarines. *Rodney* at 7.11 pm felt confident enough to send a signal to *King George V*, confirming that she could, after all, hang on until morning: 'RODNEY had 1600 tons of oil on hand at 1800. We use at present speed 23 tons per hour and 19 tons per hour at 20 knots. Clyde and Gibraltar are within my endurance if present course and speed are continued until 0800 tomorrow.'[28]

As he departed the scene at 7.19 pm in *Somali* the commander of *Rodney*'s escorting destroyer, Captain Caslon, sent apologies by visual signal: 'Very sorry to have to leave you at the end of the long chase. I still hope for your triumph.'[29] *Mashona* left *Rodney* soon after, while *Tartar*, with more fuel, was staying longer, still waiting for the *Piorun* to turn up and take over escort duties.

Rodney had by now fallen in astern of the fleet flagship, a familiar and welcome sight to Tovey. Tovey signaled her at 8.28 pm, advising: 'Accurate station keeping not necessary in order to save fuel.' A minute later *Rodney* made a request for the younger battleship to slow down: 'KING GEORGE V's 22 knots is a bit faster than RODNEY's and we are dropping distance.'[30] The reality of the situation had been clear to everyone for some time, for in an earlier exchange of light signals *King George V* had remarked to *Rodney*: 'Our only hope is for BISMARCK to be slowed up by torpedo bombers.'[31]

Chapter 17

Into the Jaws of Death

With the humiliation of their bungled attack a few hours earlier still stinging, every one of *Ark Royal*'s aviators knew they could not leave the Fleet Air Arm to be remembered for letting *Bismarck* get away. The need for their second strike to succeed was unparalleled in naval warfare and the young aviators knew it. They burned with determination not only to avenge *Hood* but also to restore their reputation. It was fortunate they flew the Swordfish, probably the only aircraft that could have pulled itself into the air in such weather conditions.

For the second attempt, seventeen Swordfish were arrayed on the *Ark*'s flight-deck, including two reserves in case mechanical problems prevented any of the fifteen actually selected for the attack from taking off. The strike aircraft were tightly packed in threes, arranged in herringbone pattern, with the foremost trio around 150ft abaft the ship's island. *Ark Royal* was sailing down wind, away from *Bismarck*, in order to make life a little easier for the aircraft handlers to push the Swordfish into place and attach torpedoes.

Ark Royal then turned almost 180 degrees, heeling dramatically as she came beam on to the wind and run of sea, waves hammering her hull, spray leaping up. The ship reduced speed from eighteen knots to ten, as the low take-off speed of the Swordfish combined with the gale gusting across the flight-deck did not require harder steaming. She lifted up high and then pitched violently into troughs, bows buried under an angry sea. Sheets of spray swept across the flight-deck as the aviators made their way to their aircraft, climbing into them at around 7.00 pm. Engines started five minutes later, roaring and sputtering into life; the first aircraft to take off was Swordfish 5A, at ten minutes past seven. Swordfish sitting on the flight-deck centre line rolled straight ahead while the two aircraft either side taxied forward with handlers on their wings turning them. Once on the centre line the pilots gave it maximum throttle, only releasing the brakes on signal from the flight deck officer (FDO), Commander Pat Stringer. Green flag held aloft, buffeted by the gale and only saved from being blown overboard by rock-solid sea legs, he also wore a safety harness on a very long line just in case. The FDO studied the movement of the ship intently, calculating the optimum moment to unleash each Swordfish, Commander Stringer's flag dropping when he judged the bows were digging into the sea. This ensured that by the time a Swordfish arrived at the point of take off, the front of the ship would be rising again. 'Splash' Carver, huddled against the weather in the observer's position behind Tim Coode, later explained the process: 'If arriving there in the "bows-down" phase one might be deluged by a sheet of spray at the "moment critique" and also, of course, it is more satisfactory to appear to be rising into the sky than to be diving towards the ocean.' The sailors on the flight-deck handling the aircraft were by now accustomed, with typical British dogged determination, to the sheer awfulness of a stormy Atlantic. While a number had oilskins, some were protected against the elements merely by blue overalls – but with as many layers as possible underneath. Everybody was bare-headed, except for the FDO and the petty officers assisting him, who had caps clamped to their heads, with chin-straps down to stop them being ripped away. Steaming boots provided some grip, but it was a tricky business standing upright. Should an aircraft handler be taken by a gust of wind he might try to hang on to something, or failing that, pray he was tumbled into the walkway that ran around the edge of the flight-deck, rather than be snatched overboard, never to be seen again.

A terrible death. Warmed by their exertions pushing the Swordfish into place, but still wringing wet, wiping water from their eyes and cheeks stinging from the freezing rain, somehow the handlers persevered. Once brought up, the Swordfish were secured to the deck then, after the engines sputtered into life, untied. However, the wheels were prevented from rolling until the right moment by chocks, two to each one. The 'chockmen' had the unenviable task of lying on the flight-deck, a tide of water washing over them, raw hands frozen. At a signal they took away each forward chock, then, as the aircraft began rolling tugged away the rear ones, running to the refuge of the flight-deck waist, dragging the chocks behind them. 'Splash' Carver thought the *Ark*'s Swordfish took off 'in conditions of sea and pitch which would only be acceptable in an operational emergency – which this certainly was!' One of the aircraft never made it to launch, its bitterly disappointed young observer, Sub Lieutenant Leonard Mann, of 820 Naval Air Squadron, lamenting it had suffered slight damage to its tail wheel. He noted disconsolately: 'An aircraft carrying the enormous weight of a torpedo has to be in absolutely perfect condition ...'[1] One of the two reserve Swordfish was brought forward, restoring the strike force to fifteen. At least it was still light, but the cloud was down to less than 1,000 feet. This time, to ensure there were no attacks on British warships, the pre-mission briefing had made it clear *Sheffield*, some twenty-six miles closer to *Bismarck*'s position than the *Ark*, should be found first and used as a way-point to target. Keen not to repeat 'the debacle of the previous attack'[2], the Swordfish soon found themselves over *Sheffield* in a tight formation, with nobody lost, flying below the lowest layer of cloud. As observer of the lead aircraft, Carver had to translate *Sheffield*'s directions to target, being told by light signal that *Bismarck* lay at 120 degrees, twelve miles away. Some of *Sheffield*'s lookouts and anti-aircraft gun crews could not help but point the way to the German ship. Using powerful optics, the cruiser's Midshipman Repard could just make out Swordfish on their attacking runs: 'They teetered heavily up into the scudding clouds. A few minutes later vast flashes from *Bismarck*'s guns silhouetted a Swordfish and lit up the smoke and spray which dulled her outline.'

Climbing back into cover due to the very thick cloud over *Bismarck*, the attack group had split up into five sub-flights of three aircraft, for it was far safer to manage three aircraft in such poor conditions than keep fifteen together in close proximity during the transit. It was always the intention that once the target was reached, each sub-flight would use its initiative in disrupting the ability of *Bismarck* to concentrate her anti-aircraft fire. With sub-flights coming in from different directions, the German ship would inevitably end up exposing her most vulnerable zones to attack while trying to cover herself by turning towards incoming torpedoes. However, for this to work properly the various sub-flights had to make their runs in quick succession, to avoid giving *Bismarck* time to orientate herself for the next attack. Coode's sub-flight was the first in and so Carver found himself approaching on *Bismarck*'s port beam, prepared for the worst. Radar-controlled anti-aircraft guns had already opened fire on the Swordfish as they approached in cloud. Now the aircraft dropped out of the cloud base, which was at just 700 feet, some two and a half miles from the target, *Bismarck*'s close range anti-aircraft weapons sparkling. Carver was both impressed and frightened by the sheer volume of 'glowing billiard balls flashing past', but Coode held steady and maintained his altitude, waiting until about 1,200 yards out before dropping his torpedo and turning away, skimming as low as possible, according to Carver at 'nought feet'. As happened with the attack by Swordfish from *Victorious*, the German gunners found it extremely difficult to hit the British aircraft, the bad weather also helping the aviators to escape destruction. Carver later explained: 'As we had been attacking across a NW gale of about 40 knots our aircraft were going sideways at nearly half their forward speed and this probably confused the German gunners ...'[3]

Unfortunately for the leading sub-flight *Bismarck* was able to change course to port and so combed the tracks of the first three torpedoes.

The Swordfish began to straggle by *Sheffield*, her lookouts spotting one, then two emerging out of the gloom, flying by very slowly, on the same level as the ship's bridge. Sailors on *Sheffield*'s upper deck took their steel helmets off, waving them in the air and giving the passing aircraft 'a terrific cheer'.[4]

Torpedoes were clearly gone and, as the planes passed, aircrews could be seen smiling; one aviator even gave a thumbs up. The sound and sight of the

Swordfish fading, attention switched back to *Bismarck*, a rain squall dissipating to reveal more Swordfish going in. James Stewart-Moore's sub-flight cleared the cloud, coming in at *Bismarck* from ten miles off her port bow, joined by another Swordfish as they turned in for the attack run, making four aircraft altogether. Stewart-Moore was dismayed by the haphazard nature of the attack, feeling it was 'rather forlorn'. Nagging him was the fact that 'success in torpedo attacks depended on the aircraft being able to put down enough torpedoes in a short interval to make it impossible for the ship to avoid them.'[5] He felt that with only four torpedoes coming in from his attack, *Bismarck* would be able to evade them quite easily. The five minute run, with apparently no other incoming Swordfish to distract the battleship's anti-aircraft gunners, saw the sky filled with shell bursts and all the hot shrapnel that entailed. Stewart-Moore was reminded of the Light Brigade's charge into the Valley of Death immortalized in Tennyson's famous poem about the notorious Crimean War incident. The slow speed of the Swordfish, pushing against the strong headwind, made it look like the British aircraft were hanging in the air. The insane bravery of it all was clear to both the aviators and the Germans trying to kill them. Surely Tennyson himself would have thought it apt to also write of the courageous Swordfish aviators:

> Storm'd at with shot and shell,
> Boldly they rode and well,
> Into the jaws of Death,
> Into the mouth of Hell

Finally, the four Swordfish got close enough to drop their torpedoes, turning away on maximum throttle to get the hell out of it, 'dodging like snipe'[6] as they made their bid to escape *Bismarck*'s flak barrage.

Alan Swanton's Swordfish was part of Stewart-Moore's formation. Descending to 100ft above the waves as they made their run in on *Bismarck*, Swanton thought the enemy ship, by then not more than half a mile away, looked 'big and black and menacing...stabbing red flame in our direction'.[7] Swanton maintained a speed of 100 knots and aimed the nose of his aircraft for *Bismarck* amidships. His observer, Sub Lieutenant Gerry Woods, was trying to give advice, yelling to be heard above the combined cacophony of the aircraft engine, rushing air and bedlam of anti-aircraft fire. Swanton – regarding Woods' advice as 'the usual sort of observer rubbish' – ignored him and concentrated on the target: 'I pushed the "tit", the torpedo fell away, and the aircraft seemed to jump up into the air.' Turning away, the enemy looked like they might get the measure of Swanton: 'There was a series of flashes, and flak ripped through the underside of the fuselage.' However, the aircraft kept flying and he put on more knots to get as far away as swiftly as possible. The four

Swordfish were close together and not more than 150ft above the waves; feeling they were now out of range of enemy anti-aircraft fire, his pilot asked Stewart-Moore if he could slow down. There was a 'terrific crash' right below them, with five of *Bismarck*'s 15-inch shells striking the water. Stewart-Moore recalled of this terrifying moment: 'I did not have to tell the pilot to open up again as were already going like the proverbial bat.'[8]

As the 15-inch shells plunged in, Alan Swanton yelled: 'Christ! Just look at this lot.' *Bismarck*'s main armament was actually firing on a flat trajectory, the shells falling right in front of his aircraft, 'pushing up 100 foot mountains of water.' Swanton pressed his flying column gently forward and took the aircraft out even lower and faster through the smoke and collapsing spray, hoping finally to get beyond the range of the German guns. Woods gave Swanton his course back to *Ark Royal*, remarking that their TAG, 'Flash' Seager had been wounded, but it looked like it was not too serious. Woods noticed that his pilot had also been hit, the wound given away by a dark stain on one shoulder as blood seeped through Swanton's flying suit. Told that he had been wounded, Swanton's chose not to admit he was enduring considerable discomfort, responding: 'No problem. I'm perfectly okay.' However, he did shout back down the voice tube that it would be 'nice' to get back to the ship.

The first three Swordfish to attack, led by Lieutenant Commander Coode, flew south and loitered at a distance of between three and four miles to see how the rest fared. However, it was difficult to observe anything at all due to the low cloud, driving rain and spume blown from wave tops. From the observer's cockpit behind his pilot, Carver saw *Bismarck* trying desperately to avoid being hit by altering course drastically. The tracer fire was heavy and gun flashes blossomed across the silhouette of the German battleship. They did not spot any torpedo impacts. Coode ordered his TAG to make a wireless report to Force H, saying that he believed no hits had been scored. The Swordfish made their way back one by one to the carrier. When Coode brought his aircraft in to land, at just after 11.30 pm, twilight's last gleaming had not yet faded. Despite the wildly pitching deck, the highly experienced Coode was able to recover to the ship safely. However, three Swordfish were not so lucky, crashing on landing. Meanwhile, Gerry Woods advised *Ark Royal* by signal that his shrapnel-riddled aircraft and its wounded occupants, Swanton and Seager, required an emergency landing. Twenty minutes later Swanton made what he described as 'a bit of a controlled crash', adding proudly 'but I was able to walk away from it!' While he may have managed to bravely clamber out of his Swordfish, Swanton was clearly in a bad way and was helped to the sickbay.

Meanwhile, the aircrews assembled in the operations room to process their experiences in a debrief, Stewart-Moore hearing 'a sorry tale of small, ineffectual attacks'. There were claims from various pilots that they may have hit the *Bismarck*, but it seemed there was no evidence for any significant damage. Like the *Victorious* aviators before them, it appeared they had tried and failed.

In *Rodney*, Dalrymple-Hamilton told his men via the public address system that *Ark Royal*'s second attack had failed. His voice dissolving into silence, he was simply overcome with weary disappointment after the strain of the past few days. The battleship captain leaned against the magnetic compass stand on the bridge, trying repeatedly to light his pipe and failing, a telling sign reflecting the sheer frustration and nervous exhaustion of the moment.[9] However, the situation soon changed dramatically. A new set of signal flags was hoisted on the nearby *King George V*. Eagerly scrutinized and joyously received, they instructed *Rodney* to alter course in order to intercept the enemy. Immediately, Captain Dalrymple-Hamilton was suffused with new energy and in his eyes 'deep and sunk after the strain and disappointments of the last few days [there was] an eager fire.'[10] It seemed *Ark*'s aviators had achieved a miracle after all.

The key moment had been witnessed from *Sheffield*, Midshipman Repard wiping moisture from his binoculars as he watched the Swordfish going in, seeing that one 'aircraft was very low near her [*Bismarck*]. There was a big column of water, briefly dull red at its base near her stern.'[11] Another sailor in *Sheffield* claimed to have seen a 'gigantic column' of spray and a 'blue flame' at *Bismarck*'s stern.[12] There were three hits on *Bismarck*, two forward of the aft turrets but making no significant impact on the German battleship's protection, whereas the other wrecked her steering. Who actually inflicted the decisive hit was not clear. Behind the controls of a Swordfish in 818 NAS's first wave was Sub Lieutenant John 'Jock' Moffat, who, as he brought his aircraft closer and closer to the huge bulk of *Bismarck* was awestruck and scared by the amount of flak thrown at his flimsy aircraft: 'If you are facing a ship that size, twice as big as your own ship and they are firing everything they have at you, it is simply unbelievable. The stuff was coming in at such a rate I don't mind admitting that I was petrified. It was coming so thick and fast that I was inclined to duck in my cockpit and, in fact, I think I did so.'

Moffat's observer, Sub Lieutenant Dusty Miller, calmly talked him in to a point where he could drop the torpedo with a fair chance of hitting *Bismarck*, studying the wave pattern so the torpedo could be dropped in a trough rather than a crest and hopefully run deep. 'Behind me the observer was leaning over the side of the aircraft and, bear in mind this took only seconds, said via the voice pipe that connected us: "Not yet". Then he says "let her go!" so I dropped the torpedo. By this time we are about 1,500 yards from *Bismarck* and I thought that the thing was so big we couldn't miss.' Uppermost in Moffat's mind as he made his exit was the fact that banking and turning would require height and that could spell disaster: 'I am at wave top height; that is, with the wheels of the aircraft just above the waves. How am I going to get turned in that situation? If I am going to turn then I will have to lift myself up or a wing tip will hit the waves. And if I lift myself up and bank the aircraft *Bismarck*'s gunners get a bigger target. So, I make a ski turn, sort of sliding around, giving it full whack, every bit of power and full rudder. And so I juddered around and got out of there. When I got the aircraft turned away, I looked back and *Bismarck* had turned to starboard and my torpedo had followed.'[13] Lieutenant Stanley Keane who had joined Coode's sub-flight bringing his Swordfish in on the port side, also looked to be a strong candidate for the crucial hit while two other pilots, Lieutenant DF Godfrey-Faussett and Sub Lieutenant Ken Pattisson may also lay claim to having crippled *Bismarck*. As his sub-flight leader, Godfrey-Faussett led Pattisson down from 9,000 ft on *Bismarck*'s starboard side. With shrapnel beginning to shred his aircraft, Pattison levelled off at 90ft above the waves, less than 1,000 yards out from *Bismarck*. Deciding the anti-aircraft barrage was a little too fierce to hold straight and true all the way in, Pattisson threw his aircraft from side to side in an attempt to make it harder to hit. Torpedo away, Pattisson did not see its impact, but others claimed to see an enormous fountain of water spring up at the battleship's stern. A modest man, Pattison would only ever admit it was 'highly probable' that his torpedo did the fatal damage. The controversy over who actually delivered the blow continues to this day.[14] Whatever happened in that half hour, from 9.00 pm to 9.30 pm, *Bismarck*'s bid to escape the revenge of the Royal Navy had failed.

A wounded beast, *Bismarck* showed her fury by firing on *Sheffield*, the first 15-inch shells falling about three miles from the cruiser. Then *Bismarck* straddled the cruiser with four 15-inch shells, two of them landing about forty yards off her starboard beam, exploding on hitting the surface of the sea, indicating high explosive. The others were even closer, one of *Sheffield*'s sailors noting they were 'about fifteen yards off our port quarter, the air was filled with flying splinters and fragments of shell.'[15] The cruiser turned away violently 'under full wheel at top speed' , laying down a smokescreen to mask her retreat. There were casualties aft, particularly among her anti-aircraft gun crews, *Sheffield*'s halyards were on fire and a mast was cut by shell splinters as well as sparks flying from severed electric cables writhing on the deck.[16] A jagged chunk of shrapnel hit the stand supporting Midshipman Repard's binoculars, the young officer staring in horrified fascination at the lump of hot metal hissing in a puddle of water at his feet. However, *Bismarck* had not turned voluntarily on *Sheffield*, for, with her rudder jammed by the torpedo hit she had no choice.

High above, this turn of events was noted by Swordfish on shadowing duty. Their reports reached *Ark Royal* shortly after a signal from *Sheffield*, which was read over the voice pipe to the aviators in the operations room. They had been discussing the possibility of a night attack on *Bismarck*, or at least a dawn assault. Absorbing *Sheffield*'s report, they now heard the German battleship was heading north at an estimated six knots. This could only mean *Bismarck* had suffered damage to her steering, for why else would she be steering *towards* the British battleships?

Tovey instructed *Rodney* to reduce speed to 19 knots, in order to save fuel for the battle ahead. Admiral Somerville suggested bringing *Renown* north to join the other two British capital ships, but Tovey declined. He was anxious not to expose the battlecruiser to the same danger as *Hood*. Tovey also did not want *Renown* to be mistaken for *Bismarck* approaching in the darkness. *Rodney* was disadvantaged in a gun battle in anything but clear weather, as she did not possess gunnery radar, whereas *Bismarck* did. Recognizing this handicap, Lieutenant Commander Crawford tried, in true British style, to cobble something together. 'We had air warning radar, one of the first two sets that were fitted in ships at all, but they were no good for ranging. So we were entirely dependent on our rangefinders ... In fact the night before the action I spent [time] with our telegraphist, seeing if he could devise any method – he knew about wireless waves, and this sort of thing – of putting out any form of jamming signal, which might possibly jam the enemy's radar ...'[17] Unfortunately, this enterprising bid to gain a technological edge failed. While the British battleship's gunnery officer coped with his frustration, teenage Midshipman GR Shaw, on the eve of his first action, found news of the torpedo hit that destroyed *Bismarck*'s steering filled him with all the naive, boyish excitement you would expect. He wrote in his journal that evening: 'Nothing better could have happened, and if she holds this course we have definitely trapped her.'[18]

Chapter 18

Vian's Dilemma

Throughout the drama of the Swordfish attacks, the ships of Captain Vian's 4th Destroyer Flotilla had thrown themselves into stormy seas, engines straining for maximum revolutions on the screws. In a turbulent following sea, the massive swell rolling under the ships lifted their sterns; screws thrashing impotently, rudders clear of the water, the destroyers yawed alarmingly. Vian was well aware that *King George V* was by now most likely denuded of destroyer escort, due to the latter running low on fuel and being sent away to replenish. As his ships made their dash towards the Home Fleet flagship, he devoured signals detailing twists and turns in the drama. *Cossack* had picked up the sighting report of the RAF flying boat that had rediscovered the fugitive German ship. Scrutinizing the *Bismarck*'s position, course and speed Vian became convinced she was heading for a port in the Bay of Biscay, which would be attained by the following day unless somebody damaged her.

Marrying this information with what he knew or could guess about the dispositions of various British units, Vian believed his flotilla was the surface action force with the best chance of intercepting *Bismarck* that night and slowing her down. Provided luck was with the 4th Flotilla, they might just manage it. However, there was still the risk of leaving the fleet flagship exposed. In trying to halt *Bismarck*, Vian might leave *King George V* and even *Rodney* at the mercy of U-boats. The fact that German submarines were in the vicinity had already been broadcast via a signal at 5.30 pm from Vian. Specifically addressed to the Admiralty, Tovey, Somerville and *Sheffield*, it told of *Sikh*'s sighting of a periscope as she and the rest of the 4th Flotilla thundered south.[1] The stark reality of that threat had, unbeknownst to the British, already been illustrated by the case of a U-boat that had *Ark Royal* in her sights even as her Swordfish attacked *Bismarck*. The British carrier was only saved from destruction because U-556 had already expended all her torpedoes. Both *Renown* and *Ark Royal* were also without any screen due to their destroyers being sent away to refuel. Fortunately, at 8 pm on 26 May, Lieutenant Herbert

Wohlfarth, captain of U-556, was consumed with frustration rather than celebrating a kill.

He watched through his attack periscope, as the British ships passed by, stamping his foot on the deck in an absolute rage.[2]

In *King George V*, Admiral Tovey was looking at the dilemma from the other end, concluding that while he needed the additional comfort of destroyers, above all the Royal Navy needed to stop *Bismarck*. If *Ark Royal's* Swordfish could not do it – news of their success had not yet broken – then Vian's destroyers truly were the next best option. Losing a British capital ship or even having one damaged in the aftermath of *Hood's* loss would be an utter disaster for the British cause. There again, if the Germans concentrated their four most deadly surface raiders – *Bismarck, Scharnhorst, Gneisenau* and *Prinz Eugen* – into one battlegroup the British could possibly be sunk anyway. Bearing in mind the trouble caused by *Bismarck* and *Prinz Eugen*, what might four German raiders on the highs seas achieve? In *Cossack*, still pondering his best course of action, Vian similarly reflected that if either *King George V* or *Rodney* were torpedoed, thanks to the lack of a destroyer screen, then *Bismarck* would get clean away and his country would suffer a catastrophic defeat. Despite this, *Bismarck* was a prize he could not resist.

Vian decided he knew Tovey's mind and the admiral would expect him to steer for the enemy; so, as he later revealed, 'we plumped for heading straight towards *Bismarck*.' Due to the need for complete radio silence, Vian did not advise Tovey 'or anybody else' of the decision.[3]

The weather was growing worse by the minute, with maximum speed still required to reach *Bismarck* despite the threat of severe damage to ships and peril to the men in them. Vian's destroyers were by now yawing up to 140 degrees from their intended course. Station-keeping in line astern was impossible, some ships falling back and others coming forward, picked up by the giant hand of a violently surging sea. Vian knew this was a dangerous game for his little ships and their sailors. There were injuries and at least one fatality: 'Reports reached me of men being hurt, and in one case of being washed overboard, but there was nothing to be done.'[4] Such things had to be weighed against the greater good – and that required sacrifice to avenge *Hood* and deal a killer blow to Germany. By 9 pm on 26 May the destroyers were less than 100 miles from *Bismarck*, conditions improving enough for *Cossack's* lookouts to spot the hazy silhouette of *Ark Royal* between rain squalls before the weather clamped down again. The Swordfish were making their attack on *Bismarck* by then, but results, if any, were far from clear. Ken Robinson at his action station next to *Cossack's* pom-pom gun had watched as the night sky in the far distance flickered 'with tracers, in lots of different colours, like a fireworks display.'[5] But then Vian's destroyers picked up signals revealing *Bismarck* was now heading north, straight for them, possibly suffering from steering problems and pushed whichever way the sea and wind desired.

Back in the UK, news that *Bismarck* had probably been crippled came as a great relief to a group of RAF aircrews, for they had been assigned to what from their perspective amounted to a suicide mission. Six Wellington bombers of 221 Squadron and six Whitley bombers of 502 Squadron, both types loaded with 500lbs armour-piercing bombs, were being held at St Eval airfield in Cornwall as a last resort option. The crews had been 'volunteered' to fly if it looked like the Navy had failed and *Bismarck* would after all make a French port. The bombers would be sent off to find *Bismarck*, with the aid of whatever shadowing information the Navy could pass on, and then make a desperate attempt to destroy or cripple her. Whether they made contact with *Bismarck* or not, at the maximum extent of their range and beyond the ability of the aircraft to make it home due to lack of fuel, they were to ditch near one of the allegedly many RN vessels out there on the ocean. It was a mad plan, and the aircrews quite rightly did not rate their chances of survival. Fortunately, their cousins in the Fleet Air Arm had now, hopefully, decisively crippled the would-be target. The odds were the Navy would be able to finish the job without a RAF bomber sortie into the unknown. However, with the affair not yet settled for good, the bombers and their men were still held at St Eval, just in case. The aircrews fervently prayed they would not be needed and, in their mess that evening raised a glass or two in salute to the Fleet Air Arm's Swordfish crews.[6]

Not long after 9.00 pm, Vian's flotilla encountered *Sheffield* steaming hard in the opposite direction, the destroyers continuing south. The cruiser signalled *Bismarck* was ten miles astern. Captain Larcom added: 'Good luck.'

The 4th Destroyer Flotilla raced on at 18 knots, the spray leaping so high the ships' lookouts were frequently blinded.[7] An hour later, as dusk dissolved into darkness, the Polish destroyer *Piorun*, on the 4th Flotilla's port wing, hoisted a flag declaring 'enemy in sight'. No sooner had she done this than there was an orange flash in the mist, shells falling close to *Maori*. The flotilla scattered, *Piorun* hurling 4.7-inch shells at *Bismarck* as she turned away. Vian instructed his destroyers to pull back. A plan of action needed to be devised, with *Maori* and *Cossack* only narrowly avoiding a collision in the mountainous seas as they put their helms hard over, withdrawing to a safer distance. Vian told his vessels to arrange themselves in a box formation around *Bismarck*, warship-grey Lilliputians tying down a Nazi Gulliver. *Cossack* took up position directly astern, maintaining a speed of 18 knots despite the gale. As the destroyers worked their way around to shadowing positions they had to be careful not to stray too close, which *Piorun* did, although this may have been more by design than accident, provoking the Germans into opening fire. During this encounter, which lasted almost ten minutes, *Piorun*'s captain, Commander Eugeniusz Plawski, ordered a signal flashed to *Bismarck*: 'I am a Pole.' This let the enemy ship, which had started its sortie from a port in occupied Poland, know that the nation the Nazis devastated and conquered in September 1939 would not let the act go without retribution. *Bismarck*'s response was three salvoes of 15-inch fire, one of them straddling the Polish destroyer, which, having restored national honour, wisely zigzagged away, making smoke furiously. Thereafter, in the darkness and heaving seas, *Piorun* lost contact. Despite valiant efforts to find and then attack *Bismarck* again, this time with torpedoes, she was unable to make any more gestures of defiance. *Zulu* also found herself too close, dodging both 15-inch and 5.9-inch shells, but while gun flashes could be seen the enemy ship herself was not visible, a sure sign to the destroyer men that *Bismarck* was using gunnery radar.

In *Cossack*, Vian – a seasoned sailor with mental and physical powers unimpaired by the sort of seasickness that might have afflicted lesser men – saw the situation with absolute clarity. He decided that, while *Bismarck* was slowed down by her present difficulties, which her crew would be working hard to rectify, she was nonetheless potentially still able to evade the British battleships. He summed up his course of action: 'Our destroyers attack, reduce enemy's speed still further and bring in the heavy ships to deliver the coup de grâce.'[8] It was the sort of classic scenario he had tackled many times during exercises in the Mediterranean before the war, but, as Vian observed with a touch of irony, in those pretend engagements the destroyers always succeeded in slowing the target down and the friendly battleships duly did their bit and sank 'the enemy'. This, however, was a real shooting war, with sea conditions somewhat different to the comparatively placid Mediterranean. There was also no moon, which made it even harder either to see the target or avoid collisions among Vian's own ships. Had such weather been encountered during peacetime, then an exercise would have been called off, for fear of destroyers being irrevocably damaged. Vian was also, of course, well aware that gunnery radar would enable *Bismarck* to hit his ships regardless of whether or not they were in vision. Fortunately, *Bismarck*'s speed slowed considerably to around 12 knots, her steering problems clearly severe, forcing her north-west towards the pursuing British battleships, rather than south-east to safety. Vian hoped Admiral Tovey might try and close with his capital ships to initiate a night action, enabling the destroyers to curtail their arduous shadowing duty. He also recognized Tovey would be well advised to wait until morning, for in such weather and at night it would be difficult to ascertain which ship was enemy and which British. In the heat of battle mistakes could easily be made. Vian judged the chances of his destroyers sinking *Bismarck* were negligible and their primary mission was shadowing, but neither option was easy, with his men already exhausted and hours of danger ahead of them. The German battleship had shaken her shadowers off before and she might do so again.

Vian was fearful of 'nothing but empty water to show the Commander-in-Chief in the morning.' Mounting some form of attack would therefore serve two purposes: maintaining close contact with the enemy and ensuring *Bismarck*'s gun crews got no rest before the big fight. Vian gave orders via a wireless signal for a synchronized torpedo attack. At 11.42 pm, as *Cossack* moved in but was still around four miles from *Bismarck*, the German ship opened fire. *Cossack*'s radar operator called out a number of contacts on his screen, which were *Bismarck*'s 15-inch shells in flight, heading towards his own ship. Vian found this 'disconcerting', making for 'some unpleasant moments until the shells plunged into the sea, exploding with a violent concussion and throwing up huge pillars of water, which seemed to tower above us.'[9] Shell splinters tore *Cossack*'s aerials away and damaged the ship's motorboat, the destroyer turning away to avoid further damage or worse. For a period Tovey and the Admiralty had to rely on shadowing reports from other ships in the flotilla. *Bismarck* stitched the air with a rainbow shower of tracer shells and bullets, her anti-aircraft guns opening fire on a shadowing Swordfish.

While Adolf Hitler was busy digesting briefings that told him *Bismarck* would probably not reach safety, Winston Churchill made the short journey from the Cabinet War Rooms, a set of underground command bunkers beneath Whitehall, over to the Admiralty. Descending into its equally subterranean War Room, Churchill settled in to watch as signals came in from ships closing on *Bismarck*, which were used to update massive charts.

Churchill spotted the Controller of the Navy, Admiral Bruce Fraser, entering and holding a discussion with Admiral Dudley Pound, the First Sea Lord. The Prime Minister subsequently asked Fraser: 'What are you doing here?' Fraser replied: 'I am waiting to see what I have got to repair.'[10]

As Controller, Fraser was responsible for the construction and repair of warships, overseeing their delivery to the front line. He was aware of damage to *Prince of Wales* and in the War Room to check on her status, bearing in mind she was one of only two brand new battleships in the Royal Navy. Fraser would be anxious to know where *Prince of Wales* was and get her released from operations so she could be repaired. News of damage to any other warships was also of great interest. Churchill would spend four hours in the War Room on the night of 26 May, leaving only when he was content the Navy had firmly fixed *Bismarck* for destruction.

At around midnight, *Zulu* feared she had lost contact altogether and, plunging forward to try and regain it, was alarmed to find *Bismarck* very close indeed, only some 5,000 yards away. *Zulu* was subjected to intensive fire from both 5.9-inch and 15-inch guns, retiring to a safer distance. Some forty minutes later, she encountered *Cossack*, which, due to earlier damage, was still only able to communicate via light and signal flag. Vian instructed *Zulu* to mount independent torpedo attacks on *Bismarck*. A co-ordinated attack would not be possible in the prevailing weather. The German battleship's erratic behaviour did not make it any easier – one moment she was doing 12 knots, the next stopped dead in the water while yet another attempt was made to fix her steering. During the night action the British destroyers had to keep their speed down to avoid serious damage, while frequent rain squalls could reduce visibility to a few yards. One by one they lunged in anyway, turning so their amidships torpedo tubes could bear and, once the fish were away, retreating making smoke furiously. *Zulu* lunged in at 22 knots, Midshipman Sam Hammick seeing the sea as 'a glare of starshell and search lights' with everything bathed in the orange glow of gun flashes. The destroyer was 'bucketing along through a head sea' smoke pouring out of her funnels, with 'spray streaming over the bridge in solid sheets.' Hammick could hear shrapnel 'pattering on the decks and see the sparks it made as it hit the steel.'[11] *Zulu* unleashed her torpedoes at a range of 3,000 yards and thought they might have hit. *Maori* was next, observers in *Zulu* spotting a fire on *Bismarck*'s forecastle, while *Cossack*'s bridge team believed they saw an explosion 'when *Maori*'s torpedo arrived'[12] while the destroyer herself reported an 'extensive fire on forecastle'. *Cossack* then *Sikh* tried their luck. In Vian's ship, telegraphist Eric Farmer felt his adrenalin pumping: 'Now was our chance. *Cossack*, full speed ahead, went in to attack. We are spotted and *Bismarck* opens fire on us. The first salvo was fifty yards short. The next one burst over the bridge causing everyone to duck. The range was less than a mile now. A sharp turn, several swishes as the torpedoes are fired …'[13]

In reality the flotilla leader actually launched three torpedoes from a range of 6,000 yards, anti-aircraft gunner Ken Robinson recalling of the attack: 'We went in head to sea and fired a spread of four torpedoes. At the time, we thought one of them had hit.'[14] Having tried her luck, *Cossack* did not hang around. 'After the attack we turned and with the sea up our stern, sped away at what seemed to be the fastest we ever went, with the stern sea throwing us all over the place.'[15] Farmer and everyone else in *Cossack* heard 'a very loud explosion; and a large flash is observed in the after part of *Bismarck* as one of our fish hit.'

Cossack discovered that one her torpedoes had not left its tube, so the destroyer went in again, Farmer tensed for the German storm of fire.

'The range closed rapidly as we sped in. Another sharp turn, another heavy smoke screen, and we are away again … a huge sheet of flame was seen to come from *Bismarck*. It is not known whether our second run had been a success, or whether the flash came from the 15-inch guns of the enemy. Anyway the fish had all gone and *Bismarck* had been stopped.' *Zulu* reported: 'Enemy on fire and stationary.'

However, in reality *Bismarck* was not halted because of the destroyers, but more due to her desperate efforts to fix the earlier damage to her steering. The night harassment by Vian's ships, combined with the fatal damage to her steering and cumulative fatigue from days of being pursued and harried by

British ships and aircraft, had destroyed any hope in *Bismarck* of a successful outcome. The torpedo hit on *Bismarck*'s stern had blasted an enormous hole, with steering compartments flooded, preventing repeated attempts to sort the problem out internally. A team of sailors sent to operate a hand rudder gave up due to the amount of water in the relevant compartment. Attempts to plug the hole in the hull with collision mats similarly failed. Divers sent into flooded steering rooms tried their best, but they could not free the rudders and were withdrawn exhausted. Lindemann's attempts to effect steering via the propellers similarly failed. Of the repeated efforts to give *Bismarck* back mastery over her fate, Müllenheim-Rechberg noted mournfully: 'When he [Lindemann] did succeed in deflecting the ship from her course to the northwest, her jammed rudders brought her back into the wind.'[16] It was suggested divers should be sent over the side to blow the rudders off. But the sea was so rough it was decided not to waste lives in vain attempts to apply this solution. As Müllenheim-Rechberg later explained, blowing the rudders off from inside the ship was equally risky and might even damage the propellers, robbing *Bismarck* of the ability to move at all. The young gunnery officer, pondering the fact that while the ship could still steam she had to go in the direction the sea and wind pushed her. Every extra knot beyond that needed to keep the ship from yawing could only narrow the distance between *Bismarck* and her pursuers. He noted bitterly: 'We were relieving Tovey of the job of pursuit.'[17]

Admiral Lütjens at 11.42 pm had sent a doom-laden signal to the German high command: 'Ship incapable of manoeuvres. Will fight to the last shell. Long live the Führer.' A further sign of the abject despair aboard was Captain Lindemann making a broadcast saying sailors could take whatever they liked from the ship's stores. Older men, some of whom had seen action in the First World War, realized their chances of surviving the forthcoming battle were slim to say the least, while the young ones clung to the idea that perhaps the Luftwaffe or U-boats might come to *Bismarck*'s aid. They had a last supper of goods liberated from the stores and ship's canteen: tinned ham, cheese in tubes, chocolate, pineapple chunks, all washed down with brandy, the latter acquired despite not being among goods they were permitted to take. There was no limit to the cigarettes they could have, while Swiss watches, after-shave, pocket-knives and even fountain pens were all up for grabs.[18] Rescue for *Bismarck* was impossible. The *Gneisenau* and *Scharnhorst* of course were unable to sail due to being under repair at Brest. U-boats were forced to stay dived to avoid damage from gales and, being submerged, had their speed reduced, while *Bismarck* was also too far out to benefit from air cover. Using the PA system, Lütjens spoke to the battleship's crew: 'The German people are with you, and we will fight until our gun barrels glow red-hot and the last shell has left the barrels. For us seamen, the question now is victory or death!' One of *Bismarck*'s officers later remarked that a senior rating in his department looked extremely dejected following the broadcast and believed 'it was really all over'.[19] The chances of making it through the gathering British fleet were reckoned to be nil. Some have described this speech as causing 'wild, unrestrained fear'[20] in *Bismarck*'s men. Members of Lütjens' staff donned lifejackets and the ship's own officers openly expressed the opinion that she was doomed. Some said it would have been far better if Lütjens had said nothing. According to one of *Bismarck*'s machinist petty officers the words of Admiral Lütjens 'had a devastating effect. Deep depression enveloped the whole crew.'[21] At 11.58 pm Lütjens had signalled that *Bismarck*'s men would 'fight to the last in our belief in you my Führer and in the firm faith in Germany's victory.' One minute later, however, on the orders of the less fatalistic Captain Lindemann, *Bismarck* signalled: 'Armament and engines still intact. Ship however cannot be steered with engine.' Hitler sent a signal to Lütjens, which said: 'I thank you in the name of the German people.'[22] He added a message for the crew: 'The whole of Germany is with you. What can still be done will be done. The performance of your duty will strengthen our people in the struggle for their existence.' Twenty-eight minutes later, Lütjens sent a signal to the C-in-C German Navy, proposing Lieutenant Commander Schneider, *Bismarck*'s gunnery officer, should be awarded the Knight's Cross for sinking HMS *Hood*. At nine minutes to 3.00 am, C-in-C German Navy would signal *Bismarck* that the Führer had confirmed the Knight's Cross to Lieutenant Commander Schneider, adding: 'Heartiest congratulations'. It was not much consolation in the circumstances.

Lookouts in *Sheffield* were reporting flashes in the distance, which was *Bismarck* responding to the British attacks. Tovey ordered via wireless signal that starshells should be fired every half an hour, hopefully illuminating where *Bismarck* was for the Home Fleet as it waited for the new day to begin its final assault. *Cossack* by then had a jury-rigged radio aerial, so she could again transmit and receive wireless signals. It was a pretty alarming trade, for often the destroyers' starshells ended up making themselves more visible to the enemy than *Bismarck* was to them. *Zulu*'s Midshipman Hammick recorded a particularly dangerous incident: 'Once we were straddled by two of *Sikh*'s starshells and the minutes that followed before we could get out of the light were extraordinarily tense!' Meanwhile, Force H boss Admiral Somerville was keen to get in on the action, reserving a slim hope that *his* brave boys could still play a key role, signalling *Ark Royal* at 3.05 am: 'At what time will striking force take off? With any luck we may finish her off before Home Fleet arrives.' Quarter of any hour later *Ark Royal* flashed back: 'Aircraft ready now but consider attack should not be launched until they can differentiate between friend and foe, shortly after 0600.'

Nothing could provide a starker contrast to the German admiral's earlier dreadful message to the troops than Tovey's effort to prepare his men for battle.

To bolster the ship's company of his flagship, before their do or die clash, he drafted a message that was posted throughout the ship and also read out over the public address system.

To. K.G.V.
   The sinking of the *Bismarck* may have an effect on the war as a whole out of all proportion to the loss to the enemy of one battleship. May God be with you and grant you victory.
                    JT 26/5/'41[23]

At 3.53 am, Vian sent a wireless message to Admiral Tovey that summarized what he believed was *Bismarck*'s fighting state: 'The enemy made good between 0240 and 0340 a distance of eight miles and is still capable of heavy and accurate fire.' Twenty-two minutes later Vian signalled his intention to fire rounds of high explosive, fused to explode in the air, as it seemed starshells were not visible enough in the filthy night.

In the Hvalfjord in Iceland, aboard *Electra* the officers were enviously studying signals from Vian to Tovey, nobody reading them with more interest than Cain, the torpedo specialist. He thought the 4th Flotilla's night action was 'the sort of show in which *Electra* could have excelled, and our jealousy was expressed in the slightly spiteful chuckles with which we greeted the signal that *Bismarck* was "still capable of sustained and accurate fire".'[24] But, of course, admiration for the bravery and tenacity of their fellow destroyer men kicked in, too, for they knew how difficult it was to mount any kind of attack in the conditions faced by the men of the 4th Flotilla.

At 4.59 am, Tovey asked for destroyers in Vian's flotilla to send a call sign signal, using 'sufficient power for homing', to enable their shadowing positions, and therefore *Bismarck*'s approximate location, to be calculated. The Home Fleet had to be ready to strike when the new day came. Dawn arrived at 5.00 am, rain squalls drifting across the storm-tossed seascape, but at times as much as ten miles visibility was possible.[25] *Piorun* was ordered back to Plymouth by Vian, for her fuel was dangerously low and her landlubber ship's company, mainly composed of Polish soldiers, could probably do with a respite from the savage sea. Vian was also worried *Piorun* might try something daft to further avenge the fate of Poland, explaining that he felt 'brave Captain Plawski would take unjustifiable risks if he regained contact in the morning.'[26] Even so, the Polish destroyer captain, still brimming with a burning desire to hit back at the hated Germans, loitered for an hour longer before complying with Vian's orders.

Tired, red-rimmed eyes in *Zulu* scanned the horizon, trying to sight the enemy who must be nearby but was not yet visible – most likely, so the destroyer men thought, because *Bismarck* was lurking in a squall and preparing to blow

Clockwise from top left:
Bismarck, the pride of
Hitler's navy, seen from
astern (*US Naval Heritage and
History Command*); Admiral
Gunther Lütjens, leader of
the ultimately ill-fated sortie
by *Bismarck* in May 1941
(*IWM A14897*); HMS *Prince
of Wales* at speed (*Strathdee
Collection*); the cruiser HMS
Suffolk, looking bedraggled
after months on patrol in
Arctic waters, but still with
guns trained to tackle all
comers (*Strathdee Collection*)

Above: Captain Ellis of HMS *Suffolk* shoots mines from the bridge of his ship. During the *Bismarck* chase he banned his officers from shooting a goose that flew alongside the cruiser for some hours (*IWM A4212*)
Right: A lookout aboard HMS *Suffolk* maintains a chilly vigil over the ice of the Denmark Strait (*IWM A4226*)
Below: Admiral Tovey, left, talks to Captain Leach on the quarterdeck of *Prince of Wales* at Scapa Flow (*IWM A3891*)

Left: A view of *Bismarck* from *Prinz Eugen*, on 21 May 1941, as the two ships sat at anchor in Norwegian waters before attempting their Atlantic breakout (*USNHHC*)

Below: HMS *Norfolk*, as seen from HMS *Suffolk*, under a glowering sky off Iceland as she heads for the Denmark Strait (*IWM A4316*)

Bottom: Destroyer HMS *Electra* during a replenishment at sea prior to the Second World War (*IWM HU 98803*)

Top: HMS *Cossack*, which led the destroyer attacks of 26/27 May on *Bismarck*, despite atrocious sea conditions (*Royal Naval Museum*)

Above: *Cossack*'s Ken Robinson, who witnessed the *Bismarck* Action from the destroyer's upper deck (*Ken Robinson/HMS Cossack Association*)

Left: The supremely aggressive Captain Philip Vian on the bridge of HMS *Cossack*, Lewis gun visible to left of image. Vian led the 4th Destroyer Flotilla, using his initiative to mount a high-speed dash into action against *Bismarck* (*IWM A1595*)

Opposite, above: One of the 14-inch guns of Home Fleet flagship HMS *King George V*'s A turret being sponged out. Churchill was critical of the calibre of main armament used in the KGVs, which he regarded as lacking punch (*Private Collection*)

Opposite, below: The British Premier had more confidence in the hard-hitting 16-inch guns of HMS *Rodney*. HMS *Hood* is seen under two of *Rodney*'s 16-inch guns, late 194 at Scapa Flow (*IWM A111*)

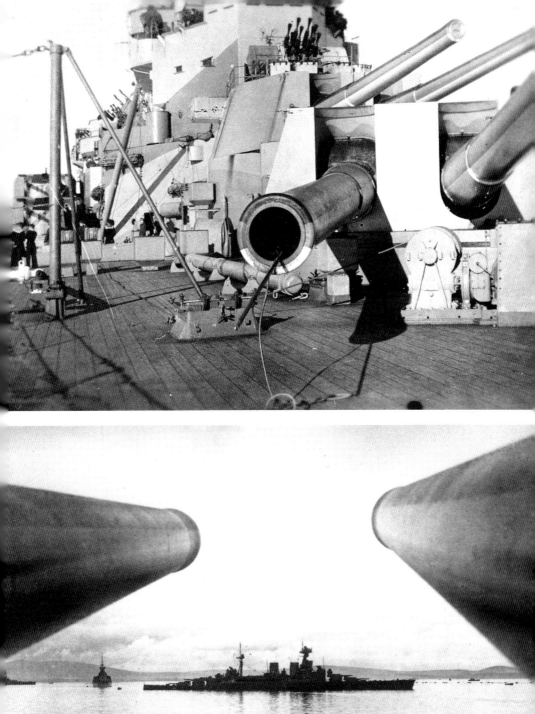

Left: The photograph that for many decades has been considered the last image of *Hood*, taken from *Prince of Wale* on 23 May 1941, between 6pm and 8pm (*IWM HU70516*)
Below (inset): *Bismarck* belches smoke as she fires at *Prince of Wales*, 24 May 1941 (*USNHHC*)
Below, across spread: *Hood* fighting *Bismarck* and already on fire after suffering serious hits. This epic painting by Paul Wright RSMA is entitled *Empire Day, 1941* as 24 May the date of the battle, was Empire Day, making it ironic that *Hood* should be destroyed on the very day Britain's globe-spanning imperium was celebrated (*Commissioned by Ron Feltham and donated to the Royal Naval Museum*)
Opposite, above: A previously unpublished and puzzling photograph taken from HMS *Norfolk*, possibly showing *Hood* exploding, although various factors may contradict this. See Appendix 5 (*Royal Naval Museum*)
Opposite, inset: Dartmouth cadets who attended the naval college in 1937-40, including *Hood* survivor William Dundas (seated, far left) and Henry Leach (standing, top row, second from left) whose father commanded *Prince of Wales* during her fight with *Bismarck* and the pursuit (*The Britannia Museum/BRNC*)

Above: Cheesy grins for the camera, as the crew of a 5.25-inch gun turret aboard *Prince of Wales* take a breather in the immediate aftermath of the action with *Bismarck* on 24 May 1941. They are holding a shell inscribed with a message to the enemy, and also what looks like wreckage (*IWM HU70519*)
Below: The Swordfish of 825 NAS crowd the rain-lashed flight deck of *Victorious* as they are prepared for the attack on *Bismarck* on the night of 24 May 1941 (*Fleet Air Arm Museum*)
Opposite, below: The forward 8-inch guns of *Suffolk*, elevated and ready for action during the *Bismarck* chase (*IWM A4335*)

Above: A Swordfish from 825 NAS, of HMS *Victorious*, skims low over the waves during the attack on *Bismarck* of 24 May 1941 (*Painting by Dennis Andrews. For more details, e-mail: admin@warshipart.com*)

Left: The valiant Eugene Esmonde, who led the 825 NAS Swordfish strike on *Bismarck*, a brave effort even if it caused little damage (*Fleet Air Arm Museum*)

Right: Les Sayer, whose Swordfish had its fuselage ripped open, but still went on to deliver its torpedo (*TAG Association*)

Above: Exhausted crew of a 4-inch gun aboard HMS *Suffolk* catch a few precious moments of sleep (*IWM A4207*)

Below: The next to last photograph of *Bismarck*, taken from *Prinz Eugen* before the German cruiser made her break from her big brother. Seen on 24 May, *Bismarck* apppears to be down by the bows due to flooding caused by a hit from *Prince of Wales*. A decisive penetration by one of the British battleship's 14-inch shells, its crucial nature was not realised at the time, for it deprived *Bismarck* of fuel as well as slowing her down due to the ingress of water (*USNHHC*)

Bottom: View from the TAG's position of a Swordfish, showing HMS *Ark Royal*, on 24 May 1941, as Force H sails north to intercept *Bismarck*. Another Swordfish is ready to launch (*IWM A3827*)

Above: A pre-war shot of cruiser HMS *Dorsetshire* fulfilling her role as guardian of a far-flung empire (*Author's Collection*)

Right: Admiral Sir James Somerville, charismatic boss of the Gibraltar-based Force H (*Royal Naval Museum*)

Below: *Bismarck*'s prey – an Atlantic convoy, protected in this illustration by the sloop HMS *Egret*, whose ship's company in May 1941 feared they would soon have to sacrifice themselves in a hopeless battle with the German raider (*Dennis Andrews. For more details of painting, e-mail: admin@warshipart.com*)

Above: Force H flagship HMS *Renown* steaming north on 24 May 1941, as seen from a circling Swordfish torpedo-bomber of *Ark Royal* (*IWM A3824*)
Above inset: A Swordfish returns to *Ark Royal* after one of the attacks on 26 May 1941 (*IWM 4100*)
Below: Fleet Air Arm aviators who took part in attacks on *Bismarck*, seen here in good spirits aboard *Ark Royal* (*IWM A3831*)

Above: Swordfish 5G of *Ark Royal*'s 818 Naval Air Squadron, which took part in the strike that stopped *Bismarck* from reaching Brest (*IWM A3819*)

Right: Swordfish pilot Alan Swanton, who was wounded during the second attack on *Bismarck* of 26 May 1941 (*Fleet Air Arm Museum*)

Below: A well known photograph, taken from another British warship, of *Rodney* firing on *Bismarck* during the final battle. Smoke from *Rodney*'s 16-inch guns drifts away in the centre. To the left a dark trail of smoke on the horizon shows *Bismarck* is gripped by raging fires (*IWM MH15931*)

Above, left: *Bismarck* survivors, desperate to be rescued, cluster below HMS *Dorsetshire*. Only a lucky few would be saved (*IWM ZZZ3130C*) **Left:** Gigantic shell splashes astern of *Bismarck* during the final battle (*IWM MISC50790*)

Above: The End of the *Bismarck* shows the German battleship on fire and surrounded by shell splashes (*Painting by Paul Wright RSMA. For more information e-mail: p.wright1@btinternet.com*)

Below: President Roosevelt and Prime Minister Churchill (both seated) take centre stage for the Sunday church service on the quarter-deck of HMS *Prince of Wales* at Placentia Bay, August 1941 (*IWM A4812*)

Left: Joe Brooks, who impulsively leapt over the side of *Dorsetshire* to help *Bismarck* survivors reach salvation. Once back aboard ship, Brooks found himself asked to justify going Absent Without Leave by the hard-driving Captain Benjamin Martin (*Royal Naval Submarine Museum*)

Below: Just over six months after she took part in the pursuit and destruction of *Bismarck*, the *Prince of Wales* (top in image) weaves to try and avoid Japanese bombs and torpedoes during the South China Sea battle of 10 December 1941, in which both she and battlecruiser *Repulse* (bottom in image) were lost. This fulfilled the prophecy of a *Bismarck* survivor that, while his battleship and many of her men might have been claimed on 27 May, it would soon be the turn of British ships (*USNHHC*)

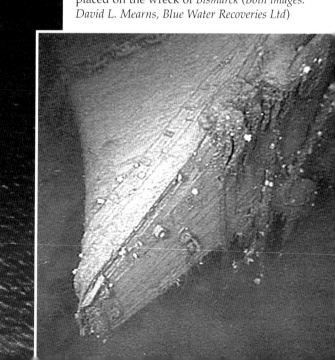

Above: *Bismarck*'s grave revealed. One of the German battleship's 5.9-inch gun turrets, with a hole punched in it, probably by an 8-inch shell from *Norfolk* or *Suffolk*

Below: The bows of *Hood*, on the bottom of the Denmark Strait, as revealed by an expedition to find the wrecks of the British battlecruiser and *Bismarck*. World-renowned undersea explorer David Mearns located and investigated both warships in 2001. *Hood* survivor Ted Briggs laid a plaque to honour his lost shipmates on the battlecruiser's wreck. A memorial plaque was also placed on the wreck of *Bismarck* (*Both images: David L. Mearns, Blue Water Recoveries Ltd*)

them out of water. Then the German battleship was spotted 8,000 yards dead ahead of *Zulu*, with a list of about 30 degrees, the 4th Flotilla's destroyers turning away to loiter at what they hoped was more healthy distance. Vian reported in a signal to Tovey at 7.01 am that *Bismarck* had opened fire, but failed to score any hits. In the aftermath an eerie calm settled over the scene, described by *Zulu*'s Midshipman Hammick as 'two hours of quiet while we wandered about the sea, watching *Bismarck* steaming along the horizon, and waiting for our own fleet to arrive.'[27] The weather cleared and the young naval officer was pleased to see 'a bright blue sky and a clear horizon had taken the place of the grey mists and driving clouds.' In the German battleship, there was no pleasure taken in the same vista, for it meant the approaching enemy would have a good view to a kill. From *Cossack*, at around 8.55 am Eric Farmer saw 'a heavy explosion and after a few seconds a huge sheet of water rose alongside *Bismarck*.' He declared: 'The big ones had arrived and the final stage of the engagement was on.'[28]

Chapter 19

A Desperate and Deadly Race

Through the voice pipes from the magazine and shell handling room below HMS *Rodney*'s X turret came the sound of singing and cheering as men learned battle was close at hand.[1] Infused with enthusiasm by an announcement that *Rodney* and *King George V* would meet *Bismarck* in a matter of hours, Royal Marines were giving weapons they served some last minute tender loving care. Sub Lieutenant Sopocko watched 'thick, greasy work-roughened hands slide tenderly over the glistening steel', ensuring there was not even the slightest speck of dust.[2] Despite such excitement, Sopocko lay down for a nap between the breeches of two loaded 16-inch guns. At 6.55 am, via a visual signal from *King George V*, Admiral Tovey told *Rodney*: 'At dawn I intend to close and look for the enemy.'[3] In two subsequent signals, the first at 7.08 am, Tovey instructed his old ship[4] to keep station 1,200 yards from *King George V*, 'or more as you desire and adjust your bearings', so giving *Rodney* the tactical freedom *Hood* had denied *Prince of Wales*. In this way Tovey applied tactics he had thought of ordering Admiral Holland to employ during the fateful encounter in the Denmark Strait. Now, three days later, the odds were in the Royal Navy's favour, with a crippled single opponent. Tovey was simply determined to give Dalrymple-Hamilton the room he needed to bring all of *Rodney*'s nine 16-inch guns to bear.[5] They, and not *King George V*'s main armament, were likely to inflict the decisive blows. Striking a note of caution, Tovey also advised *Rodney*: 'If I do not like the first set-up I may break off the engagement at once.' He added: 'Are you ready to engage?' After so many hundreds of miles pushing her old frame and engines to the limit, *Rodney* most certainly was.

By that morning John Ruffer, a Lieutenant of Royal Marines in *Norfolk*'s gunnery director, was in an almost trance-like state of light-headedness, having been at action stations for three days and nights. Via his very powerful glasses he had witnessed *Hood* blow up, the attack by torpedo-bombers from *Victorious* and also the pyrotechnics of destroyer attacks the night before. Now, when he most needed to be alert, to be pin-sharp as the cruiser's spotting officer, reporting fall of shot so the gunnery officer could correct *Norfolk*'s aim, he felt most peculiar. He recognized it was the result of 'prolonged exhaustion', having only had the odd nap since the ship first went to action stations.[6] After losing *Bismarck* two days earlier, *Suffolk* had been sent off to find and destroy waiting German supply ships,[7] while *Norfolk* steamed south at moderate speed, just in case she was needed. On the night of 26 May, as *Ark Royal*'s second strike went in, Captain Phillips decided it was all or nothing, ordering full speed despite concerns about *Norfolk*'s rapidly decreasing reserves of fuel oil. At 8.15 am on 27 May, a battleship was sighted ahead, some eight miles away, the narrow silhouette showing it was end on. But which ship? *Rodney? King George V? Bismarck?* In the gunnery director Lieutenant Ruffer used his 'magnificent glasses' to gain a sharper impression of the mystery ship, trying to rouse himself from a fatigued indifference to whatever his fate might be. He saw 'a bleak dawn, with a flicker of a watery sun to come, low down through the driving clouds. It was blowing a full gale, with a heavy sea running.' Within moments the men in *Norfolk*'s gunnery director were in no doubt the enemy was dead ahead. The gunnery officer exclaimed: 'There she is!'

He ordered Ruffer to ensure the 8–inch guns were properly laid on *Bismarck* and ready to fire, snapping the young marine out of his trance.

Ruffer reported: 'All guns ready.'

This was it: whether he lived or died would soon be settled. He saw the enemy vessel rolling and pitching, with 'water streaming off her fo'c'sle as she lifted to each gigantic wave. She was an enormous and splendid ship.'

That *Bismarck* lay ahead was conveyed to Captain Phillips on the bridge, the gunnery director team expecting *Norfolk* to turn away from the enemy at any moment and take up a shadowing position. However, the cruiser maintained her course and speed of 20 knots, leading those in the gunnery director to speculate the German giant had been mistaken for *Rodney*. On the bridge a telegraphist was ordered to flash a friendly recognition query at the battleship with a signal lantern. Sensing he was attempting to communicate with an enemy vessel, the young sailor turned to the chief yeoman of signals, pointing out that he suspected he was being asked to signal the '**!!**! *Bismarck*.'[8]

But the senior rating was not one to disobey orders and told the youngster to carry on signalling. Up in the gunnery director the likelihood of destruction if *Norfolk* carried on with her current course and speed prompted 'Guns' to instruct the sailor handling voice pipe communication with the bridge: 'Tell them that the vessel is *Bismarck*. Make sure they get it!'

Despite the rating yelling himself hoarse, nobody on the bridge felt inclined to pay any attention to the frantic protestations coming out of the voice pipe.

Finally, the peril of the situation was realized and Captain Phillips ordered the wheel hard over, *Norfolk* showing *Bismarck* a clean pair of heels after coming too close for the second time in four days. Fortunately, the German ship's gunners were too fatigued to bother firing at the retreating cruiser.

A message came up the voice pipe enquiring why nobody in the gunnery director position, with all those high-powered glasses at their disposal, had seen fit to pass on that it was *Bismarck* and not *Rodney*? Lieutenant Ruffer saw the sailor on the voice pipe turn 'a rich plum colour' with anger, but instead of firing back a broadside of expletives he slammed the lid down, growling that he couldn't wait for the day when he had high enough rank to 'kick something other than the ship's cat'. *Rodney* and *King George V* were spotted coming into view from the west, at around 8.30 am, Rear-Admiral Wake-Walker from *Norfolk* signalling Tovey: 'Enemy bears 130 degrees 16 miles. On tin hats!'[9]

In *King George V* Midshipman Dalrymple-Hamilton gained great comfort from the sight of his dad's ship and her powerful 16-inch guns. But, he confessed, 'as a boy, a young midshipman, to think my father was driving along just astern was an odd sensation.'[10] Dalrymple-Hamilton was in the secondary armament gunnery control position for the port 5.25-inch guns, very high up above the battleship's bridge, in a metal box shaped a little bit like a mushroom. He was rate officer, tasked with keeping track of the heading of a target, how fast it was estimated to be going and whether it was coming towards or going away from his ship. *King George V*'s battle ensigns had been hoisted the night before, one of them right above Dalrymple-Hamilton's head. He heard 'the most frightful crackling', the ensign having wrapped itself around an item of electrical equipment, causing something to short and 'there were great flashes coming out'.[11] The men in the gunnery director control position could not retrieve it, so, as it was considered bad luck to try and remove a battle ensign once it had been hoisted prior to action, it had been left there.

Geoffrey Marr, navigating officer of *King George V*, was blessed with an excellent view of the British battleships racing towards their fate, as he was in the flagship's emergency conning position. *Rodney* and *King George V* were 'running before the gale, decks cleared for action ... big silk battle ensigns streaming from every masthead, like knights in armour riding out to meet their adversaries on the jousting field.'[12]

Tovey had hoped to work his way south and west of *Bismarck*, obtaining the advantage of having the German battleship silhouetted against the north-east horizon as the sun rose. With his ships in the darker south–west, and with rain squalls hopefully further obscuring visibility, Tovey knew it would be heavy work for the German gunners. He had not achieved this, for *Bismarck* still lay to the south, while due to her damaged steering she was heading north-west.

With *Bismarck* having been at action stations for four days and harassed throughout the night by Vian's destroyers, the British admiral still hoped the sight of two powerful enemy battleships would shake the Germans to the core, making their aim hesitant and inaccurate. In *King George V* there was a real sense of the impending clash representing another turning point in history in which the weather played its part, once again providing England's navy with an edge. An officer in the ship's company noted *Bismarck* 'could only steam into the wind' due to 'a fresh gale from the north-west so that she was forced to head straight for us.' Wind had scattered the Armada in 1588. A gale had propelled Hawke's ships into Quiberon Bay in 1759 and dashed Conflans' ships to pieces on the rocks. In 1940, calm seas had enabled Operation Dynamo to succeed in plucking hundreds of thousands of British and allied troops from the shores of France. The flagship officer felt moved to observe: 'There are many other examples in our Naval History and they cannot be purely by chance.'[13]

As *King George V* sped towards her showdown with *Bismarck*, visibility varied between fifteen miles and three or four, as rain squalls continued to intrude. The ship's primitive gunnery radar obtained an echo from what it was reckoned could well be *Bismarck*, although sometimes such a contact could turn out to be a phantom, merely a reflection caused by waves.[14]

King George V's chronicler explained that throughout the British flagship 'the hands had been at action stations all night, taking it in turn to doze off beside their guns or station.' Events in modern naval warfare came so suddenly, and often out of the blue, that it wasn't possible that morning to allow the Home Fleet flagship's men to 'go below for a breakfast, so cocoa, soup, sandwiches, cake and ship's biscuits were issued to the quarters.'[15]

In *Rodney*, the impending clash was a cause for nagging anxiety, her air defence officer, Lieutenant Donald Campbell noting the likelihood of a savage fight to the finish was 'a cold uninviting prospect to weary men already shocked by loss of *Hood* and three days and nights of alarms, excitement and disappointment.' Full of apprehension, Campbell expected to see *Bismarck* at any moment and his heart jumped when 'dimly seen, a ship ghosted out of a rain squall ten miles ahead; in my control binoculars a warship with elevated guns ...' This was not the enemy, but rather *Norfolk*, which, as *Rodney* sailed past, seemed to Campbell like 'a hound on the trail of a wounded buffalo'. The cruiser 'waited for the hunters and pointed the way.'[16] As the two British battleships lunged towards their fate, Lieutenant Campbell reflected he would not have much to do except observe the forthcoming battle, for his anti-aircraft weapons were merely on stand-by, in case the reported 200 Luftwaffe aircraft seeking to protect *Bismarck* came over the horizon. Many of the AA weapon crews had actually been reassigned below decks to damage control parties. Campbell and his team in the Air Defence Position (ADP) could expect a front-row, though somewhat exposed, view of the forthcoming drama. Perched inside an unarmoured box, which, like the top layer of a wedding cake, crowned *Rodney*'s 'Octopoidal' – a massive eight-sided bridge tower unique to *Rodney* and *Nelson* – their view would be enhanced by high-powered binoculars. Due to the need for an unrestricted view of surrounding skies, Campbell and his team were even above the 16-inch gunnery director position. 'It was a privilege, which at that time I could well have done without,' he observed sardonically. Having earlier thought *Norfolk* might be the enemy, Campbell finally gained sight of his ship's opponent: 'A curtain of rain on the horizon parted and there, on the dull rim of the sea, as a grey shape, insignificant in size at that range, with weapons as powerful and ready as ours to bridge it ... twenty-eight thousand yards ... fourteen miles ... the target: *Bismarck*.' As that same rain squall passed, from the perspective of those at the other end of the fight it revealed a sight to make their blood run cold. For, lying straight ahead, were two Royal Navy capital ships: one a new *King George V*, the other a Nelson Class vessel. *Bismarck*'s men knew how to fight the former – they had, after all, made one of them run away a few days earlier – but the other British ship, armed with 16-inch guns, while old, was no doubt *Rodney*, the formidable opponent they had earlier been relieved to believe stood no chance of catching them. The Swordfish attack had changed all that. Yet, while she was outnumbered two to one, and had already received critical damage, *Bismarck* was still newer than *Rodney*, better armed than *King George V* and had already proved her lethality by destroying *Hood*.

But this was not a game of trumps, with *Bismarck*'s various statistics weighed off against those of the British capital ships to compute the possibility of a win due to armament, armour, fighting record and so on. The German ship had lost her ability to steer but even worse, so it appears, the heart had gone out of her crew. Lütjens' sombre speeches over the broadcast system had depressed *Bismarck*'s men, while their captain's words had lifted them, but work on trying to fix the rudder had stopped hours earlier. The older sailors recognized that they were sentenced to death. Stress and sheer fatigue overwhelmed many of them, and they lay down to sleep at their action stations.

With everything ready for action in his aft fire control station Lieutenant von Müllenheim-Rechberg decided to make one last tour of the ship. In the wardroom he found some officers lost in dark thoughts clustered around a table, one of them remarking: 'Today my wife will become a widow, but she doesn't know it.'[17] Müllenheim-Rechberg decided this was all too depressing and headed for the bridge, expecting to find Captain Lindemann more resolute and determined to fight for survival. However, he found the captain in his lifejacket. The gunnery officer had to look twice to make sure his eyes were not deceiving him. This did not seem like the Lindemann he knew. The captain was eating breakfast, staring off into the far distance, and did not acknowledge Müllenheim-Rechberg's salute. The young officer, who had at one time been Lindemman's personal adjutant and therefore knew him well, waited for the leader he admired so much to say something. 'I would have given a great deal for a word from him, one that would have told me how he felt ... but there was only silence ...'[18]

Earlier, when engineering officer Lieutenant Commander Gerhard Junack had telephoned Lindemann to express concern about the strain being put on the ship's turbines, the captain had shocked him with the response he gave to a request for the 'slow ahead' order. 'Ach, do as you like,' Lindemann sighed dejectedly.[19] Leaving the bridge, Müllenheim-Rechberg descended to the ship's charthouse, finding the 'atmosphere in there was ghostly'. Looking around, the only light coming from a single lamp over the chart table, he thought that he was alone. Taking a look at the chart, he saw the position where the torpedo hit had wrecked *Bismarck*'s steering clearly marked. 'From there on, a serpentine line showed out our swerving course to the northwest, into the wind. Where the line stopped must be where we were at the moment.'[20] This bemused him. If the chart was completely up-to-date, why was there nobody still running the plot? Glancing around, peering into the gloom, he finally picked out the charthouse occupants lying down in the shadows awaiting their fate. Spooked, Müllenheim-Rechberg made his exit and headed back to his aft fire control position action station. He went via the upper deck, going past some of the Bismarck's anti-aircraft weapons where he encountered Lütjens and a staff officer, standing aside to let them past, this time his salute being returned by the senior officer. Müllenheim-Rechberg expected the admiral to spare some morale-boosting words but even though Lütjens literally brushed by him, nothing was said. From the jubilation at *Hood*'s sinking, which Lütjens had two days earlier declared covered *Bismarck*'s men in glory, achieving military as well as psychological value – the admiral was proud to have destroyed a ship he labelled 'the pride of England' – it appeared he had rapidly sunk into melancholy acceptance that death rather than victory would be the ultimate fate of the pride of Hitler's navy.[21]

In confronting *Bismarck*, the two British battleships brought to an end a pursuit that had lasted five days and covered 1,750 miles. The finale would be like a Western shoot-out on an epic scale. More than 5,000 Britons and 2,365 Germans would be locked in combat. Whoever was quickest on the draw would win. High up in *Rodney*'s ADP, Lieutenant Campbell studied the enemy, fully realizing, with a mixture of fear and awe, that it would be 'a desperate and deadly race for the first telling blow, devastating in its effect and shattering to morale.' When it came time for the traditional prayer before action over the speakers, sometimes a battleship's 'sin bosun' could be caught out. The key moment might come when the padre was not near enough to the microphone to make it in time. Such was the case now in *Rodney*. Having struggled through the ship, leaving only moments before battle was joined, the padre contented himself with the shortest and plainest of invocations. 'Oh God, remember that we will be very busy today,' he intoned over the speakers, 'and though we may forget you, please don't forget us.'[22] Throughout the ship, many ordinary matelots put their trust not only in God but also in the 'Seaman's Pocket-Book'[23], ensuring a copy of it was placed where it could protect their 'vitals', one of *Rodney*'s ratings explaining that 'everyone made sure he had his handbook in his pocket.'[24]

Captain Dalrymple-Hamilton, dozing cradled by an upright chair that enabled him to sleep standing up on the bridge, was gently nudged awake by the navigating officer, who told him: 'Gunnery Officer says *Bismarck* in sight, sir.' Seemingly unperturbed by this news, Dalrymple-Hamilton responded crisply: 'Why hasn't he opened fire?'[25]

The normal procedure was for the gunnery officer to ask permission, but Dalrymple-Hamilton obviously felt there was no point in ceremony when facing such a deadly opponent, so the message to open fire without further delay was passed back. In the ADP, Lieutenant Campbell saw *Bismarck*'s shape change, as she somehow managed a turn to starboard, opening arcs of fire to bring all eight 15-inch guns to bear. Campbell calmly assessed the German gunnery officer's likely tactics: 'As with *Hood*, he must have calculated that his third salvo would strike and he might live. It had to. He would know of the tremendous punch of *Rodney*'s 16-inch shells ... *Rodney* had to be knocked out if there was to be any hope of survival.'

Sitting alongside Campbell in the ADP, junior rating G Conning was both terrified and excited, glancing at *King George V*, which to him 'seemed to be hanging back.' Meanwhile, second gunnery officer, Lieutenant Peter Wells-Cole was blessed, or cursed, depending on your point of view, with one of the best seats in the house. Like young medic Sam Wood in *Prince of Wales* during the earlier battle in the Denmark Strait, Wells-Cole was in his ship's armoured conning position. *Rodney*'s Octopoidal was so well protected the command team of the ship had stayed there, on the bridge, rather than troop down to the conning position. Should the principal fall-of-shot spotting officer, Lieutenant Henry Durell, up in the 16-inch director control position, be killed then Wells-Cole would take over. In the meantime, over the internal communications network, he listened in to what was being said by Durell. Absorbing the scene of battle, Wells-Cole saw 'a horrid morning, with a strong north-westerly gale, a heavy sea and the sky very grey. I recall seeing a dim, grey shape to begin with, which turned out to be *Bismarck*. It gradually got closer and you could distinguish very clearly her four turrets.'[26]

In the main gunnery director, Lieutenant Commander Crawford was applying himself to the task of bringing down hammer blows of vengeance upon *Bismarck* as rapidly as possible. He found range-finder conditions were far from ideal, for *Rodney* was vibrating badly due to her high speed charge, spray hurled up as bows thrust the sea aside. Crawford's expert eye told him the ranges supplied by his instruments were incorrect. Therefore he guessed the distance to target, with *Rodney* throwing the first punch at 8.47 am, firing one gun from A turret for range before unleashing a salvo. *King George V* hurled her first salvo of 14-inch shells at *Bismarck* sixty seconds later, while the German ship replied at 8.49 am. In the British flagship Midshipman Dalrymple-Hamilton saw 'enormous mushrooms of flame' erupting on *Bismarck*'s silhouette and thought: 'I hope she's firing at *Rodney*.' He instantly felt guilty. 'I shouldn't be thinking that,' he told himself. 'The old man's in *Rodney*.'[27] Using powerful binoculars he watched shells falling around his father's ship: 'The *Rodney* disappeared in the most enormous shell splashes ... and we thought she'd been hit, in fact she wasn't.' Dalrymple-Hamilton saw *Rodney*'s guns fire and then dip to be reloaded, the noise of his father's ship firing reaching his ears as 'vroom vroom'.[28]

Eager to get in the fight, *Dorsetshire*'s Captain Martin judged he might try his luck, but his cruiser had to check fire when *Cossack* crossed between her and *Bismarck*. The destroyer's men had watched as *Rodney* began her assault 'firing 16-inch salvoes, which they decided were hitting home. Then came the *King George V*. The *Bismarck* was fighting furiously to get away, but she could not do any more than 8 knots.'[29] Ken Robinson scanned the scene from his position on *Cossack*'s pom-pom anti-aircraft weapon: 'There were large White Ensigns flying all over the place and the *Bismarck* was sporting two large swastika flags. Shots were soon hitting the *Bismarck*, who returned fire with her 15-inch guns.'[30] During the action, unless called forward to make a torpedo attack, destroyers were required to keep out the way, and circled on the periphery keeping watch for U-boats. In the *Tartar*, still on the scene after escorting *Rodney*, Lieutenant Ludovic Kennedy had also studied *Bismarck*, thinking her 'the most powerful, majestic, graceful' warship he had ever set eyes on.[31] Earlier, exhausted officers grabbing some sleep in *Tartar*'s wardroom, slumped in chairs and sprawled on the deck, had their off-watch snooze disturbed by an excited shipmate storming in shouting: 'It's begun!' The intruder had witnessed smoke erupting from *Rodney*'s guns, hearing the rumble a few seconds later.[32]

Aboard *Rodney*, Midshipman Shaw scrutinized the enemy through his binoculars and thought the German vessel looked 'a huge ship'.[33]

Deep inside one of *Rodney*'s engine rooms, Frank Summers, a French sailor who helped out during the evacuation of Dunkirk, then decided to join the Royal Navy, was playing a vital role in improving the British battleship's chances of hitting *Bismarck*. With the vibrations from the big guns pulsating through the hull he was controlling the ship's throttle, both decreasing and increasing the speed of the ship, under orders to keep 'as steady as possible to facilitate the gunners gaining a good aim.'[34] Any increase or decrease in the ship's speed had to be conducted with care, as smoothly as possible, to avoid throwing off the aim of the gunners.

Twenty-year-old engine room artificer Charles Barton was working in nearby boiler rooms, on stand-by in case something such as a fan or a pump broke down. A failure in any one of the critical engineering systems during the slugging match could be fatal for *Rodney*. However, the shock to the old lady caused by her own guns firing posed the risk of serious burns, for Barton found 'every time the big guns fired you had to step to one side because flames would come out of the boilers, due to the change in pressure forcing flaps open.' Furthermore, he found that when '*Rodney* fired her 16-inch guns, she slid sideways in the water so, if you were standing on a metal plate without screws fitted, you could find yourself thrown off.'[35]

At one point the ventilation fan in the A (port side) engine room broke down, making it so hot people going up and down ladders had to wrap dusters around their hands to avoid getting burned by the metal rails. Throughout the pursuit of *Bismarck* and now in the culminating shoot-out, *Rodney*'s engines were pushed to their limits, kept going by the sheer determination and valour of her engineering department, a number of whom fainted due to dehydration.

One of the battleship's engineering officers, Lieutenant Commander Eric Walton, declared *Rodney*'s propulsion machinery 'couldn't have been much more clapped out'. At one stage the engineers resorting to 'pouring water on top of parts that were getting hot, just pumping sea water straight on top to cool them down.'[36] Super-heater tubes inside the boilers had to be mended 'on the run'[37], with leaks plugged in order to prevent *Rodney* losing power at a critical moment. At one stage the tubes were leaking so badly that the boiler in question was shut down and a diminutive sailor was sent in to repair the holes, saved from death by cold water hoses spraying water inside and being wrapped in wet sacking.[38]

Stoker Alfred Brimacombe was on hand to trouble-shoot in the boiler rooms but found himself ordered to assist an officer who had fainted due to the heat. The twenty-year-old sailor manhandled his officer up ladders and through hatches to get him somewhere less hot. He gently laid the officer down 'on the deck in the stokers' mess-deck to recover where sickbay attendants would look after him.' Returning to the engine room, Brimacombe thought he could feel *Rodney*'s torpedoes being fired underfoot, with the battleship dipping her bows and then rising up again once the tinfish were away.[39]

At his action station in the starboard engine room, engineering artificer Ken George could only guess at what was happening but fortunately, from time-to-time, Captain Dalrymple-Hamilton's calm voice came over the speakers, providing a drily humorous commentary, both informing and reassuring the many men unable to see events unfold. '*Bismarck* has given us the honour of choosing us as its first target,' he told them.[40]

As *Rodney* was still approaching *Bismarck* head-on, her X turret could not yet bear, but Sub Lieutenant Sopocko used the periscope with which he was supposed to check its guns were laid on target, to watch the other two turrets at work. As *Rodney*'s 16-inch guns fired, the young Polish officer saw 'a sea of flame and then a pall of black smoke', the floor of X turret trembling under his feet. Shell spouts surrounded *Bismarck*, which, according to Lieutenant Campbell were 'great pillars of water soaring 200 feet', that were 'ghost-like and silent, rising and fading. [They] dwarfed and hid the enemy.'[41] *Rodney*'s 6-inch guns could now join in and *Bismarck*'s 5.9-inch calibre secondary armament also began to fire. In *Rodney*'s armoured conning tower Lieutenant Wells-Cole was feeling the full force of battle. Although 'behind a lot of thick armour', he was extremely close to the 16-inch guns, using binoculars to study *Bismarck* through the unglazed slit. Wells-Cole found the noise and blast 'incredible', adding, 'you could feel it through your body.' Having initially felt frightened, after a while, Wells-Cole found he acclimatized, calmly weighing up which side of *Rodney* the enemy shell was going to land. He felt it was 'sort of exhilarating, seeing our shells going out and theirs coming in.'[42] The *Bismarck* was, as anticipated, employing exactly the same pattern as used to destroy *Hood*: one salvo under and one over, to bracket the target, then, hopefully, a hit, which, with good fortune, might destroy the enemy in a cataclysmic explosion. At 8.58 am the German battleship straddled *Rodney* with her third salvo, the nearest shell 20 yards abaft the bridge, shrapnel slicing into the thinner armour covering that part of the superstructure and going through the navigator's cabin.

Campbell and his team 'cowered when they [*Bismarck*'s 15-inch shells] exploded with tremendous impact, right alongside, port and starboard, drenching us with stinking water.' The ADP 'shuddered to clanging metal when a chunk of shell ripped through its thin steel to wreck the gun-ready lamps, fire buzzer, check-fire gong, and gouging a great furrow in the heavy steel main support, split the trainer's telescope right down the middle but harming none.' Unfortunately, so Campbell reported, a sailor picked up 'three pounds of jagged metal and dropped it with a yell; his hand badly burned by the almost red-hot splinter.'[43]

In *King George V*, teenage sailor Harold Thompson had earlier scanned the horizon with binoculars, both hoping and dreading he would spot *Bismarck* looming large. And then, there she was: the killer of *Hood*, wallowing in the heavy swell, making hardly any progress after being crippled by the Swordfish strike. Thompson's unimpeded view of the climax in the Royal Navy's dogged pursuit of the German battleship did not last for long. *King George V*'s 14-inch guns roared, sending out thick rolling clouds of smoke, completely enveloping his action station in the gunnery director tower above the bridge. Usually he was below decks, behind the armour plating, in a shell and cordite charge handling space on the starboard side of the ship, helping to feed ammunition up to a 5.25-inch turret, but Thompson had been seconded to the gunnery director tower and was feeling more than a little exposed to enemy fire.

To him the loss of *Hood* had been 'a blight on the Navy', which had to be avenged. Now, seeing *Bismarck* occasionally through the smoke, he thought her 'an impressive sight'.[44] His job was to ensure the main sights for the 14-inch guns were level and on target, not easy with vibration from weapons firing and the general motion of the ship. An officer nearby struggled to make out the impact of the high explosive shells, catching only occasional glimpses of *Bismarck* through the smoke. Suddenly, above the deafening noise of the guns, this officer exclaimed: 'Good God! The shells are just bouncing off her.' The order was given to use armour piercing. *Bismarck* was going to be a tough nut to crack. Alongside Harold Thompson in the 14-inch gun director position was eighteen-year-old Ordinary Seaman Douglas Turtle, who was very grateful to be wrapped up warm in a long navy blue scarf sent to the ship by schoolchildren in the Midlands. Those in action stations exposed to the elements were given first pick of such 'home comforts'. Turtle believed he was the only one up there with warm feet, for his brother-in-law had managed to acquire a pair of well insulated RAF aircrew flying boots, also sent out to him. Turtle and the others had been closed up in the gunnery control tower – which he likened to a 'tin box' – for five days and nights. The long-suffering Turtle recalled his team was not allowed to leave 'under any circumstances. In this small area we ate, endeavoured to sleep on and off, and carried out our personal requirements as best we could in a bucket!'[45] Soon after the ship opened fire, one of *King George V*'s hits was reported as 'entering the base of *Bismarck*'s fore superstructure; a bright flame burnt for some seconds.'

The splashes of the British capital ships' near misses rose 'as high as the enemy's foretop'.[46] At around 9.00 am *Bismarck* decided to give *King George V* some attention: 'a whistling noise was heard over the bridge and then the splashes of heavy shells were seen some 400 yards over.' *Bismarck*'s outline was wreathed in heavy cordite smoke, gun flashes flickering within 'a dull orange glow'.[47]

On the Admiral's bridge, the fleet gunnery officer, as is the tradition, declared the estimated time of flight from *Bismarck* to target, but was asked by a grimly amused Admiral Tovey to desist, as he said it was better not to know the exact moment when a 15-inch shell would 'hit him in the stomach'.[48]

There would be a number of near misses but the 'nearest approach to a hit' on *King George V* was a shell from one of *Bismarck*'s 5.9-inch guns, which 'burst about 50 yards short of the conning tower'.[49]

In *Rodney*, G Conning was not impressed with the actions of the fleet flagship, noting rather acidly: 'KGV swung starboard and drew away. At the time we said she was yellow.'

This was, however, due to the fact that the chosen tactics aimed to make the most of each ship's fighting qualities; for, by pulling back, *King George V* avoided getting in the way of *Rodney* at the most vital moment, the latter still seeking to land the big killer punch. Admiral Tovey, using glasses to watch the hits – or lack of them – on *Bismarck* used the internal telephone system to urge Captain Patterson on the battleship's compass platform: 'Close the range! Get closer! I can't see enough hits.'[50]

Midshipman Dalrymple-Hamilton was finding the battle both exhilarating and frightening, all at once: 'It was so intensely exciting and sort of nerve-wracking – you did not know what to expect next, particularly when we heard some of the shells going over, and one was colossally tensed up ... it was the most dramatic moment of my life ... well, I've had one or two others, but it was a very dramatic time ...' His tender young ears soon adjusted to the extraordinary noise of battle, which was a surprise. 'During the 14-inch gun trials of *King George V*, I used to hate the noise and find it quite shattering, but in the action I never noticed it. Of course I was only too pleased to hear one's own guns going off, but it made no impression on me at all ...'[51]

The cruisers were only entering the fray when their actions did not conflict with *Rodney*'s. Captain Martin again tried to bring *Dorsetshire* into the fight at 9.02 am,[52] when his ship was still on the edge of her effective range. Salvoes of the cruiser's 8-inch shells hurtled towards the German battleship in quick succession, *Dorsetshire* turning broadside on and letting rip with all eight guns. Flame rippled down her sides, dirty yellow-brown smoke enveloping the cruiser's upper works. In such terrible weather conditions, with spray obscuring optics, range-finders found it difficult to achieve precision. Captain Martin, exposed to the elements on *Dorsetshire*'s bridge, expected the full fury of the *Bismarck* to be turned on his ship at any moment. He studied the enemy through his binoculars, each time spray covered the lenses turning to a junior rating standing nearby who passed him a dry set.[53] *Dorsetshire* began getting the range and scoring hits. Meanwhile, in the cruiser's gunnery control position an excited commentary was provided by a young officer for the rest of the ship's company, via the public address system. As shell spouts rose around *Bismarck*, he exclaimed: 'There's a good straddle! Got her that time ... battleships are hitting her. There are some whacking great fires on her now.'[54] It seemed a lot of explosions were taking place deep inside *Bismarck*; shell bursts could just be made out but the blast appeared to go inwards. From *Rodney*, Midshipman Shaw saw *Bismarck* firing on his own ship with her X turret equivalent. Her Y turret equivalent was 'out of action' while the German ship's A turret appeared to be trained on *King George V*, which was on *Bismarck*'s port beam. Principal armament turrets in British warships were known, going aft, as A, B, X and Y (in *Rodney*'s case, though, there was no Y turret) while in *Bismarck* the equivalents were Anton, Bruno, Caesar and Dora. The *Rodney* was crossing *Bismarck*'s starboard bow, Midshipman Shaw estimating the range was now 'down to 3,600 yards', with the British battleship's 16-inch guns 'taking devastating effect'.

The men operating *Rodney*'s weapons were mere cogs in a huge machine of war – seeing nothing except the machinery inside their own turrets, concentrating hard on not doing anything that might lead to a gun jam. Len Walters, captain of the centre 16-inch gun in A turret, was glad of a job that

174 Killing the Bismarck

fully absorbed him mentally and physically, providing no time to ponder the danger to his own life, or lives his gun might be claiming in the enemy ship. In front of Walters were two steel boxes, and in them levers used to load the 16-inch gun. The rhythm of destruction would be embedded in his memory forever: 'First of all you take a lever and lock the gun at three degrees, then you move a lever and the breech opens. A big blast of air clears smoke and fumes from the breech, then you pull the next lever and tilt a tray down in front of the gun itself. The tray has a 16-inch shell on it. You push the next lever and a hydraulic rammer comes, pushing the shell right into the gun.' Withdrawing the rammer, a charge of cordite was then pushed up snugly behind the shell. 'Close the breech, then push the lever forward and retrieve the slide, meaning the gun is no longer locked and the gun follows the pointer, which is controlled by the gunnery officer up top ... It takes a couple of minutes to load. With the 16-inch guns you don't fire them all together ... two outside guns of A turret would fire with the middle gun of B turret – three shells [plus] two shells of X turret. That means five shells in the air. While they are being loaded, the guns that have not been fired will be on target. When loading the centre gun of A turret, the outer two will fire and vice versa. You don't fire a broadside unless absolutely necessary ... it causes so much damage to the ship. Even three, four and five guns firing together really shakes the ship up.'[55] At 9.10 am *Rodney*'s battle observer, a Paymaster Lieutenant tasked with taking notes on the action as it progressed, wrote: 'Our salvoes falling well together astern of *Bismarck*,'[56] but the British shells – both *Rodney*'s and *King George V*'s – began to register killer blows.

Well protected in the *Bismarck*'s aft gunnery control position, Müllenheim-Rechberg heard the British hits as 'harumphs'.[57] Many casualties were being suffered among the German battleship's anti-aircraft gunners. Because their services were not needed, rather than being stationed deep below decks as damage control teams, they were being held in 'protected rooms',[58] which were situated within the superstructure on the upper deck. These were not armoured and could not even resist shell splinters, never mind direct hits.

Rodney's Lieutenant Campbell observed that *Bismarck*'s 'forward defences in main armament had ceased to exist but not her secondary armament, which spat defiantly, nor her aft big guns which engaged the flagship [*King George V*] holding off at long range.' Between 9.10 am and 9.13 am, *Rodney* fired three torpedoes from her starboard bow-mounted tube and then three more, from the port tube, between 9.14 am and 9.16 am.

By 9.15 am *Bismarck* was sliding by *Rodney*'s port side, the British vessel making a turn to starboard to deliver a broadside with all three 16-inch turrets, achieving at least one hit. *Bismarck*'s return fire was ragged and infrequent but her aft turrets managed a salvo. In reply, *Rodney* straddled *Bismarck* again at 9.21 am, all the while closing down the range. Between 9.13 am and 9.27 am,

14-inch or 16-inch shell hits started a fire in the power plant on *Bismarck*'s port side and also penetrated the main deck, detonating ready-use ammunition.[59]

The reality is that within around half an hour of the action beginning, British gunnery denuded *Bismarck* of the ability to co-ordinate her defence, because the vital communications circuits linking her command team with the gunners were all outside the ship's heavily armoured citadel, along with electrical power cables and other life support systems. Only the engine rooms, deep within the citadel,were left in a functioning condition.

Hits from *Rodney*, *King George V*, or a Royal Navy heavy cruiser, penetrated one of the German ship's 5.9-inch gun turrets, causing an explosion that blew its roof off and considerable damage to the superstructure. Midshipman Shaw thought that while *Bismarck* was battered and bloody her lines still exerted a powerful fascination: 'She looked very impressive – huge splashes coming up all 'round her, while she came on towards us, the seas sweeping off the huge flare in her bows.'[60] *Norfolk* had been playing a part in *Bismarck*'s death since 9.04 am, her 8-inch guns firing whenever the target could be seen amid shell splashes, one of the cruiser's shells managing to eliminate *Bismarck*'s for'ard fire control. Lieutenant Ruffer had been urged by the gunnery officer to take his time about spotting fall of shot, the key thing being to identify which shells were going over (and therefore creating splashes *behind* the enemy) and which were under (splashes *in front* of *Bismarck*). Ruffer complained that in such heavy seas it was going to be difficult to keep his glasses on the enemy and *Bismarck* was so huge that no 'overs' would be visible. The gunnery officer advised him to keep shortening the range until he saw shell splashes for all the guns fired in a particular salvo this side of *Bismarck*. Then he could correct the range until they hit. The double 'ting' of the firing gong indicated guns ready to fire and, after a few seconds heavy with anticipation, the gunnery officer squeezed the trigger, firing the 8-inch guns in unison.

Ruffer felt the noise was 'louder than any thunderclap', the concussion 'tremendous' and he felt the ship give 'a long and ferocious shake'.

Ruffer also said of this: 'There is a momentary cloud of swirling hot brown gas, and the 8-inch shells are on their way, at more than double the speed of sound.' During the final battle, *Norfolk*'s guns would fire every twenty seconds. Despite this hellish cacophony, the exhausted rating who had shouted himself hoarse earlier down the voice pipe remained fast asleep, having been given permission to get his head down. Very much wide awake, from his position in *Norfolk*'s gunnery director, John Ruffer saw a large shell explode inside *Bismarck*, possibly one of *Rodney*'s 16-inch. It had a spectacular effect on the surrounding seascape: 'The water for half a mile beyond was momentarily and instantly lashed into a white foam as a result of the penetration and explosion of the shell.' He saw that the enemy's guns were in disarray and then another shell struck the back of a turret and 'in a flash of time the whole of the rear armour of that turret was driven forward.' As flames leapt higher than *Bismarck*'s mainmast, Ruffer fully expected the German battlewagon to explode, but the conflagration died down. *Bismarck*'s aft turrets fired a salvo again, achieving a near miss on *Rodney*'s starboard side. Lieutenant Commander Crawford reckoned the range to *Bismarck* was 'about 4,000 yards' and *Rodney* was 'pumping stuff into her pretty hard'. And then he saw something remarkable: 'through binoculars, at very short range, where you've got a flat trajectory, you can see your own shell going out, away from you. And I saw three shells from *Rodney* going towards *Bismarck*, and I saw two shells from *Bismarck* coming towards us, passing in mid-air. It was a sort of eerie sight for these things [were] going at whatever it was, 2,000 foot per second, and looking as if the *Bismarck* shells were going down the barrel of each binocular. But they plunged into the sea a long way short.'[61]

From the perspective of *King George V*, standing further out to avoid getting in *Rodney*'s way, it seemed *Bismarck*'s predicament was beyond salvation, for around 9.20 am 'she began to blow off steam, black smoke began to pour out of the funnel and a strong fire started amidships. Half her armament appeared to be out of action and what remained was firing intermittently and erratically. She had a heavy list to port, which at 0925 became most noticeable.'[62]

With *King George V* closing in as *Rodney* herself shortened the range, the British fleet flagship's secondary armament of 5.25-inch guns were ordered into action, very swiftly scoring 'a considerable number of hits'. Those spotting the fall of shot from *King George V* had 'no doubt that these guns, with their high rate of fire, had a devastating effect on the superstructure and upper deck of the enemy.'[63]

Hard at work supplying the guns of a starboard 5.25-inch turret with ammunition was Marine Henry Bridewell, who had not anticipated that his ship's secondary armament would even be required to take part. The action would surely have taken place at distances beyond the maximum range of the 5.25-inch weapons? 'Nevertheless,' said Bridewell, 'I soon found myself pushing the brass cylinders up through the hole in the deck head above me at about five-second intervals. When my right arm suddenly turned numb I found difficulty in maintaining the required momentum. The fellow standing next to me, serving the left hand gun, took over from me when his gun ceased firing because of a damaged cylinder jamming the breach. Later I found a sizeable bruise on my elbow where I had somehow knocked the "funny bone" on something. I don't know what, where or how, but that's how it was, and I felt somewhat peeved at letting the side down, even though it made no overall difference.' For those in exposed positions on the British flagship's upper deck, the sound of their own guns firing 'soon became so customary that it was no longer noticed' although, 'occasionally when the turrets fired on extreme bearings, their blast rattled round the superstructure, causing discomfort to the personnel and minor damage to the ship.'[64] However, the 5.25-inch guns of *King George V* fired only briefly during the engagement because their smoke was preventing the spotting officer in the 14-inch gunnery director from seeing his target.

Conditions in *Rodney*'s torpedo compartment, down in the bows of the ship, were becoming somewhat difficult. The vibrations from 16-inch guns firing were extraordinary, Chief Petty Officer F Pollard finding that everything rattled, including his teeth. When enemy heavy shells fell close to the ship, light bulbs shattered and rivets in an overhead tank popped, resulting in the torpedo men being doused by a shower of cold water. The noise of enemy shells hitting the sea – magnified because the compartment was below the waterline – proved most disconcerting. Fortunately, the chance to fire torpedoes took peoples' minds off the danger. There was even excitement, for nobody in the team that maintained and loaded *Rodney*'s tinfish had believed their ship would ever get close enough to an enemy to actually use them.

Pollard was full of admiration for his youngsters labouring so diligently in horrendous conditions. While their average age was just twenty-one, they performed like seasoned war veterans.[65] Soon the last light bulb shattered, plunging them into darkness relieved only by a trio of two-volt battery lamps and torches. Despite this, the torpedo men carried on, the jamming of the starboard sluice door causing only a momentary pause before all efforts were switched to getting a torpedo loaded into the port tube.

Chapter 20

The Brutal Business of War

R*odney* was now closing down the range even further, running parallel to *Bismarck* and scoring two good hits, at 9.29 and 9.30. A 14-inch shell from *King George V* managed to wreck the hydraulics of *Bismarck*'s Anton turret, causing its guns to droop. From *Norfolk*, Lieutenant Ruffer looked on aghast, yet enthralled by the gruesome spectacle: 'As she [*Bismarck*] lifted sluggishly, the water could be seen pouring out of enormous holes in her side, followed by flames. Her [gunnery] director … a structure as big as the average drawing room … was struck, turned into a flat tin can in an instant, and then seemed to flutter away like a leaf caught by a gale, over and over until it disappeared.' *Rodney*'s Lieutenant Campbell, described this same moment of decapitation as *Bismarck*'s 'main director sailing into the air like a great dustbin lid.' *Dorsetshire* later claimed she destroyed this key piece of *Bismarck*'s superstructure, but the reality may have been that more than one British ship actually delivered the hits.

From his perspective in *Rodney*'s X turret, Sub Lieutenant Sopocko saw *Bismarck*'s range-finder structure and upper bridge 'lean over and collapse'. This devastating blow, surely the result of a 16-inch shell strike, must have killed whoever remained alive in *Bismarck*'s command team, further eroding her ability to fight.

Midshipman Shaw's perspective on these moments was no less horrifying:

'Her aloft director was peeled off and went spinning into the sea – the top of her funnel disappeared – men poured out on to the quarter deck and dropped into the sea.' As *Rodney*'s 16-inch shells slammed into the enemy ship Shaw saw some of *Bismarck*'s men blown 'high over the bridge', like tiny rag dolls spinning into the sky. But the German battleship still had some fight in her, for the Dora turret, while unable to train, was firing at *Rodney* as the latter crossed its line of sight. This was soon punished, for it was 'hit and silenced a second later.'[1]

Lieutenant Commander Lewis, looking on from one of *Rodney*'s torpedo director positions, was simultaneously transfixed and repelled by the sheer, awesome killing power of *Rodney*. He reckoned that his ship fired her last 100 rounds of 16-inch at only 3,000 yards, which was point blank in battleship terms.

In *Bismarck*'s aft gunnery director position, Müllenheim-Rechberg had been without the ability to direct his guns since his targeting optics had been shattered, and he had instructed the Caesar and Dora turrets to fire independently. By 9.31 am these two turrets had fallen silent and *Bismarck* had taken on a pronounced list to port, with smoke and gas seeping into the aft gunnery director position, forcing Müllenheim-Rechberg and his team to pull on gas masks. Entering the rest of the ship was out of the question because it had been turned into a 'raging inferno'[2] Müllenheim-Rechberg wondered if Lindemann were still alive in the ship's forward command post and in charge of the ship. There had been no contact from the forward part of the ship since the beginning of the action, but *Bismarck* had clearly been hit a number of times forward. The telephone rang and Müllenheim-Rechberg heard the voice of an officer in the forward fire control station who informed him it was being evacuated due to gas and smoke. He rang off before Müllenheim-Rechberg could ask any questions.

This confounded the young gunnery officer who had presumed when control of the aft guns was handed to him earlier that it was because the forward fire control system was already out of action. He wondered if it had been used to direct the secondary armament, or perhaps had been used 'as a place of refuge?' Müllenheim-Rechberg got on the telephone again and began ringing around various parts of the ship, getting no answer, except from the *Bismarck*'s damage control centre. 'Who has and where is the command of the ship?' he asked the rating on the other end. 'Are there new orders in effect?'[3] The man told him that the damage control centre was being abandoned and he was the last man there. He was getting out now.

One officer in *King George V* noted that by 9.45 am 'the enemy, who was yawing considerably, exposed his starboard to view for the first time.' He carried on: 'Observers noticed at least three large fires amidships and a large hole in the bows near the waterline. The few guns, which were left, were firing spasmodically and gallantly. The range came down to some 3,000 yards and three hits in one salvo were clearly seen. Two entered the deck at the base of the superstructure and one appeared to take the whole of the back off B turret; an enormous sheet of flame enveloped the turret.'[4]

Around this time, somebody noticed that *King George V*'s Polish midshipmen were suddenly absent from their action stations. A search was mounted for them and they were discovered by their lockers below decks 'sharpening knives and bayonets, as they thought that a boarding was imminent with a chance to pay off old scores.'[5]

Those aboard in a position to witness the closing moments of the battle 'could see all nine shells going through the air and all of them entering the

Bismarck', for in a bid to finally finish off the German behemoth, it had been decided to risk some broadsides of all *Rodney*'s 16-inch guns.

Far from exulting in the murder and mayhem *Rodney* was dealing out, Lieutenant Commander Lewis thought it 'a disgusting sight'. He continued: 'We picked off some of the men who were trying to jump into the sea with [deliberately placed] shells from our 6-inch turrets…we could see the [*Bismarck*'s] turrets and bits of the upper deck blowing up in close sight and we could see the crew diving into the sea to escape from the holocaust onboard. It was frightful.'

Up in the ADP, Campbell watched the dismemberment of *Bismarck* with disgusted fascination, *Rodney* using her freedom of manoeuvre to hit *Bismarck* from all angles. These were moments of unrelenting destruction: 'Salvo after salvo; *Rodney* steamed through, ahead, astern, alongside … Now we had the bull by the nose, using our superior speed to cross and re-cross her undefended bows. *Bismarck* was down by the head, making about eight knots. Slowly she swung round, her forward guns at crazy angles …' Campbell stared with horrified fascination at a 'blazing inferno where the whole rear of her B turret had been blown out.'

Glancing down at *Rodney*'s long forecastle, he watched the 16-inch turrets move in unison under the direction of Lieutenant Commander Crawford in the gunnery control director position beneath his feet. The long gun barrels, paint stripped from them by flames, were dipping and rising, as each one was loaded and then laid on the target. Campbell thought them 'like the antennae of giant deadly insects' but in this case they spat fire and vomited huge clouds of smoke. The shock wave was like being clubbed. He felt his entire being under assault: 'Stunned and horrified, sickened by the carnage and dreadful impact on the senses, at the power of modern artillery, I watched with wide-eyed fascination.' The battle was like an obscene game of skipping stones played by giants: supersonic blurs that were *Rodney*'s big shells hitting the sea, tumbling and crashing through *Bismarck*'s sides or carving a path of destruction across her upper works.

The range was now down to 2,000 yards, and the 16-inch guns fired more slowly, Midshipman Shaw hearing *Rodney*'s gunnery officer 'shout down to the bridge that he was taking his time and firing deliberately to complete the devastation.' Shaw heard the thunderous roar of *King George V*'s main guns, noting later that he 'caught an occasional glimpse of her, mostly on a parallel course to the enemy but at twice our range.' Then he spotted what he believed was *Renown* on the horizon, seeing her fire 'a few salvoes but [she] soon stopped, we were too close for safety.'[6] *Rodney*'s secondary armament barked and Lieutenant Campbell saw 6-inch shells 'burst on her [*Bismarck*'s] armour like eggs on a wall.' He watched one shell hit after another plough into *Bismarck*'s bridge, provoking a 'yellow-white flame, so hot it consumed its own smoke, licking up her whole forward superstructure, incinerating any that still lived.' Most intriguingly of all, he spotted what looked like a white light sending a Morse code signal from *Bismarck*'s mainmast and wondered, 'was it surrender?' But a heavy hit cut short the message, sending 'the whole ponderous stalk … spinning in the air to crash over the side.'[7] The morale of the *Bismarck*'s crew prior to the battle was shaky and in various accounts there have been references to panic when the finality of the ship's predicament set in on the morning of the battle. It only took forty minutes or less to reduce *Bismarck* to a floating hell, littered with ripped apart corpses, her interior an inferno and letting in huge amounts of water. Lieutenant Campbell's speculation that *Bismarck* was trying to surrender was shared by at least one other sailor in *Rodney* with a clear and close-up view of the action via powerful optics. In the gunnery director, Tommy Byers had, from 9.30 am, noticed men jumping overboard and then he spotted something curious – a black flag flying from *Bismarck*'s main yardarm, a means of calling for 'Parley'. The black flag is used to signify a plea for surrender, because a white flag still looks like a battle ensign from a distance.[8]

Byers also noticed a man waving semaphore flags and reported this to Lieutenant Commander Crawford, sitting above him in the upper tier of the 16-inch gunnery director tower, 'but he did not want to know.' The Irish sailor also saw *Bismarck* 'flashing her signalling lights, sending us a Morse message.' Also reporting this to Crawford, he received a sharp response: 'If they are asking to surrender it is too late for that now. Don't report anymore.'[9] Suitably admonished by the gunnery officer, Byers returned to observing the fall of shot, finding the man waving the semaphore flags again, only to see him 'blown into the air by a 16-inch shell.' Byers felt very sad for the German, but he knew 'it was them or us'.

A sailor in *Dorsetshire*, AE Franklin, also possibly saw light signals from *Bismarck*, but did not comprehend what they meant, possibly because he was not using high-powered optics.[10] *Dorsetshire* had delivered broadside after broadside against the enemy and then there was a lull, the thunder and smoke of the guns dissipating on the wind. *Bismarck* fired only spasmodically, but Franklin spotted a signal light flashing what he thought was 'its message of defiance'.

Dorsetshire moved in closer, the range between her and the mortally wounded *Bismarck* coming down to around two thousand yards. The German battleship's secondary armament trying in vain to hit her, the cruiser turned her full fury on the German 5.9-inch batteries, putting some out of action. It is reckoned *Dorsetshire* fired two hundred and fifty-five 8-inch shells in all, scoring fifty hits, considering herself and *Rodney* to be the principal punishers of *Bismarck*. The British cruiser did not receive any damage at all, which later in the minds of her men made the slaughter inflicted on the enemy all the worse. On the bridge of *Rodney*, one of the ship's chaplains was so appalled that, in front of the other officers and men, he begged the battleship's captain to stop. His plea received a coldly furious response, Dalrymple-Hamilton ordering him below decks with an admonition to 'mind his own business'.[11]

Rodney's commanding officer had grown increasingly frustrated as his ship's broadsides, 'fired at close range, although spectacular, failed to produce any disruptive effect, neither did the fires raging all over the ship cause a major explosion.'[12] Nobody liked the brutal business of war, least of all him, but it was not possible to stop until the enemy was utterly destroyed.

An officer dedicated to doing his duty on behalf of a nation fighting for its survival, Dalrymple-Hamilton was also capable of great empathy for fellow mariners under a dreadful onslaught. It must have been a stomach-churning experience, hence his fury at the chaplain actually betraying his own misgivings. From *King George V*, the son of *Rodney*'s captain watched men running along *Bismarck*'s upper deck and jumping into the sea: 'We were awfully close, and everybody was expecting that she'd strike her flag, we could see the swastika flying very plainly from her mainmast, but she never did, and so...we just went on firing. I mean there was nothing else to do – my father was horrified by this, actually, he told me afterwards, but you see, until she struck her flag you just did not know how badly she was damaged.'[13]

Royal Marine Len Nicholl was a sight setter, operating the training and elevation of a 6-inch turret in *Rodney*, one of nine men crewing it under the direction of a sergeant of marines as gun captain. The turret had a sighting port covered with a steel lid that was taken off during action, so there was nothing to hinder Len's view of *Bismarck*, not even glass. As *Rodney* continued to pour shells into the German battleship, including those from the two 6-inch guns in Len's turret, his job was to make sure they were right on target. He wore earphones that allowed him to take instructions from an officer directing secondary armament – Len adjusted the guns' aim, also paying heed to dials indicating direction and angle of elevation. While the 6-inch guns could operate under their own 'local' control, as could the 16-inch, the gunnery director usually controlled when they fired after it was indicated they were laid on target. The 'be ready' bell would 'ding-ding' and the guns roar a few second later. As one of those whose duty it was to look at the enemy – compared with hundreds of his shipmates who saw nothing but the inside of the ship – Len Nicholl could scarcely believe what he was seeing. As *Rodney* and the other British ships kept on hitting 'it was such a rough sea such that every time *Bismarck* was pushed under the water the flames would go out, but then she would come up again and the flames would start again.' Some of *Rodney*'s gunners felt they were so close to *Bismarck* they could have hit her with a hurled spud, although this was of course an illusion caused by the magnification of their optics.[14]

A most inopportune handicap afflicted *Rodney*, namely the loss of her main gunnery control computer, thanks to a Royal Marine putting his boot through the machine.[15] This accident took place down in the ship's transmitting station, a nodal point for calculations of range and deflection combined with data coming in from the gun turrets. This was then resolved on the computer, the information fed up to Lieutenant Commander Crawford to correct or confirm his own targeting assessment. The Royal Marine bandsman's boot broke one of the computer's electric motor drives. Up in the gunnery director position, Crawford was perturbed to see the range reading run down to zero, later observing, with typical British understatement: 'Well, one soon realized there was something basically wrong ...'

After barely a moment's hesitation, Crawford switched to the old tried and tested 'clock' and a Dumaresq machine.[16] According to Crawford these were 'the types of fire control instrument devised in about 1908 or 1909, and were used in the far-off days before the First World War, and which we merely carried as a sort of secondary device.' Therefore, as Crawford revealed, he 'opened fire on a guessed range' and entered the final phase of the engagement using fire control instruments four decades old. He felt 'it was adequate at that sort of range.' Regardless of the lack of a modern fire control computer, dreadful punishment was still being meted out. The *Bismarck*'s foremast was hit and brought down; her hangar wrecked and aircraft set on fire; one of *Rodney*'s 16-inch shells slammed into *Bismarck*'s forward canteen, killing 200 men.[17]

Shells clanged as they ricocheted off the *Bismarck*'s Dora turret, ammunition for the anti-aircraft guns was detonating and corpses were piled high behind one of the 5.9-inch gun turrets – men killed by shell splinters that scythed across the upper deck as they tried to take cover.[18]

A shell from *Rodney*'s main armament ripped into the barbette of the Dora turret and a massive detonation in the magazine was only prevented by flooding. *Rodney*'s Lieutenant Campbell saw the Grim Reaper take his toll and tried to make out the finer detail: 'About thirty men in pairs, carrying what? Smoke floats? Life rafts? I don't know. The solid mass of her X turret, some hundreds of tons, above them, vanished with a blinding flash over the side and her quarterdeck was left bare and smoking.'[19] At 9.52 am, *Rodney* fired all nine guns, of which up to six may have actually scored hits on *Bismarck*.[20] They caused absolute carnage but in many cases shells were still going straight through. With *Rodney* as close as 2,750 yards, one of her 16-inch shells also managed to penetrate *Bismarck*'s armoured belt, below the waterline between Bruno turret and the bridge.[21] *Rodney*'s 16-inch and 6-inch shells were turning the helpless *Bismarck* into a charnel house.

The conditions were like something from the worst nightmare visions of hell: 'The blood trickled down sticky and slow, through hatches and gangways on to the tween-decks, where it gathered in horribly colourful puddles: the blood of the dead, the dying, the maimed, the amputated ...'[22]

From *Norfolk*'s position, *Rodney* – between the cruiser and German battleship – appeared to be steaming almost alongside *Bismarck*. This forced the cruiser's gunnery officer to call for fire to be checked and, as an added precaution, *Norfolk*'s guns were put on maximum elevation. However, earlier, *Norfolk* had been admonished by *Rodney*'s captain, who signalled when some of the latter's 8-inch shells landed rather too close for comfort: 'This is me you're shooting at, not BISMARCK.'[23] Sailors and marines in the cruiser saw five 16-inch shells 'clearly visible' tear through the air and hit the German ship. As these shells exploded, John Ruffer saw that '*Bismarck* heeled slowly to port, away from the gigantic blow she had received. As she recovered and began to roll slowly back to starboard, the *Rodney* fired her other salvo of four.' All of these 16-inch shells hit *Bismarck* and 'two bits of metal, very large and white-hot were blown off her: one bit was sailing smoothly through the air, with the other bit revolving slowly beside it.'

Striking the sea close to *Norfolk*, they 'threw up two large spouts of water', while in the distance shell splashes formed a 'ghastly necklace' around *Bismarck*. Amid the collapsing spray, the German battleship's superstructure seemed to be white hot, especially amidships, with heavy fires visible through a gaping hole. Ruffer saw *Bismarck* shudder to continuous hits: 'The ship was being shot to pieces.'

He observed a torpedo hit *Bismarck* aft, sending flames across the deck and throwing up a column of water, which was 'flecked with black' – a large group of men wiped out and carried away. This may have been *Rodney*'s first torpedo hit. Through his binoculars, Ruffer was amazed to see on *Bismarck*'s hull huge imprints of shells, which had hit the water and then skipped into the German ship, hitting her side-on, armour 'driven inwards'. *Bismarck* was somehow 'steaming through the water', however 'the whole movement of the vessel was sluggish. She was clearly finished but had no means of surrendering. She had to be sunk!' Two minutes later *Rodney* was only one and a half miles from *Bismarck*, and turned to starboard, slowing down to make sure all nine 16-inch guns were on target. Alongside Lieutenant Campbell in the ADP, junior rating G Conning thought *Rodney*'s 16-inch armour-piercing shells looked like fiery tennis balls, with some 'going through her bows and out the other side', bouncing and twirling into the distance until they splashed. *Rodney* couldn't switch to high explosive shells as they had been off-loaded because she was going into refit at Boston.

King George V was five miles ahead, firing as and when she could be sure her shells would not endanger *Rodney*. The British flagship's 14-inch shells did hit *Bismarck* frequently but often failed to penetrate.[24] But did it matter? *Bismarck* was clearly finished. Observers in *Dorsetshire* watched a 'beautifully placed' salvo from *Rodney* inflict more major damage to *Bismarck*. Thick, black smoke was pouring out of the dying German battlewagon and being blown down the whole length of the ship on her port side.[25] *Dorsetshire* closed right up on *Bismarck*, red mist before the cruiser men's eyes as they exulted in delivering revenge on behalf of *Hood*. AE Franklin thought *Bismarck*'s 'beautiful outline [was] like a huge racing yacht with razor like bows.' *Dorsetshire* was bows on bows with *Bismarck*, and now turned slowly to port, opening arcs of fire for her entire armament, artfully using *Bismarck*'s own smoke as a screen. AE Franklin felt the adrenalin pumping through his veins: 'Bang! Bang!! Bang!!! Salvos of broadsides are pouring into the *Bismarck* [and] we see great havoc being wrought…all her secondary armament of 5.9-inch guns are brought to bear on us, but they are aiming high. The shells whizz over the top of the ship – then a fish – a touch of the helm and it passes harmlessly by our port side, the spray showing plainly the track of the torpedo.'[26] This was probably from HMS *Rodney*, for between 9.51 am and 9.55 am she fired three more tinfish, with another at 9.57 am, so the likelihood of one going maverick and coming close to a British ship was fairly high.[27] *Rodney*'s torpedo officer, Lieutenant Commander Roger Lewis, claimed one of these torpedoes hit the *Bismarck* at around 9.58 am, and Sub Lieutenant Sopocko, still observing via his periscope in X turret, believed he saw more than one torpedo hit at the height of the action. Captain Dalrymple-Hamilton was convinced his ship had achieved an historic first – a hit with a torpedo by one battleship on another in combat – and told his men so over the public address system during the battle.[28] *Norfolk* fired torpedoes at 10.10 am, claiming two hits out of the four tinfish launched.

Meanwhile, the back blast from the *Rodney*'s guns was formidable, having already shattered a number of bridge windows. Captain Copinger's helmet was ripped off his head, sending it spinning across the bridge to strike a seaman hard on the chest, knocking him over. As he went down, the sailor cried out: 'I'm dead … I've been hit!' Hauled back to his feet, he was informed he had 'only' been felled by a flying steel helmet. Looking on, Captain Dalrymple-Hamilton thought the seaman's fears for his life were valid, as being struck by the helmet was 'rather like being hit by a falling cock-pheasant'.[29] Using his periscope, Sopocko scanned *Bismarck*, which was now entirely filling the view through his optics. The details of destruction were shockingly clear. He counted more than fifteen holes in the German battleship's starboard side, smoke pouring out of some, others just agape. Sopocko was filled with anger and amazement at what he regarded as stubborn, fanatical Nazi resistance causing so many men to die needlessly. Observing from *Rodney*'s armoured conning tower, Lieutenant Wells-Cole was equally dismayed, feeling 'it was really quite horrible' as he watched men leaping from *Bismarck* into the shrapnel-lashed sea. He was profoundly horrified: 'It was something you had to accept as part of the brutal business of war but it was still a form of murder, an extremely brutal experience, but we had to try and sink her.' *Rodney* turned to carry out a run down *Bismarck*'s port side, the British battleship's Midshipman

Shaw using binoculars to take in the gruesome spectacle of the pride of Hitler's fleet turned into 'a grand but ghastly sight'. He saw water pouring from holes in *Bismarck*'s bows as they lifted from the sea, the 15-inch guns 'lying drunkenly at all angles, upper-works smashed and blazing.' This vision of Hades also included black smoke pouring out of what was left of *Bismarck*'s funnel, while there were flames 'licking' around the barbettes of her 15-inch turrets and Shaw saw 'numerous flashes denoting our shells were hitting, while "shorts" and "overs" threw up cascades of water all 'round the doomed vessel.' And, while Shaw saw some of *Bismarck*'s men emerge on her upper deck to abandon ship 'a group of officers could be seen still standing on the wing of her bridge.'

At 10.13 am *Rodney*'s battle observer noted a salvo 'explodes amidships enemy' while up in the ADP Lieutenant Campbell was praying for it all to stop. The scene unfolding before his eyes was like something from a hellish medieval painting, showing wretched sinners being cast into Lucifer's realm. He would never be able to erase the images from his memory: 'Smoke and flame gushed from a hundred places like blood from a riddled carcass and a stream of men ran and stumbled about her decks or jumped into the shell-torn sea. It was slaughter, ruthless, without mercy, a brutal, necessary killing. I remember calling out: "Oh God, why don't they stop?"'

With his calls for it to stop still ringing around the inside of the ADP, suddenly the guns fell silent, Campbell thankful his pleas had been answered. Now there was an equally unsettling silence, filled only with 'the keening of the wind in our halyards, the rush and wash of the sea ...'[30]

On *Rodney*'s bridge it was Captain Dalrymple-Hamilton himself, equally sickened by the slaughter, who had declared: 'we've had enough, cease fire.'[31]

From *King George V*, they could see 'men jumping off the quarterdeck; the ship was a blazing wreck, so cease fire was ordered at 1021.'[32] *Rodney* by then was getting low on ammunition anyway, with cordite for the 6-inch guns running out. Standing next to his captain on the battleship's bridge, Lieutenant Commander Lewis was in the grip of an adrenalin rush that he was glad of, because it helped him ride through realization of the devastation his own ship had delivered upon the enemy. From *King George V*, Midshipman Dalrymple-Hamilton swept his glasses along the vanquished foe. *Bismarck* was listing dramatically to port and he could see the roof of her B turret had been blown off, which he thought must have been caused by a hit from one of *Rodney*'s 16-inch shells. 'She was smoking all over and, looked as if she was completely done ...'[33]

During combat the focus for hundreds of men below decks within *Rodney* had been feeding shells and cordite charges to the ship's hungry guns. With the guns falling silent, it was time to feed the ship's company a hot meal, so Stoker Alfred Brimacombe made the long climb from the engine room to a compartment adjacent to the battleship's boat-deck. There he opened a valve on a fuel tank that supplied diesel to the galley so the cooks could start their work.

As he did this, Brimacombe stared out a porthole and saw something that has haunted him ever since: '*Bismarck* was lying on her side and there must have been hundreds of men in the water ... not like one line of men, but a whole mass of them, all down the length of the *Bismarck*. I could see some of them were waving, we were that close. In *Rodney* we had heard so much about *Bismarck* being unsinkable and she was a very formidable ship, of that there is no doubt. I think the German boys in the water expected us to pick them up, but we couldn't do that, sadly not possible for a battleship in those conditions ... Even to this day in my mind, I sometimes see those men in the water by that sinking ship. It is an image that has stayed with me all my life, but then I think about all the lads lost in *Hood* and all our other ships in the war, and it takes the edge off it.'[34]

Chapter 21

In at the Kill

A*rk Royal*'s aviators were determined to enter the fray again at first light on 27 May, with Tim Coode leading a strike group of a dozen Swordfish. During the night, the weather deteriorated, *Ark*'s bows really digging in, green sea cascading across the forward part of the flight-deck. Weather had not prevented them from delivering the blow that stopped *Bismarck* getting away, so why should it now? *Ark*'s flyers were mad keen to be in on the final showdown. 'Splash' Carver summed up their mood as 'cock-a-hoop and very keen to get airborne and be in at the kill.'[1] However, they had to cool their heels when the anticipated 6.30 am take-off time came around, for weather conditions made it too dangerous even for the sturdy Swordfish to get safely airborne. Around three hours later it was judged the risk could be taken and aircraft launched. Their orders were to attack *Bismarck*, then disperse and guide disparate warships of the Royal Navy to the scene of battle, so they too could add their firepower. The Swordfish were flying into a strong wind and so took forty minutes to reach *Bismarck*, which was initially just 'a large smudge of black smoke on the horizon'. Then, as they got closer, gun flashes could be seen.[2] Carver saw laid out below a deadly diorama, with *Bismarck* already 'a burning, smoking cauldron wallowing in the heavy seas, but still making headway at a few knots', her executioners circling. Observer Sub Lieutenant Leonard Mann, who had been unable to fly the previous day, was now successfully aloft in Swordfish 4G, finding it difficult to make out what was happening, for at first sight this naval battle appeared 'as meaningless and chaotic as is a yachting race to an uninitiated.'[3] He saw *Bismarck* 'enveloped in a kind of private fog-bank of thick black smoke.' Furthermore: 'After flying around for a few minutes, however, we could see that *Bismarck* could be considered "written off", though it was my impression that, at this stage, she was still firing, but I may have mistaken the bursting of shells from our own battleships for flashes from *Bismarck*'s guns – in that black murk it was impossible to be certain.' The Swordfish crews were dismayed to be fired upon by one of their own warships, Carver noting with disgust poor aircraft identification skills. Surely it did not take much brainpower to understand that single-engine biplanes in the middle of the Atlantic could only be Swordfish? Carver used a signal lamp to contact *King George V*, making sure the fleet flagship knew they were British aircraft. He received no response for a couple of minutes but when it came, the message was 'keep clear'.

From *Cossack*, Ken Robinson saw *Bismarck*'s ensign fluttering defiantly despite her being turned into a hellhole. It was an image that would remain imprinted on his memory for the rest of his life: 'She was a right mess. There was a lot of flame and smoke. The ship was just a mass of wreckage under all that fire and smoke. I wouldn't like to have been aboard her.'[4] Elsewhere in the same destroyer, Eric Farmer thought the enemy battleship's demise was a dreadful business. It was 'a sorry sight to see Germans racing along the deck to jump over the stern. They would sooner be in the open sea which was very rough, than in *Bismarck*, which was by now nothing more than a floating hell ship … Finally the big guns dropped down like dead flowers and ceased firing at our ships, who kept at it … She was on fire, and, at last, stopped amidst a cloud of steam.'[5] Once the guns had fallen silent the Swordfish came down to just a few hundred feet above *Bismarck*, circling for a quarter of an hour. The view afforded to Carver revealed the desperation of those left alive in *Bismarck*: 'Men were jumping over the side and there was a trail of them in her wake. Her leaking oil had some effect in calming the seas for it was still blowing a very full gale.'

With their ship ceasing fire at around 10.15 am the men of *Dorsetshire* gazed in horrified awe at the stricken enemy, which was 'a blazing mass of metal rolling helplessly in the heavy seas, her stern obscured by a great pall of black smoke.'[6] Leading Seaman Bert Gollop thought '*Bismarck* was in an unbelievable shambles but refused to sink…it must have been hell aboard her.'[7] So now it was down to the British cruiser to end the German battleship's agony. With the big ships withdrawing, she moved in for the kill after being ordered to do so by Admiral Wake-Walker who had taken the following signal from Admiral Tovey as his cue: 'Any ships with torpedoes are to use them on *Bismarck*.' Captain Martin amazed his men by making an utterly dispassionate statement of his intentions over the public address system: 'I am going to put torpedoes into the *Bismarck*'.[8]

Dorsetshire moved in for the final act against the dying giant, a torpedo leaping from the cruiser's tubes at a range of only 2,400 yards. It plunged into the sea, lunged above the surface but then carried on, hitting the German ship's hull on the starboard side, producing a 'dull red explosion'.[9] As a precaution against any potentially lurking enemy submarines *Dorsetshire* zigzagged and then fired another 21-inch torpedo. AE Franklin saw 'a tremendous explosion', believing both 'fish' must have 'planted themselves in the bowels of the *Bismarck* far below the waterline amidships. *Bismarck* appeared to shake from bow to stern, like a piece of tissue paper and then rights herself as though nothing had happened, but her guns are silent...'[10] *Dorsetshire* crossed *Bismarck*'s bows, launching another torpedo at a range of around 2,600 yards, this time into the port side, causing *Bismarck* to shudder, German sailors tumbling into the sea. Franklin watched the final moments unfold from his vantage point on the British cruiser's upper deck: 'It was useless to fire our other fish, for gradually we saw the *Bismarck* heel over on her side. Some of her guns firing and then, with a sudden lurch, she turns uppermost her hull being red hot as it appears upon the surface, some raging inferno within burning out the heart of the ship ... "The pride of Hitler's Fleet" sank stern first and the waves covering her after a glorious fight against odds ... *The Hood* has been avenged.'

From his Swordfish, still circling overhead, Sub Lieutenant Mann had watched as 'white smoke appeared to pour out from *Bismarck* amidships. For a few seconds this provided a strange contrast to the thick black smoke.' Mann turned to read a message being sent via semaphore flags by his flight leader's aircraft, but then his pilot shrieked down the voice pipe, 'She's sinking!' Switching his gaze back to *Bismarck*, Mann saw the German battleship had heeled over dramatically, to about thirty degrees. For a few moments he could see 'her funnel and her enormous bridge quite clearly, then she slipped sideways down into the sea. From the time when she heeled over, not more than fifteen seconds elapsed before there was no sign of *Bismarck*'s existence. She had been afloat, a damaged wreck, and within ten seconds even the disturbance of the sea was beginning to die down.' Just a few survivors had slithered off her capsizing hull to fall into the 'chill, heavy seas'[11] as *Bismarck* slid under. From his Swordfish 'Splash' Carver estimated between 300 and 400 Germans in the water. The men in *Dorsetshire* saw 'the tip of the bows above water for a short time'. Captain Martin ordered a signal sent as 'Most Immediate', which told the world: 'Torpedoed *Bismarck* both sides before she sank. She had ceased firing but her colours were still flying.'

German survivors would later claim that they had received orders to scuttle the ship and this is what finally put *Bismarck* out of her misery, rather than *Dorsetshire*'s torpedoes. It is a point that has been hotly contested ever since.[12]

In *Rodney*, making her way north, Lieutenant Commander Lewis was busy making a telephone call via the ship's main switchboard, to ask the warrant officer electrician what needed fixing in the electrical system, when he heard a midshipman exclaim: 'She's gone!' Turning around, Lewis saw only empty ocean where *Bismarck* had been just seconds ago. With *Bismarck* gone, the Swordfish dispersed, some circling over where she had been, hoping to help spot survivors and also keep U-boats away. The Swordfish of Sub Lieutenant Mann swooped low over *Dorsetshire*, the young naval officer thinking she was 'a strange sight, with two large ensigns, one on each mast, and an enormous cheering crowd on her decks.' Lifting his eyes to the horizon he spotted *King George V* and *Rodney* heading north: 'Like all battleships in a heavy sea [they] looked like a couple of hippopotami splashing about.' The Swordfish turned away, their torpedoes still attached, as they had obviously not been needed. Due to enduring bad weather conditions, and risk of an explosion during landing, *Ark*'s aircraft were again ordered to jettison them. The remaining Swordfish formed a circuit, circling over Force H until it was their turn to land, but, finding themselves seemingly under fire from their own ships, 'scattered like frightened chickens'.[13] However, the anti-aircraft gunners of *Renown*, *Ark* and *Sheffield*, were actually firing at a couple of Luftwaffe Heinkel III bombers, forced by the barrage to drop their bombs some way out from the task force. Mann, whose Swordfish was just about to land as the firing erupted, spotted what he believed to be a Focke-Wulf Condor 'simply surrounded by shell bursts', the German aircraft disappearing as fast as it could over the horizon. As the Swordfish touched down, a Heinkel 'popped out of cloud at about 2,000ft, and dropped a bomb about 200 yards away on the starboard quarter', which Mann believed was about as close as the Germans came to hitting *Ark* that day. The rest of the Swordfish got back into their circuit and for some it was a bumpy return, with damage sustained. Aboard *Sheffield*, having a few moments earlier been directing his anti-aircraft gunners in seeing off the Heinkels, Midshipman Repard now used his glasses to get a close-up view of aircraft landing. The continuing gale force winds were making it very difficult for one aircraft: 'The batsman ordered the pilot of the Swordfish, hanging over the deck like a hoverfly, to cut his engine and he immediately dived for cover, anticipating an explosion. The plane hit the deck and slid sideways into the netting, pursued by ground crew struggling to grab it.'[14] John Moffat's view of *Ark Royal* would have terrified a less cool-headed aviator, for as he came in to land the ship was rising and falling at an alarming rate. 'I don't know of any other aircraft that could land and take off from a carrier in a howling gale,' he said. 'The Swordfish had a low landing and take off speed. It wasn't a fast machine and even down to 60 knots you would still have control, which is unique. When I brought my aircraft in to land, one moment I was looking at the flight-deck, the next the quarter-deck and then the screws.'[15]

As *Ark Royal*'s aircraft touched down, below decks in the sickbay Swordfish pilot Alan Swanton, who had walked away from his wreck of a plane the previous day but then had to be rushed to the sickbay for treatment to his wounds, had just woken up. He found his observer, Gerry Woods, by his cot, the bearer of good news. Woods explained how *Cossack* and the other destroyers had harassed *Bismarck* throughout the night, Swanton hearing that *Ark* launched another strike group that morning, but they arrived as *Dorsetshire* was delivering her torpedo attack. Now the Swordfish could be heard returning to the ship with all the thumps, rattles and scrapes that entailed. Woods told

Swanton that their aircraft was in a bad state, for he had 'stopped counting holes when he had reached 200!' It was a comparatively new aircraft as well, with 'less than forty hours on the clock', but would never fly again, destined instead to be a source of spares for the *Ark*'s other Swordfish.[16] The pilots and observers were meanwhile enjoying 'a little celebration' involving alcohol in the wardroom, for they knew there was 'negligible prospect of being required to fly again that day.'

Carver and the others 'felt an overwhelming satisfaction that *Hood* had been avenged.'[17] However, the British naval aviators also had 'the highest admiration for the extremely gallant fight that *Bismarck* put up against impossible odds once she had been crippled.'[18]

Chapter 22

A Necessary Killing

The *Rodney*'s gunnery officer had, more than most, seen what the guns of his battleship were doing to the enemy. With the ceasefire, Lieutenant Commander Crawford descended to the chart house in the bridge, catching sight in the far distance of *Bismarck*'s final seconds, thinking her overturned hull looked like a giant whale. He felt a sense of relief that a vessel which had threatened to wreak such havoc in shipping lanes had been disposed of. Crawford did not feel joy or any lingering hatred for the enemy, just a sense of sadness. As far as he was concerned, 'a gallant ship had gone, and a lot of gallant people had gone, although they were our enemies.' However, Crawford, who would rise to high rank in the Royal Navy post-war, was also frank about the brutal, bloody business of destroying *Bismarck* being entirely necessary.

'We couldn't leave her floating about there, and go away,' he explained. 'And of course we were in the very difficult position ... both ourselves and *King George V* were running extremely short of fuel ... some of the people who weren't actively doing [anything] had many more feelings than possibly I did, about whether we ought to be still firing at her. I had a job to do, which I had to get on with. I did not really have enough time to think very much about the moral side of it.' Crawford was not impressed with the performance of British shells: 'I don't honestly think that our ammunition was very good ... you could either set the armour-piercing shell to delay or non-delay, according to your target. Normally against an armoured ship you always fired with the delay setting, because you hoped to get the shell exploding inside the ship, where it'd do the maximum damage. And at one time the *King George V* – we'd separated, widely, and she was on the other side of *Bismarck* – reported that some of our shells were going through the ship and exploding outside. And I then gave the order to set the shell to non-delay. But I believe if our shells had been really efficient we ought to have blown the ship up, however good her armour. Eventually, it was a rather bloody business.' After the war, when asked if the *Bismarck* had stopped firing would *Rodney* have followed suit, Crawford replied: 'No, our job was to sink her. And our job was to sink her as quickly as possible.'[1]

Finally emerging from below decks, engineering officer Eric Walton headed for *Rodney*'s wardroom to swap stories with his shipmates. As he talked to others it was clear there was a difference between those who had actually witnessed the action and those closed up below. Officers who'd seen *Bismarck* torn apart 'were prepared to be sick'. Walton was nauseated by hearing them describe what they had witnessed, hearing that *Rodney* was so close by the end, she could not get her guns depressed low enough to hit the German vessel.[2] One of his shipmates told him: 'So, we had to open up the range to three miles in order to hit her. Every time we fired our broadside, and we were firing broadsides in the end, the whole [of *Bismarck*'s] upper deck was just cleared of people.' Walton found there was 'no sense of jubilation at all. It was just a feeling of "well, she has gone and we were there and then we left in a hurry because of the risk of submarines".' Walton felt: 'It was extraordinary ... You were just, in some ways, almost sorry. There was great respect for the Germans. They had fought a very brave battle. That was an understatement.' It was a brutal job that had to be done. Even Lieutenant Campbell, who had been appalled at the sheer horror of the battle's final stages, believed the Royal Navy had shown the sort of fighting steel Britain would need to survive: 'There was little honour or glory in the battle; we dealt mercilessly with a pirate who would have been equally ruthless with helpless merchant ships had her mission been successful.'

In *Rodney*'s lower deck, however, there was great jubilation, prompted by sheer relief at surviving – perhaps not something the gentlemen of the wardroom, particularly those who had seen the slaughter up close, regarded as tasteful. But, among ordinary sailors, especially those who had witnessed the battle at first hand, there was again admiration for the enemy's stubborn fight.

G Conning remarked: 'It must have been hell inside the German ship and I salute those men.' Junior rating Richard Hughes, who normally operated a two-pounder anti-aircraft gun, but had been assigned to a damage control party below decks, was under no illusions that suitable revenge had been achieved. 'A load of us had the *Hood* in mind, as she was an old friend of ours,' he said. 'I don't think there was over jubilation but there was at the back of our minds that it was a good job done.' He thought, with only three survivors from *Hood* 'there was a balance there which we seemed to accept.'

As he made his way through *Rodney*, Sub Lieutenant Sopocko encountered both happiness and fatigue. The Polish officer was full of admiration for his British shipmates: their good humour in the face of adversity; determination to achieve victory; cool head under fire; generosity of spirit towards their enemy. Jack Austin, one of *Rodney*'s Royal Marines, was appalled by the loss of life in *Bismarck* but agreed there was a sense of the British demanding and receiving their pound of flesh, even though it was a pretty grim thing. He conceded: 'We lost a lot of good sailors in the *Hood*, but there were also a lot of good German sailors lost in the *Bismarck*, or in the water afterwards. What a bloody waste.'[3]

Austin was disgusted by the behaviour of *Rodney*'s executive officer in the wake of battle. He seemed more concerned with clearing up the shock damage in the battleship than giving her men a pause to reflect on their good fortune. 'After we were stood down I went to the marines' mess deck. It was a shambles, with fanshafts hanging down, lockers overturned, cups and plates all over the place. Just then the Commander came through on his way aft. A word of praise? Not on your life. All he said was: "It's where you bloody live, get the place cleaned up!"' Having been in an action station where he saw the horror unfold with his own eyes – fully aware of the slaughter inflicted on the Germans – the executive officer was possibly angered by the jubilation he found below decks, expressing his irritation by ordering the men to tidy up. Meanwhile, in *King George V*, the young officers of the gun room seemed primarily concerned with their empty stomachs. They tucked into corned beef sandwiches and downed 'quite a lot of cocoa', although Midshipman Dalrymple-Hamilton confessed he would have preferred a beer.[4]

Standing before MPs in their makeshift meeting place in Church House, Prime Minister Winston Churchill was finding it painful to relate the details of the loss of *Hood* and subsequent pursuit of *Bismarck*. That morning a desperate Admiralty signal, drafted on the orders of Churchill or even written by him, had been sent to Admiral Tovey, provoking fury in the Home Fleet. Transmitted at 11.37 am, fortunately after *Bismarck* had been sunk, the inflammatory message suggested that, if necessary, Tovey's battleships should be sacrificed. This appalling missive stated: 'We cannot visualize the situation from your signals. *Bismarck* must be sunk at all costs and if to do this it is necessary for *King George V* to remain on the scene, then she must do so, even if it subsequently means towing *King George V*.'[5] The stupidity of this signal was quite amazing, bearing in mind *King George V* was both fleet flagship and the only fully operational modern battleship in the Royal Navy. There were U-boats on the prowl and, should *King George V* have ventured close to the French coast in pursuit of *Bismarck*, the Luftwaffe could have launched mass air attacks. She would probably have been sunk, and not only her entire complement possibly killed but also the admiral and his staff. Had Tovey been willing to follow such an insane course of action he might well have decided sacrificing *Rodney* was a better bet, for while she had bigger guns she was older, therefore perhaps less of a material loss. There would still have been huge loss of life, not just among the ship's company but also the hundreds of passengers *Rodney* was meant to be conveying to Canada ahead of her refit in the USA. Fortunately, neither *Rodney* nor *King George V* had to face the risk of being towed home because they, and the cruisers, did the job and left the scene with enough oil to reach the UK. Tovey and his staff initially thought the signal was a joke, but became enraged when they realized it was serious. After the war Tovey would describe it as 'the stupidest and most ill-considered signal ever made'.[6]

Fortunately, Winston Churchill was able to present MPs with some welcome good news, rather than a revelation that *King George V* or *Rodney* had been sunk. The parliamentary correspondent of a newspaper covering proceedings on 27 May noted the faces of some MPs were 'white with suppressed excitement' as Churchill laboriously made his way through the story of the hunt for *Bismarck*, speaking from notes on scraps of paper. He was playing for time, so he could give the sorry tale of *Hood's* loss a happy ending. After explaining how he believed *Hood* had been blown apart by a shell penetrating her magazines, Churchill expressed the hope that destroying *Bismarck* would help the Royal Navy better maintain a blockade of Germany. He told MPs *Bismarck* was being engaged but he did not know the outcome yet, although it appeared the German battleship could not be sunk by gunfire and that she would be 'dispatched by torpedo'. Churchill continued: 'It is thought that this is now proceeding, and it is also thought that there cannot be any lengthy delay in disposing of this vessel. Great as is our loss in the *Hood*, the *Bismarck* must be regarded as the most powerful, as she is the newest, battleship in the world.'[7] The Prime Minister produced no more scraps of paper, and it appeared his account of the *Bismarck* episode was at an end.

He sat down and an MP asked how it was, after the lessons of Jutland, that *Hood* had not been fitted with extra protection over her magazines. The Prime Minister explained *Hood* had last been fully refitted in 1931, that it was known she was not heavily enough armoured, but it had not been possible to carry out this work. The MPs turned to other business, but suddenly Brendan Bracken, the Prime Minister's Parliamentary Private Secretary, parted a group standing by the entrance to the makeshift debating chamber.[8] He walked over to the front bench on the government side of the hall. A note was passed along to the Prime Minister. Churchill took a quick look and rose, glancing at the Speaker to indicate he needed to address MPs. For even the Prime Minister to rise while the Speaker was on his feet was a serious offence against Parliamentary protocol, but Churchill persisted: 'I do not know whether I might venture to intervene, with the very greatest of respect ... I have just received news that the *Bismarck* is sunk.'[9] The MPs erupted into cheers that took a very long time to subside. Churchill later observed of this moment: 'They seemed content.'[10]

In Liverpool there was jubilation among the Wrens[11] who worked in 'The Dungeon' – a bunker beneath the city centre's Derby House office block in which the Royal Navy had its Command Headquarters for co-ordinating transatlantic convoys. Displayed on a massive table was a 'situation map' of the Atlantic, on which were marked the positions of the convoys and also, over the past few days, the movements of ships engaged in the pursuit of *Bismarck*, as well as the German battleship herself. The Wrens in 'The Dungeon' had, in the course of decoding signals and updating the 'situation map', followed every twist and turn in the drama. They had been shocked by *Hood*'s loss and the fact that only three men survived. They understood the need for revenge. Now they were ecstatic, one Wren on duty when *Bismarck* sank explaining why it was a necessary killing: 'When you are in a war for survival, you can only rejoice when the enemy suffers losses. You have a totally different perspective from pundits writing history years later.'[12]

At the Admiralty's Bletchley Park code-breaking centre, in the Buckinghamshire countryside, the great moment when captured Enigma machines finally enabled boffins to begin their process of completely penetrating German naval codes had yet to arrive. However, other enemy wireless signals traffic was being intercepted, scrutinized and deciphered, particularly as Wehrmacht and Luftwaffe codes were already broken. The interception of a signal from a senior German air force officer, General Hans Jeschonnek, asking the location of his son, a midshipman in *Bismarck*, and also the subsequent reply from a Luftwaffe HQ that the vessel would soon reach Brest, enabled Bletchley to tell the Royal Navy the German battleship was not heading north, but rather south.[13] A brilliant young mathematician named Jack Good[14] was greeted with excellent news on arriving for his first day's work in Bletchley's Hut 8 – the home of the naval code analysts – on the morning of 27 May. Good learned that Bletchley was being saluted for its influence on the pursuit and destruction of the German battleship. 'For the good of our morale, we were given a number of tidbits about the results of our work,' he revealed. 'We were told it had led directly to the sinking of the *Bismarck*.'[15]

Out in the Atlantic, the aftermath of *Bismarck*'s sinking saw desperate calls for salvation from hundreds of German survivors fighting to stay afloat amid oil and debris in a strength-sapping cold sea. Captain Martin gave the order for *Dorsetshire* to stop by the biggest group of survivors and start rescuing them, despite fears of U-boat attack and the likelihood of a Luftwaffe assault.

The sea was too turbulent for the cruiser to lower boats but many of *Bismarck*'s men were incapable of hauling themselves up rope ladders. Leading Seaman Bert Gollop, in charge of a side party, told his team to throw down lifelines, but when ropes and nets were lowered many of the Germans were too numb to grab hold of them. Leaning over the guardrails, *Dorsetshire*'s sailors urged *Bismarck*'s men to try harder and not to gather around some ropes while ignoring others. It was impossible to haul up a clump of survivors but a single man on the end of a line was a different matter. The Germans had lifejackets, which gave them buoyancy but in a number of cases this meant they were easily swept away by the swell. A few 'dripping, shivering men, many of them little more than cadets'[16] managed to make it up the towering sides of the County

Class ship, but, as Bert Gollop remarked, 'the difficult part was the fact we had a waistline[17] of thirty feet and had to haul them up.'

AE Franklin described the flurry of action as *Dorsetshire*'s men extended 'willing hands' to help the enemy. 'The battle finished, the humanitarian instinct rises above the feeling of revenge and destruction,' he observed. 'The foe is beaten and hearts go out in sorrow to them that are in the water. Ropes come from nowhere. Willing hands rush to haul inboard the survivors. More ropes, more hands. Various groups of sailors hauling with all their might; one then another and then three are hauled inboard ... willing hands give artificial respiration [while] the more serious cases are taken to the sickbay where doctors and other willing hands give succour to the fallen foe.'

Acting on impulse, Midshipman Joe Brooks leapt over the side to see if he too could provide salvation. He tied lines around exhausted survivors and on Brooks' signal these men were pulled up and onto the cruiser. But it all came to a halt twenty minutes after it started, when there was a submarine scare, Captain Martin giving the order for slow ahead to remove *Dorsetshire* from peril.

Leading Seaman Gollop heard someone yell from the bridge: 'Cease rescue operations. A U-boat has been sighted.'[18]

The cruiser's navigating officer had spotted a 'smoky discharge in the water'[19] about two miles away on the starboard bow, which he believed could only have been caused by a lurking German submarine.[20]

Along with others, Gollop shouted to Brooks that the ship was pulling away. Sub Lieutenant Allon Smith, a good pal of the young midshipman, pleaded with him to get back to the ship. A heaving line was thrown down but would Brooks be too exhausted from his efforts to get back aboard his own ship? 'Brooks grabbed it, took a turn around his oily, slippery body and was pulled through the churning water to safety.'[21]

The cruiser accelerated through floating knots of Germans who cried out in despair, faces etched with agony as their only means of survival sped away. Horrified British sailors staring over the side knew they were leaving fellow mariners to a slow, excruciating death, so they 'worked fast and furiously to save as many as possible. They threw everything into the sea that came to hand which might provide a lifesaver for the poor wretches to cling onto.'[22] Royal Marine gunner Geoff Kitchen found it 'heartbreaking to hear their cries'.[23]

Some of the Germans hung stubbornly onto the ropes, only letting go when they were washed away by the ship's foaming wake. One lucky soul was pulled up and over the side even as the cruiser accelerated away.

There appeared to be a lot of stokers among the survivors, which surprised *Dorsetshire*'s men, who wondered how on earth they made it out of *Bismarck*'s engine rooms. When later interrogated, these men 'had no idea how they had reached the water', some venturing the unlikely explanation that they had been 'blown there by the blast of a torpedo'.[24] However, one of the *Bismarck*'s survivors, engineering officer Gerhard Junack, would later confess to a British naval officer that until he had emerged from below decks he had no idea of the slaughter. 'He said that really they weren't aware the ship was receiving all this frightful damage. The engines were still running, the lights were still on, and then suddenly they got this order to abandon ship. And then his trouble started and he had a frightful time getting up from down below because of all the damage that had been done, and eventually he got into the sea.'[25]

Meanwhile, damage caused to *Dorsetshire*'s upper works by German shrapnel and the blast from her own 8-inch guns had to be cleared up, including the remains of shattered boats but 'a sense of grim satisfaction, even of elation, was felt throughout the ship.'[26]

Midshipman Brooks had collapsed in an exhausted heap and, as he recovered below decks, on the bridge his friend Sub Lieutenant Smith was handed a piece of paper from Captain Martin. He was told to present it to Brooks. It said: 'You are to report your reasons in writing as to why you were absent without leave from HMS *Dorsetshire* at 1030 on Tuesday, 27 May 1941.'

On receiving this missive Brooks' reaction was: 'Oh, sod it.'

He turned over and went to sleep.[27]

Maori had stayed behind with *Dorsetshire* to pick up survivors and now both headed north to join the rest of the Home Fleet. As the fourth gunnery officer, Müllenheim-Rechberg was the most senior out of four *Bismarck* officers pulled from the sea. He had received no order to abandon ship, nor had he heard about the instruction to scuttle the ship. He kept his men inside the well-protected aft gunnery director position until after the enemy's guns had fallen silent and *Bismarck*'s anti-aircraft ammunition had stopped detonating. By the time he emerged to make his bid to escape the sinking ship, Müllenheim-Rechberg found *Bismarck* was listing very heavily to port and was already down by the stern, with big waves rolling across her. Many men who leapt into the sea on *Bismarck*'s port side or were washed overboard were dashed against the ship and killed. Taking in the scene around him, Müllenheim-Rechberg was amazed to see nothing left of the anti-aircraft guns, which had been completely torn away from their positions by enemy fire. There was scorched, twisted metal lying everywhere and gaping holes in the deck and superstructure. White smoke poured out of the holes, indicating raging fires below. Climbing over debris and leaping across holes, Müllenheim-Rechberg headed past the Caesar turret, finding its guns on maximum elevation and trained to port, apparently unharmed. Dora was a blackened wreck, the right hand 15-inch gun shredded by a shell hit. Scanning the surrounding seascape, Müllenheim-Rechberg was shocked to see *Rodney* so close, with her 'nine guns still pointing mistrustfully at us. I could look down their muzzles.'[28] He reckoned at that range *Rodney* could not have missed *Bismarck*, but he did not fear she would open fire again, for the German battleship was obviously reduced to a wreck. Waiting until the

Bismarck had begun to capsize, Müllenheim-Rechberg ordered his men to snap off a salute to 'fallen comrades' and shouted at them to jump into the water. They swam as fast as they could to avoid being sucked down and then watched as *Bismarck* slowly turned over and sank by the stern, Lindemann apparently standing at the stem, tall and proud, saluting as he went down with his ship. Müllenheim-Rechberg and his little group were swept past several knots of survivors, enabling him to exchange words and glances with shipmates, most of whom he never saw again. Fortunately, he soon sighted *Dorsetshire* and, urging his group of survivors on, they struggled across to the British cruiser.

Shortly after being rescued, Müllenheim-Rechberg was given permission via a note from Captain Martin, to visit *Bismarck*'s other survivors, most of whom were being held in a recreation space just aft of the forecastle.[29] Martin suggested to Müllenheim-Rechberg that he should find out if there was anything the prisoners needed and, if available, the ship would supply it. The young *Kriegsmarine* lieutenant was also brought to the cruiser's bridge, entering into a discussion with Captain Martin, during which he made clear his disapproval of *Dorsetshire*'s leaving so many men in the water. Müllenheim-Rechberg 'was quickly put in his place by the more experienced Captain Martin who made it plain that the issue was not open for discussion.' Martin explained forcefully that the presence of U-boats left him 'no choice but to consider his men and his ship as his first priority.' Müllenheim-Rechberg grudgingly accepted that, in the circumstances, it was the correct course of action for *Dorsetshire*.[30]

Naval surgeons in the cruiser fought to save the life of *Bismarck*'s Gerhard Luttich who had somehow managed to make it aboard despite losing a leg and suffering severe burns. Their efforts were in vain and he passed away on 28 May, his funeral at sea to be conducted the following morning. It was agreed that an Imperial German Navy ensign the ship possessed could be used to cover his shroud. There would be no manifestations of the Nazi regime.[31]

The funeral service took place on the cruiser's quarter-deck, with British sailors arrayed one side and *Bismarck*'s men the other. One of *Dorsetshire*'s men described the ceremony: 'A guard of honour fired three volleys over the body. At 9.20 am the ship's engines stopped, the chaplain concluded his short service, and the body splashed to its final resting place in the sea. Facing each other across the quarter deck there was no animosity in the faces of the men, just a little sadness that this man had to die.'[32] During their time aboard *Dorsetshire*, the Germans were docile, at least to begin with, partly, of course, due to the mental shock of losing their ship and the physical effects of their ordeal, which took them some time to shake off. *Dorsetshire*'s matelots were friendly, understanding the Germans were sailors just like them and had fought bravely, to the bitter end. However, in some Nazi defiance soon came to the surface. During one incident 'an officer, stark naked, was handed a clean shirt, he drew himself up, coldly gave the Nazi salute – and then his bare heels slipped on the wet soapy floor and he toppled backwards.'[33] However, on the whole, as one *Dorsetshire* sailor related, 'the German survivors were given every care and attention that the ships' resources could provide. The brotherhood of the sea was evident, even between victor and vanquished.'[34]

In *King George V*, Marine Henry Bridewell had found that when it was broadcast *Bismarck* was sinking, 'previous misgivings' were transformed into 'elation'.

Not long after he heard the British fleet was leaving and that attempts to rescue *Bismarck* survivors had been called off due to the possible presence of a U-boat. This caused Bridewell 'disquiet' – probably he was imagining what it must have felt like to be left behind, bobbing in the sea facing only the certainty of a slow death. However, Bridewell's guilt on behalf of his navy soon abated when he learned more: 'The majority of us had seen nothing at all of the action, we knew nothing at all of *Dorsetshire*'s presence or of her valiant rescue efforts, until hearing about them on the radio some two or three days later. Better and proper information at the time would at least have allowed us each to make our own more realistic appreciation. So that was the *Bismarck*, that was! It seemed to be all over before it started to many of us. Few of us really knew much about it, though we must be excused for thinking that we did at the time.'[35]

For the first time in several days the men of *Norfolk* were relaxed from action stations as their ship also headed for the Clyde. Lieutenant Ruffer was released from the gunnery director, making his way down to the wardroom. There he found little by way of elation. The young marine helped himself to a sandwich, sitting in a daze munching it until there was an air attack alert, which he and his shipmates wearily responded to, heading for their action stations once again. Only the thought of fighting for their lives in the water like *Bismarck*'s men motivated them to move their weary bones. The *Kriegsmarine* may have received a bitter lesson in the supremacy of the Royal Navy, its ability to soak up major losses and still retain the strategic upper hand, but the Luftwaffe apparently begged to differ. As the Home Fleet withdrew from the scene of its triumph over *Bismarck*, Goering's planes made their presence felt, even if it was a rather half-hearted effort. Four German bombers made attack runs, but thought better of trying to part the curtain of steel put up by the combined anti-aircraft guns of the British fleet. *Rodney* shot one of them down. By this time *Dorsetshire*, carrying her eighty-five *Bismarck* survivors, and *Maori*, with twenty-five, had caught up with the rest of the Home Fleet, finding the destroyers of Vian's 4th Flotilla in attendance.

Cossack had saved one *Bismarck* 'survivor', in the form of a tabby cat, which was dubbed 'Herr Oscar' and had been spotted, fur all oil-matted and shivering, riding some wreckage.[36]

Aboard the destroyer *Electra*, still at anchor in Icelandic waters and waiting to escort *Prince of Wales* to Rosyth Dockyard, they read signals detailing *Bismarck*'s destruction with admiration for the foe's brave fight against the odds. They also felt satisfaction at the result. The destroyer's men were exhausted by the sheer nerve-wracking, epic nature of what they had just been through: the charge north with *Hood* and *Prince of Wales*; the cataclysm of the battlecruiser's loss; providing salvation for just three survivors; meeting the battered *Prince of Wales*; living the night action by Vian's destroyers through intercepted signals; the final battle, again as long-distance spectators via intercepts. They had prayed the German battleship that destroyed *Hood* would not get away and now, so *Electra*'s Lieutenant Cain noted: 'Retribution had overtaken her, and very gallantly had she suffered it; fighting to the last. *Bismarck* had outlived our friend the *Hood* by just three days. To us the time had passed like an eternity.'[37]

Chapter 23

Ghosts at the Feast

On arrival in Iceland Sam Wood went ashore from *Prince of Wales* with the severely wounded officer Esmonde Knight, who was to be flown back to the UK in a Royal Air Force bomber, destined for an eye hospital in Edinburgh. There was a suggestion Wood should go all the way with him. However, it transpired he would not be needed and Wood was grateful for this, for he was 'dressed only in a duffel coat and sea boots with no hat'[1] and feared a ticking off for being improperly attired ashore. Instead Wood took a taxi to the fjord where *Prince of Wales* lay at anchor. Joining some other medics, who had also been escorting casualties, he persuaded Royal Artillery gunners manning an anti-aircraft position to send a signal to the battleship requesting a boat. Meanwhile, *Prince of Wales* had received temporary repairs to her battle damage and was now listed to port – achieved by transferring oil in her tanks – in order to lift suspected shell holes above the water. Two 8-inch shell hits from *Prinz Eugen* had ruptured armour in the hull above the ship's propeller shafts.[2]

Water that had flooded into the stern was pumped out and the holes were patched up. Once considered seaworthy, *Prince of Wales* weighed anchor and set sail for Rosyth Dockyard, accompanied by *Electra* and other destroyers. News of *Bismarck*'s destruction broke during the voyage to Scotland, with Joseph Willetts witnessing the moment it reached the ship. He was called to the cipher office, as Paymaster Lieutenant Commander McMullen – brother of the gunnery officer – required him to take a signal down on a message pad. It was marked urgent, 'for immediate dissemination'. Deciphering it, McMullen became excited, telling Willetts to lock up the office while he took the signal to Captain Leach. As he departed, McMullen advised Willetts to then make his way to the upper deck 'because the Captain will be clearing lower deck.' By the time he got there Willetts found it already crowded, with sailors and marines milling around until a Royal Marine bugler sounded the 'Still'. Leach told his men: 'I have just received a message from the Admiralty, which I must read to you: "The *Bismarck* is sunk."' Once the cheers had subsided Leach added: 'Gentleman, I'm sure that you will agree that this is the end of a very gallant ship.'³ Sam Wood was among those celebrating, feeling the ghosts of fellow sailors and marines in *Hood* could now rest easier: 'We felt elated that our efforts had not been in vain and revenge had been extracted for the loss of the *Hood* and our shipmates lying off Cape Farewell.' Captain Leach called McMullen – the gunnery officer – up to his day cabin, to discuss if it was feasible for the ship to take part in the hunt for *Prinz Eugen*, which was thought to be still at sea. Leach intended sending a signal to the Admiralty informing their Lordships that *Prince of Wales* was ready for action again. During their discussion Leach and McMullen asked for clarification of Y turret's status, but the message they got back was not positive: the complex mechanism was still giving trouble and was effectively out of action. That meant the ship was out of the game until after major work in a dockyard. On arrival at Rosyth, *Prince of Wales* found the Forth Railway Bridge packed from one end to the other with thousands of people. They had been following the *Bismarck* drama in the newspapers and listening to radio bulletins, so from the moment *Prince of Wales* came into sight, they 'cheered and cheered and cheered and cheered all the way' during her progress under the bridge and up river to the dockyard.⁴ After the ship went into dry dock, to everybody's horror another shell hole was discovered, twenty-seven feet below the waterline on the starboard side. At the time Lieutenant Brooke was duty officer, pondering the fact that the middle watch⁵ was *always* deadly dull, when he heard 'the sound of frantic feet' coming up a ladder towards where he was in the ship's quarter-deck lobby. Lieutenant Dick Wildish, an engineer who was also the ship's damage control officer, appeared, very agitated and announcing his awful find. Due to a gauge on a control panel Wildish had already been able to tell during the 24 May battle that something must have penetrated an aft compartment and flooding had taken place. Once the dry dock was empty and the ship resting securely, Wildish decided to go down and have a look, taking a senior rating with him. Discovering a large hole 'just above the ship's bilge keel', they decided to climb in to see what they could find. Like archaeologists getting ever deeper into a pharaoh's tomb – the light of their torches probing the glistening sides of rarely explored compartments – they clambered through a series of jagged holes, following the path of the shell. Its trail of destruction ended at a dent in an armoured bulkhead. Using a boat hook Wildish probed the dark, dank bottom of the compartment until it glanced off something. Shining the torch down, to his absolute horror he saw what was clearly an unexploded 15-inch shell, a surprise present from *Bismarck*. On hearing all this from Wildish, Lieutenant Brooke ran aft through the ship, leaping over hatch combings, to the captain's cabin, waking Leach and other senior officers. They were soon 'buttoning coats over pyjamas',⁶ all hurrying down to the bottom of the dry dock to carry out their own inspection of the unwelcome lodger. Lieutenant Commander McMullen inspected the hole, finding that it was fifteen inches in diameter and assessing it was 'where one of

Bismarck's shells had gone into the sea short of the ship, had swum like a torpedo, had gone through the ship's side …'

Who would get the delicate job of removing the live 15-inch enemy shell from *Prince of Wales*' innards? McMullen and the torpedo officer, Lieutenant Commander RF Harland, tossed a coin to decide whether it should be gunners or torpedo men. McMullen lost, so the gunnery officer and his 'splendid gunners' got on with the job, working under extreme pressure on two counts: firstly, not to set the shell off; secondly, to enable the ship to be properly repaired and at sea again to face the next German surface raider breakout. Hearing this tale Sam Wood ventured: 'What a victory *Bismarck* would have had if that shell had exploded, the *Hood* and *Prince of Wales* [claimed] in one battle.' Lieutenant Brooke thought it 'astonishing luck' the shell had not detonated. Had it done so it would have been a calamity, for it lay in 'very close proximity to both oil fuel and diesel oil, could at best have started a major fire and blown out the side of the ship.' Furthermore, he reflected, the magazine of the ship's Y turret 'was only yards away and at worst there could have been an explosion in all too faithful emulation of the *Hood*.'[7]

Lt Commander McMullen considered that, while removing the 15-inch shell appeared a risky venture, it had already been tested to the extreme and had not gone off. After hitting the sea and penetrating the hull, it had punched through two vertical bulkheads, smashed through three-inch armour and then dropped into the bottom of the ship. Therefore, McMullen concluded, 'if that hadn't exploded the shell, then OK, if we treated it gently, we were alright.' The nose cap was never found, so perhaps the fact that it had detached from the 2,000lbs of explosives had saved the ship? Manhandling a manually operated 14-inch shell grab down into the bowels of the ship, the gunners used it very gently to pick up the enemy ordnance. McMullen measured the shell's diameter, just to make sure it truly was 15 inches. He then held a discussion with the dockyard staff and they cut a hole in the bottom of *Prince of Wales* big enough for the grab, suspended on the end of a chain, to lower the shell through and lay it gently on the bottom of the dock. Job done, Lieutenant Commander McMullen asked Captain Leach to come and have his picture taken with the offending shell. After having *Bismarck* chalked on it, the shell was placed carefully in front of Leach, McMullen and the proudly beaming gunners for their photo shoot.

While she was at Rosyth, *Prince of Wales* was visited by AV Alexander, First Lord of the Admiralty, who was taken to the wardroom, where he met the ship's officers. Captain Leach introduced him to the battleship's gunnery officer. Alexander demanded: 'Did you hit her, boy?'

McMullen replied: 'I'm pretty certain we did hit her because we …'

'Did you hit her or did not you?'

'The thing is, with armour piercing shell, sir, the shells go …'

'Did you hit her, boy?'

'I think we ...'[8]

Losing patience, Alexander turned his back on McMullen, leaving the gunnery officer's pride sorely bruised. An uncomfortable silence hung over the wardroom until the First Lord's private secretary intervened, explaining he was ushering Alexander away to a pressing appointment in Edinburgh.[9]

McMullen thought Alexander had wanted him to say: 'Yes, I saw three hits and an enormous explosion.' But, of course, naval warfare was not that clear cut. McMullen hoped he'd be able to meet Alexander again after the war and tell him: 'Yes, we did hit her.' He never did get that opportunity.

On the whole, and despite their superb reception on reaching Rosyth, the ship's company of *Prince of Wales* felt marginalized from the celebrations of the *Bismarck* victory, one in which they had truly played their part. As reflected by Alexander's rough handling of McMullen, the impact of her gunnery was not appreciated at the time, and the politicians felt Britain's newest battleship should have done better. Therefore, the glory went to other ships – *Ark Royal*, *King George V*, *Cossack*, even *Victorious* – while *Prince of Wales* and *Rodney* were pushed to one side. In the latter's case, it was probably a matter of not wanting to be reminded that it had taken the guns of a ship built in the 1920s to take *Bismarck* apart while the Home Fleet flagship's 14-inch weapons were less effective. The men of *Prince of Wales* felt particularly hard done by, having coped with all their mechanical problems, suffered deaths and yet, so they thought, delivered telling hits on *Bismarck*. 'We are all a bit bitter as the papers have got hold of the wrong end of the stick,' Lieutenant Brooke wrote to his parents in early June 1941. He explained that his own ship was not, as claimed by Nazi propaganda, left in a sinking condition. Brooke still paid tribute to the German battleship: 'She did marvellously well and was apparently unsinkable by gunfire in a short time. The penny press and all their vulgar exaltation (apart from natural jubilation) and not knowing anything about it, rather annoy me.'[10] Brooke felt the press had inadvertently bought into the Nazi propaganda.

In the wake of his considerable victory, Admiral Tovey received a telephone call aboard *King George V* from the First Sea Lord, Admiral Sir Dudley Pound, who told him Captain Leach and Rear-Admiral Wake-Walker were to be court-martialled for withdrawing the *Prince of Wales* while engaging the *Bismarck* and *Prinz Eugen*. Admiral Tovey was angered by this suggestion, considering Captain Leach, in charge of a new ship with severe teething problems, had done as well as could be expected. Despite suffering serious hits *Prince of Wales* had, in fact, continued to shadow *Bismarck*. Had he been foolish enough to engage *Bismarck* and *Prinz Eugen* at close quarters, Captain Leach could easily have thrown the lives of his own sailors away on top of the dreadful loss of *Hood*'s. Admiral Tovey told his boss: 'If the Admiralty is going to do that, then I will resign and act as Prisoner's Friend[11], because I consider he did absolutely the right thing.'

On receiving this shot across his bows, Admiral Pound ultimately decided to opt for the only other course of action: saluting the bravery of Captain Leach by awarding him a medal, the Distinguished Service Order (DSO). Rear-Admiral Wake-Walker received the Commander of the British Empire (CBE) 'for distinguished services in the masterly and determined action in which the German battleship *Bismarck* was destroyed.'[12]

Unaware of threats against their beloved captain, the *Prince of Wales'* sailors and marines felt they had made it to easy street. Scapa enjoyed some magnificent weather that summer, and on such occasions every scuttle would be open, sailors on the upper deck in working parties soaking up the sun. One particular day there was a good line in banter going between matelots and members of the Royal Marine band who were, as one *Prince of Wales* rating put it 'at the wrong end of a lot of crude sayings…advice such as what to do with their trumpets.'[13] But the marines were used to it and took it in good heart, getting on with their band practice despite the chorus of mickey-taking. The high spirits dissipated, however, when the order was given for all scuttles to be closed and the ship put at twelve hours notice to sail. The buzz went around that someone very important would soon be coming aboard, and everybody was advised they would not be permitted to stand about on the upper deck 'in an unseamanlike manner'. The destroyer *Oribi* soon pulled alongside the ship and there on the smaller warship's open bridge was Winston Churchill himself, with top brass from all three branches of the UK armed forces. The Prime Minister would be aboard for nearly three weeks, as would the First Sea Lord – the two men who suggested Captain Leach should be court-martialled. And here they were a matter of weeks later, shaking hands with Leach, the scene observed by Lieutenant Brooke, who was officer of the watch. Joseph Willetts also saw Churchill come aboard ship: 'He'd got his cap slightly to one side, with the cap badge not quite in the middle … And a big cigar.' The idea for a trip across the Atlantic for a summit meeting between Churchill and Roosevelt 'in some lonely bay or other'[14] had first been raised in late July, when the Prime Minister and American envoy Harry Hopkins enjoyed a chat as they sunned themselves in the back garden of 10 Downing Street. The location selected was Placentia Bay, Newfoundland, the date to be August 9, or thereabouts.

At a station near Chequers, the Prime Minister boarded a special train for Scapa Flow, and, as night fell on 4 August, once he was securely aboard, *Prince of Wales* carved her way out into a moderate Atlantic swell. The ship's company soon learned she was heading for Newfoundland but not exactly why. Churchill spent a lot of time on the battleship's bridge, smoking cigars, and whenever one was stubbed out in an ashtray, a sailor would spring forward to dispose of it. The remains of the Prime Minister's cigars were squirrelled away 'as a trophy'.[15] Despite his threat to court-martial Captain Leach over failing to renew the action with *Bismarck* just over two months earlier, Churchill found the battleship's captain 'a charming and lovable man and all that a British sailor should be.'[16] By 5 August the seas were so heavy Churchill moved from spacious quarters at the stern of the ship – afflicted with severe vibration due to thrashing propellers directly below – to the Admiral's Day Cabin in the bridge tower. This became his headquarters, where he slept and worked. On orders of Admiral Pound the destroyer escort was left behind because, typically, the smaller ships could not maintain high speed in such heavy seas. It was felt best not to slow the battleship down to let them keep up, for fear of U-boat attack. There were also concerns that if news leaked out about Churchill racing across the Atlantic in a battleship, *Tirpitz* might be sent to kill him, such was the anxiety about a sequel to the *Bismarck* drama. Calling briefly at Iceland to top up oil tanks, *Prince of Wales* picked up a new destroyer escort, in the form of two Canadian vessels, *Restigouche* and *Assinibone*, plus *Ripley*, the latter one of fifty ancient First World War-era former US Navy destroyers on lend-lease to the Royal Navy. *Prince of Wales* wound herself up to her top speed of 28 knots but in calmer seas the escorts could keep up. In his War Room, established in a surplus office, Churchill, political advisors and senior officers met regularly to discuss the progress of the war and future strategy. The positions of Allied warships and convoys were marked on a large chart, including that of *Prince of Wales* herself. There was also a massive map of Russia, which showed developments in the recently erupted conflict between the Soviet Union and Nazi Germany. Looking at the chart one day, Lieutenant Brooke commented on a U-boat that he saw had been 'sunk'. A strangely familiar voice remonstrated with Brooke, chiding him by remarking: 'Only British submarines are sunk. German U-boats are destroyed.'[17] Behind him Churchill had quietly entered the War Room.

The need to maintain radio silence, to avoid giving away the ship's position, forced the Prime Minister to take a break from his usual hyperactive work routine. He was unable to shape events if signals could not be sent out from the ship. The weather also intervened. Relegated to reading CS Forester's *Captain Hornblower R.N.*, the Prime Minister also occupied himself by taking exercise, making circuits of the battleship's quarter-deck. However, it was often out of bounds due to heavy seas, so Churchill made circuits of compartments in the bridge tower, finding excellent exertion in clambering up and down the ladders. In the evenings there were post-dinner film shows, including *Lady Hamilton*, starring Laurence Olivier as Nelson, which dealt in part with the Battle of Trafalgar. Afterwards the Prime Minister told *Prince of Wales'* men, thinking of the *Bismarck* action: 'Gentlemen, I thought this film would interest you, showing great events similar to those in which you have been taking part.'[18] They enjoyed having 'the Prime' about the ship, dressed in his Trinity House uniform and cap. He was occasionally glimpsed in his blue denim, all-in-one 'siren suit', which Lieutenant Brooke thought, combined with a portly figure and 'cherubic face', made the British war leader look like 'a huge baby in rompers'.[19]

Traces of the *Bismarck* action were still to be found around the ship, despite her time in dockyard hands. Journalist HV Morton, specially selected to cover the trip, but forbidden from filing any news reports for the duration of the time he was with the Prime Minister's party, was given a young officer's cabin. Showing the journalist to his temporary home, over one of the propeller shafts – which juddered appallingly due to the ship's constant high speed – the officer pointed to a slight bulge in the deck by the bunk, explaining with great pride: 'That's where a *Bismarck* shell came in. It did not do much damage, but it's left a bump, as you can see.' Asked if he had seen action against *Bismarck*, the officer exclaimed: 'Rather! We got in some good shooting, but we were called off just as things were getting exciting. We were very fed up at the time.'[20]

Another trace of the battle was to be found in the wardroom, in a form that quite astonished Morton, who wrote: 'Above the bar a piece of white steel had curled round and hung from the roof like a wood shaving. It was a relic of the *Bismarck* action.' He was informed that a decision had been made not to repair that damage, but to leave it as a memento.

Morton also heard the story behind the padre's prayer before battle. The Rev. WG Parker told him that just before action was joined on 24 May Captain Leach had called him to the bridge, pointing out that the battleship might need a little divine help. Parker was asked to read a particular prayer to the ship's company over the public address system, the one that began, 'O, God, thou knowest how busy I am…' Parker told Leach it was called 'Sir Jacob Astley's Prayer before Edgehill' and that he just happened to have a copy of the words in his cabin.

The captain urged him to hurry back and fetch it. So, with everyone on edge expecting to hear and feel the roar of the guns, 'there came to every corner of the ship, from the engine-room to the crow's nest, the sound of the Chaplain's voice'.[21] If he overheard the padre spinning this yarn for the attentive journalist, Colin McMullen probably smiled in recollection at his frustrating wait for the prayer to finish so he could open fire.

The weather having calmed not long after Iceland, *Prince of Wales* made good progress, reaching waters off Newfoundland on Saturday, 9 August 1941. Three American destroyers came out to lead the British battleship into Placentia Bay, a vast enclosure of water with a mouth fifty-five miles wide and stretching nearly a hundred miles inland. Its heavily wooded, hilly shores were tightly populated with fir and larch but there was no sign of human life. However, an impressive American force soon emerged out of the mist, at its centre the cruiser *Augusta*, with President Roosevelt aboard. Overhead circled US Navy seaplanes, while flanking *Augusta* were the battleship *Arkansas*, cruiser *Tuscaloosa* and various destroyers, all with pristine paintwork and gleaming brass.

America was still a nation at peace even though the US Navy was already covertly involved in battling U-boats in the Atlantic.[22] *Prince of Wales*, by contrast, was weather-beaten, her hull rust-streaked, guns flame-seared, decks pitted and brass work painted over; and of course she carried the reputation of having fought *Bismarck*. The ship's company, the majority now fallen in on parade on the upper deck, were told ' behave as you normally do' when it came to mixing with their American cousins. Meanwhile, as *Prince of Wales* drew level, Roosevelt took his hat off in salute, while Churchill raised a hand to his cap. The British battleship came slowly to rest close by *Augusta*, running out her anchor cable with a loud rattle, the splash signifying she had assumed her co-starring role alongside the American cruiser. Churchill and his team stayed momentarily on the quarterdeck, gazing across at the President and his entourage who were arrayed under an awning on the cruiser's forecastle. Boats were soon bustling to and fro, staff officers and diplomats finalizing arrangements for a meeting aboard *Augusta* in a couple of hours' time. Loitering in the background, observing all these details as is the journalist's habit, Morton spotted a tall, lean naval officer whom he had not seen before and on approaching him learned it was the ship's commanding officer. Captain Leach had spent the entire passage on the bridge, making sure he properly discharged his duty of carrying the Prime Minister across the Atlantic safely. Morton asked Leach about this awesome responsibility, provoking only 'an eloquent glance of tired blue eyes and a weary but contented smile'.[23] Still aboard *Prince of Wales*, Morton watched as Churchill later went over to meet Roosevelt in *Augusta*, both men surrounded by their top military officers, the British PM presenting a letter from the King to the President before it was smiles and handshakes all round. Churchill was puffing on a cigar and Roosevelt drawing on a cigarette as they disappeared below decks for talks, trailing a faint cloud of smoke. That afternoon a flotilla of small boats carrying a cargo of gifts to the men of *Prince of Wales* puttered across the bay. Aboard were 1,500 boxes containing goodies, one for every man aboard the battleship. Inside each the British sailors and marines found packets of Lucky Strike cigarettes, two apples, an orange and a hunk of cheese together with a card, which explained: 'The President of the United States of America sends his compliments and best wishes.'[24] The President believed he was giving the British things they craved. However, while cheese and fruit was appreciated, the cigarettes were, according to Willetts, not exactly welcome for 'no Englishman ever smokes Lucky Strike cigarettes.' Even in wartime, he thought, British cigarettes were still better than anything the Yanks could provide. There were plenty of visits by British sailors to American warships and vice versa, enhancing the burgeoning 'Special Relationship'. With American ships 'dry', visits to the *Prince of Wales* by US Navy ratings featured more than a few tots of rum being downed. Willetts and many others saved their tots to give the Americans a treat: 'our rum was wonderful stuff – thirty per cent over proof. It was against all regulations to keep it at all – every man was supposed to drink his own rum immediately it was issued. We had an eighth of a pint per person per day if we accepted it. So we made a point of keeping our rum until these Americans came on board. And then we invited them down into our own messes … And they appreciated it. Some of them appreciated it a little bit too much.'

A bugle call sounded from *Prince of Wales*' speakers, signalling the 'Still' for everybody to cock an ear to an important broadcast: 'The President of the United States will now visit the ship and inspect the ship. All personnel except those engaged in this particular visit will you please remain below deck.'[25]

The main event during the President's visit on Sunday, 10 August, was a church service on the battleship's quarterdeck, presided over jointly by naval chaplains from the two countries. Sitting at its centre were the President and Prime Minister, the former in a wheelchair – as a young man Roosevelt had contracted polio – the latter in a comfortable armchair. Around 5,000 British and American sailors and marines were gathered around the leaders, all intermingled informally rather than arrayed strictly by country and division. In the middle of this Joseph Willetts reflected not only on the diversity of the American nation, but also of his own country, for there were 'Welsh, English, Scottish, Irish' aboard *Prince of Wales*. The Americans 'came from every state' including 'all the black fellows and Chinese that were Americans and we all stood together'.

They sang hymns printed in an Order of Service, well known to sailors of both countries, concluding with 'Oh God, our help in ages past'. Roosevelt was a navalist and *Prince of Wales*' men were delighted he wanted a tour of their ship. They took him around the upper deck in his wheelchair, the President giving every detail his keenest attention. Hatches in the backs of the turrets were open so he could see the guns that had fired on *Bismarck* and *Prinz Eugen*. Roosevelt was very interested in the technicalities of engaging enemy warships, in how guns had performed. Explaining the action from his point of view, Lieutenant Commander McMullen slipped in the story of how *Prince of Wales* nearly opened fire on the US Coast Guard Cutter *Modoc*. The President responded: 'Gee, if you'd sunk that ship I would have found it very difficult to explain to the Great American Public.'[26] To further illustrate the battle and the damage *Prince of Wales* suffered, they showed Roosevelt the photograph of Captain Leach and the gunners with the *Bismarck* shell. The President was next taken to the wardroom, for lunch with Churchill, their respective staff officers and a selection of the battleship's own officers, including Captain Leach and Lieutenant Commander McMullen, some thirty-six people in total. The menu was everything a President would expect from a British Prime Minister who enjoyed his food, and a far cry from Hitler's frugal vegetarian meal aboard *Bismarck* three months earlier. They dined on: smoked salmon and caviar; turtle soup (bottled, bought in plentiful quantities at a London shop because it was not regulated by rationing); roast grouse (loaded aboard the train that brought the Prime Minister north from London in Scotland as the grouse shooting season had started on August 1); and Coupe Jeanne d'Arc, a dessert featuring cherries bathed in champagne.

As Roosevelt's visit drew to a close the ship's company were advised over the speakers: 'The President of the United States is now leaving us – all those that wish, will they please come on to the upper deck to say goodbye.'

The battleship's upper deck was packed solid with sailors and marines eager to bid the President farewell. Roosevelt was soon settled in an armchair on the forecastle of the destroyer *McDougal*. With Churchill amid the throng, the *Prince of Wales'* Master at Arms shouted: 'Three cheers for the President of the United States.' Every man on the upper deck raised his cap and roared: 'Hip-hip hooray, hip-hip hooray, hip-hip hooray!'[27] With the echo of cheers fading away across the bay and the destroyer backing very slowly away from *Prince of Wales*, President Roosevelt's reply was clearly heard: 'Thank you gentlemen.' Joseph Willetts noticed Churchill 'standing abreast the quarterdeck with his cap raised, was too full to speak. And there was a tear on the cheek of the Prime Minister of England.' Turning away, Churchill was engaged in conversation by some of the ship's officers. Waving a hand expansively to indicate the peaceful vista stretched out around them, he declared: 'On this lovely day, the sun shining as it is on this beautiful harbour, surrounded as we are by American men of war, it is difficult for you and me to realize that we are fighting for our very lives.'[28]

The *Bismarck* action and the critical way in which it demonstrated Britain could fight and win after a string of military defeats on land must have been a powerful boost for a President who recognized that sooner or later he would need to bring his nation fully into the war against fascism. The Atlantic Charter he and Churchill had agreed at Placentia Bay was the foundation for the so-called Special Relationship that still endures to this day, tested in battle not only in the Second World War but also through the Cold War, conflicts in the Middle East and on the battlefields of Afghanistan. Back in summer 1941, *Prince of Wales* was the manifestation of a maritime superpower that remained predominant for just a few years more before being replaced by the USA. The text of the Atlantic Charter stated that the President and Prime Minister were making known 'certain common principles in the national policies of their respective countries on which they base their hopes for a better future in the world.' Aside from not seeking territorial expansion, the USA and UK agreed to democracy, free trade and the 'final destruction of Nazi tyranny', the latter a remarkable commitment when Hitler had yet to declare war on America.[29] The two nations were also committed to ensuring there should be peace among nations secure in their own borders, within which their citizens could live 'in freedom from fear and want'. There was also a commitment to the freedom of the seas, and the charter vowed to see the world rid of heavily-armed aggressor states.[30]

That evening, with the Prime Minister safely out of the way ashore, the officers of *Prince of Wales* welcomed their counterparts from the US Navy to dinner in the wardroom after which there were raucous mess games. During the evening an American officer turned to Lieutenant Commander Anthony Terry and remarked amid the alcohol-fuelled hilarity: 'I guess you boys take this war very lightly?'

Laughing, Lieutenant Commander Terry responded: 'Oh, rather, why not?"

For that particular officer, laughter in the face of adversity masked the fact that he had survived the sinking of the battleship *Royal Oak* at Scapa Flow and had recently lost his home in Plymouth to the Luftwaffe's blitz of the city.

Terry had, of course, also seen *Hood* blown apart.[31]

The following day was taken up with more talks between the military and political leaders of the two nations as well as meetings between the Prime Minister and the President. Late on the afternoon of 12 August the *Prince of Wales* weighed anchor, her business at Placentia Bay concluded. Now she must dash back across the Atlantic to deliver the human dynamo at the centre of the British war effort safely home.

At 7.30 am on 13 August, Captain Leach made a broadcast that illustrated how fraught with danger their voyage might be, for he explained news of the Prime Minister's meeting in Newfoundland had reached Germany. Both U-boats and the Luftwaffe could be expected to make an effort to attack and sink *Prince of Wales*. Leach urged the whole ship's company, to be 'on their toes', particularly those involved in anti-aircraft and anti-submarine duties or damage control. He concluded: 'If ever there was a time when the utmost vigilance is required, it is upon this voyage.'[32] With destroyers screening her, *Prince of Wales* steamed at top speed but fortunately there was no sign of either enemy submarines or aircraft. The Prime Minister had strained a leg muscle and so was confined to bed for a few days. He still managed to attend the evening film shows in his 'baby grow', finding Donald Duck in *Fox Hunting* and Laurel and Hardy's *Saps at Sea* mildly entertaining. It took a lot to keep the Prime Minister inactive for long, and his quarters in the bridge tower placed him rather too close to the nerve centre of the ship. Instead of waiting for signals to be deciphered and brought down to him, Churchill would often make his way up to the signals office, pacing up and down, waiting impatiently for signals to be deciphered and thrust into his eager hands. Being in close company with the Prime Minister only endeared him more to ordinary sailors like Joseph Willetts. 'He used to come down in the morning with his duffle coat on and sometimes you could see that he was just wearing a pair of pyjamas underneath it, and he had on his Royal Yacht Squadron cap, which was always over one ear.

More often than not he was smoking a big cigar. And we were told implicitly that we were always to stand to attention and give him gangway. If he came on the upper deck, he'd say: "Sit down, gentlemen" and they'd sit down on the deck or whatever they could find. And there he'd be sitting among us smoking one of these big cigars and having a yarn with the lads. It was contrary to all discipline but he did it. There was nobody to tell him not to do it.' On the way across, a convoy was sought out for Churchill to gaze upon the sea trade that kept the war effort pumping. The battleship made a high speed pass through the centre of the seventy-two-ship formation, mariners on all sides cheering their lungs out for 'Winnie'.

Six days after leaving Newfoundland, and following a brief call in Iceland, *Prince of Wales* reached Orkney, where a special firepower demonstration gave the Prime Minister a taste of the sound, smell and power of the battleship's full range of weapons. Before he left, Churchill addressed the ship's company, who were gathered on the long forecastle, thanking them for their part in making history. He finished his speech with a flourish the sailors appreciated – pulling a cigar out and clamping it between his teeth with a great grin on his face. Years later, Churchill would recall of the Sunday service held on the quarterdeck of *Prince of Wales* in Placentia Bay that thousands of young British and American sailors sang a selection of stirring hymns, including *For Those in Peril on the Sea*. Every word seemed to stir the heart. He felt it was 'a great hour to live' but, hinting at the cruel fate that would befall *Prince of Wales* just four months later, Churchill also wrote: 'Nearly half those who sang were soon to die.'[33]

Chapter 24

Bitter Harvest

L egend has it that, after a *Bismarck* officer was hauled up over the side of HMS *Dorsetshire*, plucked from a watery grave by the willing hands of his enemies, he told his British rescuers: 'Us today, you tomorrow.'[1] And so it was in the months and years which followed that his prediction came to pass for a number of the ships, their sailors and marines, who had pursued the mighty German battleship.

It was late when Winston Churchill's doctor, Charles McMoran Wilson, encountered the Prime Minister's secretary, Mrs Hill, coming out of the PM's bedroom. She seemed relieved to see him. 'He has just heard some very bad news,' said Mrs Hill, indicating that he should go in. McMoran Wilson suggested, as the Prime Minister disliked being fussed over by a doctor at the best of times, it might be best to leave him alone. But Mrs Hill insisted: 'I think he would like to see you.'

Churchill was sitting on the edge of his bed, head in his hands, seemingly in a daze.

'You know what has happened?' he asked, looking up.

'No.'

The Prime Minister explained that the Japanese had sunk both *Prince of Wales* and *Repulse* off Malaya.[2] Gone was the battleship that fought so valiantly against *Bismarck* in the Denmark Strait and which had carried him to Placentia Bay in August 1941, then rode shotgun on a Malta convoy before being sent to the Far East to safeguard Singapore. Both capital ships were lost in the South China Sea, on 10 December 1941. The First Sea Lord had advised Churchill not to send them to Singapore, but he overruled Admiral Pound, hoping the sight of those magnificent ships would deter the sons of Nippon. It was Admiral Pound who broke the news to the Prime Minister, ringing him in the early hours of 10 December. Setting aside a tray of paperwork to pick up the handset of a telephone on a bedside table, Churchill thought the First Sea Lord's voice sounded odd, the first intimation something bad was about to be revealed. Churchill heard Pound cough and gulp, his words at first faint.

'Prime Minister, I have to report to you that the *Prince of Wales* and the *Repulse* have both been sunk by the Japanese – we think by aircraft.'

It was simply unbelievable, even after all the other shocking ship losses during 1941 in the Mediterranean.

'Are you sure it's true?' the Prime Minister asked.

'There is no doubt at all.'

Churchill was plunged into turmoil, later confessing: 'In all the war I never received a more direct shock.'[3]

Who could have imagined the Japanese would deliver such a blow? They had sunk or damaged eight American battleships at Pearl Harbor on 7 December but, until *Prince of Wales* and *Repulse* were sent to the bottom, no capital ship on the open ocean had ever been destroyed by aircraft. Being sent to the Far East, so far from home, was not something the men of *Prince of Wales* regarded with great enthusiasm. Having spent so much time in the thick of the action, however, the long voyage did at least offer an opportunity for relaxed gunnery training, including on the anti-aircraft weapons, and to practise more traditional seamanship skills previously neglected. The accepted wisdom was, anyway, that the Japanese were not very good aviators. Lieutenant Commander McMullen attended an intelligence briefing in which it was claimed they could not fly at night because they had such poor eyesight and therefore could not see in the dark. How on earth would they manage to hit a battleship with a torpedo? But, while *Prince of Wales* was in dry dock at Singapore, the Japanese made a night attack. Nine aircraft, flying in perfect formation, dropped bombs on the naval base. As the Japanese planes were frozen in a searchlight, the anti-aircraft guns of *Prince of Wales* joined the flak barrage, but scored no hits. Soon news began flooding in of a surprise attack on Pearl Harbor. It seemed the Japanese were not only good pilots, they had aircraft and weapons capable of sinking battleships.

Force Z, as *Prince of Wales*, *Repulse* and their escort destroyers were known, set sail from Singapore on 8 December, after hearing reports of Japanese transport ships heading for Malaysia. Shortly before the *Prince of Wales* left, Captain Leach invited his son, Henry, serving in the cruiser *Mauritius*, then in dock at Singapore's naval base, to dinner aboard the battleship. It was the first time they had met since Christmas 1940, when the captain had been horrified to learn his son was drafted to *Prince of Wales* and arranged a transfer. Leach the younger thought his father was distracted by some gnawing anxiety, which he caught a hint of when Captain Leach suggested taking on the Japanese was a mission against the odds. A couple of nights later, father and son met for a swim at the naval base swimming pool and afterwards had drinks with the commanding officer of *Repulse*, Captain William Tennant. Two hours after Henry Leach said goodbye to his father, *Prince of Wales* set sail. The future Falklands War-era First Sea Lord later wrote of that parting: 'I never saw my father again.'[4]

Bad weather initially hid the British vessels from Japanese scouting planes, but when it cleared they were cruelly exposed. The only real defence against determined air attack would have been fighters from an aircraft carrier sailing with the two big ships, but the vessel assigned to that role had run aground in the Caribbean and was instead in dry dock for repairs.[5]

Hard-pressed in the Mediterranean and in the Atlantic, and particularly with convoy runs to Russia, which had just started, the Royal Navy had been unable to find another carrier to send.

Flying from bases in Indo-China, eighty-five Japanese aircraft attacked Force Z at 11 am on December 10, the first wave of bombers passing over *Prince of Wales* to attack *Repulse*. Later, both ships were assailed by torpedo-bombers approaching on the bow and stern. *Prince of Wales* suffered hits in her stern that damaged her steering and propellers. As she started listing to port she turned around in a huge circle, shuddering under a constant onslaught. *Repulse* succumbed first but by that stage *Prince of Wales* was a sitting duck, with seemingly endless waves of Japanese aircraft coming in. She was soon beyond hope and the 'abandon ship' order was given. Many of the seriously wounded, who would not be able to escape, were taken to the battleship's small chapel, where the ship's dentist was doing what he could to ease their pain. As he moved among the wounded, the floor of the chapel slick with blood and vomit, the dentist was approached by a sailor, who told him: 'Sir, the Captain says that you should please come onto the upper deck and get away.' The dentist thanked the sailor but shook his head. 'Tell Captain Leach thank you very much, but I'm not going to leave my patients.' The Rev. Wilfred Parker, who had delivered the prayer before the Battle of the Denmark Strait on 24 May 1941 was tending to wounded elsewhere. Both men went down with the ship.

Boy Seaman Alan McIvor, who had used his wits to get an 8-inch shell from *Prinz Eugen* ejected from his gun turret, was wounded in the head. Fortunately he was able to leave the ship without even getting his feet wet, walking along a plank that had been laid across from the battleship's stern to HMS *Express*, an escort destroyer, which had come alongside.

Eighteen-year-old Marine Peter Dunstan, who somehow managed to struggle up from below decks, was shocked at the angle to which the ship was listing. Momentarily bemused by the unfamiliar chaos that had gripped his usually well ordered ship – smoke and flame everywhere, wreckage cluttering the deck and men staggering about clutching wounds, shouting their heads off – he just stood there until somebody shouted, 'Jump!'

Managing to pull himself onto a raft with a number of others, Dunstan turned to watch as the ship rolled over, spotting senior officers still standing on a bridge wing. They were gone within an instant, taken down to oblivion in a frothing, churning sea.[6] Captain Leach had to be one of them, and his corpse was spotted later floating in the water, but not recovered.

Junior rating Joseph Willetts had also escaped to *Express* and then watched *Prince of Wales* slowly turning turtle, he believed still with hundreds of sailors trapped inside her hull. He saw those who had made it to the upper deck, but had yet to jump, trying to scramble clear, a few falling into the sea where some ingested oil and soon died. The Japanese had by now stopped their onslaught, and the ocean was littered with dead and wounded. Willetts decided he had to do something to help. Hanging on to a stanchion with one hand, he dropped over the side of *Express* to offer his other hand to survivors in the water. In this way, one by one, he saved some of them from a watery grave. But eventually, his strength ebbing away, Willetts had to be hauled back up on to *Express*. He found himself next to a petty officer gunner, seemingly without injury, who was standing perfectly still watching *Prince of Wales* begin to slide stern first under the waves. The petty officer looked at Willetts and said: 'I'm going back ... I'm not going to leave the lads there.' The senior rating jumped over the side and swam the 100 yards back to the *Prince of Wales*, just so he could be sucked down with his shipmates.

Lieutenant Commander McMullen was taken down with the ship, but then, like Ted Briggs of *Hood*, popped to the surface. He got into a Carley float with four ratings whom he found singing the Volga Boat Song to keep their spirits up: 'Yo heave ho! Yo heave ho! Once more, once more, Yo heave ho!'

Arriving just too late to matter, Buffalo fighter aircraft wheeled overhead. Shocked survivors shook their fists and hurled abuse skywards, cursing the RAF for failing to protect them against the Japanese. And so, *Prince of Wales* – sent to try and prevent an attack by Japan on British colonies in the Far East – was lost on a forlorn mission bitterly opposed by senior officers, but forced on the Royal Navy by Churchill. *Prince of Wales* took 327 of her officers and men with her to the bottom of the South China Sea, while a further 513 went down with *Repulse*, the ship Admiral Tovey had sent away to refuel in May 1941 rather than risk her in a battle with *Bismarck*. The two great ships were dinosaurs killed by gnats.

Electra had gone east with *Prince of Wales*, her fate seemingly still intertwined with the battleship that she had been in company with during the *Bismarck Action*. As such, she accompanied the battleship and *Repulse* on the ill-fated foray to prevent the Japanese landings. Her men looked on horrified as Japanese aviators, unlike their Italian and German counterparts, proved adept at high-level bombing, scoring a hit on *Repulse* which saw black smoke belching out of a large hole in her deck.[7] Then, the destroyer men watched as torpedo-bombers skimmed low over the sea from all directions, *Electra* trying in vain to place herself between them and the British capital ships and shooting down a Japanese aircraft. First *Repulse* succumbed, and then *Prince of Wales* stopped dead in the water, mortally wounded. This time, rather than receive the thunderbolt of disaster via signal, as had been the case with *Hood*, the destroyer's sailors saw the dreadful spectacle unfold before their eyes. *Prince of Wales*, which had escaped to fight another day on 24 May, just over six months earlier, began to sink. This time *Electra* could save more than just three lives. Provided she got there in time, she could offer salvation to many more.

After ordering the terrible news to be conveyed via signal to Singapore, Commander May took his destroyer in, finding *Express* was already nestled alongside *Prince of Wales* taking off survivors. Therefore *Electra* went in search of survivors from *Repulse*, pulling them from an oil-covered sea in various states of distress.

As *Prince of Wales* rolled over, bilge keel threatening to capsize *Express*, the destroyer backed away, fortunately speedily enough to avoid that fate. Watching from *Electra*, Lieutenant Cain saw 'a whirlpool, spread over the water in brief fierce testimony of the violence of her passing ...' It wiped men 'from the sea like chalk figures from a slate.'[8] *Electra* was able to pull several hundred survivors from the sea and carried them to Singapore, more than making up for the paltry few she had saved from *Hood*.

Nine months to the day from *Bismarck*'s sinking, *Electra* was claimed. Her death ride came during the Battle of the Java Sea on 27 February 1942, as she aimed to protect *Exeter*, the latter having suffered a crippling hit in a boiler room. *Exeter* needed time to get moving again. American and British destroyers made a smokescreen to hide the crippled British cruiser from the enemy and waited for the attack that would surely come. Cain contemplated mens' attitude to mortal danger, the feeling of personal immunity 'that other ships sank, and that other men died, but that we were immortal'.[9] How else could he and his shipmates have survived so long? *Exeter* was finally able to get underway again and retire from the scene. As the Japanese came forward in strength Allied cruisers and destroyers counter-attacked, *Electra* vanishing into the smokescreen and seconds later breaking through the other side. For a few brief moments, the only sound was her engines and the noise of the sea parting in huge bow waves. Every man aboard was grimly silent, waiting for first sight of the enemy. *Electra* appeared to be alone, but then cutting across her path came the menacing silhouettes of a Japanese light cruiser and half a dozen heavy destroyers. *Electra* charged bravely on, exchanging fire with the enemy. Three devastating hits slammed into the British destroyer – one cutting off communication between the bridge and the rest of the ship, another wrecking the electrical system forward, the third exploding in the aft boiler room. *Electra* came to a halt with steam and smoke pouring through multiple holes. The Japanese fighting line had disappeared, but a single enemy destroyer came back to finish *Electra* off. Cain, swearing blue murder, ordered torpedoes fired, a forlorn attempt to blunt the enemy attack. None hit. *Electra*, with no central gunnery control and no power forward was a sitting duck as the heavily armed Japanese warship circled, taking out turrets one by one. Fire took hold aft, preventing any shells from being passed back to Y turret, the only one left in action, which soon ran out of ammunition, its gun falling silent. A message came down from Commander May on the bridge: 'Prepare to abandon ship.'

Many officers and men who had been astonished, and deeply dismayed, by the lack of survivors from *Hood* were to be among those claimed by the sea that day. Cain was hit in the legs by shrapnel, the wail of the Japanese shell ringing in his ears as he continued trying to get a Carley float into the water despite his wounds. Fortunately for Cain he did not escape in it, for the Japanese destroyer decided on some target practice against the *Electra*'s floats and their survivors, achieving a direct hit on the one Cain helped put over the side. He escaped on another, which fortunately avoided the attention of the merciless enemy. Only fifty-four of *Electra*'s 144-strong ship's company survived. Commander May was not among them, choosing to go down with his ship. He appeared on the bridge, giving those in the water an encouraging wave just seconds before *Electra* sank. Cain heard 'one gentle sigh from our ship as she plunged below, her torments ended', the White Ensign flying proudly from her gaff. The American submarine *S38* rescued *Electra*'s survivors, ten of them so ill they had to be left in the care of Dutch doctors in Java, while the other forty-four, including Cain, made it to Australia aboard a small steamer called *Verspeck*. They reached Fremantle on 10 March, nine days after *Exeter* was sunk in a sequel to the Battle of the Java Sea, the cruiser meeting her end in the Sunda Strait. After taking shelter at Surabaya to effect further temporary repairs, *Exeter* set sail on 28 February, in the early hours of 1 March sending a signal picked up by a British destroyer, reporting sighting three enemy cruisers. Unable to make more than sixteen knots, *Exeter* was easy meat for the Japanese warships, which reduced the British cruiser to a floating wreck via gunfire before sending in a destroyer to torpedo her. Fifty-four of *Exeter*'s men went down with her, while 651 survivors were rescued and taken prisoner by the Japanese. Meanwhile, in Australia, some of *Electra*'s survivors were put on the Ceylon-bound liner *Nankin*, which was intercepted by the German raider *Thor*. Cain and others were among those transferred to a Japanese destroyer off Java, not far from where their ship had been sunk. They were to spend three years as prisoners. Also subjected to the degradation and brutality of captivity in Japanese hands were men from *Prince of Wales*, captured after fighting on land in defence of Singapore. A number of them died in captivity, one more sweep of the scythe that is war's bitter harvest.

Like the Swordfish of *Ark Royal* who put paid to *Bismarck* nearly seven months earlier, those infernal Japanese aircraft that destroyed *Prince of Wales* dropped torpedoes and bombs that cost a fraction of what it took to create a vessel with the awesome firepower of a battleship. In both cases a few impudent torpedoes found the battleships' unprotected Achilles heel – their steering and propulsion. Like Achilles crashing to the dusty plain beneath the walls of Troy, the myth of battleship omnipotence had been slain. However, the ships the torpedo-bombers flew from – the new capital vessels that replaced battleships as rulers of the seas during the Second World War – were also not invulnerable. *Ark Royal* was sunk in the western Mediterranean by a single torpedo fired by *U-81* but she did not go down straight away, for her crew managed to get tows across from two tugs. However, in transferring the majority of the ship's company to the destroyer *Legion* key damage control personnel went, too, and it was not possible to return them. The structure of *Ark* – the vast hangar running through the entire length of the ship – also enabled flooding to take hold rapidly. In the early hours of 14 November, with fire breaking out and water ingress creating an irretrievable list of 35 degrees, those left aboard abandoned ship, all save one sailor who went down with *Ark*. A number of the aviators who flew in the Swordfish attacks from *Ark Royal* did not survive the war. The leader of the strike from *Victorious*, Eugene Esmonde, was killed on 12 February 1942, leading 825 NAS on a mission to prevent the *Scharnhorst*, *Gneisenau* and *Prinz Eugen* from breaking through the English Channel to Germany – the notorious 'Channel Dash'. Esmonde's aircraft suffered a hit as he made his torpedo run in the Channel, going down in flames. None of the other aircraft made it, all but five of the eighteen aviators in the squadron losing their lives. The Germans had learned how to shoot down Swordfish. Esmonde's body was eventually washed up in the Medway and he was posthumously awarded the Victoria Cross. Eight of the forty-three Fleet Air Arm aviators who took part in attacks launched by *Ark Royal* against *Bismarck* later lost their lives. Among them was Tim Coode, who led the successful strike on the night of 26 May, killed in early 1943. Based ashore at a naval air station in east Africa, his aircraft caught fire and crashed during a night low-flying sortie. David Godfrey-Faussett was also killed, during a flying accident at night in March 1942, his Swordfish plunging into the North Sea off Easthaven.[10]

Ever the fighter, it took four days for *Cossack* to give up the fight after she was struck by a torpedo fired by *U-563* west of Portugal. On 23 October 1941 *Cossack* was helping to escort a UK-bound convoy, the fatal hit suffered just forward of the bridge on the destroyer's port side, blowing off her bows and 'about a third of the forward section of the ship'.[11] She suffered 159 deaths[12] and her twenty-nine survivors were picked up by fellow British escorts *Carnation* and *Legion* as well as the Free French warship *Commandant Duboc*. The following day a salvage team, including some of *Cossack*'s own men, was put aboard from *Carnation*. They strove valiantly to save the ship: 'The fires were put out and bulkheads were shored up. The ship was lightened by throwing loose equipment, ammunition etc. overboard. Working under Commander E Halliwell, the engineering officer and senior survivor, they managed to get the main engines going again, although they could only proceed stern first, heading back to Gibraltar very slowly.'[13] They managed to stabilize the situation and on 25 October a tug from Gibraltar duly arrived and a tow was successfully put across. Towed stern first into steadily worsening seas, the salvage team was taken off during the night but could not get back aboard, the tow being slipped on 27 October, leaving *Cossack* slipping below the angry waves. Among the men lost in *Cossack* was telegraphist Eric Farmer who left such a graphic account of the *Bismarck* Action. The survivors took passage home to the UK in another veteran of the *Bismarck* Action, battleship *Rodney*, which had spent some time based at Gibraltar as flagship of Force H. Vian had departed *Cossack* that June, on promotion to Rear-Admiral and was tasked with organizing protection for convoys to northern Russia. When it came to the rest of Vian's heroic destroyers of the 4th Flotilla, they were all lost in 1942: *Maori* was sunk by air attack in harbour at Malta, 12 February; *Zulu* sunk by air attack, off Tobruk, 14 September; *Sikh* sunk by enemy shore batteries, at Tobruk, 14 September.

Like *Dorsetshire*, the destroyer *Maori* had of course rescued *Bismarck* survivors and similarly, she too fulfilled the German officer's grim prediction of 'us today, you tomorrow'. But her casualties were light and only one man was killed when a Luftwaffe bomb penetrated and exploded in her machinery space in the early hours of the morning, a fire detonating a torpedo magazine blowing the ship apart. Fortunately the ship's company was sleeping ashore rather than aboard ship. *Maori* broke in two, with her bows and stern poking above water. Because it was a hazard to shipping in the middle of Malta's busy harbour, the wreck was raised and moved to a creek. After the war in Europe ended *Maori*'s wreck was raised yet again, towed out to sea and consigned to a permanent grave in deep water.[14] In August 1942, *Zulu* and *Sikh* had joined forces with two other warships and RAF aircraft to hunt down and kill *U-372* off Haifa. Both Tribal Class destroyers met their end during an ill-starred venture to put ashore a Royal Marine raiding force at Tobruk. Just after 5.00 am on 14 September, as the ships moved in to carry out the landings, a searchlight illuminated *Sikh* and an 88mm gun in a Luftwaffe anti-aircraft battery opened fire, displaying its lethality against targets other than aerial ones. Shells ripped into *Sikh* in several places in quick succession, putting her propulsion out of action and setting off the ammunition and demolition charges belonging to embarked marines. Her bridge was also wrecked. Sister ship *Zulu* attempted to tow *Sikh* out of trouble but was hit several times herself, abandoning the idea. *Sikh* was scuttled shortly after 7.00 am, 115 of her men lost and many others taken prisoner. After withdrawing from the range of enemy guns, *Zulu* sought protection from the cruiser *Coventry*. A few hours later enemy dive-bombers plunged from the clouds, leaving *Coventry* so badly damaged she had to be scuttled by fire from *Zulu*'s guns. Hardly had *Zulu* left this disaster in her wake, with *Coventry*'s sailors joining Royal Marines packed aboard her, when no less than eighteen enemy dive-bombers attacked at once and from all directions. With a bomb destroying her engine room, the doomed warship was left dead in the water. Even then her end did not come quickly. With most of those aboard evacuated to another British warship, a valiant attempt was made to tow *Zulu* to safe harbour, all the while under enemy air attack, but the situation was soon rendered hopeless. *Zulu* turned turtle and sank just inside the breakwater at Alexandria, the Royal Navy's main base in the eastern Mediterranean. Thirty-seven of *Zulu*'s men lost their lives.

The plucky *Piorun* – the English translation of her name means Thunderbolt – saw plenty of action after her encounter with *Bismarck*, participating in the escort force for the big Operation Halberd convoy run to Malta of autumn 1941, which also involved *Prince of Wales*. After further service in the Mediterranean, by 1944 *Piorun* was part of the Home Fleet, coming through the remainder of the war unscathed. Having originally been commissioned into the Royal Navy as HMS *Nerissa*, the *Piorun* was handed back to Britain in 1946, becoming HMS *Noble*, and was sent for scrap nine years later. The most immediate casualty in the aftermath of the *Bismarck* Action among the British warships that took part was the Tribal Class destroyer *Mashona*, sunk by German aircraft west of Ireland on 28 May 1941. Returning to the UK to refuel, having withdrawn as escort for *Rodney* in the closing stages of the chase, forty-six of her ship's company went down with her, but the remaining 184 were rescued by destroyers *Tartar* and *St Croix*, the latter a Canadian ship. Her own side delivered the final blows that sent *Mashona* to the bottom, for even though she had capsized, the destroyer still wouldn't sink. *Tartar* therefore put a torpedo into *Mashona* and, finally, *St Croix* and the destroyer *Sherwood* shelled her.[15] Another of *Rodney*'s escorts, *Somali*, fell victim to *U-703* off Bear Island on 20 September 1942, the destroyer's middle blown out by a torpedo explosion. Forty-seven of her men died with their ship. *Achates*, which had escorted *Hood* on her fateful foray, was sunk by enemy guns during the Battle of the Barents Sea, on 31 December 1942, while three members of *King George V*'s destroyer screen were also lost due to enemy action: the Australian-manned *Nestor*, scuttled after receiving severe damage during air attack, off Crete, 16 June 1942; *Intrepid*, sunk by air attack, at Leros harbour, 27 September 1943 and *Inglefield*, sunk by German air attack, off Anzio, 25 February 1944. At least fifty men died in those destroyers. *Punjabi*, another member of the Home Fleet flagship's screen for much of the pursuit of *Bismarck*, was the most bitter loss among these ships, for she was sunk north of Iceland on 1 May 1942 as the result of a high speed collision in mist with *King George V*. The *Punjabi*'s depth charges detonated as she was cut in two and her aft end pushed under by the battleship, explosions inflicting additional damage to the flagship's bows and taking lives. Forty-nine of the destroyer's men were killed, but somehow 205 survived, most due to the fact that her forward section stayed afloat for a short time, while some were plucked from the water by other units of the fleet.[16] *King George V* needed two months of repairs at Liverpool before she could resume duties as Home Fleet flagship. She survived the war, seeing action against the Japanese in the closing stages of the Pacific War and ultimately being scrapped in the late 1950s. *Rodney* recorded one of the most illustrious combat records of any British warship during the Second World War, seeing action on the Pedestal convoy run to Malta, duelling with Vichy French shore batteries during the Allied invasion of North Africa, and supporting the thrust up through Italy before conducting a number of key bombardments in support of British and Canadian troops fighting hard to break out of the D-Day beachhead in Normandy. Following a bombardment mission against the German occupiers of Alderney, *Rodney*'s last mission was to deter *Tirpitz* from attacking a convoy to Russia in late 1944. Serving for a time as Home Fleet Flagship, she was decommissioned in late 1945 and sent to the breakers before the end of the decade. The battlecruiser *Renown*, Somerville's[17] Force H flagship, saw out her war in the East Indies Fleet, using her guns to bombard the Japanese. Her last high profile assignment was at anchor in Plymouth Sound, in early August 1945, when she hosted a meeting between King George VI and President Harry S Truman, who had become the American leader after President Roosevelt's death that April. *Renown* was scrapped in 1948.

Of the cruisers that came into conflict with *Bismarck* in May 1941, only *Dorsetshire* was lost to enemy action for the other three – *Sheffield*, *Suffolk* and *Norfolk* – all survived the war to be sent for scrap after hostilities ceased, the last of them (*Sheffield*) not disposed of until the late 1960s. In *Dorsetshire*'s case, the end came on 5 April 1942, in the Indian Ocean, under a hail of bombs from Japanese carrier aircraft. She sank stern first after sustaining ten hits and near misses that created catastrophic damage and great slaughter. The first wave of Japanese aircraft approached from dead ahead – knowing this was the blind spot for the cruiser's anti-aircraft armament. The fate for many of *Dorsetshire*'s 234 dead was every bit as horrific as that suffered by *Bismarck*'s men. The ship was on fire almost from stem to stern, mangled anti-aircraft guns drooped over the cruiser's side, while eviscerated corpses hung from the rigging. The upper deck was slick with blood. There were bodies piled up by the same guardrails over which *Bismarck*'s men had been helped just under a year earlier. With bombers having dealt the death blows to the ship, Zero fighters swept up and down, machine-gunning anyone who dared to move on the upper deck. Hatches and steel doors were jammed shut through distortion caused by the shock of the bomb hits, ensuring a dreadful death for many. A *Dorsetshire* survivor recorded: 'Men could be heard banging on the steelwork and shouting frantically. It must have been especially frightening for those unfortunate to realize that their chances of survival were nil. They would be entombed in a communal steel coffin. Others below who found that ladders to exits had been blown away, scrambled up pipes and other fixtures to get out onto the upper deck.'[18] The survivors spent thirty hours in the water before being rescued by Royal Navy destroyers. Some of the men lost in *Dorsetshire*[19] had been drafted to her from *Prince of Wales.*[19] One *Dorsetshire* survivor was particularly traumatized by seeing some of these young sailors, a number badly wounded, just give up and lie down on the cruiser's upper deck, waiting for the ocean to end their pain.

When it came to those other workhorses that participated in the broader pursuit of the *Bismarck* and *Prinz Eugen*, there were heavy casualties. Of the cruisers that rode shotgun on *King George V* and *Victorious*, the *Galatea* was sunk by an enemy submarine, west of Alexandria, on 14 December 1941, while *Hermione* also fell victim to a U-boat, south of Crete on 16 June 1942. *Neptune* was lost in a minefield, off Tripoli, on 19 December 1941. The cruiser *Edinburgh*, which was pulled away from convoy escort duty to join the hunt, ended up sunk by German destroyers and a submarine attack in the Barents Sea on 2 May 1942. *Manchester*, which patrolled between Iceland and the Faroes, just in case the German raiders tried to break out that way, was scuttled after being damaged by torpedoes off Kelibia on 13 August 1942. The loss of life in those five cruisers totalled 1,470, more than were killed in *Hood*. Only one man survived out of *Neptune*'s complement of 764.

It was the carrier *Victorious* that had the longest active service life of all the British warships involved in the *Bismarck* action. After seeing service on the Russian convoys, including a vain attempt by her Albacore torpedo-bombers to sink *Tirpitz,* when the latter made a rare deployment to sea in spring 1942, *Victorious* spent time in action with American naval forces in the Pacific. She returned home to take part in further, equally unsuccessful, strikes against *Tirpitz*, which was by spring 1944 holed up in a Norwegian fjord. By May 1945, *Victorious* was with the British Pacific Fleet, weathering Kamikaze attacks off Okinawa, being struck more than once but thanks to her armoured flight-deck able, after several hours' successful damage control, to resume strike and fleet protection missions. Extensively reconstructed post-war, *Victorious* made it into the jet age, in the early 1960s entering the Arabian Gulf in a display of power that deterred an Iraqi invasion of Kuwait. For the Labour government of the late 1960s, keen to divest Britain of its big carriers to save money in order to buttress the Welfare State, the serious fire that struck *Victorious* in the early hours of 11 November 1967, as she completed a major refit at Portsmouth Dockyard, was most opportune. One sailor lost his life fighting the blaze but, absorbing this blow, the ship's company set to work with the dockyard to ensure *Victorious* would be ready to re-commission into the front line fleet on 24 November. However, it was then revealed by the captain that the veteran carrier would instead be paid off to save money. In the midst of a Fleet manpower shortage, such a move enabled her sailors to be drafted to other ships. A ceremony went ahead, but took the form of a wake, in celebration of the long life of a ship that had first tasted action against *Bismarck*, more than twenty-six years earlier.

Just as *Victorious* had evolved from being a ship that embodied Britain's need to defend itself against the menace of German and Japanese fascism, to one that policed the withdrawal from empire and was fit to fight the day the Cold War turned hot, so former foes from the Second World War had by the late 1960s become allies. Common cause against the Soviet threat helped Britain and West Germany to forget about the old enmity, and veterans of both sides in the *Bismarck* episode forged friendships. In May 1974 a combined group of *Dorsetshire-Maori* veterans travelled to Germany to take their place at events to mark the thirty-third anniversary of the battle. Bill Braddon, who had seen action in *Dorsetshire*, felt moved enough to record the event on paper. He described the pilgrimage aboard a North Sea Ferry to Hamburg as an opportunity for British sailors 'to meet their old enemies and pay homage to the crew of the *Bismarck*.'[20] On 25 May, some of the *Bismarck* veterans met their former enemies at the ferry terminal, escorting them to the Hotel Wagner. Dropping their bags in their rooms, the British veterans had a wash, shave and changed. That afternoon they went to the main railway station to get a train to the *Bismarck* memorial, located at nearby Friedrichsruh, on the family estate of the statesman the ship was named after. Braddon wrote: 'At our destination we walked off the station with our German hosts, over the cobbles and a level crossing, down a leafy lane of spruce, pine and aromatic shrubs, past the Bismarck estate entrance to the lodge gatehouse at the Memorial site where the wreaths with their long purple streamers were awaiting us.' Pinning war medals on their blazers, veterans from both nations picked up the wreaths and 'proceeded to the shrine'. Braddon continued: 'Our progress was comparatively noiseless over the dark brown, almost black, loam and eventually we turned a sharp bend and into a square of hard rolled earth and stone slabs bounded by chains on posts. In the centre was a large stone four feet high, one end embedded in a floral border, with the BISMARCK crest on the front.' The assembly of relatives, old shipmates, onlookers and invited guests listened in respectful silence to a brief German-language service, which was translated into English as it progressed. Braddon, who was carrying the *Dorsetshire-Maori* wreath, felt it 'a privilege to be able to pay homage to the brave in that simple and hallowed spot.' He believed veterans of both countries formed 'an understanding'. They posed together for photographs and then began the walk back to the railway station where something quite extraordinary happened. 'Whilst waiting to return to Hamburg we had a glimpse of Admiral Doenitz standing on the edge of the platform. Now eighty-three years old he appears in the background on these occasions and then glides away again into the shadow of the trees. They call him the Grey Ghost.' Doenitz, who had succeeded Hitler as the leader of the Third Reich for a few days in May 1945, before capitulating to the Allies, had been the commander of the U-boat arm prior to heading the *Kriegsmarine* from January 1943. What did he reflect on during such occasions? That the surface raiders were a wasteful diversion from the U-boat arm, which in the wake of *Bismarck*'s loss was the main weapon against Britain? Or did he just mourn the loss of so many young lives, regretting the whole adventure? Back in Hamburg the British and German veterans, together with their invited guests, sat down to break bread together and bury the past in comradeship. At nine the following morning, possibly nursing some spectacular hangovers reminiscent of their younger days, the veterans went by coach to Kiel and later to the main German naval war memorial where more wreaths were laid. Braddon recorded the moment: 'A bosun's pipe shrilled out the "still" and a muted trumpet played 'Ich hatt einen Kamarade ('I had a Comrade'). Very reminiscent of thirty-three years ago when I heard it played on a mouth organ on the quarterdeck of *Dorsetshire* as we buried a German sailor at sea.' The veterans adjourned for lunch at Kiel Naval Base, where they were guests of the West German Navy, honoured with a tour of the guided-missile destroyer *Lütjens*, named in honour of the admiral who died in *Bismarck*. Returning to Hamburg, the veterans sat down to another evening of memory-swapping, tall stories, dinner and drinks. They no doubt recalled the same night more than three decades earlier when destroyer *Maori* had been locked in battle with battleship *Bismarck* in the wake of the key torpedo hit on the German battleship's steering. The following morning – the actual anniversary of the battle – sailors from *Dorsetshire* and *Maori* stood shoulder-to-shoulder with the men they had pulled from the sea, paying their respects to the dead of both sides at the main war memorial in Hamburg itself. At 1.00 pm, as *Prins Hamlet* – the ferry on the Hamburg-Harwich run – pulled away from the jetty, the last survivors of *Bismarck* gathered en bloc on the jetty, despite the pouring rain, to wave adieu to men who had saved them from a watery grave on 27 May 1941.

> He went like one that hath been stunned,
> And is of sense forlorn:
> A sadder and a wiser man,
> He rose the morrow morn.

> Samuel Taylor Coleridge,
> *The Rime of the Ancient Mariner*

Notes

Author's Introduction
1. From Christopher Hibbert's obituary, published in *The Daily Telegraph*, 23 December 2008.
2. In writing this introduction, and considering this element of what I am trying to convey, it struck me that the British frame of mind – at least among senior officers such as Home Fleet boss Admiral Tovey and HMS *Rodney* CO Captain Dalrymple-Hamilton – is reflected in the famous Powell and Pressburger movie, *The Life and Death of Colonel Blimp*. The chief intellectual and emotional argument at the heart of that 1943 production was that the British, accustomed to waging war with a measure of gentlemanly conduct, had to adopt ruthlessness, and even brutality, they might ordinarily shrink from, in order to defeat the Nazis. Hardened and supremely aggressive though they were, the British commanders engaged in the pursuit and destruction of *Bismarck* would, like Blimp, have found it deeply distasteful. Unlike Blimp, they would have recognized it was essential to abandon gentlemanly conduct in the heat of battle in order to win, for to lose would, potentially, have had horrific consequences for millions of people. As I suggest in the Introduction, that didn't mean they could not show humanity in the aftermath of battle or regret about what they had been forced to do.

Prologue: The Hoodoo Ship
1. McMullen, IWM Sound Archive. The watertight doors dividing compartments in warships are secured using not only a locking system controlled by a wheel in the centre of each one, but, as an added measure to ensure a seal, by rotating clips around the edges.
2. Slang for the padre – called 'Sin Bosun' because he steered sailors' prayers to Heaven.
3. Joseph Willetts, IWM Sound Archive.

Chapter 1: Made with Blood and Iron
1. Captain Troubridge, *Report to British Embassy*, National Archives. Some biographical details in main body text, including his invocation to naval cadets, are taken from a profile in the October 1980 edition of *The Naval Review*. Troubridge also features in Donald McLachlan's *Room 39*. In the Second World War,

Troubridge commanded the carrier *Furious* during the Norwegian campaign of April 1940. Returning to the naval intelligence world, he headed a secret unit that simulated what the German high command might do next. By the summer of 1941, Troubridge was in command of battleship *Nelson* when flagship for Force H but his skills as a carrier captain soon saw him return to naval aviation, commanding a series of carriers and strike forces. By the end of the war he was head of the Fleet Air Arm. Knighted and made a Vice-Admiral, Troubridge was forced by ill health to retire from the Navy in 1949, dying the same year, aged just fifty-four. Many thought he might well have become First Sea Lord were it not for his early demise.

2. Plan Z envisaged the *Kriegsmarine* creating a fleet that by 1947 would include eight battleships, a dozen battlecruisers, four aircraft carriers and around 250 submarines as well as dozens of cruisers. A formidable force, but surely an economically unrealistic plan, bearing in mind Hitler's desire at some stage to take on the Russians, which would require the majority of resources for the land and air forces. Anyway, the British and French would have sought to equal, if not surpass, such a naval expansion. Two battleships even bigger than *Bismarck*, at 62,497 tons deep load and with eight 16-inch guns, were laid down for the *Kriegsmarine* in the summer of 1939. Plan Z was axed when war broke out in September 1939, the steel from *Bismarck*'s successors ultimately used to construct submarines.

3. Captain Troubridge, *Report to British Embassy*, National Archives.

4. This British attempt to restrain German rearmament under Hitler, following the latter's renunciation of the Versailles Treaty terms in 1935, allowed the German to build a navy up to thirty-five per cent of the Royal Navy (in tonnage terms).

5. Captain Troubridge, *Report to British Embassy*, National Archives.

6. Von Müllenheim-Rechberg, *Battleship Bismarck*.

7. Cajus Bekker, *Hitler's Naval War*.

Chapter 2: Germany's Masterly Deception

1. A series of treaties sought to prevent a repeat of the naval arms race that was one of the causes of the First World War. It was hoped that allocating tonnage of different types of warships could satisfy the major naval powers. However, the rise of militarism and fascism in Japan, Italy and then Germany led to their governments cheating on new warship displacements, which were clearly in violation of the agreements, even if nobody would admit to it. As the international situation deteriorated, the various agreements fell by the wayside. After the initial Anglo-German Naval Agreement of 1935, there was a second, agreed in 1937, which sought to incorporate elements of the restrictions proposed in the London Naval Treaty of 1936.

2. Donald McLachlan, *Room 39*.

3. McLachlan cites these figures, provided to the Foreign Office by the German Embassy, in *Room 39*.

4. The Germans were permitted to build a navy thirty-five per cent the size of the Royal Navy in tonnage terms but were allowed to create a submarine arm forty-five per cent of the size of Britain's equivalent (again, in tonnage terms).

5. McLachlan, *Room 39*.

6. Ibid.
7. Churchill was First Lord of the Admiralty between 1911 and 1915, achieving great things (for instance, creating the Queen Elizabeth Class super-dreadnoughts) and also meeting disaster (the ill-fated Dardanelles campaign was his brainchild).
8. Churchill, *The Second World War Vol I* (*The Gathering Storm*). Sir Samuel Hoare was at the time new in the post. Like Churchill, Hoare was aware of the urgent need to build new battleships, pushing through the orders for the first three King George V Class ships. Today the figure quoted by Churchill (£7,000,000) would equate to £258,860,000.
9. According to the National Maritime Museum's account of the battleship's life, the vessel was originally to have been named *King George VI*, as it is British tradition to name the first capital ship built after coronation of a new monarch for the relevant King or Queen. However, the new king in this case asked for the first in class to be named after his father instead. As the text indicates, a subsequent battleship honoured the reigning king instead.
10. Churchill, *The Second World War Vol III*.
11. With a displacement of 56,500 tons (deep load), they would have been spectacular vessels. The Lion Class battleships were to mount nine 16-inch guns as their main armament – the same heavy punch as the Nelson Class, and like them with three guns in each turret. However, rather than having all three turrets forward, one would have been aft. The shell proposed, was, however, heavier than that fired by the Nelsons. In the end, Britain could not find the resources to finish them, and it became clear that creating battleships that could survive modern threats was simply not possible without huge expense (if at all).
12. Tovey writing to Admiral Cunningham, quoted by Stephen, *The Fighting Admirals*.
13. Roskill, *Churchill and the Admirals*.
14. Today the Polish commercial shipping and naval port of Gdynia, twinned with Plymouth, which was the base port city of HMS *Prince of Wales* during the Second World War. Between 1870 and the end of the First World War, Gotenhafen was a port in the German Empire, and hence a top target for recovery by Hitler.
15. Berthold, *The Sinking of the Bismarck*.
16. *Interrogation of Survivors, February–November 1941*, National Archives.
17. Fritz Otto Busch, *Prinz Eugen*. Busch served in the cruiser during the May 1941 Exercise Rhine sortie.

Chapter 3: Storm-Tossed Sentinels
1. Quoted in the author's HMS *LONDON*.
2. Monsarrat, *The Cruel Sea*.
3. Holystoning is the process of cleaning the planking of the upper deck by the use of a piece of sandstone, a task usually carried out by junior ratings on their hands and knees.
4. Peacetime levels of cleanliness and smartness.
5. R Wood, IWM Department of Documents. Wood served in the Arctic veteran cruiser HMS *London*.
6. Rivets provided natural flexibility ('give') that those with welds did not possess, hence *London*, which had been rebuilt with sections of her hull welded rather than riveted suffered structural damage that other County Class warships did not.

7. R Ransome-Wallis, *Two Red Stripes*.
8. They were known as 'treaty cruisers', limited by international agreements to 10,000 tons and 8-inch guns and therefore restricted in the amount of armour they could carry.
9. Lieutenant Commander BW Smith, IWM Department of Documents.
10. Commander CT Collett, IWM Department of Documents.
11. Russell Grenfell, *The Bismarck Episode*.
12. Naval slang for lookouts.
13. HMS Norfolk*'s Gunnery and R.D.F. During Operations Against* Bismarck, National Archives.
14. Ibid.
15. DA Hibbit, IWM Department of Documents.
16. Ibid. Like many sailors Hibbit kept a secret and forbidden diary. As related in the author's book featuring the fighting life of the cruiser *London* (see bibliography) Hibbit was to continue serving on the staff of the 1st Cruiser Squadron when a former Commanding Officer of *Prince of Wales*, Louis 'Turtle' Hamilton, took command.
17. Lt Cdr BW Smith, IWM Department of Documents. Lt Cdr Smith gave his take on how this historic moment unfolded in a humorous letter home to his family mailed within days of the *Bismarck* action.
18. Cdr CT Collett. IWM Department of Documents.
19. Forward gunnery control position.
20. Captain Ludovic Porter, IWM Department of Documents.
21. Reported in Grenfell, *The Bismarck Episode*.
22. Hibbit, IWM Department of Documents.
23. HMS Norfolk*'s Gunnery and R.D.F. During Operations Against* Bismarck, National Archives.
24. Captain Ludovic Porter, IWM Department of Documents.

Chapter 4: Raise Steam with All Despatch
1. Exchange recorded by CR Benstead in HMS *Rodney at Sea*.
2. For more on this remarkable officer and HMS *Rodney*, see the author's book, HMS *RODNEY*.
3. Transcript of interview for the documentary series *The Battleships* (2001). See sources.
4. In early January 1941 German bombers achieved several near misses on *Victorious* as she neared completion.
5. Transcript of interview for the documentary series *The Battleships*.
6. Ibid.
7. Dalrymple-Hamilton was rendered permanently deaf in one of his ears.
8. Transcript of interview for the documentary series *The Battleships*.
9. Ibid.
10. In early 2009 it was claimed that a revived Cammell Laird yard was a contender to build the flight-decks for two new 65,000-ton aircraft carriers for the Royal Navy, one of which is to be named *Prince of Wales*.
11. The White Star line commissioned the *Bismarck* as the RMS *Majestic*, the 57,000-ton ship being retired from service in 1936. She was destined for the scrap yard until

bought in 1937 by the Admiralty for mooring alongside at Rosyth as a training school for junior ratings. The trainees were soon accommodated ashore, which was just as well, since the Luftwaffe destroyed the former *Bismarck* during an air raid on Rosyth, in late September 1939. She sank at her mooring and was only scrapped in 1943, after being raised from her watery grave. A relative of the author was trained as a rating in *Caledonia*, but was later killed in the Mediterranean during the Second World War, while another member of the author's family was a civilian doctor appointed to provide medical services to Rosyth dockyard, including *Caledonia*.
12. The citadel can be described as a gigantic, heavily armoured box that sits inside a battleship's outer skin, enclosing the vitals of the ship, including its ammunition magazines, main command and control systems as well as life support and weapons systems.
13. Willetts, IWM Sound Archive.
14. Of between 1,600 and 2,000 men – depending on whether or not an admiral and his flag staff were embarked.
15. *See* Prologue.
16. Detailed by Henry Leach in his autobiography, *Endure No Makeshifts*. Leach writes that if he had served in *Prince of Wales* when his father was her CO, this would have 'invited allegations of nepotism'. He also says that had he been appointed to the battleship he might also have suffered 'unduly harsh treatment' to 'negate such allegations'.

Chapter 5: Heavyweight with a Glass Jaw
1. Coles and Briggs, *Flagship Hood*.
2. Britannia Museum/Britannia Royal Naval College.
3. An encounter detailed in the author's HMS *Rodney*, which quotes this description from HMS *Rodney at War*, the ship's own account of her service in the Second World War.
4. Graham Rhys-Jones, *The Loss of the Bismarck*.

Chapter 6:. The Navy's Here
1. D.K. Brown, *Nelson to Vanguard*.
2. In today's money (2010) a Tribal Class destroyer would cost £17,750,400.
3. *The Life of L03*, a chronicle of *Cossack*'s life. HMS *Cossack* Association document. *See* Sources for further details.
4. Martin Stephen, *The Fighting Admirals*.
5. Sherbrooke commanded the Royal Navy's destroyers during the Battle of the Barents Sea on New Year's Day 1942, showing great courage in the face of formidable odds. He was seriously wounded when his command ship, *Onslow*, was badly damaged. Sherbrooke refused to leave the bridge until the fight was won. For showing such extraordinary gallantry in the face of the enemy Sherbrooke was awarded the Victoria Cross.
6. Coles and Briggs, *Flagship Hood*.
7. KFW Rail, IWM Department of Documents.
8. Coles and Briggs, *Flagship Hood*.
9. Vian, *Action This Day*.
10. Ibid.

11. Ibid.
12. *The Life of L03.*
13. Vian, *Action This Day.*
14. *The Life of L03.*
15. Vian, *Action This Day.*
16. Ibid
17. Max Arthur, *The Royal Navy 1939 to Present Day.*
18. *The Life of L03.*
19. TJ Cain, 'HMS *Electra.*
20. Ibid.
21. Ibid.
22. Within the Royal Navy, indeed within the ship herself, and well away from tender public ears, HMS *Hood* was also known as 'The Seven Bs'. This is explained on the excellent HMS *Hood* web site (www.hmshood.com) as standing for *Britain's Biggest Bullsh*ttingest B*stard Built By Brown.* *Hood* was built by the John Brown yard on the Clyde and of course for many years was the biggest warship in the world and the showboat for purveying the public relations image of Rule Britannia, hence the salty nickname.

Chapter 7: Rushing to their Destiny
1. Sam Wood, RNM. It is likely that, however, Captain Leach described *Prinz Eugen* as a Hipper Class cruiser, rather than by name as it was not certain which one was out with *Bismarck.*
2. TJ Cain, HMS *Electra.*
3. Coles and Briggs, *Flagship Hood.*
4. Ibid.
5. Magazine of HMS *King George V*, RNM.
6. This was actually the 7.22 pm signal from *Suffolk*, but passed on to the Admiralty by *Norfolk*, intercepted and decoded by ships throughout the Fleet.
7. Coles and Briggs, *Flagship Hood* – both signals.
8. Harriman and Abel, *Special Envoy to Churchill and Stalin 1941 – 1946.*
9. Ibid
10. Richard Hough, *Former Naval Person.*
11. Harriman and Abel, *Special Envoy to Churchill and Stalin 1941 – 1946.*
12. Churchill, *The Second World War, Vol I.*
13. Churchill, *The Second World War, Vol II.*
14. The Royal Navy's operational centre was the Admiralty Citadel, London, a rather large, and ugly blockhouse with walls around 20ft thick on Horse Guards Parade, behind the actual Admiralty building. Its construction was carried out in the period 1940–41. The Citadel extended underground, too.
15. Test rounds that simulated the process of loading and firing.
16. Coles and Briggs, *Flagship Hood.*
17. Fibres and fragments of dirty clothing penetrating the body at the same time as shrapnel or bullet could cause infection.
18. Exchange detailed by Briggs in *Flagship Hood.*
19. In *Flagship Hood* Briggs provides a description of Holland on the bridge and also of his character.

20. Coles and Briggs, *Flagship Hood*.
21. Ibid.
22. This was *Prince of Wales'* Colin McMullen, who related in a taped interview for the Imperial War Museum Sound Archive that after the war the Home Fleet boss made this revelation while paying him a visit at home.
23. Coles and Briggs, *Flagship Hood*.
24. Ibid.
25. TJ Cain, HMS *Electra*.
26. Ibid.
27. Coles and Briggs, *Flagship Hood*.
28. Ibid.

Chapter 8: Death of a Battlecruiser
1. Cain, HMS *Electra*.
2. Magazine of HMS *King George V*, RNM. This speech to the men of *King George V* could alternatively have taken place at Scapa Flow, in January 1941, when Churchill came aboard to see off Lord Halifax on his way across the Atlantic in the battleship to take up the post of British Ambassador to the USA. *Also, see* Chapter 10.
3. On receiving a semaphore or light signal warships were meant to acknowledge they had received and understood the signal by sending back 'C' after each word. By flashing 'I-M-I' the *Prince of Wales* was saying that she did not understand the final word (or words in this case) of the open fire message. As suggested, McMullen was telling Admiral Holland that he was targeting the wrong ship.
4. McMullen, IWM Sound Archive.
5. For more on this *see* Chapter 22.
6. Müllenheim-Rechberg, *Battleship Bismarck*.
7. Coles and Briggs, *Flagship Hood*.
8. Ibid.
9. Geoffrey Brooke, *Alarm Starboard!*
10. Unrotating Projectile (UP) Rocket Launcher, a notoriously unreliable and unstable anti-aircraft weapon that was designed to sew a so-called 'aerial minefield', with mines floating on the ends of wires suspended from parachutes, which blossomed from each rocket. An utter failure, it is thought more British lives were claimed than enemy.
11. Coles and Briggs, *Flagship Hood*.
12. *Prinz Eugen*'s shooting was the most likely culprit.
13. Tilburn to Board of Inquiry, National Archives.
14. Ibid.
15. Tilburn says one thing in *The Royal Navy 1939 To the Present*, but told the inquiry something else.
16. Coles and Briggs, *Flagship Hood*.
17. Captain Leach to the Admiralty inquiry.
18. Tilburn to inquiry.
19. Ibid.
20. Max Arthur, *The Royal Navy 1939 To the Present*.
21. Tilburn to the inquiry.
22. Ibid.

23. Account given by Dundas in *Flagship Hood*.
24. Exchanges recorded in *Flagship Hood*.
25. Coles and Briggs, *Flagship Hood*.
26. Sequence of events detailed by Briggs in *Flagship Hood*.
27. Fritz-Otto Busch, *Prinz Eugen*.
28. Von Müllenheim-Rechberg, *Battleship Bismarck*.
29. Max Arthur, *The Royal Navy 1939 To the Present*.
30. As recounted by Cain in HMS *Electra*.
31. Tilburn to the Admiralty inquiry.
32. Account given by Dundas in *Flagship Hood*.
33. According to Bruce Taylor, in *The Battlecruiser* HMS *Hood*, without this phenomenon, which shot all three survivors to the surface on what was the ship's port side, *Hood* might have gone down with no survivors.
34. The 2001 expedition led by David Mearns to find both the wrecks of *Hood* and *Bismarck* discovered that the B turret and conning tower had been blown off by a massive explosion forward. See Appendix 1, *Busting the Myths*.
35. Timings recorded in the papers of Ludovic Porter, IWM Department of Documents.

Chapter 9: The Entrails of Hell

1. Letter to Ludovic Porter from JD Brown of the RN Historical branch, IWM Department of Documents. *For more on this topic, see* Appendix 3.
2. Fritz Otto-Busch, *Prinz Eugen*.
3. Geoffrey Brooke, *Alarm Starboard!*
4. It took Knight two years to recover, and even then he only regained partial sight. Knight's most memorable silver screen role was Captain Fluellen in Laurence Olivier's *Henry V* (1944). He went on to play the part of Captain Leach in the 1960 British movie *Sink the Bismarck!*
5. Brooke, *Alarm Starboard!*
6. Fifteen-year-old McIvor had joined up in March 1939, in his home city of Belfast, but without first seeking the permission of his father, who fought in the First World War as a US Marine Corps sergeant but was now a Constable in the Royal Ulster Constabulary. 'Do your parents know you are down here joining the Navy?' the recruiting officer asked. 'Sure, they do,' lied Alan. The recruiter knew his dad, for PC McIvor's beat went right past the recruiting office, and so blew the whistle on the teenager's enlistment, offering the chance to cancel it. When young McIvor got home he found his dad waiting for him. Enquired a stern-faced PC McIvor: 'I believe you have joined the Royal Navy?'

    'I have,' came the wary reply. But, instead of being angry, his dad seemed to accept the idea. The former marine observed: 'Well … it's done now.'

    Probably he recognized that sooner or later he would lose his strong-willed son to the Navy. Alan's mother was not very pleased, but the fact that war might yet be avoided in the coming months tempered her anxiety.
7. It was traditional in British cruisers and battleships for Royal Marines to man at least one turret of the main armament, in this case the Y turret.
8. The mechanism for passing shells up to the turrets of the King George V Class ships was complex. Instead of going straight up in a lift, the shell was put in the

ring – a little bit like a truck on a roller-coaster track – and the shell travelled up that way, helter-skelter. This enabled shells to be loaded onto the ring even if the turret was revolving. According to Captain Leach, in his report on gunnery defects during the action: 'Owing to the motion of the ship, a shell slid out of the port shell room and fouled the revolving shell ring while the latter was locked to the trunk and the turret was training. The hinge tray [on which the shell was placed] was severely buckled, putting the revolving shell ring out of action.' Other turrets in *Prince of Wales* suffered similar problems. Even a slight lack of alignment could lead to trays being buckled and the shell ring becoming jammed.
9. Geoffrey Brooke detailed his experiences during the Battle of the Denmark Strait in his autobiography, *Alarm Starboard!*
10. The 'heads' is naval slang for the toilets, derived from the fact that in the days of the sailing navy, sailors and marines used to go forward to the head of the ship to do their business, via a hole over the waves.

Chapter 10: After-Shock
1. Harriman and Abel, *Special Envoy to Churchill and Stalin 1941 – 1946.*
2. Churchill, *The Second World War Vol III.*
3. Ibid.
4. Among those lost in *Hood* were four Australians who had answered the call to defend the mother country. David Hall, George Hall (the former not related to the latter) together with Ian Startup and John Shannon volunteered when the Royal Navy asked for 'gentlemen' with experience of yachting to come forward under the Dominion Yachtsmen Scheme. The four Aussies joined *Hood* in early 1941. Their names are on the commemorative plaque, which was placed on the battlecruiser's wreck in 2001 by Ted Briggs, during the Mearns expedition. Brief details of the four men's experiences are contained in the April 2009 issue of the Sea Power Australia regular publication 'Semaphore', entitled *'The Yachtsmen and the Mighty Hood'*.
5. Churchill, *The Second World War Vol III.*
6. Quoted by Sopocko in *Gentlemen, The Bismarck Has Been Sunk.*
7. Vian, *Action This Day.*
8. Tragedy would strike the Kerr family again, as the *Hood* captain's son, Russell, a Captain in the 82nd Tank Regiment, lost his life in Burma, late March 1945.
9. Donald, *Stand By For Action.*
10. TJ Cain, HMS *Electra.*
11. Ibid.
12. Ransome Wallis, *Two Red Stripes.*
13. Account published by the UK's WWII Experience Centre. *See* Sources.
14. Recounted by Kennedy, *Pursuit.*
15. KGV Association, *Memories – Life Aboard King George V.*
16. *Battleships* transcript.
17. Account given by Tilburn in Max Arthur's *The Royal Navy – 1939 To The Present Day.*
18. Coles and Briggs, *Flagship Hood.*
19. It has been speculated by some that much of the force of *Hood*'s explosion went into the water, the catastrophic event venting its power not only horizontally and vertically from stern to stem, but also by ripping out the bottom of the ship. This

would possibly explain the lack of noise. One officer in *Prince of Wales*, Lieutenant Commander AH Terry, who observed *Hood*'s demise using high-powered glasses, reported being able to see inside the ship, through the frames where plating had been blown off, as the battlecruiser's middle section rolled over.

20. Churchill, *The Second World War Vol III*.
21. Ibid.
22. Ibid.
23. Ibid.
24. Ibid.
25. John Colville, *The Fringes of Power*.
26. Coles and Briggs, *Flagship Hood*.
27. *The Royal Navy – 1939 To The Present Day*.
28. Coles and Briggs, *Flagship Hood*.
29. *The Royal Navy – 1939 To The Present Day*.
30. Ibid
31. TJ Cain, HMS *Electra*.
32. Coles and Briggs, *Flagship Hood*.
33. *The Royal Navy – 1939 To The Present Day*.
34. TJ Cain, HMS *Electra*.
35. Ibid.
36. Ibid.
37. Arthur, *The Royal Navy – 1939 To The Present Day*.
38. *Sunday Pictorial*, 25 May 1941.

Chapter 11: The Hunters and the Hunted

1. Berthold, *The Sinking of the Bismarck*.
2. This was the boat deck fire, caused by one of *Prince of Wales'* 14-inch shell hits.
3. HMS *Suffolk* pulled her first spell of picket duty in the Denmark Strait in November 1939, on the 23rd of that month hunting in vain for the raiders *Scharnhorst* and *Gneisenau* after they broke out into the Atlantic and sank the *Rawalpindi*. During the Norwegian campaign *Suffolk* suffered grievously, only just making it back to Scapa Flow after coming under intensive air attack for several hours, receiving a hit by a single German bomb. The cruiser's quarterdeck was under water and she was forced to steer by her screws, harassed by the Luftwaffe all the way back to Orkney. Thirty-two of her men were dead, with a further thirty-eight wounded. Major repairs were necessary, *Suffolk* not returning to service until March 1941 when she was immediately sent to waters off Iceland.
4. Porter, IWM Department of Documents.
5. McMullen, IWM Sound Archive.
6. Collett, IWM Department of Documents.
7. BW Smith, IWM Department of Documents.
8. Porter, IWM Department of Documents.
9. The armoured box on top of the bridge superstructure in which sat the team controlling the 6-inch main armament.
10. Fritz-Otto Busch, *Prinz Eugen*.
11. The shells of *Prince of Wales* failed to hit their target – two of her 14-inch guns failing again – and *Bismarck* was not keen on joining battle.

Chapter 12: Swordfish Strike

1. *Kenya, Aurora, Hermione* and *Galatea*.
2. Magazine of HMS *King George V*, RNM.
3. It did not explode. However, having survived the Crimean War, Thomas Esmonde died at the age of forty-four, in 1873, after being hit in the eye by a tree branch. He suffered a lethal infection, a bitterly ironic fashion for a VC winner to lose his life.
4. The aviator's brother, Lt Cdr John Esmonde served in the destroyer *Zulu*, which was also involved in the *Bismarck* chase; therefore both brothers ended up being involved in torpedo attacks on the German battleship.
5. *Victorious* had a double bottom that was designed to provide additional protection against underwater explosions. Speed of turning rudder was exceptional, without too much heel, enabling the ship to head into the wind as swiftly as possible to launch aircraft. The original anti-aircraft weapons fit was substantial, taking the form of sixteen 4.5-inch guns, six eight-barrel pom-pom mountings and multiple .50-calibre machine guns. The 4.5s were specially designed to fire at low elevation across the flight-deck, enabling the full weight of their firepower to be brought to bear against attacking enemy aircraft on either beam. The flight-deck armour was three inches thick. The hangar space was enclosed in what Michael Apps describes in *Send Her Victorious* as an 'armoured shell', with flash-proof doors and a self-contained fire-fighting system.
6. At a stroke, the Royal Navy removed the Italian main battle fleet from the Mediterranean for many months. The Japanese studied the Taranto raid carefully, later making it the model for the naval air assault against the US Navy's Pacific Fleet at Pearl Harbor in December 1941.
7. Account given in Max Arthur's *The Royal Navy 1939 to the Present Day*.
8. Carver, FAAM.
9. *The Royal Navy 1939 to the Present Day*.
10. Ibid.
11. Collett, IWM Department of Documents.
12. Porter, IWM Department of Documents.
13. *The Royal Navy 1939 to the Present Day*.
14. Ibid.
15. Sayer, *Tag on a Stringbag*.
16. Robertson, *Channel Dash*.
17. Müllenheim-Rechberg, *Battleship Bismarck*.
18. Wellings, *On His Majesty's Service*.
19. Sayer, *Tag on a Stringbag*
20. The torpedo dropping speed was 90 knots at an altitude of 90 feet.
21. Sayer and Ball, *Tag on a Stringbag*.
22. Wellings, *On His Majesty's Service*.
23. Apps, *Send Her Victorious*.
24. Captain Harrington gave an account of his part in the *Bismarck* Action, entitled *The Bismarck Breakout*, in Issue 23, 1990, of the newsletter of the HMS *Victourious* Association.
25. Sayer and Ball, *Tag on a Stringbag*.
26. Müllenheim-Rechberg, *Battleship Bismarck*.
27. McMullen, IWM Sound Archive.

28. Michael G. Walling, *Between a Rock and a Hard Place*.
29. HMS Norfolk*'s Gunnery and R.D.F. During Operations Against Bismarck*, National Archives.
30. Wood, RNM.
31. Porter, IWM Department of Documents.

Chapter 13: A Day of Fearful Gloom

1. Quoted by Colville in *The Fringes of Power*. It is a curious twist of fate that the Troubridge family name should enter the *Bismarck* story more than once.
2. Cdr Kenneth Edwards, *Men of Action*.
3. Although Churchill, as First Lord of the Admiralty, presided over the Navy during the calamitous Norwegian campaign of spring and summer 1940, as Prime Minister, Neville Chamberlain carried the can and resigned. This cleared the way for Churchill to become PM.
4. Colville, *The Fringes of Power*. This was far from the case, the Germans failing to mount a successful seaborne landing while the Royal Navy suffered grievous losses holding them off under Luftwaffe onslaught.
5. McMurtrie, *The Cruise of the Bismarck*.
6. For more on *London's* search and destroy mission see the author's HMS *LONDON*.
7. Magazine of HMS *King George V*, RNM.
8. Winston's Specials [WS] were troop convoys sent to reinforce the North African theatre and also Indian garrisons.
9. Not revealed in Vian's own *Action This Day*, but details of code provided to Grenfell by Arbuthnot and published in *The Bismarck Episode*.
10. Vian, *Action This Day*.
11. Ibid.
12. Ronald Bassett, HMS *Sheffield*.
13. *The Destruction of the Bismarck* a typescript account of the action, RNM.
14. Carver, FAAM.
15. Swanton, FAAM. Alan Swanton, a farmer's son who suffered from dreadful hay fever, got the flying bug after a trip in a glider, subsequently joining the Royal Navy in 1939. Gaining promotion after the *Bismarck* Action, Swanton ended up commanding several naval air squadrons. He saw action in the Mediterranean, attacked the *Tirpitz* in her Norwegian lair and led strike missions against the Japanese at the end of the war while flying Avenger dive-bombers from the carrier *Implacable*. He saw the devastation wrought on Hiroshima by an atomic bomb blast and during the Korean War of the early 1950s led numerous bombing missions. Luck stayed with Swanton throughout his career, for an Avenger he was flying in the Pacific crashed on launch, the carrier pushing it under and cutting the aircraft in two. Swanton and his crew escaped and were rescued by a destroyer. Swanton was back flying sorties the following day. Retiring from the Navy with the rank of Commander in the late 1960s he was a highly decorated officer, winning a Distinguished Service Cross and Bar and the Distinguished Service Order, as well as a Mention in Dispatches for his various exploits. In his *Daily Telegraph* obituary, published in early 2003 shortly after his death, and written by Captain Peter Hore RN, it is mentioned that Swanton once gave his Army officer brother a 'lift' in his

Swordfish. Swanton's brother remarked that 'it was hard to imagine anything less likely to wound a battleship.'

16. *The Destruction of the Bismarck* a typescript account of the action, RNM.
17. Chesneau, *Aircraft Carriers*.
18. Peter C Smith reveals in his book, HMS *Renown*, that when the battlecruiser's men later heard their ship was being held back from engaging *Bismarck* they cheered. The fate of *Hood* had filled many of them with a dread of doing their duty, although some brave souls were ready to have a go no matter what.
19. Somerville came from a naval family, with one forebear, Lieutenant Mark Somerville killed in action as long ago as 1758, while another was the legendary Admiral Samuel Hood, mentor of Nelson. A naturally shy man, but with a mischievous sense of humour, James Somerville, who joined the Navy at the age of fifteen in 1897, was by 1912 an instructor at the Torpedo School in Portsmouth. During the First World War he served in the battleship *Marlborough* and also ashore in the Dardanelles campaign. By the mid-1920s Somerville was Commanding Officer of the battleship *Benbow* and later Captain of *Warspite*. Rising ever higher on the promotion ladder, by the late 1930s Somerville was Commander-in-Chief, East Indies. However, he was diagnosed with tuberculosis and invalided out of the Navy. Not content to sit on the sidelines as the country slid to war, Somerville sought a second opinion and was awarded a clean bill of health. With a pressing need for experience and skill at sea, in early September 1939, Somerville was returned to the active list and given command of Force H.
20. Macintyre, *Fighting Admiral*.
21. Ibid.

Chapter 14: Steering to Intercept Enemy
1. This large and varied group of passengers included RAF aircrew going to Canada for training, British sailors headed eventually for the Falklands, Canadian troops heading home and even medical cases, including shellshock victims. All were destined for Halifax, Nova Scotia, which was meant to be *Rodney*'s first port of call before going to Boston. Strapped to *Rodney*'s upper deck were four thousand boiler tubes, armour plate and anti-aircraft weapon mountings, all to be used during the refit. Additionally, below decks was a quantity of Britain's last gold reserves and even some of the famed Elgin Marbles, going to Canada for safe-keeping. All in all, *Rodney* was carrying people and items surely not suited to potential involvement in a major battle.
2. Wellings, *On His Majesty's Service*.
3. Ibid.
4. Ibid.
5. Inside even a twentieth century British warship messengers ran in bare feet to get greater grip. This custom dated back at least as far as the era of Nelson, for example in HMS *Victory* at Trafalgar gunners and others went barefoot.
6. Sopocko, *Gentlemen, The Bismarck Has Been Sunk*.
7. Wellings, *On His Majesty's Service*.
8. It has been claimed that data meant to be applied to a gnomonic chart was plotted on a Mercator chart instead, therefore giving the wrong position for *Bismarck* and suggesting she was heading north. On a gnomonic chart a straight line is what it

appears to be – a straight line providing the shortest track between one point and another. I consulted a naval officer friend who provided me with the following explanation of the difference between a gnomonic and Mercator chart which even the most landlubberly person (including myself) should hopefully be able to understand:

> Think of an OS map where Plymouth is represented on a piece of paper, which is okay for getting from the northern outskirts of the city to the Hoe but actually on larger scale, say for long voyages at sea, a route from A to B would be distorted because the Earth isn't flat. A Mercator projection presents the Earth as a cylinder, which mostly corrects this distortion and is better for navigation. However, as you get closer to the poles, the distortion becomes infinite, so no good for, let's say, navigating the North-West passage. Alternatively, think of the shortest distance between two points: if you could fly from northern Plymouth to the Hoe you wouldn't notice any distortion unless you were a very clever crow. Over longer distances you want to steer the shortest route and use as little fuel as possible. On a voyage of less than about 600 miles don't bother with a Mercator – use an OS map. On the surface of the Earth – and here I mean oceans – the shortest distance between two ports is a great circle, but to steer a great circle you need to adjust your actual heading regularly – typically a degree or so each twenty-four hours on an ocean passage. The next shortest distance that enables you to steer the same course without alteration is a rhumb line. Mercator represented all rhumb lines as straight lines, which is OK if you are under sail and subject to the vagaries of the wind and currents. But – and this goes back to the infinite distortion nearer the poles – this distorts the size and shape of large objects, so Greenland appears on a Mercator chart to be larger than Brazil. A gnomonic (that's Greek, not a gnome who invented it) shows all great circles as straight lines, which eliminates the distortion of large objects (i.e. Greenland and Brazil) but useless for ocean or aero navigation. So if you find your pilot using a gnomonic chart, get off!

However, Ludovic Kennedy, while writing *Pursuit* consulted Captain Frank Lloyd, Fleet Navigating Officer with Tovey in *King George V*, who told him that the flagship did have gnomonic charts. Lloyd remarked that only a fool would have tried to plot direction finding bearings using a Mercator – D/F needs straight line plotting to achieve triangulation. It appears the error crept in because the gnomonic charts in *King George V* did not have true North readings for each of the intercept stations providing the data, so therefore had to try and calculate it themselves using a protractor. This led to errors creeping in, which the Admiralty's more experienced plotters avoided. Tovey had, of course, requested that their analysis was not passed on to him, just the data. Fortunately, the fleet navigating officer was able to double-check his team's interpretation and realized something was wrong.

9. Wellings, *On His Majesty's Service.*
10. Churchill, *The Second World War*, Vol III.
11. Carlo D'Este, *Warlord.*
12. In one of those strange twists of history, a previous HMS *Prince of Wales* was the ship that took Calder home to face court martial, so ensuring the ship missed the battle of Trafalgar in October 1805.

13. Churchill, *The Second World War*, Vol III.
14. Colville, *The Fringes of Power*.

Chapter 15: Remorseless Determination
1. Palmer, IWM Sound Archive.
2. Creasy, *Action Stations*.
3. Biographical details carried on the front of the *Daily Mirror*, 28 May 1941, as part of a story headlined 'Navy "Boy" Sank Her', referring to *Dorsetshire*'s part in destroying *Bismarck*.
4. John Cannon and Bert Gollop, *A County Class – The Epic Story of* HMS *Dorsetshire*.
5. Johns and Kelly, *No Surrender*.
6. *A County Class*.
7. The main galley cooked the hot meals and a nominated sailor from each mess-deck throughout the ship came to get the food. Getting it back hot to his hungry shipmates was another matter. In today's Navy there is central messing, which means the sailors go to dining halls located next to the galley for their food. Good food has always been fundamental to good morale aboard ship.
8. *A County Class*.
9. Ibid.
10. Ibid.
11. *Action Stations*.
12. Sam Wood, RNM.
13. TJ Cain, HMS *Electra*.
14. RNM.
15. RNM.
16. Churchill and Gilbert, *Winston S. Churchill*, Companion Volumes.
17. Ibid.
18. Wellings, *On His Majesty's Service*.
19. Journal of Midshipman Shaw, BRNC.
20. Exchange contained in Wellings, *On His Majesty's Service*.

Chapter 16: Sorry for the Kipper
1. *The Destruction of the* Bismarck, RNM.
2. Liar Dice was a gambling game, with the traditional 'cards' on the faces of the die. It is said to have been brought to Europe by the Spanish conquistadores, who based it on a game they encountered in South America.
3. Carver, FAAM.
4. Article by James Stewart Moore in *The Times*, 22 May 1991.
5. HMS *Sheffield* account, RNM.
6. He gave a short account in a letter to *The Times*, 27 May 1991, a photocopy of which is held in the FAAM.
7. The practice of 'zogging' was also used to communicate between Swordfish and may have been used on this occasion. When consulted by the author about this, Kenneth Davies of the TAG Association, who served in the Indian Ocean during the Second World War, explained that 'zogging' was a substitute for Semaphore 'by which TAGs or observers could (just about) communicate with other aircraft in

mid-air from their open cockpits or sometimes with ships.' He added: 'We were taught it when training but I don't know anybody who claims to have used it in action. I used an Aldis lamp. I find it difficult to believe that with all the mayhem which was going on around *Bismarck* that anyone had the time, inclination or a steady enough platform to use it then.'

8. For details of the *Prinz Eugen*'s fate see Appendix 3.
9. James Stewart Moore, *The Times*, 22 May 1991.
10. Reported in HMS *Sheffield* by Ronald Bassett.
11. The tactic to avoid being hit by a spread of torpedoes was to turn a warship toward the oncoming torpedoes, therefore presenting the toughest, and narrowest, part of the hull to the on-coming weapon and being able to steer decisively to evade it. This was obviously much better than turning away, presenting the vulnerable stern, with its rudder(s) and propellers, as well as being unable to see the torpedo. It was called combing because the spread of torpedoes would be like the teeth of a comb, with the ship seeking to go between them.
12. Repard, letter to *The Times*.
13. Ibid.
14. Ibid.
15. His account is contained in *Some Survivors' Narratives*, a document compiled by the HMS *Cossack* Association.
16. *King James Version*, Kings, 10:7. 'Howbeit I believed not the words, until I came, and mine eyes had seen it: and, behold, the half was not told me: thy wisdom and prosperity exceedeth the fame which I heard.'
17. Swanton, FAAM.
18. James Stewart Moore, *The Times*, 22 May 1991.
19. Magnetic warheads had been used on the torpedoes dropped by Swordfish during the attack on Taranto, but the targets there were ships at anchor in a sheltered harbour.
20. As related by Stewart-Moore in *The Times*.
21. Magazine of HMS *King George V*, RNM.
22. Ronald Bassett, HMS *Sheffield*
23. *Sheffield* account, RNM.
24. Ibid.
25. Ibid.
26. Ronald Bassett, HMS *Sheffield*.
27. As with other signals quoted in this book's *Bismarck* chase chapters, sourced in Wellings, *On His Majesty's Service*.
28. Ibid.
29. Ibid.
30. Ibid.
31. Tovey to *Rodney* at 5.24 pm, as related by log of signals in Wellings, *On His Majesty's Service*.

Chapter 17: Into the Jaws of Death
1. Letter from Sub Lt Leonard Mann to his parents, held by the FAAM. According to Mark Horan's account of the action four aircraft from 810 NAS took part in the actual attack, four from 818 NAS and seven from 820 NAS. *See* Note 14, *below.*

2. Carver, FAAM.
3. In the end only three of the fifteen Swordfish suffered damage and none were lost.
4. *Sheffield* account, RNM.
5. Article by James Stewart Moore in *The Times*, May 1991.
6. Ibid.
7. Swanton, FAAM.
8. Stewart-Moore, *The Times*, May 1991.
9. Sopocko, *Gentlemen, The Bismarck Has Been Sunk*.
10. Ibid.
11. Letter to *The Times*, 27 May 1991, a photocopy of which is held in the FAAM.
12. *Sheffield* account, RNM.
13. Account given by Moffat in an interview with the author, June 2009.
14. John Moffat, the last surviving *Ark Royal* aviator to have taken part in the strike on *Bismarck*, wrote a book with the prolific Mike Rossiter that was blessed with the contentious title *I Sank the Bismarck* (published in 2009). *See* Bibliography. Moffat himself was somewhat embarrassed, but said he could not argue with the publisher's desire for a mass market title regardless of the finer points. This, however, outraged Ken Pattisson's son, the Olympic gold medal-winning yachtsman, Rodney Pattisson, who wrote to the *Daily Telegraph* newspaper protesting about Moffat's claim. Published on 23 June 2009, just days after Moffat's book hit the shelves, Pattisson's letter stated: 'It could not have been Moffat's torpedo that sunk [sic] the *Bismarck*.' He pointed out that Moffat attacked on the *Bismarck*'s port side, while his father went in on the starboard side. Referring to an expedition by the movie director and under water explorer James Cameron (*see* Appendix 1) that discovered a hole on *Bismarck*'s starboard side at her stern, with her rudder jammed against her 'central propeller', Pattisson's angry letter concluded: 'Moffat's torpedo, therefore, was not fired at her starboard side, so he could not possibly have crippled *Bismarck*.' Moffat and Rossiter's claim is based on an account written by Mark E Horan, called *With Gallantry and Determination – The Story of the Torpedoing of the Bismarck*, which attributes the fateful hit to Moffat. For a full version of his account visit http://www.kbismarck.com/article2.html.

There were three hits, eleven Swordfish torpedoes missed altogether while two were not dropped and had to be jettisoned before the aircraft landed back aboard *Ark Royal*.
15. *Sheffield* account, RNM.
16. Details from Repard's letter to *The Times* and also Basset, HMS *Sheffield*. The cruiser suffered fourteen casualties in total, with three dying later of their wounds.
17. Crawford, IWM Sound Archive.
18. Journal of Midshipman Shaw, BRNC.

Chapter 18: Vian's Dilemma
1. Wellings, *On His Majesty's Service*.
2. Related by Macintyre in *Fighting Admiral*. U-556 and *Bismarck* were particular friends, an amity founded on the good personal relationship between Wohlfarth and Lindemann and the fact that both vessels were built by Blohm & Voss at Hamburg around the same time. They were often berthed alongside each other and Wohlfarth promised that U-556 would always endeavour to protect the battleship, something

she was unable to do on 26 May 1941. The boat was also ordered to collect *Bismarck*'s war diary, another task unfulfilled, much to the anguish of Wohlfarth and his men. During the period 6–20 May 1941 *U-556* sank half a dozen Allied merchant vessels and damaged another, hence the absence of torpedoes when the opportunity to put one into *Ark Royal* arose. *U-556* met her end a month to the day after *Bismarck*. The submarine was cornered and depth-charged off Iceland, with five of her men killed and forty-one surviving. Wohlfarth survived, spending the rest of the Second World War as a prisoner of war, returning to Germany in 1947.

3. Vian, *Action This Day*.
4. Ibid.
5. Interview at the April 2009 HMS *Cossack* Association reunion. It is interesting to note that *Ark Royal*'s navigator was Lieutenant Commander Hector MacLean, who had been *Cossack*'s navigator during the *Altmark* incident.
6. WWII Irish Wreckology Group Study and Research, document lodged with FAAM.
7. KFW Rail, IWM Department of Documents
8. Vian, *Action This Day*.
9. Ibid.
10. Churchill, *The Second World War, Vol III*. Fraser would go on to command the Home Fleet, on Boxing Day 1943 flying his flag in the King George V Class battleship *Duke of York* at the Battle of North Cape, the last major capital ship action in European waters, in which the Royal Navy destroyed *Scharnhorst*.
11. Hammick's account, archived on BBC *Peoples' War* web site. *See* Sources.
12. Vian, *Action This Day*.
13. Eric Farmer account, HMS *Cossack* Association/Sallyann Pagett.
14. Interviewed at the April 2009 HMS *Cossack* Association reunion.
15. *Some Survivors' Narratives*, compiled by the HMS *Cossack* Association.
16. Müllenheim-Rechberg, *Battleship Bismarck*.
17. Ibid.
18. Berthold, *The Sinking of the Bismarck*.
19. Ibid.
20. Müllenheim-Rechberg, *Battleship Bismarck*.
21. Berthold, *The Sinking of the Bismarck*.
22. Jack Broom, *Make Another Signal*.
23. Magazine of HMS *King George V*, RNM.
24. TJ Cain, HMS *Electra*.
25. Hammick, *Peoples' War*, BBC.
26. Vian, *Action This Day*.
27. Hammick, *Peoples' War*, BBC.
28. Eric Farmer account, HMS *Cossack* Association/Sallyann Pagett.

Chapter 19: A Desperate and Deadly Race

1. Sopocko, *Gentlemen, The Bismarck Has Been Sunk*.
2. Ibid.
3. Wellings, *On His Majesty's Service*.
4. John Tovey was captain of *Rodney* in the early 1930s, in the aftermath of the Invergordon Mutiny, restoring the morale of the Ship's Company after that

tumultuous event. For more on *Rodney*'s part in the mutiny and also John Tovey's time as her Commanding Officer, see the author's HMS *RODNEY*.

5. Many years later Captain North Dalrymple-Hamilton revealed how crucial his father believed Tovey's decision to let *Rodney* determine her own tactics, and fate, had been: 'The main thing I remember my father saying was how grateful he was to the Commander-in-Chief for giving him freedom of manoeuvre. In the old days you fought in line. At Jutland for instance, all the ships had to keep station and then there was *Hood* and *Prince of Wales*. He was grateful to have been given freedom of action to manoeuvre his ship as he saw fit during the engagement and that this had been a very great assistance to him. They [*Rodney*] received a few shell splinters on board but that was all. They were jolly lucky in the *Rodney*. I think the nearest shell wasn't more than something like 20 feet off the bows and so they [the *Bismarck*'s shells] were quite near. Had my father not had this freedom of action, I think they would almost certainly have been hit ...' Recounted during an interview for the television documentary *Battleships* although not used in the final transmitted series in 2001. *See* Sources.

6. Personal, unpublished version of a written account of the action, *The End of the Bismarck*, sent to the author by its author, Major JEM Ruffer, RM. Subsequent material giving Ruffer's point of view also based on that account. In an accompanying note, Ruffer, who was ninety-five years old at the time [Aug 2007] told the author: 'I was in the *Norfolk* for four years during the Second World War and we ran into a bit of trouble now and again.'

7. *Suffolk* was unsuccessful, but, as recounted in the author's HMS *LONDON*, other British warships found and destroyed German supply vessels waiting in vain to support *Bismarck* and *Prinz Eugen*. For example, on 4 June, the *Esso Hamburg*, which had refuelled *Prinz Eugen* on the morning of 28 May, as the latter headed for a French port, was intercepted by the cruiser *London* and destroyer *Brilliant*. The *Esso Hamburg*'s crew were taken off and held captive aboard *London*, while *Brilliant* sank the German vessel with fire from her 4.7-inch guns after a torpedo failed to do the trick.

8. Ruffer's account.

9. Ludovic Kennedy, *Pursuit*.

10. Dalrymple-Hamilton, *Battleships* interview transcript.

11. Ibid.

12. *Daily Telegraph Book of Naval Obituaries*.

13. HMS *King George V* magazine, RNM.

14. Dalrymple-Hamilton, *Battleships* interview transcript.

15. HMS *King George V* magazine, RNM.

16. From the full account of the action provided by this officer in the HMS *Rodney* Association archive.

17. Müllenheim-Rechberg, *Battleship Bismarck*.

18. Ibid.

19. Ibid.

20. Ibid.

21. Ibid. Lütjens' broadcasts to *Bismarck*'s ship's company, including his praise for the sinking of *Hood*, were recorded in a reconstructed War Diary for the battleship. It was based on testimony of those few survivors picked up by the Germans and

returned home rather than going to British PoW camps. The admiral's melancholy is of course also recorded in Müllenheim-Rechberg's book.

22. At this time *Rodney* actually carried two chaplains, one Anglican and the other Roman Catholic, the former taking precedence and being known as the Padre.

23. Volume I of the Royal Navy's *Manual of Seamanship* was issued to every sailor joining the seaman branch and was a rather bulky, disorganized, not terribly well written compendium of essential facts that men needed to sail and run warships, from how to steer a vessel to understanding the effects of wind, anchors and cables; it even included slang. Vol I was composed of 450 pages, which explains why it was such good protection. In 1943 a simplified version was produced, at 120 pages-long, so perhaps not so useful in protecting a sailor's vital parts, but maybe easier to glean vital info from. A reprint of *A Seaman's Pocket-Book*, as the concise manual was entitled, has proved essential to the author of this book in trying to get to grips with the world of the Royal Navy. *See* Bibliography.

24. G Conning, IWM Collections.

25. As related by Crawford during his interview for the IWM Sound Archive.

26. Interview with the author, 2007.

27. Quoted in Johnston and McAuley, *The Battleships*.

28. Dalrymple-Hamilton, *Battleships* interview transcript.

29. Eric Farmer, HMS *Cossack* Association account.

30. Robinson, HMS *Cossack* Association account.

31. Kennedy, *Pursuit*.

32. Ibid.

33. Journal of Midshipman Shaw, BRNC.

34. Interview with the author, 2006.

35. Interview with the author, 2007.

36. Walton, Sound Archive IWM.

37. George Thomas, Sound Archive IWM.

38. Ibid.

39. Interview with the author, September 2009. Alfred Brimacombe was at the time of the interview aged eighty-nine and one of the last surviving veterans from the *Rodney* to have seen service in the battleship during the *Bismarck* action. He volunteered for the Navy when he was nineteen because he did not want to be called up into the Army. Born in Plymouth's historic Barbican quarter, the old haunt of the great Elizabethan seadogs Drake and Hawkins, the sea was in his blood and he was always in boats, taking part in rowing regattas and so on. After joining up on 16 May 1940, Brimacombe went for training at HMS *Royal Arthur*, Skegness. There was a need at this time for stokers, so in October 1940 he was sent to *Rodney* to join her engineering department. Assigned to the double-bottom party, his job was to move oil around in the tanks, making sure the ship was properly ballasted and draining water off the bilges. It was a strange subterranean job, almost akin to being a coal miner as he spent his time in pitch-black passages. He recalled: 'You went right down into the bottom of the ship, no lights, with just a torch to find your way and once you had done your job with the pumps and the valves you went back up.' During the *Bismarck* action he was assigned to the engine room being told by an old and bold Chief Petty Officer that they would be lucky to get out of it alive. Alfred felt *Rodney* was a highly trained and professional ship: 'They even used to train us to move

around the ship in darkness so we could find our way to our action stations without lighting.' Post-*Rodney* Alfred went on to serve in the minesweeper *Grecian*, seeing action off the D-Day beaches, where he caught sight of the battleship bombarding Germans forces in Normandy. He left the Navy in 1946 as a leading hand.

40. Interview with the author, 2007.
41. Campbell account, HMS *Rodney* Association.
42. Interview with the author, 2007.
43. Campbell account, HMS *Rodney* Association.
44. Interview with the author, 2004. Harold Thompson chose the Navy as a career over one as a musician. Harold's dad was a great fan of organ music and knew the renowned theatre organist Reginald Porter Bown. He had admired the maestro's performances between features at a cinema in Southampton. However, sixteen-year-old Harold did not fancy being an apprentice theatre organist, and so it was that one day he sat down with his father and a copy of *Pears' Encyclopaedia* to decide a future away from music. Leafing through the hefty tome, they considered all manner of trades and crafts. They even considered the Armed Forces. 'I was in the Army during the Great War...I don't think you'd fancy that,' Mr Thompson told his son. 'I wouldn't mind the Navy,' suggested Harold. Mr Thompson was happy enough with that choice, as it would place Harold far away from the kind of misery he had endured in the trenches. Harold left the family home in Surrey to attend Royal Navy engineering artificer exams at Portsmouth. Unfortunately he failed to make the grade by five marks. The Navy offered Harold training as an air engineering artificer, which did not need such high marks, or as a boy sailor. Harold chose the latter path, which of course led him to HMS *King George V* and a ringside seat for the sinking of the *Bismarck*.
45. KGV Association, *Memories – Life Aboard King George V*.
46. HMS *King George V* magazine, RNM.
47. Ibid.
48. Related by Grenfel, *The Bismarck Episode*
49. HMS *King George V* magazine, RNM.
50. Reported in the book *Men of Action*, by Cdr Kenneth Edwards, and also detailed (as here) by North Dalrymple-Hamilton in the transcript for his *Battleships* interview.
51. Dalrymple-Hamilton, *Battleships* interview transcript.
52. *Log of* HMS *Dorsetshire*, National Archives.
53. *Action Stations*.
54. Ibid.
55. Len Walters, IWM Sound Archive.
56. Battle observer's account published in both *Battleship Bismarck* (Müllenheim-Rechberg) and *On His Majesty's Service* (Wellings).
57. Müllenheim-Rechberg, *Battleship Bismarck*.
58. Ibid.
59. Skwiot and Prusinowska, *Hunting the Bismarck*.
60. Journal of Midshipman Shaw, BRNC.
61. Crawford, IWM Sound Archive transcript.
62. RNM, newspaper of HMS *King George V*.

63. Ibid.
64. Ibid.
65. Kenneth Thompson, HMS *Rodney at War*.

Chapter 20: The Brutal Business of War
 1. Journal of Midshipman Shaw, BRNC.
 2. Müllenheim-Rechberg, *Battleship Bismarck*.
 3. Ibid.
 4. HMS *King George V* magazine, RNM.
 5. Brooke, *Alarm Starboard*!
 6. This was one of the cruisers, as *Renown* did not take part in the action.
 7. Campbell, HMS *Rodney* Association archive account.
 8. When German U-boats surrendered at the end of the Second World War, on approaching British ports or groups of Royal Navy warships they flew the black flag from their conning towers.
 9. Byers transcript. *See* Sources and Appendix 2.
10. Although he could also have meant *Bismarck*'s few remaining operational guns 'flashing their defiance'.
11. Mentioned in a letter to the author from *Rodney* veteran James McLean.
12. Quote published in *Hood and Bismarck* by Means and White.
13. North Dalrymple-Hamilton, *Battleships* transcript.
14. Interview with the author, 2007.
15. This incident is related by Crawford in his IWM Sound Archive interview.
    He referred to the computer as costing a million pounds. If this was a million pounds in 1941, then today it would cost £28,720,000, a serious amount of damage. However, Crawford may have been talking a million pounds equivalent in the year the IWM interview took place.
16. A device invented at the turn of the century by Lieutenant John Dumaresq RN. It enabled the gunnery officer to calculate relative speeds and headings of his own ship and that of the enemy. The Vickers Range Clock was another mechanical device from the same era, into which data from the Dumaresq and other sources – estimates provided by using optical range-finders and information from fall-of-shot spotting officers – would be input, to provide a range to target for the gunners. These robust devices could not be put out of action by a Royal Marine's boot.
17. Skwiot and Prusinowska, *Hunting the Bismarck*.
18. Berthold, *The Sinking of the Bismarck*.
19. Campbell, account in the HMS *Rodney* Association archive.
20. Skwiot and Prusinowska, *Hunting the Bismarck*.
21. Ibid.
22. Berthold, *The Sinking of the Bismarck*.
23. Incident related by Crawford in his interview for the IWM.
24. Skwiot and Prusinowska, *Hunting the Bismarck*.
25. A.E. Franklin, IWM Department of Documents.
26. Ibid.
27. Neither *Bismarck* nor the King George V Class ships carried torpedoes. The only vessels to launch them during the climactic battle were *Rodney*, *Norfolk* and *Dorsetshire*.

28. See the author's book HMS *RODNEY*.
29. Related in *Rodney Buzz*, the magazine of the HMS *Rodney* Association, April 1997 edition. Aside from the seaman struck by the flying steel helmet on the bridge, there was only one other casualty in *Rodney*.
30. Campbell, account in the HMS *Rodney* Association archive.
31. Lt Cdr Lewis, IWM Department of Documents.
32. HMS *King George V* newspaper, RNM.
33. Dalrymple-Hamilton, interview transcript for *Battleships*.
34. Interview with the author, September 2009.

Chapter 21: In at the Kill

1. Carver, FAAM.
2. Lt Cdr L Mann, in a letter to his parents, FAAM.
3. Ibid. All quotes from Mann are from the same source.
4. Interviewed at the HMS *Cossack* reunion in Worthing, April 2009.
5. Eric Farmer account, HMS *Cossack* Association/Sallyann Pagett.
6. *Action Stations*.
7. In an e-mail to the author, 2008.
8. AE Franklin, IWM.
9. *Action Stations*.
10. AE Franklin, IWM Department of Documents. Quotes from Franklin all taken from the same source.
11. *Action Stations*.
12. For more on the controversy over whether *Bismarck* finally sank due to British actions or scuttling, see Appendix 1.
13. Carver, FAAM.
14. Repard, FAAM.
15. Interview with the author, summer 2009.
16. Swanton, FAAM.
17. Carver, FAAM.
18. Ibid.

Chapter 22: A Necessary Killing

1. Crawford, IWM Sound Archives. His response to the question about whether or not *Rodney* would have ceased firing had *Bismarck* stopped was given to an Imperial War Museum interviewer.
2. North Dalrymple-Hamilton said in his interview for the TV documentary series *Battleships*: 'And in the end *Rodney* went in to about a mile, and I suppose we [*King George V*] were in to about two miles.'
3. In a letter to the author, 2004.
4. Transcript of interview for *Battleships*.
5. As quoted by Ludovic Kennedy, *Pursuit*.
6. Ibid.
7. Churchill, *The Second World War Vol III*.
8. An Irishman, Bracken would for a short time at the end of the war be First Lord of the Admiralty. He was one of Churchill's most trusted lieutenants, though others regarded him as untrustworthy.

9. The front page of the *News Chronicle,* Wednesday, 28 May 1941.
10. Churchill, *The Second World War Vol III.*
11. Members of the Women's Royal Naval Service (WRNS).
12. Quoted by Michael Patterson in *Voices of the Code Breakers.*
13. Midshipman Jeschonnek was not among the survivors rescued.
14. Good graduated with a first class honours degree in mathematics from Jesus College, Cambridge, in 1938. He was completing his PhD in 1941 when approached to work alongside Alan Turing at Bletchley. Jack Good subsequently played a key role in penetrating German naval codes, helping to turn the tide against Hitler's U-boats in the Battle of the Atlantic. Post-war Professor Good worked in British intelligence at GCHQ, the successor to Bletchley. After moving to the USA in the 1960s, he was consulted by the movie director Stanley Kubrick about how to depict a super-computer as a central character in *2001: A Space Odyssey.* The author of this book has worked with Jack Good's nephew, Desmond – Managing Director of the successful London-based multi-media enterprise Grosvenor Vision – on a number of corporate communications projects for the Royal Navy, including a documentary on the Battle of the Atlantic (2003).
15. Quoted by Michael Patterson in *Voices of the Code Breakers.*
16. *Action Stations.*
17. The *high* freeboard of the ship at its *waist* (middle).
18. Recounted by Bert Gollop in an e-mail to the author.
19. Kennedy, *Pursuit.*
20. *Commander-in-Chief Home Fleet Despatch,* National Archives. Tovey, in his official 'Action of 27th May' report, described it as 'a suspicious object, which might have been a U-boat'. This, he felt, meant ships trying to rescue *Bismarck* survivors 'were compelled to abandon the work of rescue.'
21. Incident related to the author in an e-mail from Bert Gollop (2008) and also in Cannon and Gollop's *A County Class – The epic story of H.M.S. Dorsetshire.* See Sources.
22. Gollop and Cannon, *A County Class.*
23. In a letter to the *Daily Telegraph,* June 23, 2009.
24. *Action Stations.*
25. North Dalrymple-Hamilton. Some years after the war he was in command of the Dartmouth Training Squadron, which was visiting its German equivalent at Flensburg. In the unbroadcast portion of his interview for *Battleships* Captain Dalrymple-Hamilton revealed: 'The senior instructing officer there, I found out, had been an officer on the *Bismarck.* I asked him onboard and had a fascinating yarn with him in my cabin. He'd been in the engine room throughout the action, and he was very interesting about that.' The German officer was most likely to have been Lieutenant Commander Junack.
26. *Action Stations.*
27. Cannon and Gollop, *A County Class.*
28. This quote and also details of Müllenheim-Rechberg's escape taken from his account, *Battleship Bismarck,* which is sub-titled *A Survivor's Story.*
29. Cannon and Gollop, *A County Class.*
30. Ibid.

31. Ibid. When Müllenheim-Rechberg had his uniform taken away to be laundered, the eagle clasping the swastika was removed before it was returned to him. Another example of manifestation of the Nazi regime not being allowed aboard *Dorsetshire*.
32. Ibid.
33. Ibid.
34. Ibid.
35. *Memories*, KGV Association.
36. According to an account in the archives of the HMS *Cossack* Association Herr Oscar was 'one of the luckiest cats of all time – or unluckiest, depending on how you look at it …' Appointed as the *Cossack*'s official ship's cat, Oscar, 'a strange black cat with tabby markings' survived catastrophe again six months after *Bismarck*'s loss, being saved from the British destroyer when she too was sunk. Saved from drowning by sailors from HMS *Ark Royal*, the cat met disaster again three days later when the aircraft carrier was torpedoed. Abandoning ship along with *Ark*'s human Ship's Company, Oscar found he was regarded as a bit of a Jonah and was therefore sent ashore for good. He ended up at an old sailors' home in Belfast where, according to the *Cossack* Association, he 'lived out the rest of his days in peace' dying aged fifteen in 1955.
37. TJ Cain, HMS *Electra*.

Chapter 23: Ghosts at the Feast
1. Wood, RNM.
2. Brooke, *Alarm Starboard*!
3. Willetts, IWM Sound Archive.
4. Ibid.
5. Midnight to 4.00 am.
6. Brooke, *Alarm Starboard*!
7. Ibid. In his recorded interview with the Imperial War Museum, *Prince of Wales*' Gunnery Officer Colin McMullen revealed the fate of the shell. He explained that, on being appointed to the RN's gunnery school at Whale Island, Portsmouth, in the aftermath of the battleship's destruction, in late 1941, he asked the establishment's commanding officer if it was possible to retrieve the *Bismarck* shell. McMullen thought it could be made into a trophy to encourage high standards in gunnery and also memorialize *Prince of Wales*. However, as McMullen explained, this was not to be: 'Unfortunately by then it had been cut up. The metallurgists and so on had got all the information they could get out of it, so that [making it into a trophy] wasn't on.'
8. Exchange reported by McMullen in his recorded IWM interview.
9. Brooke, *Alarm Starboard*!
10. Letter's contents related by Geoffrey Brooke in *Alarm Starboard*!
11. Tovey was therefore threatening to, literally, stand alongside Captain Leach at any court martial and give evidence in his defence. Such a development would have potentially dealt Churchill's premiership a devastating blow. The fact that the boss of the Home Fleet was having to defend one of his battleship captains in public would have undermined national morale, handing the Nazis a propaganda coup. It would also have made the Americans call into question Churchill's judgement.
12. *London Gazette* citation. Other characters that we have met in the course of this great drama were also among those honoured. For his part in destroying *Bismarck*

Admiral Tovey was made a Knight Commander of the British Empire (KBE). Captain Dalrymple-Hamilton of *Rodney* was awarded the Companion of the Order of the Bath (CB) as was Captain Patterson of *King George V*. Rear-Admiral Wake-Walker had already been awarded the CB for previous service, hence the award of the Commander of the Order of the British Empire (CBE) for his part in the *Bismarck* Action. Awards of the CBE also were made to the captains of *Victorious* and *Ark Royal*. Captain Vian received a Second Bar to his DSO. The DSO was also awarded to the captains of *Sheffield*, *Dorsetshire*, *Norfolk* and *Suffolk*. The Distinguished Service Cross (DSC) was awarded to *Rodney*'s Lt Cdr Crawford and Lt Cdr Gatacre. The Distinguished Service Medal (DSM) was awarded to Leading Sick Berth Attendant Wood (*Prince of Wales*) and Able Seaman Newell (*Suffolk*). Among the aviators honoured, Lt Cdr Esmonde and Lt Cdr Coode were awarded the DSO, while the DSC went to Lt Carver, Lt Gick and Lt Godfrey-Faussett. The DSM was awarded to Leading Airman Sayer.
13. Willetts, IWM Sound Archive.
14. Churchill, *The Second World War, Vol III*.
15. McMullen, IWM Sound Archive.
16. Churchill, *The Second World War, Vol III*. Clearly the mercurial British war leader did not carry a grudge against Leach, or possibly, in writing his account of the war, did not wish to speak ill of the dead.
17. Brooke, *Alarm Starboard!*
18. Churchill, *The Second World War, Vol III*.
19. Brooke, *Alarm Starboard!*
20. Morton, *Atlantic Meeting*.
21. Ibid.
22. In July 1941, the Americans agreed to take over garrison duties in Iceland. They also committed their warships to escorting convoys from American to Icelandic waters.
23. Morton, *Atlantic Meeting*.
24. Ibid.
25. Willetts, IWM Sound Archive.
26. McMullen, IWM Sound Archive.
27. Willetts, IWM.
28. Morton, *Atlantic Meeting*.
29. The Nazi leader pre-empted the inevitable by declaring war on the USA on 11 December 1941, four days after the Japanese attack on Pearl Harbor, which fully brought the Americans into the war. The German declaration was inevitable, bearing in mind the huge economic and military support the USA was by then giving Britain. In the Atlantic, the practice of US Navy warships escorting convoys had already seen American blood spilled, when *U-562* torpedoed the destroyer USS *Reuben James*. She was the first American naval vessel sunk due to hostile action in the Second World War, and 115 members of her ship's company lost their lives, causing deep anger in the States.
30. The name 'Atlantic Charter' was the creation of a British national newspaper looking for an accessible way of describing a document that expressed the US-UK common aims. The actual title of the document was 'Joint Declaration by the President and the Prime Minister'. Its principles have also been used as a basis for

the United Nations aspirations, as well as the guiding light for various free trade and other agreements.

31. According to Geoffrey Brooke in *Alarm Starboard* Terry would survive another ship sunk under him, *Prince of Wales*, but not the war.
32. Morton, *Atlantic Meeting.*
33. Churchill, *The Second World War, Vol III.*

Chapter 24: Bitter Harvest

1. Related by HMS *Dorsetshire* Royal Marine Geoff Kitchen in his letter to the *Daily Telegraph*, 23 June 2009.
2. Exchange etc from account by Lord Moran, *Churchill at War 1940–45.*
3. Churchill, *The Second World War Vol III.*
4. Henry Leach, *Endure No Makeshifts.* Leach saw action in the battleship *Duke of York* during the Battle of North Cape on Boxing Day 1943 and would be First Sea Lord during the Falklands War of 1982, playing a pivotal role in persuading the British government to send a naval task force to the South Atlantic.
5. This was the brand new fleet carrier HMS *Indomitable.*
6. Recounted during an interview with the author, 1991.
7. TJ Cain, HMS *Electra.*
8. Ibid.
9. Ibid.
10. Mark E Horan and FAA SIG, see Sources.
11. Account on HMS *Cossack* Association web site.
12. Kemp, *British Warship Losses.*
13. Account on HMS *Cossack* Association web site.
14. Kemp, *British Warship Losses* and www.naval-history.net
15. Kemp, *British Warship Losses.*
16. Kemp, *British Warship Losses* and www.naval-history.net
17. Admiral Somerville became Commander-in-Chief of the Eastern Fleet in 1942, during the most difficult period of facing down rampant Japanese naval aggression. In 1944/5 he led the Admiralty's delegation to Washington D.C. but enjoyed only a few years retirement in Somerset, dying in March 1949 at the age of sixty-six.
18. Cannon and Gollop, *A County Class.*
19. Captain Martin relinquished command of *Dorsetshire* in early August 1941, so was not with the cruiser when she was lost. He finished his career as Vice-Admiral Sir Benjamin Martin. Not bad for a lower-decker. Captain Augustus Agar VC succeeded Martin in command of *Dorsetshire*. Agar had been awarded the Victoria Cross for showing extraordinary bravery in the face of the enemy when he attacked a Bolshevik cruiser at Kronstadt in June 1919.
20. Bill Braddon's account of remembrance ceremony with the survivors of *Bismarck*, RNM.

Appendix 1

Busting the Myths?

The German Navy never recovered from *Bismarck*'s loss and thereafter resorted to U-boats as its primary weapon in the war on commerce, its capital ships declining to venture very far on the open ocean. That much is uncontested, but there are other perceptions of what happened during the *Bismarck* episode that have been challenged since the day of the battle itself.

> "Who sank the *Bismarck*?"
> and there was a pause,
> "we did," a sailor said who loved applause.
> Another thought that he had laid her low,
> And all said that they had
> Struck the final blow.*

So ran some doggerel penned by a sailor in HMS *King George V* to celebrate his ship's key role in sinking the *Bismarck*, even then reflecting controversy that endures to this day over who, or what, actually sank the German battleship. What has received no real analysis – or even coverage – in accounts of the action is whether or not *Bismarck* was trying to capitulate amid the hell-fire.

Was it Possible for *Bismark* to Surrender?
The reality of war is that in the heat of battle it is notoriously difficult for soldiers, sailors or airmen to surrender without being killed in the process. All manner of calculations enter into the equation. It is not as simple as waving a white flag. There is the confusion and chaos of battle, the sheer brutality and pace of events. Then there is fear that the enemy may be using 'surrender' as a ruse to achieve advantage. Above all, the commander must safeguard his own people in the face of threats from enemy forces who may not have capitulated. Taking care of a surrendered enemy is no easy matter on a hot battlefield,

* HMS *King George V*, ship's magazine, poem entitled 'Ode to Glory'. *Source: RNM.*

never mind getting the message that they genuinely want to throw in the towel.

A battleship surrendering in the midst of combat was an event unheard of in war at sea since the days of fighting sail, when warships traded blows literally within shouting distance. The distance between British warships and the *Bismarck* was miles and there was no realistic means of clarifying if any attempt to surrender came as a result of a decision by the *Bismarck*'s command team to cease fighting, or was just a result of panic under fire in one part of the ship. *See* Appendix 2. Certainly, *Bismarck*'s two aft turrets were determined to go on fighting in the absence of contact with the command team, which was probably wiped out very early in the final battle. *Bismarck* famously went down with her colours still flying – the time-honoured sign of surrender in war at sea was for them to be struck. Aside from saluting the bravery of his foe, Tovey did later emphasize *Bismarck*'s colours were still flying when she went down. Was this because he wanted to cover himself against accusations that the British had carried on assaulting the German ship even though she was trying to surrender? *See below* – 'The Spin Masters of 1941'.

It would have been folly for the British to hesitate, particularly with mass air attacks thought imminent by up to 200 Luftwaffe bombers, and U-boats likely to make every effort to sink Royal Navy warships. And *Bismarck* could not be left to it, for she might have been salvaged and towed back to France, a very visible example of heroic Nazi endurance on the high seas, having delivered a body blow to the world's most powerful fleet and got away with it. The impact on British morale and Britain's global prestige would have been immense. Fighting a fascist military machine that had mercilessly waged war on millions of innocent people, caring little for the rules of war, the British dared not give any quarter. Britain was fighting for its life and 1,415 sailors in HMS *Hood* were denied any opportunity to surrender, nor would they have taken it. *Bismarck* had to be sunk, but simply would not go down. *Norfolk*'s John Ruffer, who saw *Rodney* rip *Bismarck* apart, wrote of her final moments: 'She was silenced, but still looked an impregnable fortress, despite the hammering she had had. Then started the most fantastic phase of all, which made the most bloodthirsty feel rather sick. We simply could not sink her, and we expected large scale air attack at any moment.' Despite the efforts of two battleships and two cruisers, 'pumping all they had into her', she would 'neither sink nor surrender'. In short, as John Ruffer summed it up: 'It was quite appalling.' Appalling, yes, but as everyone acknowledged, entirely necessary.

Could They Sink Her by Gunfire?

In the closing stages of the final battle, the *Rodney*'s Captain Dalrymple-Hamilton could see that it was a case of diminishing returns – particularly as *Rodney*'s shells were going straight through the enemy battlewagon.

Dalrymple-Hamilton's own assessment after the action was that, as his ship's shells did not set off an explosion, it increasingly became a wasted effort. If the two British battleships had stood further off, might plunging shellfire have stood a chance of penetrating so deep *Bismarck* could have been blown apart, like *Hood?* That was only a hope, not an outcome to bank on. Not only that, had the British adopted that tactic, they might well have opened themselves up to destruction, particularly when just a few days earlier *Bismarck* had apparently destroyed *Hood* with plunging shellfire. Who would want to stand off against such a formidable ship and allow her to do the same thing to *King George V* or *Rodney?* As it was, after ninety minutes of pounding *Bismarck*, Admiral Tovey saw the German battleship still stubbornly afloat even if she could no longer be described as a fighting ship. No matter how much they poured into her, *Bismarck* would not explode. Tovey memorably sent the signal, 'Cannot get her to sink with guns', but, ironically, it actually went out AFTER *Bismarck* had sunk. Possibly, Tovey was not sure at the time. The well known wreck hunter and undersea explorer David Mearns concluded after his detailed inspection – via underwater photography – of the *Bismarck*, in 2001, that the guns of *Rodney* and other British warships had comprehensively destroyed her. Together with the torpedoes, the British guns punched enough holes in the German battleship to take her down regardless of efforts by her own sailors, whom it was claimed had *really* sunk *Bismarck* by setting off scuttling charges.

The Myth of the Invincible *Bismarck*

David Mearns observed in his book *Hood and Bismarck*, co-written with Rob White, that 'events of 27 May 1941 proved that *Bismarck* was no more invincible than *Titanic.'*

The late Anthony Preston delivered a crushing verdict on *Bismarck* by including her in his 2002 book, '*The World's Worst Warships'*. Preston – a globally respected authority on naval matters – explained that *Bismarck* was ordered very quickly after the Nazis came to power in 1933, her design actually based on the Bayern Class of 1914. In common with other First World War-era designs *Bismarck* possessed a low armoured deck, leaving a lot of vital areas outside the armoured citadel, including all the communications and electrical systems. Preston judged that, during the fight of 27 May 1941, British guns 'shredded everything except the main machinery.' Therefore, *Bismarck* could just about maintain her momentum, but all her vital systems were swiftly destroyed and with them hundreds of lives. Preston claimed that, far from resisting British shells, *Bismarck*'s hull actually suffered 400 holes, although others claim that only four hits actually penetrated the armour belt, something seemingly contradicted by Mearns, who says he discovered 'quite a few outright penetrations in the armour belt on both the starboard and port sides.' Preston and Mearns agree that, prior to the *coup de grâce* with torpedoes, *Bismarck* was already flooded with thousands of tons of seawater, due to holes caused by the shells of *Rodney*, *King George V*, *Norfolk* and *Dorsetshire*. If you believe the Mearns diagnosis, it would appear, contrary to Dalrymple-Hamilton's assessment, that *Rodney*'s shells *did* cause decisive damage to *Bismarck*, enough to sink her, although too slowly for Tovey's liking.

It is ironic that for decades so many people have been in thrall to *Bismarck*, making great efforts to show that she sank herself via scuttling charges rather than British shells and torpedoes doing the job. The reality was that while *Bismarck* was an outwardly modern looking ship, under the skin she was actually of a less advanced design than even *Rodney*. And that is why, when she met capital ships more modern than the poor doomed *Hood*, Germany's fleet flagship was destroyed so utterly and why so many men died. After the loss of steering the night before, during the final battle she soon lost her communications, command and control, with her guns being gradually silenced. The choice was surrender or death.

Decisive Tinfish Hits

One of David Mearns' chief objectives was to discover whether torpedoes sank *Bismarck*. Or did they only speed up the process begun by British shells and scuttling charges? In his book *Hood and Bismarck*, Mearns says up to nine torpedoes hit *Bismarck*. Aside from the Swordfish and *Dorsetshire* hits, Mearns credits *Rodney* with a torpedo hit at around 9.40 'amidships' while *Norfolk* also fired torpedoes at *Bismarck* (10.10 am approx), two possibly hitting.

Using a Remotely-Operated Vehicle (ROV), Mearns was able to photograph the wreck. He found four 'gaping holes' in *Bismarck*, three of them reckoned to be caused by tinfish launched from the cruisers and one previously unknown strike by a Swordfish torpedo. However, the possibility that a second *Rodney* torpedo hit could have caused one of these holes is not completely outlandish, especially when you consider her 24.5-inch torpedoes packed a mighty punch. Witnesses in the British battleship counted two strikes. There is also the case of Vian's destroyers and their attacks on the night of 26 May. They have always been dismissed by the German survivors, despite destroyers themselves feeling they scored hits. What if one, or even two, of the torpedo hits found by Mearns actually belong to *Cossack* or *Zulu*? Why should the world accept the word of German survivors, none of whom were from the top tier of the command team in the ship? The Second World War Arctic Convoy veteran British naval officer, and renowned post-war historian, Captain Donald Macintyre, cautioned against accepting the word of German survivors without a decent dose of scepticism. In looking at the *Bismarck* episode in his book *Fighting Admiral*, the biography of Admiral Somerville (published in 1961), Macintyre considered whether *Ark Royal*'s Swordfish achieved more hits than admitted by the Germans. His analysis is relevant to whether or not Vian's ships experienced success as well as the additional Swordfish hit claimed by Mearns. Macintyre related that German survivors conceded only one hit from *Ark*'s Swordfish: 'Observing that they similarly denied other definitely claimed torpedo hits from destroyers during the night and taking into account the German habit of building a legend to minimize an enemy's triumph, this need not be taken too seriously. On this occasion the legend was assiduously fostered that the *Bismarck* was never sunk by enemy effort but was scuttled.'

To this day, there are those who persist in attempting to reduce the scale of the victory achieved by British sea power, through arguing the toss over whether or not Royal Navy shells and torpedoes did it, or *Bismarck*'s own men.

Ghosts of the Deep

The wreck of *Bismarck* was actually located more than a decade before the Mearns expedition, in 1989, by the same man who four years earlier discovered *Titanic*, oceanographer Robert Ballard. His inspection confirmed the terrible havoc wrought on the battleship's superstructure, but seemed to reinforce the contention that British shells and torpedoes failed to actually sink her. The stout construction of the hull and its internal protection system – lots of small compartments and longitudinal bulkheads running from stem to stern – appeared to have kept her afloat.

However, in *The Discovery of the* Bismarck Ballard observes of damage to the nerve-centre from where *Bismarck* was commanded: 'The conning tower area looks like Swiss cheese …' There was also a gigantic hole on the ship's port side, where a 16-inch shell penetration detonated *Bismarck*'s ready-use ammunition magazine. Ballard thought there would be much more damage below what he termed 'the mud line', hidden from view, especially towards the stern.

However, Ballard agreed with previous analysis – based on the claims of German survivors – that scuttling charges (alleged to have been set off at around 10.20 am) were what began the process of taking *Bismarck* under, rather than the torpedoes of *Dorsetshire*. However, timings noted for the cruiser's torpedo firings by men who served in her would appear to show she fired four torpedoes at *Bismarck*, between 10.14 am and 10.30 am, possibly with telling penetrations *before* the scuttling charges were set off. Ballard stated that he found no signs of the kind of implosions caused by pressure, when a ship sinks with some compartments still full of air. This reinforces the scuttling claim, with Ballard pointing to his survey of the *Titanic* wreck, parts of which were crushed due to not being fully flooded before sinking. However, *Titanic* was not riddled with holes and, as eyewitnesses in British ships attested, the German battleship was 'dunked' under numerous times during her final moments, allowing water to pour in via all those holes above the armour belt. *Bismarck*'s poorly constructed stern actually fell off as she capsized. The *Dorsetshire*'s torpedoes, the alleged scuttling charges, the stern breaking away and the fact that she turned turtle, with her turrets – secured only by gravity – dropping off, surely enabled more water to flood in? Ballard asserts that once the hull was submerged, it righted itself due to 'its low centre of gravity and hydrodynamic shape' but this was also achieved because the ship was by then completely flooded. Ballard reckoned that between ten and twenty minutes after she slipped below the surface, *Bismarck* hit the side of an undersea volcano, causing a massive landslide sweeping the wreck down with it. That is where she lies today, 15,700ft under the surface of the ocean, some 404 miles to the west of Brest.

Ballard decided to keep the exact location of *Bismarck* secret, but did admit her wreck lay less than two miles from where *King George V's* navigator said she went down. Ballard stated in his book: 'I don't want treasure seekers and souvenir hunters turning this war memorial into a scavenger's carnival.'

In fact quite a few of *Bismarck*'s survivors and even *Hood*'s Ted Briggs objected to Ballard seeking out the German battleship's wreck, because they believed the dead should lie in peace. However, Briggs did go back to sea, aboard the ship later used by Mearns to locate both the wrecks of *Hood* and *Bismarck*. In late July 2001, Briggs – last living *Hood* survivor – controlled a ROV as it placed a memorial plaque on the wreck of his old ship.**

In the summer of 2001, another expedition, led by Australian explorer Michael McDowell, also visited *Bismarck*, using the Russian oceanographic ship *Akademik Keldysh*, from which small submersibles carrying three people at a time were sent down to inspect the wreck. *Bismarck* survivors were aboard the mother ship and a memorial service was held over the site. Almost immediately after the Mearns expedition to the wrecks of *Hood* and *Bismarck*, Hollywood movie director and underwater explorer James Cameron embarked on his own investigation. Unlike the expeditions of Mearns and Ballard, the one led by Cameron intended to use extremely manoeuvrable ROVs to search inside *Bismarck* in a bid to settle once and for all what actually sank her. Cameron's findings appeared to debunk those of Mearns. He claimed that some of the large gashes discovered in *Bismarck*'s hull were not torpedo holes enlarged by friction during the long slide down the volcano side, but the result of 'hydraulic outburst' when the ship hit bottom. Furthermore, he claimed hits on *Bismarck*'s outer hull, below the waterline, were absorbed by a layer of protection, so therefore did not actually penetrate the inner hull.

** Briggs died in October 2008 having served as the first President of the HMS *Hood* Association on its formation in the mid-1970s. Bob Tilburn died in February 1995. He had succeeded Ted Briggs in the post of President of the HMS *Hood* Association. Both men were predeceased by William Dundas who died in late 1965 after suffering severe injuries in a car crash.

Mearns is unconvinced by Cameron's findings, telling the author of this book in October 2009: 'I haven't changed my opinion that the British gunnery, including torpedoes, dealt the telling blows that made the ship sink. If you look at the timing between when the scuttling charges went off and when the ship actually sank it is clear that the scuttling action could have only advanced the sinking by a few minutes at most. It is like a boxer who is already falling to the canvas but is hit once more as he is going down.'

McDowell and the *Akademik Keldysh* returned to the site of *Bismarck* in the summer of 2005, conducting a number of dives. Among those descending in a submersible to gaze at *Bismarck* was ocean adventurer Robert M Williams, who had also visited *Titanic* on the seabed. What he saw haunts him to this day and surely emphasizes that, in the end, it is the *human* cost that matters, not the technicalities of a vessel's loss. As the MIR submersible Williams was aboard approached the battleship's hull, lights picked up hundreds of boots scattered across the seabed. Williams wrote of his deep-sea visit to *Bismarck* that his first thought was they might have been kicked off by 'frantic swimmers' but then he realized, 'like *Titanic*, the symmetry of pairs brings the reality that most of these were worn by their owners to their final resting place.' He added: 'Neatly arranged in their final pose as they each came to rest on the bottom, the memory of these boots and uniforms is one that will remain with me until the day I die.'

Such a sight dispels the myth that *Bismarck*'s end was anything but tragic, or that the sacrifice of human lives on such a scale, and in such circumstances, can ever be glorious. Bert Gollop, the *Dorsetshire* sailor who helped save some of *Bismarck*'s men in the aftermath of battle, had this to say about the debate on what exactly sank the German vessel: 'At one of our reunions some Germans told us they had opened the sea cocks, while others said it was impossible to do so. Either way it made no difference to the end.' Bert was right, in that *Bismarck* was destroyed as a fighting unit, ninety-five per cent of her ship's company either killed in the slaughterhouse that she became during combat, or drowned later.

North Dalrymple-Hamilton, who had a private conversation with one of the *Bismarck*'s surviving officers after the Second World War, reflected: 'We always said she was sunk. The Germans, I think, sometimes for the honour of Germany, said they scuttled her...When we [*King George V* and *Rodney*] left, I mean she was an absolute hulk, so I would say almost certainly she was sunk. I think the scuttle story was just something that the Germans thought sounded better.'

Scuttled or sunk by Royal Navy guns and torpedoes, the fact is that, with *Bismarck* gone, the surface raider threat to Britain's lifeline was removed. During the course of a few days in May 1941 thousands of British and German servicemen died, with Britain's reputation as Ruler of the Seven Seas challenged, her reputation damaged, but her oceanic grip not yet loosened.

262 Killing the Bismarck

The German fleet would never again seriously challenge the Royal Navy's dominance, at least on the surface of the sea, though fear of what *Tirpitz* might do if she ever broke out into the Atlantic demanded a close watch. It required at least two British battleships and a carrier to be on constant stand-by in the Home Fleet and therefore unavailable for operations elsewhere.

Government Neglect of the RN Killed *Hood*

The sense of shock in Britain at the loss of *Hood* was profound, the mood black. For three days the general population knew little of the determined efforts to avenge her. Between the wars, HMS *Hood* had arguably been the most famous Royal Navy capital ship, renowned for her graceful combination of size, speed and armament. She had spent much of her career showing the flag around the globe, so her destruction also had an impact overseas. *Hood* was THE symbol of Royal Navy suzerainty over the oceans. Her sinking signalled that the British no longer possessed that uncontested supremacy. In the wake of her loss, Britain was diminished in the eyes of the world. Even as the pursuit of *Bismarck* continued, no less a person than Admiral of the Fleet Lord Chatfield sought to provide a reality check and inject some brutal realism into the after-shock. When it came to warship construction, Chatfield – a former Comptroller of the Navy and retired First Sea Lord – of course knew what he was talking about. He also knew the flaws of battlecruisers well, having seen many friends die when *Indefatigable* and *Queen Mary* blew up at Jutland, during which battle his own ship, the battlecruiser *Lion*, also suffered a hit that almost destroyed her. A quarter of a century later, Chatfield was clearly concerned people would think there was something inherently wrong with the design of British warships. In a letter to *The Times* published on 26 May 1941 – two days after *Hood*'s loss and the day before *Bismarck*'s destruction – Chatfield disputed the newspaper's recent assertion in a leader that *Hood* was the largest *and* most powerful warship afloat.

He acknowledged she was the largest, but stressed *Hood* 'was constructed 22 years before the *Bismarck*. In those twenty-two years engineering science, and the power-weight ratio, have changed beyond recognition.' Secondly, Chatfield pointed out, it could not be said *Hood* was destroyed by a lucky hit. He explained there were a number of other magazines in a capital ship in addition to the four large ones deep in the vessel below the main turrets. This assertion was a precursor to later analysis that her demise had been triggered by a hit on one of her ready-use lockers or secondary armament magazines, creating a chain reaction reaching into the bowels of the ship, literally tearing *Hood* apart. It would also mesh with another theory, namely that *Hood*'s destruction was caused by an explosion of gas after a 15-inch shell, or shells, penetrated the hull under the water, beneath the armoured belt, sparking off a fire in cordite stored in the aft 4-inch and 15-inch magazines. Chatfield's *Times* letter stated: 'If, therefore, a heavy shell penetrates the armour at the angle of descent given by long ranges, the chance of one of the magazines being ignited is quite considerable.' Next, Chatfield pointed out that, after the First World War, and therefore after *Hood*'s construction, it was decided that a fast capital ship could not really afford to sacrifice armour protection to attain high speeds. Therefore, 'speed was sacrificed to ensure protection against sudden annihilation by shell, torpedo or bomb.'

In his final point Chatfield explained that further advances, even since the construction of *Nelson* and *Rodney*, allowed greater speed to be squeezed out of heavily armed and armoured battleships. Chatfield laid the blame for *Hood*'s loss on those who had conspired to rob the Royal Navy of proper resources during the inter-war years. If the Navy had been properly funded, *Hood* could have been modernized, with greater protection added during a major refit, or a modern, fast battleship might instead have replaced her. Chatfield concluded that the loss of *Hood* 'was not the fault of the British seamen. It was the direct responsibility of those who opposed the rebuilding of the British Battle Fleet until 1937, two years before the second great war started. It is fair to her gallant crew that this should be written.'

Chatfield's verdict pre-empted the official inquiries into *Hood*'s loss, which came to conclusions not a lot different from his *Times* letter of 26 May 1941.

On investigating *Hood*'s wreck in 2001, David Mearns concluded that a 15-inch shell from *Bismarck* had penetrated the battlecruiser aft, detonating an explosion in ammunition magazines that swiftly spread forward, setting off the forward magazines. There was a massive explosion aft, the centre of the battleship was burned out and another massive explosion forward, with *Hood* torn into pieces as if by a giant hand twisting and tearing apart soft, warm bread. One theory gaining credence thanks to the Mearns expedition is that a German 15-inch shell swam under water and penetrated the hull *below* the armour belt. That is exactly what happened to *Prince of Wales* in the same engagement. Except, as we have seen, the latter was lucky in that her unwelcome visitor did not explode. Had it done so, in close proximity to *Prince of Wales'* own aft ammunition magazines, the Royal Navy might have lost another battleship and a further 1,500 men on that fateful morning.

The Spin Masters of 1941

At the time, *King George V*, *Victorious* and *Ark Royal* got their share of glory, as we have seen, for the roles of the fleet flagship and the valiant Fleet Air Arm aviators made good copy and their tales were easy for the general public to understand. *Rodney*, *Prince of Wales*, the destroyers of the 4th Flotilla and the cruisers in comparison got little individual credit for their exploits. Captain Dalrymple-Hamilton was forced to admonish one senior admiral for suggesting *Rodney* should salute *Victorious* for her part in sinking *Bismarck*. Dalrymple-

Hamilton told him: 'Sir, you are standing on the quarterdeck of the ship that sank the *Bismarck*.' Did the spin masters of the day heighten other aspects of the pursuit and kill because they appeared more gallant, much cleaner than the dirty business of execution? Tovey's attempt to pay a tribute to the gallantry of the enemy was certainly suppressed as an inconvenient salute to the foe at a time of great crisis. In his summary of the action, the Home Fleet commander said: 'The *Bismarck* had put up a most gallant fight against impossible odds, worthy of the old days of the Imperial German Navy, and she went down with her colours still flying.' That passage was not made public in 1941, an example of news management familiar to us today, but perhaps a necessary excision when fighting a war of national survival. When it came to the British playing down their own achievements, it was perhaps *Prince of Wales* that suffered most, as her gunnery officer, Colin McMullen, acknowledged when interviewed many years later. He observed: '*Prince of Wales* played an absolutely vital part in this operation and has never really been given credit for her part in it.' McMullen believed his ship's sailors never made much of a fuss, as they felt it would draw attention to the fact that *Hood*'s shooting was so poor and that she was firing at the wrong ship (i.e. *Prinz Eugen* rather than the more lethal *Bismarck*). 'It would be nice for *Prince of Wales* really to at last be given the full credit for what she did,' said McMullen in his post-war interview for the Imperial War Museum Sound Archive. 'She went out with the bugs not out of turrets, but the men in the turrets achieved three hits, two of which were very serious, and which altered the whole operation from the Germans' point of view. If we hadn't hit her she could have gone on with her raiding operation.' The reason why Lütjens headed for France was the damage inflicted by *Prince of Wales*' 14-inch shell hits. Had *Bismarck* headed home around the northern route after sinking *Hood* she might not have been caught. Similarly, had she not been damaged she could have disappeared into the vastness of the Atlantic, rather than make the obvious move of heading for a Biscay port. Of course in the immediate aftermath Winston Churchill wanted to court-martial the captain of *Prince of Wales* and the admiral in charge of the cruisers, so he would not have approved of them grabbing the glory after he felt they had failed to show sufficient aggression in the wake of *Hood*'s loss. The British Prime Minister was a master of spin. During the First World War, when the rest of the government and naval high command was in a state of paralysis over how to break mixed news about Jutland, it was he who organized a press release highlighting the strategic victory achieved by the Royal Navy, despite heavy losses that compared badly with those of the Germans. And it was, of course, Churchill who highlighted the truly amazing feats of the RAF's 'Few' during the Battle of Britain. The achievements of the 'Many' in the Royal Navy, whose ships had lurked in ports waiting to go out and destroy the Nazi invasion fleet in the summer of 1940, received little, if no, attention. *Rodney* was one of those vessels that watched and waited during the long hot summer of the Battle of Britain. In May 1941 she was the ship that went in to do the point-blank dirty work with *Bismarck*. Churchill would have noted Tovey's notorious signal declaring that he could not sink *Bismarck* with guns alone. He would have been dismayed that his faith in the 16-inch gun power of *Rodney* appeared to be ill-founded, while fears for the 14-inch power of the new battleships were apparently proven. Better not to draw attention to that, then. But let us not imagine British gunnery was a failure. DK Brown pointed out in *Nelson to Vanguard* that between 300 and 400 British shells, out of 2,871 fired at her, actually hit *Bismarck*, which proved no more resistant to damage than Royal Navy ships. Furthermore, Brown described *Bismarck*'s armour arrangement to be 'old fashioned', which did 'as well as could be expected' but that it was 'not magical'. British gunfire may not have sunk *Bismarck* – at least not as quickly as Tovey needed, with fuel running low and enemy air and submarine attacks anticipated – but it *did* destroy the German battleship as a fighting unit. Utterly. Plenty of 14-inch, 16-inch and 8-inch shells did their worst inside *Bismarck*. The German ship, by contrast, scored not a single hit on any of the British battleships or cruisers with either her primary or secondary armament. Likewise, *Bismarck*'s anti-aircraft weapons failed to shoot down a single Swordfish. No amount of spin – British, German or any other – no myth-making, then or now, can cover up those incontestable facts.

The Need to Move AND Fight

Consider the fates of three battleships. At Jutland, in May 1916, the super-dreadnought *Warspite* took more than two dozen heavy shell hits, but even though she suffered a temporary steering failure that saw her going in circles in front of the entire German battle fleet, she soon repaired herself and steamed out of trouble. *Prince of Wales* was sunk in the South China Sea not because she could not weather the Japanese assault *per se*, but because she received shattering blows on her steering and lost mobility. In fact, neither *Bismarck*, *Warspite* nor *Prince of Wales* lost the ability to *fight* – or at least not instantly – and all three were able to soak up heavy punishment. Some of the *Bismarck*'s guns kept firing until close to the end, and *Prince of Wales* fought off many Japanese air attacks, while *Warspite*'s combat capability was never seriously threatened. Only one of them retained the do-or-die capability of being able to move *and* fight. That was *Warspite*. She was incredibly lucky throughout a combat career that spanned two world wars. Two days before *Hood* was blown up, *Warspite* was weathering a determined Luftwaffe air assault off Crete, sustaining a single bomb hit that killed thirty-eight men and wounded thirty-one. She was so badly damaged she had to be sent to Puget Sound in the USA for repairs. *Warspite* also got away with it when a German glider-bomb hit her off Salerno in 1943 but passed right through to explode in the water underneath. *Warspite* was crippled but survived the war to end her days scrapped on a Cornish beach. When the cards fell, both *Bismarck* and *Prince of Wales* were, ultimately, dealt unlucky hands. In losing their steering, they lost mastery over their own fate and, like wounded buffalos crashing onto their knees, were set upon and killed by the predators that pursued them to destruction.

Some Myths Take Longer to Slay Than Others ...
It's worth noting that, had *Warspite* faced torpedo-carrying aircraft at Jutland, like *Bismarck* and *Prince of Wales* did, aircraft delivering exterior (and irreparable) shattering blows to her steering, then she too would have gone down. As it was, *Warspite*'s problems, aside from two dozen heavy shell hits, were self-inflicted and also self-repaired. She was able to limp home from battle, shrugging off torpedo attacks from U-boats. Surviving the attentions of pursuing enemy aircraft would have been another matter and, in both *Bismarck*'s and *Prince of Wales*' case, anti-aircraft defence was woefully inadequate, although, as the loss of the Japanese super battleships *Yamato* and *Musashi* proved at the end of the war in the Pacific, no matter how big, how well protected or how many anti-aircraft guns a battleship had it was doomed in the face of concerted air attack. The myth of battleship invincibility, even in the face of air attack, which was adhered to by admirals of all navies, was busted not during the Second World War, but rather when the British launched naval aircraft from platforms built on top of the turrets of pre-dreadnought battleships prior to the First World War. A rather literal demonstration of the aircraft's ascendancy over the battleship big gun and it *only* took another three decades for *Bismarck*'s loss to demonstrate that even allegedly outmoded Swordfish torpedo-bombers could lay the mightiest battlewagon low.

The Royal Navy's Dark Secret?
In returning to consider the true nature of the final battle in which the Royal Navy killed *Bismarck*, we have to ask if it could be described as a dark secret, which nobody who saw it up close wished to address in detail. There may be some truth in that, but rather than a dark secret, surely it simply wasn't right to exult in the slaughter inflicted on a ship that, by the time *King George V* and *Rodney* had been battering her for half an hour (or less), had no centrally co-ordinated defence? There is the tendency in some quarters to minimize the British part in actually sinking *Bismarck*, indeed there is outright denial in some cases, that anything but scuttling charges could have put the Nazi battlewagon down, while perversely highlighting the sheer horror of the butcher's shop that the German ship became due to the Royal Navy's gunnery. The flipside of the coin is that, for many of the British ships involved, it was a case of glory denied out of respect for the dead. The act of killing *Bismarck* was clearly not

something those who saw what it entailed close-up wanted to boast about too much. Just as it has become the fashion to deny the Royal Navy thirsted for revenge in the wake of *Hood*'s destruction, so it became the custom simply not to talk about the dirty, disgusting – but fully necessary – killing of *Bismarck*. In his recent book, *I Sank the Bismarck*, Swordfish pilot John Moffat makes an observation that does not chime with the reality at the time. 'Many people have said that we attacked *Bismarck* to seek revenge for the loss of *Hood*,' writes Moffat. 'Nothing could have been further from our minds.' Surely, this is a case of modern-day sensibilities enhanced by the mellowing effect of time passing?

As seen in the eyewitness accounts contained in this book, this was certainly not true of his fellow aviators in *Ark Royal*, nor of sailors and marines in other ships. As briefly discussed in this book's Author's Introduction, revenge was, in fact, the pre-eminent motivation. Moffat is right to point out that *Ark*'s aviators risked their lives in attacking *Bismarck* because it was their job to do so, as well as for the security of the nation and the pride of their Service. However, to pretend that vengeance was not a major motivating factor is another example of myth making. Just as a soldier fights primarily for the mate he shares his foxhole with, or for the other members of his platoon, so sailors fight for their shipmates in their own ship and in vessels in which they once served, or in which they have pals. Nelson understood this perfectly – hence his cultivation of a Band of Brothers to take Napoleon on. That great admiral also understood there was no point in waging war unless it was to the bitter end, executed with the utmost aggression. It is, of course, typical that once the killing was done the British sailors would do their best to save the same men they had a few moments before been trying to kill. British servicemen and women are to this day known for their compassion, even towards the most fanatical enemy, as a can be seen from the way in which the UK military treats Taliban wounded alongside its own in Afghanistan. However, that does not mean the British are not also irresolute in bringing those who commit murder – even if state-sanctioned in a time of war – to justice. And that is what the Royal Navy did in killing the *Bismarck*.

To ignore the reality of what happened to *Bismarck* on 27 May 1941 is to do those men who died an injustice, to betray future generations who will not have received a lesson from history on the true horror of war at sea. Nor will they have been taught the virtues of heroism in the face of adversity, especially in the wake of disaster on the scale of *Hood*'s loss.

Silent Saviour
It is not a Royal Navy tradition to brag. Not for nothing is it known as the Silent Service. In the summer of 2009, looking back at the amazing events of May 1941 in which he participated, John Moffat was resigned to the Royal Navy's not necessarily getting the credit it deserved. 'I have always said that side of the

war is under-represented in history, or at least in books on the war,' he told the author of this book. 'The Fleet Air Arm was the overlooked side of the Navy, which itself is known as the Silent Service, so you could say the Fleet Air Arm is the silent bit of the Silent Service. And I don't think the men got the opportunity to talk about it. There were so many other things happening. The *Bismarck* chase was just one more event in a big war. Don't forget, not long before, the [Swordfish aviator] lads of the Mediterranean Fleet had put the Italian fleet out of action at Taranto. We were hoping for a chance to do something equally important.'

The brave young men of the Royal Navy seized that opportunity in May 1941 and, in doing so, achieved a victory at sea when everywhere else the Nazis were triumphant, or at least on land. The myth of German invincibility suffered a blow every bit as telling as that delivered by victory in the air during the Battle of Britain. The world, and America in particular, saw that Hitler could be decisively beaten at sea, too, and therefore the struggle was worth joining. Western democracy was saved.

Appendix 2

The Byers Letters

Battleship *Rodney*'s Tommy Byers was for the rest of his life troubled by what he believed were signs of *Bismarck* attempting to surrender. *See* Chapter 20.

In late 1991, Byers wrote to Baron Burkard von Müllenheim-Rechberg, the most senior survivor from the German battleship, who had recounted his experiences in the book *Battleship Bismarck,* published in 1980. Byers told the Baron about seeing mysterious light signals that could have been *Bismarck* attempting to surrender. Byers also asked about the 'black flag' he spotted at the height of the battle. Müllenheim-Rechberg wrote back: 'I must admit that I never heard about "Bismarck" flashing something about 9.30 hours on 27 May 1941 but I shall enquire with other survivors.' Some days later the Baron conveyed his findings in another letter to Byers, in which he said: 'I have now contacted survivor Josef Statz, the only one, I believe, who in theory might have seen or heard about the *Bismarck* message, which you had mentioned.'

Statz told the Baron that he knew 'nothing of the matter'. Müllenheim-Rechberg added: 'He himself did reach the forward conning tower only at 09.40 hours, at a time when he did not see anything of a large black flag flying from the fore-yard – if only for the reason that large parts of the fore-mast had been shot away.' The Baron apologized for offering only 'meagre' information.

Statz had emerged from an action station in the damage control centre at the foot of the conning tower to find a scene of utter devastation, with much of the superstructure destroyed, and only encountered a few people still alive, with none of the senior command team among them. Like the Baron, who was enclosed in his gunnery control position in the aft portion of the German battleship, Statz was unable to confirm or deny Byers' claim because he was actually not as well positioned as the Irishman to see what was happening. Many of the survivors were from the engine rooms, deep within the *Bismarck*'s hull, or were men who crewed the aft gun turrets – both very well protected zones – and knew next to nothing about what was happening elsewhere in the ship once battle was joined.

With no one alive to give the order to abandon ship, it is possible some of *Bismarck*'s men understandably tried to surrender, especially as their morale had been destroyed by Admiral Lütjens' broadcasts and their general lack of confidence in his leadership, as recounted elsewhere in this book.

For dates of the letters, see Sources. For more discussion related to this topic, see Appendix 1.

The Mystery of *Hood*'s Torpedoes

On the topic of *Hood* launching torpedoes that may have come close to hitting *Prinz Eugen* and *Bismarck* even after the British battlecruiser had been blown apart, in the early 1970s HMS *Suffolk*'s Ludovic Porter wrote to *Prinz Eugen*'s second gunnery officer, Paul Schmalenbach. He also wrote to Stephen Roskill, the Admiralty's official historian, a former serving RN officer and war veteran. Roskill said that while tubes were still fitted in *Hood*, at the ranges and speed of the battle he doubted that any torpedoes had been launched. This was reflected in the official account written up by Roskill, in which a track chart of the Denmark Strait action did not show torpedoes launched by *Hood*. However, Schmalenbach wrote in a letter to Porter: 'This Roskill chart doesn't respect the alterations of our course caused by the message of our hydrophones of torpedoes. We reported these to *Bismarck*, who followed our change [of course] to starboard.' *Suffolk*'s former executive officer was also in correspondence with Ludovic Kennedy whose account of the *Bismarck* action, *Pursuit* was published in 1974, the same year in which Porter conducted his correspondence. Kennedy and Porter did not discuss the torpedoes issue, but in *Pursuit*, the former made it clear he doubted torpedoes had been fired. In *Pursuit*, Kennedy acknowledged that *Hood* had torpedo tubes, but believed the alleged sighting of torpedoes by *Prinz Eugen's* commanding officer, and hydrophone operators believing they heard tinfish in the water, were down to overactive imaginations. Kennedy claimed that even if *Hood* had fired torpedoes 'before blowing up, they couldn't have run the distance in time.'

In a letter to Porter dated 28 April 1975, JD Brown, of the Naval Historical Branch in the UK Ministry of Defence, pointed out that Paul Jasper, *Prinz Eugen*'s gunnery officer, had stated in a recent article that the cruiser 'turned under full helm on three occasions during the action firing while turning, although twice losing the line. At the 28th salvo (approximately 0606, basing the timing on a rate of fire of four salvoes per minute) the ship turned so far away that the forward turrets would not bear, and fire was maintained by the after turrets only until the ceasefire.' The Germans did not feel the initial battle sketch produced by Schmalenbach was accurate and it was later recomposed using data from *Prinz Eugen*'s 'computers'. Brown also said in his letter that according to *Prinz Eugen*'s captain, 'avoiding action was taken against torpedoes at 0603, 0606-7 and 0614; he "saw" the second two.' Brown went on: 'The first turn and resumption of the original course would presumably be Jasper's first two "full helm" turns and the 0606-7 turn would be that which caused him to lose the target from the forward director. The German Naval Staff Chart agrees in principle with the ship's observations.'

In a letter dated 19 May 1975 Captain Porter thanked Mr Brown for his letter, adding, 'I think one must conclude that *Prinz Eugen* did turn away three times…and that *Bismarck* conformed, for several photographs show her in the same posture firing only from the after turrets, though of course there is no first-hand documentary evidence of this. Here it is perhaps interesting to note that 30 knot, 16,000 yard torpedoes, if fired by *Hood* just before she was sunk, could have come within about a mile of the enemy line of advance.'

There was a slim chance during the engagement that *Prinz Eugen* could have used her own torpedoes against *Prince of Wales*, but, according to Graham Rhys-Jones in *The Loss of the Bismarck* (published 1999) the German cruiser's torpedo officer did not want to chance 'a shot at extreme range'. Jones, a former naval officer who commanded a frigate during the Cold War, speculates that *Prinz Eugen*'s hydrophone operators may have been guilty of a false alarm over *Hood*'s torpedoes. He writes in his book: 'There is no evidence that the *Hood* fired torpedoes although the possibility cannot, perhaps, be totally discounted.' Conversely, with *Hood* the only British warship in the engagement with torpedoes, it is equally possible that what *Prinz Eugen*'s hydrophone operators heard, and Brinkmann claimed he saw, were indeed the destroyed battlecruiser's forlorn tinfish. In writing this book I decided that, on balance, *Hood* did fire her torpedoes. *See* Chapter 9.

Exchange of letters to be found in the collection of Captain Ludovic Porter, Department of Documents, Imperial War Museum.

Appendix 4

The One That Got Away

rinz Eugen had of course parted company with *Bismarck* on the evening of 24 May, the German heavy cruiser heading south towards the Azores, making a rendezvous with one of the German tankers sent out into the Atlantic to work with her and *Bismarck*. Refuelling early on the morning of 26 May, the following day *Prinz Eugen* made a rendezvous with two other (ostensibly) merchant vessels, which were actually reconnaissance ships tasked with scouting out likely targets. However, *Prinz Eugen* was soon experiencing engine trouble, which put the rest of her mission in doubt. On 27 May there was hope in the cruiser's crew that she would possibly head north to *Bismarck*'s aid, but this was forbidden by German naval headquarters and *Prinz Eugen* was too far away to be of any use, while British strength was thought to be too great. The doleful signals traffic between *Bismarck* and naval headquarters was monitored in *Prinz Eugen*.

A black cross was marked on a chart to indicate where *Bismarck* succumbed. The estimated time of sinking – 10.40 am – was written next to the cross. News of the battleship's loss at the hands of the British fleet made the *Prinz Eugen*'s crew angry, because they had been unable to rescue their 'big brother', and they were also deeply depressed at the scale of lives lost. On 28 May, the *Prinz Eugen* made a rendezvous with the tanker *Esso Hamburg* to take on fuel oil but this was cut short at noon when smoke from an unidentified vessel was spotted on the horizon. *See* Notes, Chapter 19.

With the engine trouble threatening to worsen, a decision was taken that *Prinz Eugen* should head for a French Atlantic port, the cruiser reaching Brest on June 1. In that way she evaded destruction at the hands of the Royal Navy.

After enduring numerous attempts by the RAF bombers to destroy her, suffering major internal damage during a July 1941 raid, in February 1942 *Prinz Eugen*, together with *Scharnhorst* and *Gneisenau*, broke out from Brest and made the legendary 'Channel Dash', surprising the British who were deeply humiliated to see the three major enemy warships make it back to Germany. However, on a subsequent foray into waters off Norway, later the same month, to try and deter a feared British invasion, *Prinz Eugen* was hit by a torpedo fired by the British submarine *Trident*. In an echo of *Bismarck*'s structural weakness, a large section of her stern broke away and a number of sailors and embarked soldiers were killed. Returning to service in October 1942, misfortune dogged the heavy cruiser again. After serving mainly as a training ship, during October 1944 operations in the Baltic, conducting naval gunfire support missions in support of land forces fighting the Russians, she was in collision with the light cruiser *Leipzig*.

Escaping serious damage – although the *Leipzig* was almost cut in half – the so-called 'lucky *Prinz*' and light cruiser *Nürnburg* were the only two significant German surface warships still afloat at the end of the war. *Prinz Eugen* was surrendered to the Western Allies in May 1945. There was some argument over who she should be awarded to as a prize of war – the British wanted her because of the cruiser's part in sinking *Hood*, the Russians felt they were owed compensation for their great suffering, while the American participant in the discussion suggested *Prinz Eugen* would never have been captured were it not for the huge support given to the war effort by the USA. It was agreed that lots should be drawn from a cap and the American pulled out the winner. Today *Prinz Eugen*'s capsized wreck lies in waters off Bikini Atoll, as in 1946 she was taken to the Pacific to be expended during nuclear bomb tests at the dawn of a new confrontation, the Cold War.

Appendix 5

The *Norfolk* Photo

The full frame *Norfolk* photo, which may, or may not, show the forecastle of the cruiser in the foreground and *Hood* blowing up beyond. *Royal Naval Museum*

Is this the moment battlecruiser *Hood* exploded? Do we see her bows rearing up, the A turret firing one last defiant salvo, superstructure enveloped in smoke from a catastrophic explosion that is ripping the battlecruiser apart? Could it be the exact moment a deep penetrating shell, or shells, fired by *Bismarck* during the Battle of the Denmark Strait on 24 May 1941, claimed the lives of 1,415 men? If this image truly does reveal the catastrophe that shocked the world, filling the men of the Royal Navy with a desire to deliver vengeance upon *Bismarck*, then it is one of the most incredible images of war to be discovered in recent times. Previously the only images of the event show a smoke column on the far horizon, the accepted last photograph of the ship herself being taken on the evening of 23 May (*See Plates*). The image published here (*and also in the Plates*) is now in the collection of the Royal Naval Museum,

Portsmouth. It came to light in 2009, when Captain Peter Hore RN was researching the obituary of Second World War veteran naval officer Commander Norman Tod. It is published here for the first time, with kind permission of the RNM and Tod's family. Tod had served as Navigator in the light cruiser *Ajax* at the Battle of the River Plate, in December 1939, and was then appointed in the same post to the heavy cruiser *Norfolk*. Captain Hore explained the context of his find: 'As he grew older Tod got rid of most of his possessions, but he kept a handful of photographs torn from an album, one of which he labelled as *Graf Spee Dec '39*. Bearing in mind *Norfolk*'s part in the pursuit and destruction of *Bismarck*, He also kept copies of two well known photos, one of *Graf Spee* on fire after being scuttled on the River Plate and the other of *Bismarck* on fire and being pounded by British guns during the final battle of 27 May 1941.'

Clearly, for Tod, who had discarded so much of the material he collected during his life, keeping these three images meant they must have retained considerable sentimental value. It immediately struck Captain Hore that the *Graf Spee Dec '39* image could not be of the German pocket battleship exploding, for she had scuttled herself on the River Plate. It bore no resemblance to any images of that event and also appeared to have been taken from a type of ship that was not present at the preceding Battle of the River Plate. *Norfolk*, a County Class cruiser, was, however, present throughout the *Bismarck* Action. 'The ship in the foreground can be identified from its features as a County Class cruiser,' explained Captain Hore, who consulted naval architects' drawings at the National Maritime Museum, identifying distinctive features in the foreground of the image as belonging to *Norfolk*. The ship in the distance is clearly a capital ship enveloped in dark clouds of smoke. 'The cruiser's turrets are trained to starboard, and the position from where the photograph was shot can be located quite closely,' said Captain Hore. 'This is a picture taken from the cruiser's B Deck, by somebody standing under the port bridge wing where he could not be seen from the bridge.'

In the the mysterious *Norfolk* photo, there is an uncanny resemblance to eyewitness accounts of HMS *Hood* exploding. This possibility is seemingly reinforced by what looks like a venting of flame high above the ship, as well as what could be the battlecruiser's bows rearing up as she explodes. The cloud of gun smoke blown away to the right could be from *Hood*'s guns as they famously fire their last defiant salvo. The capital ship seems to moving at speed, her quarterdeck awash with sea, another match for *Hood*, while it seems the battlecruiser's distinctive aft gunnery control position is just visible. A look at the plot of the battle in the Denmark Strait seems to offer some supporting evidence for the amazing possibility of this being a lost image of *Hood* blowing up. The relative

Smoke from earlier salvo of A & B guns

Jet of fire

Mainmast

After gunnery director

Break in superstructure

Smoke from salvo of A & B guns

Stem

X turret

Break in superstructure

A blow-up of the portion of the image that possibly shows *Hood* exploding, with labels to indicate what we may be seeing. *Royal Naval Museum*

position of *Norfolk* and *Hood* seems about right. There is, however, one big problem with that theory – distance.

Captain Hore observed: 'Tod's previous ship, *Ajax*, got no closer than four miles from *Graf Spee* at the Battle of the River Plate, and this photograph is taken from much nearer. Therefore, aside from the foreground detail being a different kind of ship to *Ajax*, the distance again rules *Graf Spee* out. However, *Norfolk* was even further away from *Hood*, unless of course it was a trick of the camera lens or the cruiser was closer than we had previously thought.'

Captain Hore visited the Royal Naval Museum at Portsmouth to draw on the specialist skills of its Curator of Photographs, Stephen Courtney, and also called in renowned veteran maritime photographer Jonathan Eastland, to see what light he could shed on the intriguing image. During a session in the photographic archives of the museum, the three men examined the original print in some detail. Eastland's verdict was that the photograph 'perfectly fits the remit for a frame exposed and poorly focused in a hurry.' The experienced veteran maritime lensman added: 'The foreground details are sharper than the object on the horizon, the capital ship. When magnified by fifty per cent, small details are already indistinct and confused with the grain of the film. Larger objects retain

A photograph taken from *Prinz Eugen*, showing the smoke column that marks *Hood* exploding (centre, right). *US Naval Historical Center*

their form but one speculates as to what they might really be.'

Eastland agreed that it was 'unlikely' that Tod himself took the photograph. A keen student of naval history, and familiar with the episodes in the *Bismarck* Action, Eastland proposed a theory to explain how *Norfolk* might have gained a position closer than currently accepted. 'The distance of the ship shown in the photograph taken from *Norfolk* is approximately three quarters of a mile, and may be slightly less,' said Eastland. 'A chart of the Battle of the Denmark Strait, based on data from *Prince of Wales* shows the track of ships involved, putting HMS *Norfolk* in a northerly position some miles distant from *Hood* at 05.35 hrs. *Hood* blew up and sank at 06.01hrs. The chart shows an arrow over *Norfolk*, indicating her course direction at the time, and it seems from this *Norfolk* was aiming to join the main line, which included HMS *Prince of Wales*, a distance at 05.35 of about 10 miles. *Norfolk* could have been within a short distance of *Hood* some 25 minutes later.' Eastland went on: 'The problem remains that the chart we considered during our discussions at the naval museum does not bear any annotation of the exact compass course *Norfolk* was headed on at 05.35.'

Eastland's analysis of the image itself also threw both hope and doubt into the mix of whether or not this truly was a historic photograph.

'As regards the ship enveloped in clouds of dark grey smoke, magnified examination reveals an indistinct outline of a large ship travelling at speed,' commented Eastland. 'Her quarterdeck is partly obscured by a high wake. There is no evidence of gun emplacements or barrels on the after deck, the tops of which would have been seen above the waves had they been there. The housing for the end of the hangar and profile of the detector director above it, sort of fits *Hood*'s silhouette, but it is not conclusive in my view. Clouds of dark smoke are being emitted from one or more barrels of a gun firing from the foredeck. A secondary cloud from a previous barrel emission is already passing higher over the midships section of the ship. Behind this a darker and much larger cloud of smoke has erupted. There is no evidence in these clouds of flame. Behind this central midships cloud, a jet of smoke is erupting and there is already a large volume of cloud above it, which indicates this has been going on for some minutes. To the left of the jet, another vertical, but shorter, stream of smoke is visible. The darker central cloud is not typical of gun barrel firing emissions. To me it looks more like the kind of cloud effect manifest following some kind of internal and large explosion, but again, no flame is visible in the photograph. None of the photographs taken from the German heavy cruiser *Prinz Eugen*, which show *Prince of Wales* and smoke from the sunken *Hood*, include evidence of a third ship in the immediate vicinity. Considering the target distance estimated from these German photographs, some 7-9 nautical miles, it seems likely that in the few minutes *Norfolk* might have been in the close proximity to *Hood*, the cruiser would also have appeared in these images. However, in the one in which *Prince of Wales* is visible, the British battleship appears to be hull down and *Norfolk*, if she was close by to *Hood*'s position, may, by the time the photograph was taken, be further away and therefore not visible.' Eastland agreed that the photograph must have had real value to Tod, but was it taken on 24 May 1941, or later in the chase, therefore showing another aspect of the *Bismarck* Action from *Norfolk*'s point of view? In the end, Eastland decided: 'There are too many unanswered questions about the origins of this photograph to be able to draw any positive conclusions. All we can really say at this point in time is that the forecastle of *Norfolk* is plainly visible [in the foreground of the image] and there is a ship about three quarters of a mile away, travelling at speed while firing guns. The rest of it can only be speculated upon. Given that many British sailors were at sea in May 1941, during the sinking of *Hood* and the subsequent pursuit and destruction of *Bismarck*, it seems unlikely that all of the photographic evidence has come to light. There must be many hundreds of negatives and or prints still buried in attics and cupboards. This print is a good start, but I would have liked to see the original negative, as there would be far more information on it than on the print. Finding it is a bit of a forlorn hope, but you never know.'

Having looked at the image in company with Captain Hore and Jonathan Eastland, Stephen Courtney decided to compare it with others to see if there were any similarities that might help solve the mystery. Having done so, he decided: 'I would rule out this being a picture of the *Hood* blowing up. I am also of the opinion that it was not taken during the action against *Bismarck* and, indeed, that it is not of the *Hood* at all. I would have to agree that the ship from which it was taken is a County Class cruiser and that we are looking at a capital ship about a mile away. Both ships are engaging a target off to starboard. After comparing the image with others of vessels firing, it seems to be that the ship has fired a salvo from both bow and stern turrets – either four or all eight. The two smoke clouds are distinctive and back this up. Similarly, a comparison of the other smoke plume and similar photographs suggests that this is coming from a funnel, possibly letting off steam rather than from a fire or explosion. The colour of the smoke supports this, being predominately grey, smoke from explosions and fires seeming to be darker at least in part and often black in colour. The illusion of the bow lifting up is from a combination of smoke and spray. Close inspection shows that this is not likely to be a tangible object at all. The picture was taken during a stressful moment and exhibits a fair amount of camera shake. The resolution of the image is not good and there is no clear point of focus, suggesting a simple lens was used. The level of detail apparent in the ship is poor and indistinct but the general shape can be determined. The ship itself seems too short and compact for *Hood*. It closely resembles a Queen Elizabeth or Resolution class battleship, with the distinctive mainmast visible in the right place and the "funnel" smoke emerging correctly from a single or trunked funnel. We know that *Norfolk* should have been nowhere near the *Hood* during the action and *Suffolk* even further away. The gunnery control teams in *Bismarck* were keeping an eye on them to make sure that they did not close for a torpedo attack and, in any case, she does not appear in German photographs of the action, which she would if she had been in the position shown in the mystery image. I also wonder, if this was the Battle of the Denmark Strait, with *Norfolk* in close company, why the cruiser would be placed on the engaged side of the *Hood* and *Prince of Wales*, masking the latter's fire? Not a healthy place for a large cruiser with very little armour. So, if not *Norfolk* and *Hood*, what do we see? One possibility, and I emphasise that it is just one possibility, is that the photograph is from the bombardment of Dakar in September 1940. That means it could have been taken from the cruisers *Devonshire* or *Australia*, looking at HMS *Barham* or HMS *Resolution*. The four ships were on the gun line at the same time on three occasions, all firing against shore batteries and French warships in a confined area. Having studied track charts, admittedly I cannot place them in the exact positions shown in the photo, but it is still quite possible as there was a lot of manoeuvring going on. The French gunnery was very accurate. *Barham* was hit four times, *Australia* and *Resolution* at least once each. Is this what we are seeing here? *Barham* fired at the shore batteries whilst turning back to assist and the two cruisers closed to take station on either quarter. Could the image be *Barham* letting off steam whilst going to the assistance of *Resolution* or could it be *Resolution* herself? There are, I am sure, other incidents that will fit the image. Perhaps another copy of the image or another shot of the same incident may turn up in the future, with supporting information to tell us exactly what we are looking at. I may be way off the mark with this of course, but it has been fun doing a bit of detective work and that I think makes a very interesting story in itself.'

With such feedback, combined with the input provided by Jonathan Eastland, Captain Hore decided to visit the National Archives at Kew, to investigate further the chances of *Norfolk* actually being closer to *Prince of Wales* during the Battle of the Denmark Strait than previously admitted.

'I don't think this is Dakar in 1940 and I believe firmly that we have *Norfolk* in the foreground,' Captain Hore stated after the conclusion of his further investigations. 'The sea conditions, the indistinct horizon, the lighting all indicate northern latitudes. On close examination, the supposed rearing up of the broken bows is a photographic illusion. The last refuge of any hope that this is indeed the cataclysmic moment *Hood* blew up could be if *Norfolk* was actually closer than we had previously accepted. This is a false trail. The documents I studied at the National Archives prove she got no closer than 10 miles. Sketches of *Hood* blowing up as seen from *Norfolk* also exist and show the battlecruiser as a small object on the horizon. They are similar to the shots taken by a German photographer in *Prinz Eugen*, which show *Hood* blowing up as a smudge on the horizon.'

Far from being deflated, Captain Hore was even more intrigued by the prospect that while the mystery photograph is possibly not an image of *Hood* blowing up, it perhaps depicts a later moment in the Battle of the Denmark Strait: 'If *Norfolk* was travelling at 30 knots plus, she could have closed the distance between herself and the site where *Hood* blew up in less than twenty minutes. It might have taken have taken less time to take close station on a manoeuvring *Prince of Wales*, and we know that *Prince of Wales* turned towards *Norfolk* at about 06.20. The picture cannot be positively identified, but a strong possibility must be that this is *Prince of Wales*, during the Battle of the Denmark Strait, and that it was taken either by 06.30 by which time, the official history tells us, *Norfolk* was approaching *Prince of Wales*, or later that day, between 18.47 and 18.53, when, we know, *Prince of Wales* and *Norfolk* opened fire on *Bismarck* to cover the withdrawal of *Suffolk*, for sunset was not until 21.34 local time. But, whichever the occasion is, I cannot explain the column of smoke: if it is the earlier time, could this be this the remains of the exploding *Hood*?

The picture cannot be positively identified, but the possibility must be that this is *Prince of Wales*, during the Battle of the Denmark Strait. What then is the tall column of smoke in the further distance? Is this the remains of the exploding *Hood*?'

The author of this book believes it most likely shows the clash between *Bismarck* and *Prince of Wales*, on the evening of 24 May 1941. As detailed in Chapter 11 of this book, *Suffolk* was being chased by *Bismarck*'s shells back towards *Norfolk* and *Prince of Wales*, the latter preparing to sally forth against the German battleship. Their plan of attack pre-empted, *Prince of Wales* and *Norfolk* both fired at *Bismarck* to no avail, as she was at the maximum limits of the former's range and well beyond that of the latter's guns. The long-range, rather fitful nature of the exchange might explain why the sailor or marine responsible for the mystery photograph felt safe enough to venture out on to the upper deck to try his luck. As Stephen Courtney has observed, and as both Captain Hore and Jonathan Eastland agree, the detective work surrounding The *Norfolk* photo, is a fascinating process in itself.

Maps

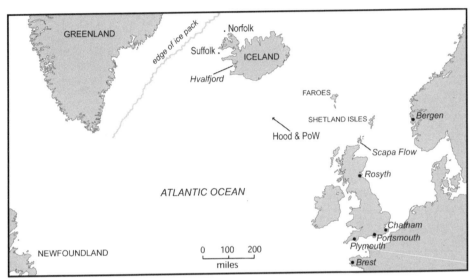

Map 1: The North Atlantic. Disposition of principal British warships at sea on 22 May 1941 that were soon to be directly engaged in pursuit of *Bismarck* and *Prinz Eugen*. *(Map by Dennis Andrews)*

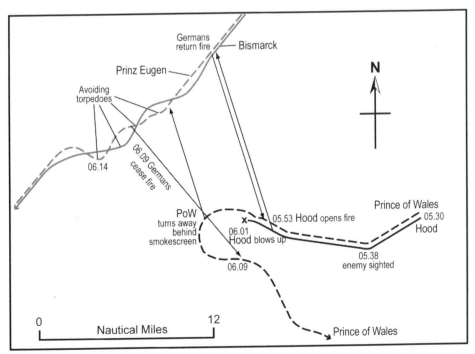

Map 2: Bismarck v *Hood.* The Battle of the Denmark Strait, 24 May 1941. *(Map by Dennis Andrews)*

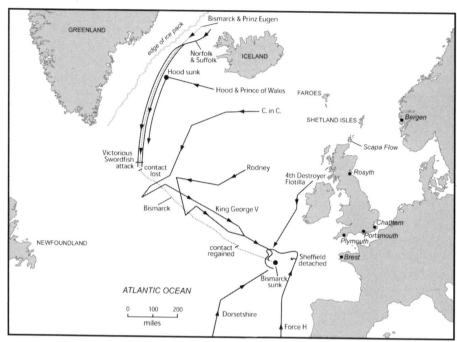

Map 3: Bismarck Action. Overview of the Royal Navy's pursuit of *Bismarck* and *Prinz Eugen* during the period 22 – 27 May 1941. *(Map by Dennis Andrews)*

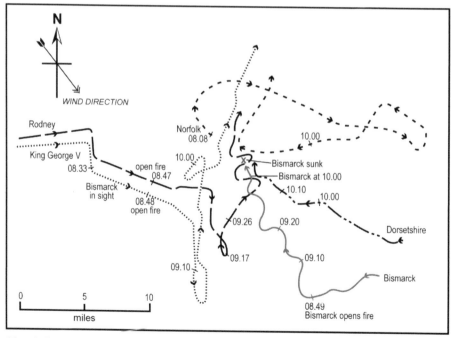

Map 4: Bismarck v Royal Navy. The final battle between the Royal Navy and *Bismarck*, 27 May 1941. *(Map by Dennis Andrews)*

Sources

Imperial War Museum (IWM) Department of Documents
The private papers of
Collett, Commander CT, 95/5/1
Conning, G, P424
Franklin, AE, 01/39/1, an account entitled *The Last of Hitler's Pride – by an eyewitness*
Hibbit, DA, 89/3/1
Lewis, Captain RC, chart showing torpedo action between *Rodney* and the German battleship *Bismarck*, Misc 177 (2683)
Porter, Captain Ludovic, 76/178/1
Rail, KFW, 03/14/1
Smith, Lieutenant Commander BW, 85/44/1
Wood, RJ, 89/3/1
Anonymous poem written by an unidentified member of the ship's company HMS *Rodney* following the pursuit and destruction of the *Bismarck* in May 1941, Misc 3213

Imperial War Museum (IWM) Sound Archive
Crawford, William (Acc No. 10673)
McMullen, Colin (Acc No. 10975/5)
Palmer, Edward (Acc No. 27742)
Thomas, George (Acc No. 15110)
Walters, Leonard (Acc No. 12788)
Walton, Eric (Acc No. 13626)
Willetts, Joseph (Acc No. 008222/04)

Royal Naval Museum (RNM)
Information Sheet No.68, *Loss of* HMS *Hood and Bismarck*
RNM 1985.755/2, Magazine of HMS *King George V*
RNM 1990.274/1, Telegram to Mrs Sarah Henshaw by Commodore of Royal Naval Barracks
RNM 1990.274/2, Buckingham Palace sympathy note to Sarah Henshaw
RNM 1987.330, Captain Dalrymple-Hamilton's congratulations to the Ship's Company of HMS *Rodney*

RNM 1992.86/10, Press cutting of a letter from T Smith, published in *The Sunday Empire News* 1 June 1958, relating the story of school children who lost pen friends in HMS *Hood*

RNM 1992.138/4, Typescript account of reunion of survivors from *Bismarck* and their rescuers [from HMS *Dorsetshire* and HMS *Maori*] in May 1975, written by Bill Braddon

RNM 1981.737, *The Destruction of the Bismarck*, a typescript account of the action, subtitled *An Unofficial Account By an Eye Witness of the Destruction of the Bismaerck* [by a member of HMS *Sheffield*'s Ship's Company]

RNM 1999.8, Typescript account entitled *The Bismarck Episode – An Eye Witness Account*, written by Sam Wood

Fleet Air Arm Museum (FAAM)

1993/266/0001, *The Bismarck Attack (Participation by the Fleet Air Arm)*, compiled by K Sims, Archivist Telegraphist Air Gunners Association (TAGA).

2000/078/0003, *Ark Royal's Operations Against Bismarck 26th and 27th May 1942*, a personal narrative by ES 'Splash' Carver

2000/678/0004, Letter from ES Carver to James Dietz, 1 June 1988

1992/375/009, Letter to his parents, from L Mann aboard HMS *Ark Royal*, 28 May 1941

2000/078/0005, *A Pilot's eye view of the Sinking of Bismarck*, by Alan Swanton

Photocopy of his account of his part in the *Bismarck* Action by James Stewart-Moore, as published in *The Times*, 22 May 1991

Photocopy/clipping of letter to *The Times*, from JDL Repard, on events witnessed from HMS *Sheffield*, 26/27 May 1941. Letter published 27 May 1991

Sink the Bismarck by John Quinn of the WWII Irish Wreckology Group Study and Research. Revised April 1996 and deposited with FAAM

National Archives (NA)

FO 371/23059, *Report to British Embassy, Launch of battleship Bismarck*, Captain Troubridge

ADM 1/11726, Board of Inquiry statements. Testimonies on the loss of the *Hood* from Captain Leach of the *Prince of Wales* and Robert Tilburn, *Hood* survivor.

ADM 53/114133, *Dorsetshire*'s Ship's Log, recording the sinking of the *Bismarck*

ADM 234/509, Flag Officer Force H Report, describing the torpedo attack on *Bismarck* by *Ark Royal*'s Swordfish

AIR 15/204, Commander-in-Chief Home Fleet Despatch, Admiral Tovey's detailed account of the action of 27 May 1941

AIR 15/415, Signal to Admiralty from *Prince of Wales*, outlining the opening action with *Bismarck* and the sinking of *Hood*

ADM 186/806 *Interrogation of* [Bismarck] *Survivors.*

ADM 234-509 HMS Norfolk*'s Gunnery and R.D.F. During Operations Against Bismarck*

Britannia Museum, Britannia Royal Naval College (BRNC)

Sinking the Bismarck, extract from Midshipman's Journal of Mid. GR Shaw, HMS *Rodney*

Interviewed by Author
(between 1991 and 2009)
HMS *Prince of Wales*
Alan McIvor
Peter Dunstan
HMS *Ark Royal*
[Fleet Air Arm]
John Moffat
HMS *Cossack*
Ken Robinson [interviewed on behalf of author by Jonathan Eastland at the
    HMS *Cossack* reunion, 2009]
HMS *Rodney*
Charles Barton
Alfred Brimacombe
Ken George
Len Nicholl
Frank Summers
Peter Wells-Coles
HMS *King George V*
Harold Thompson

Journals & Newspapers
Sunday Pictorial, 25 May 1941
Daily Mirror, 28 May 1941
News Chronicle, 28 May 1941
London Gazette, 10 October 1941, Third Supplement [detailing honours awarded by
    King George VI to participants in the *Bismarck* Action]
The Naval Review, Vol.68, No.4, October 1980
Rodney Buzz, the magazine of the HMS *Rodney* Association, April 1997 edition
The Daily Telegraph, 8 Aug 2002, 26 Feb 2003, 23 December 2008, 23 June 2009

Unpublished Documents
An Eyewitness Account of The Sinking of the The Bismarck, by Lt Donald Campbell,
    HMS *Rodney*, from the archives of the HMS *Rodney* Association [disbanded 2001]
The End of the Bismarck, by Major JEM Ruffer RM, HMS *Norfolk*
A County Class – The epic story of HMS *Dorsetshire*, by John Cannon and Bert Gollop
Transcript of interview with Captain North Dalrymple-Hamilton, HMS *King George
    V*, for the TV documentary series *The Battleships* (a Rob McAuley Production for
    Channel 4, 2001)
Transcript of interviews with Tommy Byers, HMS *Rodney*, regarding his part in the
    Bismarck Action
The Sinking of the Bismarck, article by Tommy Byers
Letter from Tommy Byers to Baron Burkard von Müllenheim-Rechberg, 15 October
    1991.
Letters from Barm Baron von Müllenheim-Rechberg to Tommy Byers, 28 November
    and 6 December 1991.

Letters to the author from *Rodney* veterans James McLean and Jack Austin

The Life of L03, [aka *The Chronology of* HMS *Cossack*] a chronicle of *Cossack's* life, between being ordered in March 1936 and her sinking in October 1941. HMS *Cossack* Association document, 2007

The Sinking of the Bismarck, A Personal Account written by Telegraphist Eric Farmer onboard HMS *Cossack*, via HMS *Cossack* Association/Sallyann Pagett

Some Survivors' Narratives, a document compiled by the HMS *Cossack* Association

Other Sources of information

The Yachtsmen and the Mighty Hood, *Semaphore* (Issue 06, April 2009), Sea Power Centre – Australia

KGV Association, *Memories – Life Aboard King George V*

Between a Rock and a Hard Place, account by Michael G Walling about *Modoc's* encounter with *Bismarck* and *Prince of Wales* and the Swordfish attack on the former, 24 May 1941

Warship Profile 18, KM Bismarck, by Paul Schmalenbach, Profile Publications, 1972

Account of *Zulu's* part in attacks on *Bismarck*, 26 May 1941, by Sam Hammick, BBC People's War. Article ID: A1991469 contributed on: 8 November 2003. See web sites below

With Gallantry and Determination, The Story of the Torpedoing of the Bismarck, by Mark E. Horan, published at http://www.kbismarck.com/article2.html

Account by Derric Breen of his time on his war service, including Atlantic convoys [May 1941] in HMS *Egret*, The Second World War Experience Centre

National Maritime Museum (NMM) Research Guide B9, Royal Navy: HMS *King George V*

History of HMS *Rodney 1939–1948*, Admiralty ship's history. Ref No. S.5775

Internet

www.naval-history.net
Outstanding archive of individual Royal Navy ship histories

www.hmscossack.org
For information and exciting first-hand stories of the men who served in British warships named *Cossack*, one of the more active and energetic ship organisations

www.hmshood.com
Stunning web site, well designed, easy to use, rich in detail, research and transcripts of documents as well as a superb memorial to a legendary warship and the men who died in her

www.fleetairarmoa.org
The main point of contact for retired Fleet Air Arm officers

www.dorsetshire.pwp.blueyonder.co.uk
Tribute to the men who went to war in a famous British cruiser, and a memorial to those who did not survive her loss

www.forcez-survivors.org.uk
Crisply presented web site memorialising the men and the ships of the ill-fated force
that tried to stop the Japanese invading Malaya

www.kbismarck.com
Supremely efficient, intensely detailed site containing every bit of trivia and
memorabilia any *Bismarck* enthusiast could want (including crew roster)

www.taga.org.uk
The story of the Royal Navy's Telegraphist Air Gunners, revealing many fascinating
facts about a special breed

www.bluewater.uk.com
For more on the work of David Mearns, the man who discovered the wreck of *Hood*
and rediscovered that of *Bismarck* during his remarkable 2001 search

www.war-experience.org
War heritage project based at Leeds, in the north of England, which gives veterans a
chance to tell us more about their experiences

www.orkneytroutfishing.co.uk
All you need to know to catch fish at Scapa Flow

www.bbc.co.uk/ww2peopleswar
Vast repository of first-hand accounts of war

http://www.coastguardchannel.com/index.shtml
Unofficial multi-media site on the US Coast Guard, including a download of Michael
G. Walling's account of *Modoc*'s brush with war in May 1941

www.rmwexplorations.com
Personal web site of Robert M. Williams, deep sea explorer, featuring an account of his
dive on the wreck of *Bismarck*

http://kgva.org/
Web site of the HMS *King George V* Association, still going strong when others have
fallen by the wayside

Some relevant museum web sites:
www.royalnavalmuseum.org
www.fleetairarm.com
www.iwm.org.uk
www.nationalarchives.gov.uk

Bibliography

Apps, Michael, *Send her Victorious*, Purnell Book Services, 1971.
Arthur, Max, *The Royal Navy 1939 to the Present Day*, Hodder & Stoughton, 1997.
Baddeley, Allan, *Royal Navy*, Frederick Muller, 1942.
Ballantyne, Iain, *Warspite*, Pen & Sword, 2001.
—— HMS *London*, Pen & Sword, 2003.
—— HMS *Rodney*, Pen & Sword, 2008.
Ballard, Robert D., *The Discovery of the Bismarck*, Madison Press, 1990.
Bassett, Ronald, HMS *Sheffield*, Naval Institute Press (NIP), 1988.
Bekker, Cajus, *Hitler's Naval War*, Macdonald, 1974.
Benstead, CR, HMS *Rodney at Sea*, Methuen, 1932.
Bercuson, David J, and Herwig, Holger H., *Bismarck*, Hutchinson, 2002.
Berthold, Will, *The Sinking of the Bismarck*, Transworld, 1960.
Bradford, Ernle, *The Mighty Hood*, Coronet, 1974.
Brodhurst, Robin, *Churchill's Anchor*, Pen & Sword, 2000.
Brooke, Geoffrey, *Alarm Starboard!*, Pen & Sword, 2004.
Broome, Jack, *Make Another Signal*, Futura 1977.
Brown, DK, *Nelson To Vanguard*, Chatham, 2006.
Brower, Jack, *The Battleship Bismarck*, Conway, 2005.
Burt, RA, *British Battleships 1919 -1939*, Weidenfeld Military, 1993.
Busch, Fritz-Otto, *Prinz Eugen*, Futura, 1975.
Cain, TJ, as told to Sellwood, A.V., HMS *Electra*, Frederick Muller, 1959.
Chesneau, Roger, *Hood*, Cassell, 2002.
—— *Aircraft Carriers of the World, 1914 to the Present*, Brockhampton Press, 1998.
Churchill, Winston, *The Second World War, Vol I–VI*, Cassell, 1948–1954.
—— & Gilbert, Martin, ed., *Companion Volumes to Biography, The Churchill War Papers, Volume Three, The Ever-Widening War 1941*, W.W. Norton, 2001.
Coles, Alan and Briggs, Ted, *Flagship Hood*, Robert Hale, 1996.
Colville, John, *The Fringes of Power*, Phoenix, 2005.
Creasey, John, ed., *Action Stations*, John Long, 1942.
Dannreuther, Raymond, *Somerville's Force H*, Aurum, 2005.
D'Este, Carlo, *Warlord, A Life of Churchill at War 1874–1945*, Allen Lane, 2009.
Donald, William, *Stand by for Action*, Seaforth, 2009.
Edwards, Kenneth, *Men of Action*, Collins, 1943.

Forester, CS, *Sink the Bismarck!*, ibooks, 2003.

Frayn Turner, John, *VCs of the Royal Navy*, WDL, 1957.

Friedman, Norman, *Naval Firepower*, Seaforth, 2008.

Gilbert, Martin, *Churchill and America*, Pocket Books, 2005.

Gray, Edwyn, *Hitler's Battleships*, Pen & Sword, 1999.

Grenfell, Russell, *The Bismarck Episode*, Faber and Faber, 1949.

Harriman, W Averell, and Abel, Elie, *Special Envoy to Churchill and Stalin 1941–1946*, Random House, 1975.

Hastings, Max, *Finest Years, Churchill as Warlord 1940–45*, Harper Press, 2009.

Hough, Richard, *The Hunting of Force Z*, New English Library, 1971.

Former Naval Person, Churchill and the Wars at Sea, Weidenfeld & Nicolson, 1985.

Jameson, William, *Ark Royal*, Periscope Publishing, 2004.

Jenkins, Roy, *Churchill*, Pan, 2001.

Johns, WE, and Kelly, R.A., *No Surrender*, Harrap, 1969.

Johnston, Ian and McAuley, Rob, *The Battleships*, Channel 4 Books, 2002.

Kemp, Paul, *British Warship Losses of the 20th Century*, Sutton, 1999.

Kemp, PK, *Victory at Sea*, Frederick Muller, 1957.

Kennedy, Ludovic, *Pursuit: The Chase and Sinking of the Bismarck*, Cassell, 2001.

Konstam, Angus, *British Battleships 1939–45 (2), Nelson and King George V Classes*, Osprey, 2009.

—— *British Battlecruisers 1939–45*, Osprey, 2003.

Leach, Henry, *Endure No Makeshifts*, Leo Cooper, 1993.

Macintyre, Donald, *Fighting Admiral*, Evans, 1961.

Macksey, Kenneth, *The Searchers*, Cassell, 2003.

Marriot, Leo, *Fighting Ships of World War II*, Airlife, 2004.

McLachlan, Donald, *Room 39*, Weidenfeld and Nicolson, 1968.

McMurtrie, Francis, *The Cruise of the Bismarck*, Hutchinson, 1942.

Mearns, David and White, Rob, *Hood and Bismarck*, Channel 4 Books, 2002.

Middlebrook, Martin and Mahoney, Patrick, *The Sinking of Prince of Wales & Repulse*, Pen & Sword, 2004.

Moffat, John with Rossiter, Mike, *I Sank the Bismarck*, Bantam, 2009.

Monsarrat, Nicholas, *The Cruel Sea*, Penguin, 2009.

Moran, Lord, *Churchill at War 1940 – 45*, Robinson, 2002.

Morton, HV, *Atlantic Meeting*, Methuen, 1943.

Müllenheim-Rechberg, Burkard, Freiherr von, *Battleship Bismarck*, NIP, 1980.

O'Hara, Vincent, P, *The German Fleet at War 1939–1945*, NIP, 2004.

Paterson, Michael, *Voices of the Code Breakers*, David & Charles, 2007.

Pears, Commander Randolph, *British Battleships 1892–1957*, Putnam, 1957.

Poolman, Kenneth, *Ark Royal*, NPI Media, 2000.

Pope, Dudley, *The Battle of the River Plate*, Pan, 1974.

Preston, Anthony, *The World's Worst Warships*, Conway, 2002.

Rhys-Jones, Graham, *The Loss of the Bismarck*, Cassell, 1999.

Robertson, Terence, *Channel Dash*, Pan, 1959.

Roskill, Stephen, *Churchill and the Admirals*, Pen & Sword, 2004.

Russell, Sir Herbert, *Ark Royal*, Bodley Head, 1942.

Sayer, Les and Ball, Vernon, *Tag on a Stringbag*, Aspen, 1994.

Schofield, BB, *The Loss of the Bismarck*, Ian Allan, 1972.

Shirer, William, *The Sinking of the Bismarck*, Sterling, 2006.

Shores, Christopher, *100 Years of British Naval Aviation*, Haynes, 2009.

Skwiot, Miroslaw Zbigniew and Prusinowska, Elzbieta Teresea, *Hunting the Bismarck*, The Crowood Press, 2006.

Smith, Peter C, *The Battle-Cruiser* HMS *Renown 1916–1948*, Pen & Sword, 2008.

Smyth, Admiral WH, *The Sailor's Word-Book*, Conway Maritime Press, 2005.

Sopocko, Eryk, *Gentlemen, The Bismarck Has Been Sunk*, Methuen, 1942.

Stephen, Martin, *The Fighting Admirals*, Leo Cooper, 1991.

—— & ed., Eric Grove, *Sea Battles in Close-up: World War 2*, Ian Allan, 1988.

Sturton, Ian, ed., *Conway's Battleships (Revised and Expanded Edition)*, Conway, 2008.

Talbot-Booth, EC, *The Royal Navy*, Sampson Low, Marston & Co., 1939.

Taylor, Bruce, *The Battlecruiser* HMS *Hood*, Seaforth, 2008.

Thomas, David A, *A Companion to the Royal Navy*, Harrap, 1988.

—— *Battle of the Java Sea*, Pan, 1971.

Thompson, Kenneth, and members of the ship's company, HMS *Rodney at War*, Hollis and Carter, 1946.

Twiston Davis, David, ed., *Daily Telegraph Book of Naval Obituaries*, Grub Street, 2006.

Vian, Sir Philip, Admiral of the Fleet, *Action This Day*, Frederick Muller, 1960.

Wallis, R Ransome, *Two Red Stripes*, Ian Allan, 1973.

Wellings, Joseph H, Rear-Admiral, *On His Majesty's Service*, Naval War College Press, 1983.

Wheal, Elizabeth-Anne and Pope, Stephen, *The Macmillan Dictionary of the Second World War*, Macmillan, 1995.

—— *The Macmillan Dictionary of the First World War*, Macmillan 1995.

Whitley, MJ, *Cruisers of World War Two*, Arms and Armour Press, 1196.

Wilmott, HP, *Battleship*, Cassell, 2002.

Winklareth, Robert J., *Naval Shipyards of the World*, Chatham, 2000.

A Seaman's Pocket-Book, June 1943, Conway, 2006.

Index

British warships and merchant vessels are indicated in italics throughout and also listed under HMS. Where necessary, non-British vessels have their nationality indicated in short form (see below).

Aus. = Australia
Fr. = France
Can. = Canada.
It. = Italy
Jp.= Japan
Pol. = Poland
Sp = Spain
Ru.= Russia
US. = United States

Ranks are abbreviated as follows:

A.B. = Able Seaman
B.S. = Boy Seaman
L.S. = Leading Seaman
P.O. = Petty Officer
Capt. = Captain
Cmdr.= Commander
Lt. = Lieutenant

Other abbreviations:

ADP = Air Defence Position, 165, 167, 168, 171, 180, 184, 186
ASV = Air to Surface Vessel, 107, 108, 138, 139
CBE = Commander of the British Empire, 207
DSO = Distinguished Service Order, 207
FDO = Flight Deck Officer, 144, 145
TAG = Telegraphist Air Gunner, 107, 112, 138, 140, 148